Frommer's®

Rome

20th Edition

by Darwin Porter & Danforth Prince

Published by:
WILEY PUBLISHING, INC.
111 River St.
Hoboken, NJ 07030-5774

ISBN 978-0-470-88727-1 (paper); ISBN 978-0-470-45121-2 (ebk); ISBN 978-1-118-00312-1 (ebk); ISBN 978-0-470-45191-5 (ebk)

Editor: Linda Barth
Production Editor: Eric T. Schroeder
Cartographer: Elizabeth Puhl
Photo Editor: Richard Fox
Production by Wiley Indianapolis Composition Services
Front Cover Photo: Temple ruins at the Forum ©Jacob Halaska / PhotoLibrary / AGE Fotostock, Inc.
Back Cover Photo: Café on the Via della Pace in the Piazza Navona district ©René Mattes / Hemis / Alamy Images

For information on our other products and services or to obtain technical support, please contact our Customer Care Department within the U.S. at 877/762-2974, outside the U.S. at 317/572-3993 or fax 317/572-4002.

Wiley also publishes its books in a variety of electronic formats. Some content that appears in print may not be available in electronic formats.

Manufactured in the United States of America

5 4 3 2 1

CONTENTS

5 WHERE TO STAY IN ROME 86

6 WHERE TO DINE IN ROME 116

7 EXPLORING ROME 147

8 STROLLING THROUGH ROME 193

9 SHOPPING 225

10 ROME AFTER DARK 238

11 SIDE TRIPS FROM ROME 246

12 FAST FACTS ROME 258

13 MOLTO ITALIANO 263

Index 274

LIST OF MAPS

ABOUT THE AUTHORS

Right out of college, **Darwin Porter** wrote the first-ever Frommer's Complete Guide, and it was devoted to Italy. (Up until then, the title had been designated as one of the Dollar-a-Day guides.) Since then, this devotee of all things Italian has covered "The Peninsula" from its Alpine peaks to its "toe" and has kept abreast of the enormous changes the country has experienced over the years. In 1982, Porter was joined in his journalistic efforts by **Danforth Prince,** formerly of the Paris bureau of the *New York Times.* This Italian-speaking disciple of Italy's art, architecture, history, and cuisine has also been personally experiencing and reporting on the glories of Italy since that time.

HOW TO CONTACT US

In researching this book, we discovered many wonderful places—hotels, restaurants, shops, and more. We're sure you'll find others. Please tell us about them, so we can share the information with your fellow travelers in upcoming editions. If you were disappointed with a recommendation, we'd love to know that, too. Please write to:

Frommer's Rome, 20th Edition
Wiley Publishing, Inc. • 111 River St. • Hoboken, NJ 07030-5774
frommersfeedback@wiley.com

AN ADDITIONAL NOTE

Please be advised that travel information is subject to change at any time—and this is especially true of prices. We therefore suggest that you write or call ahead for confirmation when making your travel plans. The authors, editors, and publisher cannot be held responsible for the experiences of readers while traveling. Your safety is important to us, however, so we encourage you to stay alert and be aware of your surroundings. Keep a close eye on cameras, purses, and wallets, all favorite targets of thieves and pickpockets.

FROMMER'S STAR RATINGS, ICONS & ABBREVIATIONS

Every hotel, restaurant, and attraction listing in this guide has been ranked for quality, value, service, amenities, and special features using a star-rating system. In country, state, and regional guides, we also rate towns and regions to help you narrow down your choices and budget your time accordingly. Hotels and restaurants are rated on a scale of zero (recommended) to three stars (exceptional). Attractions, shopping, nightlife, towns, and regions are rated according to the following scale: zero stars (recommended), one star (highly recommended), two stars (very highly recommended), and three stars (must-see).

In addition to the star-rating system, we also use seven feature icons that point you to the great deals, in-the-know advice, and unique experiences that separate travelers from tourists. Throughout the book, look for:

special finds—those places only insiders know about

fun facts—details that make travelers more informed and their trips more fun

kids—best bets for kids and advice for the whole family

special moments—those experiences that memories are made of

overrated—places or experiences not worth your time or money

insider tips—great ways to save time and money

great values—where to get the best deals

The following abbreviations are used for credit cards:

AE	American Express	DISC	Discover	V	Visa
DC	Diners Club	MC	MasterCard		

TRAVEL RESOURCES AT FROMMERS.COM

Frommer's travel resources don't end with this guide. Frommer's website, www.frommers.com, has travel information on more than 4,000 destinations. We update features regularly, giving you access to the most current trip-planning information and the best airfare, lodging, and car-rental bargains. You can also listen to podcasts, connect with other Frommers.com members through our active-reader forums, share your travel photos, read blogs from guidebook editors and fellow travelers, and much more.

THE BEST OF ROME

1

Rome is so packed with attractions that it's hard to know where to start. That's where we come in. In this chapter we present our personal, opinionated list of what we consider to be Rome's top highlights. This will get you started and point you toward some of the possibilities for designing your own vacation. Whether this is your first trip or your tenth, you're bound to come away with your own favorites to add to the list.

FROMMER'S favorite ROME EXPERIENCES

- **Walking through Ancient Rome:** A vast, almost unified archaeological park cuts through the center of Rome. For those who want specific guidance, we have a walking tour in chapter 8 that will lead you through these haunting ruins. But it's fun to wander on your own and let yourself get lost on the very streets where Julius Caesar and Lucrezia Borgia once trod. A slice of history unfolds at every turn: an ancient fountain, a long-forgotten statue, a ruined temple dedicated to some long-faded cult. A narrow street suddenly opens to a view of a triumphal arch. The Roman Forum and the Palatine Hill are the highlights, but the glory of Rome is hardly confined to these dusty fields. If you wander long enough, you'll eventually emerge onto Piazza della Rotunda to stare in awe at one of Rome's most glorious sights, the Pantheon.
- **Hanging Out at the Pantheon:** The world's best-preserved ancient monument is now a hot spot—especially at night. Find a cafe table out on the square and take in the action, which all but awaits a young Fellini to record it. The Pantheon has become a symbol of Rome itself, and we owe our thanks to Hadrian for leaving it to the world. When you tire of people-watching and cappuccino, you can go inside to inspect the tomb of Raphael, who was buried here in 1520. (His mistress, "La Fornarina," wasn't allowed to attend the services.) Nothing is more dramatic than being in the Pantheon during a rainstorm, watching the sheets of water splatter on the colorful marble floor. It enters through the oculus on top, which provides the only light for the interior. See "The Pantheon & Attractions near Piazza Navona & Campo de' Fiori," in chapter 7.

- **Taking a Sunday Bike Ride:** Only a daredevil would try this on city streets on a weekday, but on a clear Sunday morning, while Romans are still asleep, you can rent a bike and discover Rome with your own two wheels. The Villa Borghese is the best place to bike. Its 6.5km (4-mile) borders contain a world unto itself, with museums and galleries, a riding school, an artificial lake, and a grassy amphitheater. Another choice place for Sunday biking is the Villa Doria Pamphili, an extensive park lying above the Janiculum. Laid out in the mid-1600s, this is Rome's largest park, with numerous fountains and some summerhouses.
- **Strolling at Sunset in the Pincio Gardens:** Above the landmark Piazza del Popolo, this terraced and lushly planted hillside is the most romantic place for a twilight walk. A dusty orange-rose glow often colors the sky, giving an otherworldly aura to the park's umbrella pines and broad avenues. The ancient Romans turned this hill into gardens, but today's look came from the design of Giuseppe Valadier in the 1800s. Pause at the main piazza, Napoleone I, for a spectacular view of the city stretching from the Janiculum to Monte Mario. The Egyptian-style obelisk here was erected by Emperor Hadrian on the tomb of his great love, Antinous, a beautiful male slave who died prematurely. See "The Spanish Steps, the Trevi Fountain & Attractions Nearby," in chapter 7.
- **Enjoying Roma di Notte:** At night, ancient monuments, such as the Forum, are bathed in a theatrical white light; it's thrilling to see the glow of the Colosseum with the moon rising behind its arches. Begin your evening with a Roman *passeggiata* (early evening stroll) along Via del Corso or Piazza Navona. There's plenty of action going on inside the clubs, too, from Via Veneto to Piazza Navona. Club kids flock to the colorful narrow streets of Trastevere, the area around the Pantheon, and the even more remote Testaccio. The jazz scene is especially good, and big names often pop in. An English-language publication available at newsstands, *Wanted in Rome,* will keep you abreast of what's happening.
- **Exploring Campo de' Fiori at Midmorning:** In an incomparable setting of medieval houses, this is the liveliest fruit and vegetable market in Rome, where peddlers offer their wares as they've done for centuries. The market is best visited after 9am any day but Sunday. By 1pm the stalls begin to close. Once the major site for the medieval inns of Rome (many of which were owned by Vanozza Catanei, the 15th-century courtesan and lover of Pope Alexander VI Borgia), this square maintains some of its old bohemian atmosphere. We often come here when we're in Rome for a unique, lively view of local life. Often you'll spot your favorite trattoria chef bargaining for the best and freshest produce, everything from fresh cherries to the perfect vine-ripened tomato. See "The Pantheon & Attractions near Piazza Navona & Campo de' Fiori," in chapter 7.
- **Attending the Opera:** The Milanese claim that Roman opera pales in comparison with La Scala, but Roman opera buffs, of course, beg to differ. At Rome's Teatro dell'Opera, the season runs between December and June, and programs concentrate on the classics: Bellini, Donizetti, Puccini, and Rossini. No one seems to touch the Romans' operatic soul more than Giuseppe Verdi (1813–1901), who became a national icon in his support for Italian unification. See "The Performing Arts," in chapter 10.
- **Climbing Janiculum Hill:** On the Trastevere side of the river, where Garibaldi held off the attacking French troops in 1849, the Janiculum Hill was always strategic in Rome's defense. Today, a walk in this park at the top of the hill can provide an

escape from the hot, congested streets of Trastevere. Filled with monuments to Garibaldi and his brave men, the hill is no longer peppered with monasteries, as it was in the Middle Ages. A stroll will reveal monuments and fountains, plus panoramic views over Rome. The best vista is from Villa Lante, a Renaissance summer residence. The most serene section is the 1883 Botanical Gardens, with palm trees, orchids, bromeliads, and sequoias—more than 7,000 plant species from all over the world. See "More Attractions," in chapter 7.

- **Strolling Along the Tiber:** Without the Tiber River, there might have been no Rome at all. A key player in the city's history for millennia, the river flooded the capital every winter until it was tamed in 1870. The massive *lungotevere* embankments on both sides of the Tiber check the waters and make a perfect place for a memorable stroll. Not only can you walk along the river from which Cleopatra made her grand entrance into Rome, but you'll also see the riverside life of Trastevere and the Jewish Ghetto. Start at Piazza della Bocca della Verità in the early evening; from there, you can go for some 3km (1¾ miles) or more. For a stroll that takes you to sites along the river, see the "Renaissance Rome" walking tour in chapter 8.
- **Picnicking on Isola Tiberina:** In ancient times, this boat-shaped island stood across from the port of Rome and from 293 B.C. was home to a temple dedicated to Aesculapius, the god of healing. A church was constructed in the 10th century on the ruins of this ancient temple. You can reach the island from the Jewish Ghetto by the Ponte Fabricio footbridge, which dates from 62 B.C. and is the Tiber's oldest original bridge. Romans come here to sunbathe, sitting along the river's banks, and to escape the traffic and the crowds. Arrive with the makings of a picnic, and the day is yours. See the "Trastevere" walking tour in chapter 8.
- **Following in the Footsteps of Bernini:** One of the most enjoyable ways to see Rome is to follow the trail of Giovanni Lorenzo Bernini (1598–1680), who left a greater mark on the city than even Michelangelo. Under the patronage of three different popes, Bernini "baroqued" Rome. Start at Largo di Santa Susanna, north of the Stazione Termini, at the Church of Santa Maria della Vittoria, which houses one of Bernini's most controversial sculptures, the *Ecstasy of St. Teresa,* from 1646. Walk from here along Via Barberini to Piazza Barberini, in the center of which stands Bernini's second most dramatic fountain, the Fontana del Tritone. From the piazza, go along Via delle Quattro Fontane, bypassing (on your left) the Palazzo Barberini, designed by Bernini and others for Pope Urban VIII. At the famous crossroads of Rome, Le Quattro Fontane, take Via del Quirinale to see the facade of Sant'Andrea, one of the artist's greatest churches. Continue west, bypassing the Pantheon, to arrive eventually at Piazza Navona, which Bernini remodeled for Pope Innocent X. The central fountain, the Fontana dei Fiumi, is Bernini's masterpiece, although the figures representing the four rivers were sculpted by others following his plans.
- **Spending a Day on the Appian Way:** Dating from 312 B.C., the Appian Way (Via Appia) once traversed the whole peninsula of Italy and was the road on which Roman legions marched to Brindisi and their conquests in the East. One of its darkest moments was the crucifixion in 71 B.C. of the rebellious slave army of Spartacus, whose bodies lined the road from Rome to Capua. Fashionable Romans were buried here, and early Christians dug catacombs in which to inter their dead. Begin at the Tomb of Cecilia Metella and proceed up Via Appia Antica past a series of tombs and monuments (including a monument to Seneca, the

great moralist who committed suicide on the orders of Nero; and another to Pope St. Urban, who reigned A.D. 222–230). The sights along Via Appia Antica are some of Rome's most fascinating. You can go all the way to the Church of Domine Quo Vadis. See "The Appian Way & the Catacombs," in chapter 7.

- **Enjoying a Taste of the Grape:** While in Rome, do as the Romans do and indulge in a carafe of dry white wine from the warm climate of Lazio. In restaurants and trattorie you'll find the most popular brand, Frascati, but try some of the other wines from the Castelli Romani, too, including Colli Albani, Velletri, and Marino. All these wines come from one grape: trebbiano. Sometimes a dash of malvasia grape is added for greater flavor and an aromatic bouquet. Of course, you don't have to wait until dinner to sip wine; you can sample it at any of hundreds of wine bars throughout Rome, which offer a selection of all the great reds and whites of Italy.
- **Savoring Gelato on a Summer Afternoon:** Having a gelato on a hot summer day is worth the wait through the long winter. Tubs of homemade ice cream await you in a dazzling array of flavors: everything from candied orange peels with chocolate to watermelon to rice. *Gelaterie* offer *semifreddi* concoctions (made with cream instead of milk) in such flavors as almond, *marengo* (a type of meringue), and *zabaione* (or zabaglione, eggnog). Seasonal fresh fruit is made into ice creams of blueberry, cherry, and peach. *Granite* (crushed ice) flavored with sweet fruit is another cool delight on a sultry night. Tre Scalini at Piazza Navona is the most fabled spot for enjoying *divino tartufo,* a chocolate concoction with a taste to match its name.
- **Dining on a Hidden Piazza:** If you're in Rome with that special someone, you'll appreciate the romance of discovering your own little neighborhood trattoria that opens onto some forgotten square deep in the heart of ancient Rome. And if your evening dinner extends for 3 or 4 hours, who's counting? The waiters won't rush you out the door even when you've overstayed your time at the table. This is a special experience, and Rome has dozens of these little restaurants. Sample the menu at **Vecchia Roma,** Via della Tribuna di Campitella 18 (**© 06-6864604**), with a theatrical setting on a lovely square. Order spaghetti with double-horned clams and enjoy the old-fashioned ambience while you rub elbows with savvy local foodies.
- **Hearing Music in the Churches:** Artists such as Plácido Domingo and Luciano Pavarotti have performed around Rome in halls ranging from churches to ancient ruins. Churches often host concerts, although by decree of Pope John Paul II, they must consist of sacred music. When church concerts are performed, programs appear not only outside the church but also on various announcements posted throughout Rome. The top professionals play at the "big-name" churches, but don't overlook those smaller, hard-to-find churches on hidden squares. Some of the best music we've ever heard has been by up-and-coming musicians getting their start in these little-known churches. The biggest event is the RAI (national broadcasting company) concert on December 5 at St. Peter's—even the pope attends. Other favorite locations for church music include Sant'Ignazio di Loyola, on Piazza di Sant'Ignazio, and San Paolo Fuori le Mura, at Via Ostiense 186.
- **Walking from Fountain to Fountain:** On summer nights you'll find Romans—especially those who live in crowded apartments without air-conditioning—out walking from fountain to cooling fountain. Every visitor makes at least one trip to Bernini's fountain on Piazza Navona, after stopping off at the Trevi Fountain to toss in a coin (thus ensuring their return to Rome), but there are hundreds more.

One hidden gem is the Fontana delle Tartarughe, in tiny Piazza Mattei. It has stood there since 1581, a jewel of Renaissance sculpture showing youths helping tortoises into a basin. Our favorite Bernini fountain is at Piazza Barberini; his Fontana del Tritone is a magnificent work of art from 1642 showing the sea god blowing through a shell. Unfortunately, it's now against the law to jump into these fountains and paddle around as Anita Ekberg did in *La Dolce Vita*.

- **Hanging Out in the Campidoglio at Night:** There is no more splendid place to be at night than Piazza del Campidoglio, where Michelangelo designed both the geometric paving and the facades of the buildings. A broad flight of steps, the Cordonata, takes you up to this panoramic site, a citadel of ancient Rome from which traitors to the empire were once tossed to their deaths. Home during the day to the Capitoline Museums, it takes on a different aura at night, when it's dramatically lit, the measured Renaissance facades glowing like jewel boxes. The evening views of the brilliantly lit Forum and Palatine are also worth the long trek up those stairs. There's no more stunning cityscape view at night than from this hill. See "The Colosseum, the Roman Forum & Highlights of Ancient Rome," in chapter 7.
- **Shopping in the Flea Markets:** We've never discovered an original Raphael at Rome's Porta Portese flea market (which locals call *mercato delle pulci*). But we've picked up some interesting souvenirs over the years. The market, the largest in Europe, began after World War II when black marketeers needed an outlet for illegal wares. Today the authentic art and antiques once sold here have given way to reproductions, but the selection remains enormous: World War II cameras, caviar from immigrant Russians, luggage (fake Gucci), spare parts, Mussolini busts, and so on. Near Porta Sublicio in Trastevere, the market has some 4,000 stalls, but it's estimated that only 10% of them have a license. Sunday from 5am to 2pm is the best time to visit, but beware of pickpockets at all times. See "Shopping A to Z" in chapter 9.

THE best MUSEUMS

- **The Vatican Museums:** Rambling, disorganized, and poorly labeled they might be, but these buildings are packed with treasures accumulated over the centuries by the popes. There's the incomparable Sistine Chapel, such priceless ancient Greek and Roman sculptures as *Laocoön* and the *Belvedere Apollo*, rooms whose walls were almost completely executed by Raphael (including his majestic *School of Athens*), and endless collections of art ranging from (very pagan) Greco-Roman antiquities to Christian art by European masters. See p. 152.
- **Galleria Borghese:** One of the world's great small museums reopened a few years ago after a 14-year restoration breathed new life into the frescoes and decor of this 1613 palace. That's merely the backdrop for the collections, which include masterpieces of baroque sculpture by a young Bernini and paintings by Caravaggio and Raphael. See p. 179.
- **National Etruscan Museum:** Mysterious and, for the most part, undocumented, the Etruscans were the ancestors of the Romans. They left a legacy of bronze and marble sculpture, sarcophagi, jewelry, and representations of mythical heroes, some of which were excavated at Cerveteri, a stronghold north of Rome. Most startling about the artifacts is their sophisticated, almost mystical sense of design. The Etruscan collection is housed in a papal villa dating from the 1500s. See p. 180.

- **Palazzo Altemps:** A branch of the Museo Nazionale Romano contains some of the best Roman art anywhere, including the fabled Ludovisi Collection of Greek and Roman sculpture. Look for such masterpieces as the *Grande Ludovisi,* carved from a single block and dating from the 2nd century A.D. See p. 173.
- **Museo Capitolino:** At the magnificent Piazza del Campidoglio, laid out by Michelangelo, this museum complex houses some of the world's most important sculptures, including *The Dying Gaul,* a copy of a Greek original from the 3rd century B.C., and the *Capitoline Venus,* even the famous equestrian statue of Marcus Aurelius. More classical sculpture and paintings are found in the Palace of the Conservatori across the way. See p. 164.

THE best CATHEDRALS & CHURCHES

- **St. Peter's Basilica** (Rome): Its roots began with the first Christian emperor, Constantine, in A.D. 324. By 1400, the Roman basilica was in danger of collapsing, prompting the Renaissance popes to commission plans for the largest, most impressive, most jaw-dropping cathedral the world had ever seen. Amid the rich decor of gilt, marble, and mosaics are countless artworks, including Michelangelo's *Pietà.* Other sights here are a small museum of Vatican treasures and the eerie underground grottoes containing the tombs of former popes, including the most recently interred, John Paul II. An elevator ride (or a rigorous climb) up the tower to Michelangelo's glorious dome provides panoramic views of Rome. See p. 150.
- **Pantheon:** Architects have called the Pantheon "the world's only architecturally perfect building." The best preserved ancient Roman structure was built by Hadrian in A.D. 119–128 as an ancient temple (later a church). The immense dome, still intact, would remain as the largest ever built for centuries to come. See p. 169.
- **Basilica di Santa Maria Maggiore:** One of Rome's oldest and most striking cathedrals, this church dates from the 5th century. In the 14th century, the city's tallest bell tower was added. Later in the 18th century a new facade was added. Legend has it that it was gilded with the first gold to arrive from the New World. See p. 182.
- **Basilica di San Giovanni in Laterano:** The oldest Christian church within the city walls, this landmark was for years the seat of the papacy and the heart of Christianity, a role played by St. Peter's today, of course. The Emperor Constantine donated the land to the newly sanctioned sect of Christians in A.D. 314. In 1646 Borromini rescued the church from decay, creating a baroque basilica but with elements of the ancient structure kept intact. See p. 166.
- **Santa Maria d'Aracoeli:** Visits here are tied in with trips to the adjoining Piazza del Campidoglio. First mentioned in the 7th century, the church today dates mainly from A.D. 1250 when it came under the Franciscans. The Tiburtine Sibyl was said to have told the Emperor Augustus to build an "altar to the first among gods," and he dutifully constructed this *aracoeli* (Altar in the Sky). The first chapel on the right was frescoed by Pinturicchio, the Umbrian Renaissance master. See p. 167.
- **St. Paul Outside the Walls:** One of Rome's four grand pilgrimage basilicas, San Paolo Fuori le Mura was destroyed by fire in 1823 but reconstructed. The church is believed to have been erected over the tomb of St. Paul. The stunning windows appear to be stained glass but are actually made of translucent alabaster. See p. 186.

- **Santa Maria Sopra Minerva:** Built over a former Temple of Minerva, Santa Maria is Rome's only Gothic church, dating from 1280. Before entering, look for the whimsical statue by Bernini of a baby elephant on the square out front. The last chapel in the church is filled with many treasures, notably a delicious cycle of frescoes by Filippino Lippi (last chapel on the right). See p. 170.

THE best PIAZZAS

- **Piazza Navona:** Built on the ruins of the Stadium of Diocletian, this dramatic baroque square is the most theatrical in Rome, either by day or night. It's known for its trio of flamboyant fountains, including Bernini's Fontana dei Fiumi, the Fontana di Nettuno, and the Fontana del Moro. Cafes and restaurants abound on the square. See p. 170.
- **Piazza del Popolo:** Nero's ghost is said to haunt this landmark square, graced with the church Santa Maria del Popolo, one of Rome's great storehouses of ecclesiastical treasures, commissioned by the pope in 1472. The square was once the gateway to Rome for foreign visitors. A beehive of activity at night, with all its bustling restaurants and cafes, the square is crowned with an Egyptian obelisk of Ramses II (a mere 3,200 years old). See p. 178.
- **Piazza di Spagna:** First, the downside. The Spanish Steps are so overrun with tourists both day and night that you may be trampled underfoot. If not, you can appreciate their beauty. The famous steps were built in 1723 to link the church of Trinità dei Monti with the chic shopping street, Via dei Condotti, below. In the 19th century poets such as Keats and Goethe made their homes here, and artists combed the steps for prospective models, many half draped to show off their perfect bodies. See p. 175.
- **Piazza di Santa Maria in Trastevere:** This square is the heartbeat of life in the villagelike section of Trastevere with its maze of narrow, cobbled alleyways. Dominating the square is the church of Santa Maria, famous for its 12th-century mosaics by Pietro Cavallini. At night the fountain in the center, created by Carlo Fontana in 1692, is a popular meeting place on the floodlit square. See p. 188.
- **Piazza della Rotonda:** One of the greatest of all buildings from antiquity, the Pantheon, dominates this landmark square. Romans often stop here for pizza or a cup of espresso late in the evening when the tourist hordes have dwindled. Find your seat at the jumble of open-air cafe tables in front of the Pantheon and take in one of the best architectural views of a lifetime. See p. 169.
- **Campo de' Fiori:** This "field of flowers" (its English name) was once the site of executions in Rome. Now a center of artisans and craftspeople during the day, the square is filled with barhoppers at night. The piazza is also home to Rome's oldest outdoor produce and flower market, which can be visited during the day. It's also one of the few church-free piazzas in the city. In some of the old buildings surrounding the square, Vannozza Catanei, mistress of Pope Alexander VI Borgia, used to rent rooms for pilgrims flocking to St. Peter's. See p. 174.

THE best RUINS

- **Roman Forum** (Rome): Two thousand years ago, most of the known world was directly affected by decisions made in the Roman Forum. Today, classicists and archaeologists wander among its ruins, conjuring up the glory that was Rome. What you'll see today is a pale, rubble-strewn version of the once-majestic site—it's now surrounded by modern boulevards packed with whizzing cars. See p. 160.

- **Palatine Hill** (Rome): According to legend, the Palatine Hill was the site where Romulus and Remus (the orphaned infant twins who survived by being suckled by a she-wolf) eventually founded the city. One of the seven hills of ancient Rome, Il Palatino is enhanced by the Farnese Gardens (Orti Farnesiani), laid out in the 1500s on the site of Tiberius's palace. See p. 160.
- **The Colosseum** (Rome): Rome boasts only a handful of other ancient monuments that survive in such well-preserved condition. A massive amphitheater set incongruously amid a maze of modern traffic, the Colosseum was once the setting for gladiator combat, lion-feeding frenzies, and public entertainment whose cruelty was a noted characteristic of the Empire (just ask Russell Crowe). All three of the ancient world's classical styles (Doric, Ionic, and Corinthian) are represented, superimposed in tiers one above the other. See p. 158.
- **Hadrian's Villa** (Villa Adriana; near Tivoli): Hadrian's Villa slumbered in rural obscurity until the 1500s, when Renaissance popes ordered its excavation. Only then was the scale of this enormous and beautiful villa from A.D. 134 appreciated. Its builder, Hadrian, who had visited almost every part of his empire, wanted to incorporate the wonders of the world into one building site—and he succeeded. See p. 248.
- **Ostia Antica** (near Rome): During the height of the Roman Empire, Ostia ("mouth" in Latin) was the harbor town set at the point where the Tiber flowed into the sea. As Rome declined, so did Ostia; by the early Middle Ages, the town had almost disappeared, its population decimated by malaria. In the early 1900s, archaeologists excavated the ruins of hundreds of buildings, many of which you can view. See p. 255.
- **Fori Imperiali** (Rome): Lining both sides of the Via dei Fori Imperiali are the Imperial Forums, launched by Julius Caesar in 54 B.C. that includes the Temple of Venus Genetrix, dedicated to the goddess of love from whom Caesar immodestly claimed descent. On the east side are the ruins of the forums constructed by the emperors Nerva, Augustus, and Trajan. On the west side, closer to the Colosseum, you can see marble maps, ordered made by Mussolini, charting the vast outreaches of the Roman Empire in its heyday. See p. 163.
- **Trajan's Market** (Rome): Adjoining the Imperial Forum (see above), Trajan's Market in its heyday was one of the wonders of the classical world. Imagine it in all its glory when its 150 shops sold the rarest of treasures from the far reaches of the Roman Empire. The Emperor Trajan ordered his architect, Apollodorus of Damascus, to construct this avant-garde complex in the early 2nd century A.D. The market today only vaguely suggests what it used to be when it sold silks, spices, fresh fish, fruit, and flowers, a spectacle to behold. See p. 163.
- **Terme di Caracalla** (Rome): These baths lasted for 3 centuries until invading Goths destroyed the plumbing. They were ordered built by the Emperor Caracalla in A.D. 217. Back then, a noble Roman could spend the entire day at the baths, enjoying various pleasures including rubdowns with scented cloths. In its heyday, the baths also had art galleries, beautiful gardens, a big library, and even today's equivalent of a gym. One will have to imagine the magnificence of these baths before the Farnese family carted off their marble decorations in the 16th century. See p. 165.

best HOTEL BETS

- **Best Historic Hotel:** The truly grand **St. Regis Grand,** Via Vittorio Emanuele Orlando 3 (✆ **06-47091;** www.starwoodhotels.com), was created by César Ritz in 1894, with the great chef Escoffier presiding over a lavish banquet. It was the first hotel in town to offer "a private bathroom and two electric lights in every room." Its roster of guests has included some of the greatest names in European history, including royalty, naturally, but also such New World moguls as Henry Ford and J. P. Morgan. This lavish hotel is within walking distance of many of Rome's major sights. See p. 88.
- **Best Recycled Hotels:** A real discovery and a charmer, the **Inn at the Spanish Steps,** Via dei Condotti 85 (✆ **06-69925657;** www.atspanishsteps.com), is the former Roman residence of Hans Christian Andersen. It has been transformed into one of the most desirable little upscale inns of Rome, with each bedroom furnished in gorgeous, authentic period decor. Not far away, the brilliantly restored **Hotel de Russie,** Via del Babuino 9 (✆ **800/323-7500** in North America, or 06-328881; www.hotelderussie.it), was a retreat for artists, including Picasso and Stravinsky. Reclaiming its 1890s style, it's been remade as a stunning little boutique hotel with excellent service and a fabulous location right off the Piazza del Popolo. See p. 105 and p. 104.
- **Best for Business Travelers:** The restored neoclassical palace, **Exedra,** Piazza della Repubblica 47 (✆ **06-489381;** www.boscolohotels.com), stands right in the heart of Rome near the Termini. A government-rated five-star hotel, it is equipped with all the amenities, including a well-run business center. Executives will also find a helpful, multilingual staff ready to help ease their adjustment to the Eternal City. See p. 88.
- **Best for a Romantic Getaway:** A private villa in the exclusive Parioli residential area, the **Hotel Lord Byron,** Via G. de Notaris 5 (✆ **06-3220404;** www.lordbyronhotel.com), is a chic hideaway. It has a clubby ambience, and everybody is oh-so-very-discreet here. You get personal attention in subdued opulence, and the staff definitely respects that DO NOT DISTURB sign on the door. You don't even have to leave the premises for dinner; the hotel's Sapori del Lord Byron is one of the finest and most romantic restaurants in Rome. See p. 114
- **Best Classic Choice:** Ernest Hemingway and Ingrid Bergman don't hang out here anymore, but the **Hotel Eden,** Via Ludovisi 49 (✆ **06-478121;** www.hotel-eden.it), remains grand and glamorous. Views over the city are stunning, the hotel restaurant (La Terrazza dell'Eden) is one of the city's best, and everything looks as if it's waiting for photographers from *Architectural Digest* to arrive. See p. 93.
- **Best for Families:** Families gravitate to the **Hotel Ponte Sisto,** Via dei Petinari 64 (✆ **06-6863100;** www.hotelpontesisto.it), near the Piazza Navona and the Campo de' Fiori in the heart of Rome. It's a restored Renaissance palazzo offering reasonably priced family suites on its top floor with terraces overlooking the rooftops of the ancient city. See p. 98.
- **Best Moderately Priced Hotel:** So you don't have a bottomless expense account? We've got a couple of wonderful values for you. Consider the **Hotel Columbia,** Via del Viminale 15 (✆ **06-4883509;** www.hotelcolumbia.com), one of the newest properties in the neighborhoods surrounding Stazione Termini; everything is

well-maintained and comfortable. We also like **La Residenza,** Via Emilia 22–24 (© **06-4880789;** www.hotel-la-residenza.com), with a convenient location near the Villa Borghese and Piazza Barberini. Here you'll get a good price on a homey, spacious guest room. See p. 90 and 96, respectively.

- **Best Service:** Both management and staff at the **Hotel de la Ville Inter-Continental Roma,** Via Sistina 67–69 (© **888/424-6835** in the U.S. and Canada, or 06-67331; www.ichotelsgroup.com), are highly professional and exceedingly hospitable. The staff is particularly adept at taking messages, giving you helpful hints about what to see and do in Rome, and fulfilling any special room-service requests. Their general attentiveness to your needs, quick problem solving, good manners, and friendly helpfulness make this place exceptional. Room service is available 24 hours daily. See p. 104.
- **Best Location:** Everybody knows about the astronomically expensive **Hassler,** Piazza Trinità dei Monti 6 (© **800/223-6800** in the U.S., or 06-699340; www.hotelhasslerroma.com), a grand old hotel set right at the top of the Spanish Steps. But given its high prices and the fact that it's gotten a bit dowdy, we'll send you instead to the **Hotel Scalinata di Spagna** (© **06-6793006;** www.hotelscalinata.com), which is across the street at no. 17 on the same piazza and isn't so breathtakingly pricey. This intimate, upscale inn has a roof garden with a sweeping view of the dome of St. Peter's across the Tiber. When you step out your door, the heart of Rome, including its best shopping streets, is at your feet. See p. 103 and p. 106.
- **Best Views:** A great place to book a room with a view is the **Albergo Del Sole al Pantheon,** Piazza della Rotonda 63 (© **06-6780441;** www.hotelsolealpantheon.com), where you can gaze out at the Pantheon from your bedroom window. See p. 101.
- **Best for Understated Elegance:** Of course, it's not as elegant or as grand as the Excelsior, the Eden, or the Hassler, but the **Hotel d'Inghilterra,** Via Bocca di Leone 14 (© **06-699811;** http://hoteldinghilterra.warwickhotels.com), has its own unique brand of low-key opulence. Plus, it's just 2 blocks west of the Spanish Steps. The hotel's public rooms feature black-and-white checkerboard marble floors, and its upholstered lounges are filled with antiques. The fifth floor has some of the loveliest terraces in Rome, and the romantic restaurant below has *trompe l'oeil* clouds that give the impression of a courtyard terrace open to the sky. See p. 104.
- **Best in a Real Roman Neighborhood:** You can't get more Roman than the **Hotel Teatro di Pompeo,** Largo del Pallaro 8 (© **06-68300170;** www.hotelteatrodipompeo.it), which offers rooms with charming touches such as hand-painted tiles and beamed ceilings. The hotel is actually built on top of the ruins of the Theater of Pompey, where Caesar met his fate. It's on a quiet piazzetta near the Palazzo Farnese and Campo de' Fiori, whose open-air market makes this one of Rome's most colorful neighborhoods. Shopping and nightlife abound in this fascinating section of Renaissance Rome, and restaurants and pizzerias keep the area lively at all hours. See p. 100.
- **Best Value:** Rated three stars by the government, the **Hotel delle Muse,** Via Tommaso Salvini 18 (© **06-8088333;** www.hoteldellemuse.com), lies .5km (⅓ mile) north of the Villa Borghese. It's run by the efficient, English-speaking Giorgio Lazar. The furnishings are modern and come in a wide range of splashy colors. In summer, Mr. Lazar operates a garden restaurant serving a reasonably priced fixed-price menu, and the bar is open 24 hours a day. This is one of Rome's best

bargains, and you should consider checking in before Mr. Lazar wises up and raises his rates. See p. 114.

best DINING BETS

- **Best for Romance:** A great place to pop the question or just enjoy a romantic evening is **Sapori del Lord Byron,** in the Hotel Lord Byron, Via G. de Notaris 5 (© **06-3220404**), a stunner of a place that also just happens to serve the best Italian cuisine in town. The decor is as romantic as the atmosphere; it's all white lattice and bold Italian colors highlighted by masses of fresh flowers. The setting is in a Relais & Châteaux member hotel, an Art Deco villa set on a residential hilltop in Parioli, an area of embassies and exclusive town houses at the edge of the Villa Borghese. See p. 145.
- **Best of the Best:** Food critics can never agree on the best restaurant in Rome. But the more discerning cite **La Pergola,** in the Cavalieri Hilton, Via Cadlolo 101 (© **06-35092152;** www.romecavalieri.com), opening onto a panoramic view at night from its perch atop Monte Mario. The talented chef's take on Mediterranean cuisine is sublime. See p. 146.
- **Best Seasonal Menus:** Market-fresh ingredients await you at **Il Convivio,** Vicolo dei Soldati 31 (© **06-6869432;** www.ilconviviotroiani.com), one of Rome's most acclaimed restaurants. The Troiano brothers are truly inspired, shopping the markets for the best in any season and adjusting their menus accordingly. The location is in walking distance of Piazza di Spagna. See p. 127.
- **Best Offbeat Choice:** A lay sisterhood of missionary Christians from five continents operates **L'Eau Vive,** Via Monterone 85 (© **06-68801095;** www.restaurant-eauvive.it), where various popes have dined. A fine French and international cuisine is served in a subdued, refined atmosphere under frescoed ceilings. You never know what will be on the menu. See p. 129.
- **Best for a Celebration:** Romans have been flocking to **Checchino dal 1887,** Via di Monte Testaccio 30 (© **06-5743816;** www.checchino-dal-1887.com), since the early 19th century for fun and hearty food. With a bountiful array of wine and foodstuffs, every meal seems like a party. The tables are packed nightly, and the place is a local legend. You'll have fun while still enjoying some of the best cuisine in town. See p. 145.
- **Best Trattoria: Ditirambo,** on Piazza della Cancelleria 4 (© **06-6871626;** ristoranteditirambo.it), has been around so long it's cited as the most authentic and typical of Roman trattorie. Its wine list is compiled from the major winegrowing regions of Italy, and all its bread, pasta, and desserts are homemade fresh daily. Whether it's the grilled fresh fish of the day or classic Roman fare like wild boar, the cuisine is vivacious, colorful, and market fresh. See p. 124.
- **Best View:** The chic **Imàgo,** in the Hotel Hassler, Piazza della Trinità dei Monti 6 (© **06-69934726;** www.imagorestaurant.com), might be called "the rooftop of Rome." Its sweeping panorama of Ancient Rome from this hotel at the top of the Spanish Steps is reason enough to dine here. The cuisine is also sublime, the creation of a brilliant young chef who roams the world for inspiration. Even Italy's political leader, Silvio Berlusconi, can be seen here feasting on his favorite dish—pheasant ravioli with truffles. See p. 132.

- **Best Wine List:** The food is secondary to the fabulous wine list at the **Trimani Wine Bar,** Via Goito 20 (✆ **06-4469661;** www.trimani.com). One of the best tasting centers in Rome for both French and Italian vintages, this elegant wine bar offers a dazzling array of wines at reasonable prices. The Trimani family has had a prestigious name in the wine business since 1821; just sit down and let the pouring begin. See p. 120.
- **Best Value:** Twenty dollars gets you one of the finest fixed-price menus in Rome at the **Ristorante del Pallaro,** Largo del Pallaro 15 (✆ **06-68801488**). Each dish is prepared by the chef-owner, Paola Fazi, who sternly urges her diners to *"Mangia! Mangia!"* The moment you're seated at the table, the dishes start to arrive—first a selection of antipasti; then the homemade, succulent pastas of the day; followed by such meat courses as tender roast veal. Everything's included, even a carafe of the house wine. See p. 126.
- **Best for the Kids:** After their tour of the Vatican or St. Peter's, many savvy Roman families head for the **Ristorante Il Matriciano,** Via dei Gracchi 55 (✆ **06-3212327**). It's not fancy, but the price is right, and in summer you can opt for a sidewalk table. Let your kids feast on good, reasonably priced homemade fare that includes such crowd pleasers as ricotta-stuffed ravioli. At the next table you're likely to see some Vatican priests dining. See p. 140.
- **Best Continental Cuisine:** The city's finest restaurant is now **La Terrazza,** in the Hotel Eden, Via Ludovisi 49 (✆ **06-478121;** www.starwoodhotels.com), edging out a position long held by Sans Souci. You'll dine on Continental cuisine that is both bold and innovative. The seasonal menu offers the most polished, sophisticated cuisine in Rome; perhaps you'll choose a "symphony" of seafood or a warm salad of grilled vegetables. See p. 121.
- **Best Emilia-Romagna Cuisine:** The area around Bologna has long been celebrated for serving the finest cuisine in Italy, and the little trattoria **Colline Emiliane,** Via Avignonesi 22 (✆ **06-4817538**), maintains that stellar reputation among Romans. The pastas here are among the best in Rome, especially the handmade *tortellini alla panna* (with cream sauce) with truffles. The prosciutto comes from a small town near Parma and is considered by many the best in the world. See p. 122.
- **Best Roman Cuisine:** The tempting selection of antipasti alone is enough to lure you to **Al Ceppo (the Log),** Via Panama 2 (✆ **06-8419696;** www.ristoranteal ceppo.it). Try such appetizers as stuffed yellow or red peppers, or finely minced cold spinach blended with ricotta. Only 2 blocks from the Villa Borghese, this is a dining address jealously guarded by Romans, who often bring friends from out of town here. They feast on the succulent lamb chops, charcoal-grilled to perfection, or other grilled meats, such as quail, liver, and bacon. See p. 145.
- **Best Seafood:** In the heart of ancient Rome, **Quinzi & Gabrieli,** Via delle Coppelle 5–6 (✆ **06-6879389;** www.quinziegabrieli.it), serves the city's finest and freshest seafood from a restored and elegant building dating from the 1400s. The fish is simply cooked and presented, and it's heavenly. Expect everything from deep-sea shrimp to sea urchins and octopus. See p. 127.
- **Best Nuova Cucina:** Near the Vittorio Emanuele monument, **Agata e Romeo,** Via Carlo Alberto 45 (✆ **06-4466115;** www.agataeromeo.it), serves one of Rome's most inventive and creative cuisines in a striking dining room done in Liberty style. If you'd like a sampling of the best selections of the day, you can

order one of the fixed-price menus, available with or without wine. The menu reflects the agrarian bounty of Italy, with ample choices for everyone: meat eaters, fish fanciers, and vegetarians. See p. 118.

- **Best in the Jewish Ghetto:** For centuries, Romans have flocked to the Jewish Ghetto to sample Jerusalem artichokes. No one prepares them better than **Piperno,** Via Monte de' Cenci 9 (✆ **06-68806629;** www.ristorantepiperno.it), which serves savory (though nonkosher) Roman food. Of course, you can order more than these deep-fried artichokes here. A full array of delights includes everything from stuffed squash blossoms to succulent pastas. See p. 124.
- **Best Alfresco Dining:** In Trastevere, Piazza Santa Maria comes alive at night. If you reserve a sidewalk table at **Sabatini,** Piazza Santa Maria in Trastevere 13 (✆ **06-5812026**), you'll have a view of all the action, including the floodlit golden mosaics of the church on the piazza, Santa Maria, in Trastevere. At the next table you're likely to see . . . well, just about anybody (on our most recent visit, Roman Polanski). In addition to the view, you can enjoy terrific grilled fish and Florentine steaks here. See p. 141.
- **Best for People-Watching:** Join the beautiful people—young actors, models, and artists from nearby Via Margutta—who descend at night on Piazza del Popolo. Young men with their silk shirts unbuttoned alight from sports cars to go on the prowl. At **Dal Bolognese,** Piazza del Popolo 1–2 (✆ **06-3611426**), not only can you take in this fascinating scene, but you'll also enjoy fine Bolognese cuisine as enticing as the people-watching; see p. 134. In the 1950s, Via Veneto was the place to be for Elizabeth Taylor, Frank Sinatra, and other Hollywood types. Today the celebs are long gone, and Via Veneto is more about overpriced tourist traps than genuine hip. But lots of folks like to stroll this strip anyway, or enjoy the passing parade from a table at the **Cafè de Paris,** Via Vittorio Veneto 91 (✆ **06-4815631**). See p. 243.
- **Best for a Cappuccino with a View:** The best-located cafe in Rome is **Di Rienzo,** Piazza del Pantheon 8–9 (✆ **06-6869097;** www.ristorantedirienzo.com), which stands directly on Piazza del Pantheon, fronting the Pantheon. On a summer night, there's no better place to be than "the living room" of Rome, as the square before you has been dubbed, as you sit and slowly sip your cappuccino. See p. 218.
- **Best Picnic Fare:** When the weather is cool and the day is sunny, it's time for an alfresco meal. For the makings of a picnic, head for the **Campo de' Fiori** open-air market, between Corso Vittorio Emanuele II and the Tiber. The luscious produce of Lazio is on display here right in the heart of the old city. If you wish, you can purchase vegetables already chopped and ready to be dropped into the minestrone pot. There are also several excellent delicatessen shops on the square. Visit one of the shops selling freshly baked Roman bread, pick up a bottle of wine and a companion—and off you go. See p. 174.
- **Best for Celebrity-Spotting:** A chic choice is **Café Riccioli,** Piazza delle Coppelle 13 (✆ **06-68210313;** www.ricciolicafe.com), where you'll often spot models and other beautiful people having a light dinner of sashimi. See p. 128.

2

ROME IN DEPTH

Rome, according to legend, was built on seven hills. These hills rise from the marshy lowlands of the Campagna and are mostly on the left bank of the Tiber River. They include the Quirinale (seat of the modern Italian government), Esquiline, Viminal, Caelian, and Aventine—and all combine to form a crescent-shape plateau of great historical fame. In its center rises the Palatine Hill, the all-powerful seat of the imperial residences of ancient Rome, which looks down on the ancient Forum and the Colosseum. To the northwest rises the Capitoline Hill. Some historians have suggested that Rome's geography—set above a periphery of marshy and swelteringly hot lowlands—contributed to the fall of the Roman Empire because of its propensity to breed malaria-carrying mosquitoes.

Today Rome and its suburbs extend for more than 450 square kilometers, and it seems forever growing. The Tiber makes two distinct bends within Rome: below Ponte Cavour, one of the city's major bridges, and again at the history-rich island of Tiberina.

With bloodlines that include virtually every race ever encompassed by the borders of the ancient Roman Empire, the people of Rome long ago grew accustomed to seeing foreign influences come and go. Picking their way through the architectural and cultural jumble of Rome, they are not averse to complaining (loudly) about the city's endless inconveniences, yet they are the first to appreciate the historical and architectural marvels that surround them. Cynical but hearty and warm, modern Romans propel themselves through life with an enviable sense of style.

The crowds of pilgrims and the vast numbers of churches and convents exist side by side with fleshier and more earthbound distractions, the combination of which imbues many Romans with an overriding interest in the pleasures and distractions of the moment. This sense of theatricality can be seen in Roman driving habits; in animated conversations and gesticulations in restaurants and cafes; in the lavish displays of flowers, fountains, food, and architecture, the nation's trademark; and in the 27 centuries of building projects dedicated to the power and egos of long-dead potentates.

Despite the crowds, the pollution, the heat, and the virtual impossibility of efficiency, Romans for the most part take life with good cheer and *pazienza*. Translated as "patience," it seems to be the frequently uttered motto of modern Rome and an appropriate philosophy for a city that has known everything from unparalleled glory to humiliation and despair. Romans know that since Rome wasn't built in a day, its charms should be savored slowly and with an appreciation for the cultures that contributed to this panoply.

ROME TODAY

Rome is a city of images, vivid and unforgettable. One of the most striking is dawn from Janiculum Hill as the city's silhouette, with its bell towers and cupolas, comes gradually into view.

Rome is also a city of sounds, beginning early in the morning, with the peal of church bells calling the faithful to Mass. As the city awakens and comes to life, the sounds multiply and merge into a kind of *sinfonia urbana*. The streets fill with cars, taxis, and motor scooters, blaring their horns as they weave in and out of traffic; the sidewalks become overrun with bleary-eyed office workers rushing off to their desks, but not before stealing into crowded cafes for their first cappuccino of the day. The shops lining the streets open for business by raising their protective metal grilles as loudly as possible, seeming to delight in their contribution to the general din. And before long the many fruit-and-vegetable stands are abuzz with activity, as housewives, maids, widowers, cooks, and others arrive to purchase their day's supply of fresh produce, haggling over price and caviling over quality.

Impressions

In Rome you have to do as the Romans do, or get arrested.

—Geoffrey Harmsworth, *Abyssinian Adventure*, 1935

By 10am the tourists are on the street, battling the crowds and traffic as they wind their way from Renaissance palaces and baroque buildings to the famous ruins of antiquity. Indeed, Rome often appears to have two populations: one of Romans and one of visitors. During the summer months especially, Rome seems to become one big host for the countless sightseers who converge upon it, guidebook and camera in hand. To all of them—Americans, Europeans, Japanese—Rome extends a warm and friendly welcome, wining them, dining them, and entertaining them in its inimitable fashion. Of course, if you visit in August, you may see only tourists—not Romans, as the locals flee at that time. Or as one Roman woman once told us, "Even if we're too poor to

Impressions

Vile in its origin, barbarous in its institutions, a casual association of robbers and of outcasts became the destiny of mankind.

—Lady Morgan, *Italy*, 1820

go on vacation, we close the shutters and pretend we're away so neighbors won't find out we couldn't afford to leave the city."

The traffic, unfortunately, is worse than ever, restoration programs seem to drag on forever, and as the capital, Rome remains at the center of the major political scandals and corruption known as *tangentopoli* ("bribe city"), which sends hundreds of government bureaucrats to jail each year.

Political chaos remains part of everyday life on the Roman landscape. It is often assumed that anyone entering politics was doing so for personal gain. Some of that changed in the mid-1990s, when stringent penalties and far-reaching investigations were instituted by a controversial public magistrate, Antonio Di Pietro, who operated with a widespread public approval bordering on adoration. The "Clean Hands" *(Mani Pulite)* campaign he began mandated stiff penalties and led to reams of negative publicity for any politician accused of accepting bribes or campaign contributions that could be interpreted in any way as influence peddling.

Besides soccer *(calico)*, family, and affairs of the heart, the primal obsession of Rome as it moves deeper and deeper into the millennium is *il sorpasso,* a term that describes Italy's surpassing of its archrivals, France and Britain, in economic indicators. Economists disagree about whether or not *il sorpasso* has happened, and statistics vary widely from source to source. Italy's true economy is difficult to measure because of the vast Mafia-controlled underground economy *(economia sommersa)* that competes on a monumental scale with the official economy. Almost every Roman has some unreported income or expenditure, and people at all levels of Italian society are engaged to some degree in withholding funds from the government.

By 2010 *il sorpasso* seemed to have become a distant dream, as Italy, like the United States and Greece, faced a monumental debt crisis and the curse of unemployment which cannot be solved, or so it would seem.

Another complicating factor is the surfeit of laws passed in Rome and their effect on the citizens. Before they get thrown out of office, politicians pass laws and more laws, adding to the seemingly infinite number already on the books. Italy not only has more laws on its books than any other nation of western Europe but also suffers from a bloated bureaucracy. Something as simple as cashing a check or paying a bill can devour half a day. To escape red tape, Romans have become marvelous improvisers and corner-cutters. Whenever possible, they bypass the public sector and negotiate private deals *fra amici* (among friends).

Rome remains a city of contradictions. This simultaneously strident, romantic, and sensual city has forever altered the Western world's religion, art, and government. And despite all the confusion of their city, Romans still manage to live a relatively relaxed way of life. Along with their southern cousins in Naples, they are specialists in *arte di arrangiarsi,* the ability to cope and survive with style. The Romans have humanity and humor, a 2,000-year-old sense of cynicism, and a strong feeling of belonging to a particular place. The city's attractions seem as old as time itself, and despite the frustrations of daily life, Rome will continue to lure new visitors every year, including both vacationers wanting to see what's left of the glory that was Rome and immigrants seeking *la dolce vita.*

After you've done your "duty" to culture, wandered through the Colosseum, been awed that the Pantheon is still there, after you've traipsed through St. Peter's Basilica and thrown a coin in the Trevi Fountain, you can pause in the early evening to experience the charm of Rome at sunset. Find a cafe at summer twilight and watch the shades of pink turn to gold and copper, until night finally falls. That's when a new Rome comes alive, and when its restaurants and cafes grow more animated and more fun, especially if you've found one on an antique piazza or along a narrow alley deep in Trastevere. After dinner you can stroll by the fountains, or through Piazza Navona, have a gelato (or an espresso in winter), and the night is yours.

LOOKING BACK AT ROME

THE ETRUSCANS Among the early inhabitants of Italy, the most significant were the Etruscans—but who were they? Their origins are subject to debate among scholars, and the many inscriptions they left behind are of little to no help, as most are grave markers. It is thought that they arrived on the eastern coast of Umbria several centuries before Rome was built. Their religious rites and architecture show an obvious contact with Mesopotamia; the Etruscans might have been refugees from Asia Minor who traveled westward about 1200 to 1000 B.C. Within 2 centuries, they had subjugated Tuscany and Campania and the Villanovan tribes who lived there.

> **Impressions**
>
> ***The Romans would never have had time to conquer the world if they had been obliged to learn Latin first of all.***
>
> **—Heinrich Heine, *Das Buch Le Grand, In Reisebilder,* 1826–31**

While the Etruscans built temples at Tarquinia and Caere (present-day Cerveteri), the few nervous Latin tribes that remained outside their sway gravitated to Rome, then little more than a sheepherding village. As its power grew, however, Rome increasingly profited from the strategically important Tiber crossing where the ancient Salt Way (Via Salaria) turned northeastward toward the central Apennines.

From their base at Rome, the Latins remained free of the Etruscans until about 600 B.C. But the Etruscan advance was inexorable, and though the tribes concentrated their forces at Rome for a last stand, they were swept away by the sophisticated conquerors. The new overlords introduced gold tableware and jewelry, bronze urns and terra-cotta statuary, and the best of Greek and Asia Minor art and culture; they also made Rome the governmental seat of all Latium. Roma is an Etruscan name, and the kings of Rome had Etruscan names: Numa, Ancus, Tarquinius, and even Romulus.

> **Impressions**
>
> ***It is not impossible to govern Italians. It is merely useless.***
>
> **—Attributed to Benito Mussolini**

Many of the key events that shaped the rich and often gory tapestry of Italian history originated in Rome. Although parts of Italy (especially Sardinia and Sicily) were inhabited as early as the Bronze Age, the region around Rome was occupied relatively late. Some historians claim that the presence of active volcanoes in the region during the Bronze Age prevented prehistoric tribes from living here, but whatever the reason, Rome has unearthed far fewer prehistoric graves and implements than have neighboring Tuscany and Umbria.

Under the combined influences of the Greeks and the Mesopotamian east, Rome grew enormously. A new port was opened at Ostia, near the mouth of the Tiber. Artists from Greece carved statues of Roman gods to resemble Greek divinities. From this enforced (and not always peaceable) mixture of Latin tribes and Etruscans grew the roots of what eventually became the Republic of Rome.

The Etruscans ruled until the Roman revolt around 510 B.C., and by 250 B.C., the Romans and their Campanian allies had vanquished the Etruscans, wiping out their language and religion. However, many of their former rulers' manners and beliefs remained, assimilated into the culture. Even today, certain Etruscan customs and bloodlines are believed to still exist in Italy, especially in Tuscany.

The best places to see the legacy left by these mysterious people are in Cerveteri and Tarquinia, outside Rome. Especially interesting is the Etruscan necropolis, just 6.5km (4 miles) southeast of Tarquinia, where thousands of tombs have been discovered. See chapter 11, "Side Trips from Rome," for details on all these sites. To learn more about the Etruscans, visit the National Etruscan Museum (Museo Nazionale di Villa Giulia) in Rome itself (see chapter 7, "Exploring Rome").

THE ROMAN REPUBLIC Tempered in the fires of military adversity, the stern Roman republic was characterized by belief in the gods, the necessity of learning from the past, strength of the family, education through books and public service, and, most important, obedience. The all-powerful Senate presided as Rome defeated rival powers one after the other in a steady stream of staggering military successes.

As the population grew, the Romans gave to their Latin allies and then to conquered peoples partial or complete Roman citizenship, always with the obligation of military service. Colonies of citizens were established on the borders of the growing empire and were populated with soldier-farmers and their families. Later, as seen in the history of Britain and the European continent, colonies began to thrive as semiautonomous units on their own, heavily fortified and linked to Rome by well-maintained military roads and a well-defined hierarchy of military command.

The final obstacle to the unrivaled supremacy of Rome was the defeat, during the 3rd century B.C., of the city-state of Carthage during the two Punic Wars. An ancient Phoenician trading post on the coast of Tunisia, Carthage had grown into one of the premier naval and agricultural powers of the Mediterranean, with strongly fortified positions in Corsica, Sardinia, and Spain. Despite the impressive victories of the Carthaginian general Hannibal, Rome eventually eradicated Carthage in one of the most famous defeats in ancient history. Rome was able to immediately expand its power into North Africa, Sardinia, Corsica, and Iberia.

THE ROMAN EMPIRE By 49 B.C., Italy ruled the entire Mediterranean world either directly or indirectly, with all political, commercial, and cultural pathways leading directly to Rome. The wealth and glory to be found in Rome lured many there, but drained other Italian communities of human resources. As Rome transformed itself into an administrative headquarters, imports to the city from other parts of the Empire hurt local farmers and landowners. The seeds for civil discord were sown early in the Republic's existence, although, because Rome was embellished with temples, monuments, and the easy availability of slave labor from conquered territories, many of its social problems were overlooked in favor of expansion and glory.

No figure was more towering during the Republic than Julius Caesar, the charismatic conqueror of Gaul. After defeating the last resistance of Pompey the Great in

45 B.C., he came to Rome and was made dictator and consul for 10 years. He was at that point almost a king. Conspirators led by Marcus Junius Brutus stabbed him to death in the Senate on March 15, 44 B.C. Beware the Ides of March.

Marc Antony then assumed control by seizing Caesar's papers and wealth. Intent on expanding the Republic, Antony met with Cleopatra at Tarsus in 41 B.C. She seduced him, and he stayed in Egypt for a year. When Antony eventually returned to Rome, still smitten with Cleopatra, he made peace with Caesar's willed successor, Octavius, and, through the pacts of Brundisium, soon found himself married to Octavius's sister, Octavia. This marriage, however, didn't prevent him from openly marrying Cleopatra in 36 B.C. The furious Octavius gathered western legions and defeated Antony at the Battle of Actium on September 2, 31 B.C. Cleopatra fled to Egypt, followed by Antony, who committed suicide in disgrace a year later. Cleopatra, unable to seduce his successor and thus retain her rule of Egypt, followed suit with the help of an asp.

Born Gaius Octavius in 63 B.C., Augustus, the first Roman emperor, reigned from 27 B.C. to A.D. 14. His reign, called "the golden age of Rome," led to the Pax Romana, 2 centuries of peace. He had been adopted by and eventually became the heir of his great-uncle Julius Caesar. In Rome you can still visit the remains of the Forum of Augustus, built before the birth of Christ, and the Domus Augustana, where the imperial family lived on the Palatine Hill.

On the eve of the birth of Jesus, Rome was a mighty empire whose generals had brought the Western world under the influence of Roman law, values, and civilization. Only in the eastern third of the Mediterranean did the existing cultures—notably, the Greeks—withstand the Roman incursions. Despite its occupation by Rome, Greece permeated Rome more than any culture with new ideas, values, and concepts of art, architecture, religion, and philosophy.

The emperors, whose succession started with Augustus's principate after the death of Julius Caesar, brought Rome to new, almost giddy, heights. Augustus transformed the city from brick to marble, much the way Napoleon III transformed Paris many centuries later. But success led to corruption. The emperors wielded autocratic power, and the centuries witnessed a steady decay in the ideals and traditions on which the Empire had been founded. The army became a fifth column of barbarian mercenaries, the tax collector became the scourge of the countryside, and for every good emperor (Augustus, Claudius, Trajan, Vespasian, and Hadrian, to name a few) there were three or four debased heads of state (Caligula, Nero, Domitian, Caracalla, and more).

The ideals of democratic responsibility in the heart of the Empire had begun to break down. The populace began to object violently to a government that took little interest in commerce and seemed interested only in foreign politics. As taxes and levies increased, the poor emigrated in huge and idle numbers to Rome and the rich cities of the Po Valley. Entire generations of war captives, forced into the slave-driven economies of large Italian estates, were steeped in hatred and ignorance.

Christianity, a new and revolutionary religion, probably gained a foothold in Rome about 10 years after Jesus' Crucifixion. Feared far more for its political implications than for its spiritual presuppositions, the religion was at first brutally suppressed before moving through increasingly tolerant stages of acceptance.

After Augustus died (by poison, perhaps), his widow, Livia—a crafty social climber who had divorced her first husband to marry Augustus—set up her son,

Tiberius, as ruler through a series of intrigues and poisonings. A long series of murders ensued, and Tiberius, who ruled during Pontius Pilate's trial and Crucifixion of Christ, was eventually murdered in an uprising of landowners. In fact, murder was so common that a short time later Emperor Domitian became so obsessed with the possibility of assassination that he had the walls of his palace covered in mica so he could see behind him at all times. (He was killed anyway.)

Excesses and scandal ruled the day: Caligula (a bit overfond of his sister Drusilla) appointed his horse a lifetime member of the Senate, lavished money on foolish projects, and proclaimed himself a god. Caligula's successor, his uncle Claudius, was deceived and publicly humiliated by one of his wives, the lascivious Messalina (he had her killed for her trouble); he was then poisoned by his final wife, his niece Agrippina, to secure the succession of Nero, her son by a previous marriage. To thank her, Nero murdered not only his mother, but also his wife, Claudius's daughter, and his rival, Claudius's son. The disgraceful Nero was removed as emperor while visiting Greece; he committed suicide with the cry, "What an artist the world loses in me!"

By the 3rd century A.D., corruption was so prevalent that there were 23 emperors in 73 years. There were so many emperors that it was common, as H. V. Morton tells us, to hear in the provinces of the election of an emperor together with a report of his assassination. How bad had things gotten? So bad that Caracalla, to secure control of the Empire, had his brother Geta slashed to pieces while lying in his mother's arms.

As the decay progressed, Roman citizens either lived on the increasingly swollen public dole while spending their days at gladiatorial games and imperial baths, or were disillusioned patricians at the mercy of emperors who might murder them for their property.

The 4th-century reforms of Diocletian held the Empire together, but at the expense of its inhabitants, who were reduced to tax units. He reinforced imperial power while paradoxically weakening Roman dominance and prestige by dividing the Empire into east and west halves and establishing administrative capitals at outposts such as Milan and Trier, Germany. Diocletian instituted not only heavy taxes but also a socioeconomic system that made professions hereditary. This edict was so strictly enforced that the son of a silversmith could be tried as a criminal if he attempted to become a sculptor instead.

Constantine became emperor in A.D. 306, and in 330 he made Constantinople (or Byzantium) the new capital of the Empire, moving the administrative functions away from Rome altogether, an act that sounded a death knell for a city already threatened by the menace of barbarian attacks. The sole survivor of six rival emperors, Constantine recognized Christianity as the official religion of the Roman Empire and built an entirely new, more easily defended capital on the banks of the Bosporus. Named in his honor (Constantinople, or Byzantium), it was later renamed Istanbul by the Ottoman Turks. When he moved to the new capital, Constantine and his heirs took with them the best of the artisans, politicians, and public figures of Rome. Rome, reduced to little more than a provincial capital controlling the threatened western half of the once-mighty empire, continued to founder and decay. As for the Christian church, although the popes of Rome were under the nominal auspices of an exarch from Constantinople, their power increased slowly and steadily as the power of the emperors declined.

THE EMPIRE FALLS The eastern and western sections of the Roman Empire split in 395, leaving Italy without the support it had once received from east of the

Adriatic. When the Goths moved toward Rome in the early 5th century, citizens in the provinces, who had grown to hate and fear the bureaucracy set up by Diocletian and followed by succeeding emperors, welcomed the invaders. And then the pillage began.

Rome was first sacked by Alaric in August 410. The populace made no attempt to defend the city (other than trying to buy off the Goths, a tactic that had worked 3 years before); most people simply fled into the hills or, if they were rich, headed to their country estates. The feeble Western emperor Honorius hid out in Ravenna the entire time.

More than 40 troubled years passed until the siege of Rome by Attila the Hun. Attila was dissuaded from attacking, thanks largely to a peace mission headed by Pope Leo I in 452. Yet relief was short-lived: In 455, Gaiseric the Vandal carried out a 2-week sack that was unparalleled in its pure savagery. The empire of the West lasted for only another 20 years; the sackings and chaos finally destroyed it in 476, and Rome was left to the popes, under the nominal auspices of an exarch from Byzantium (Constantinople).

The last would-be Caesars to walk the streets of Rome were both barbarians: The first was Theodoric, who established an Ostrogoth kingdom at Ravenna from 493 to 526; and the second was Totilla, who held the last races in the Circus Maximus in 549. Totilla was engaged in a running battle with Belisarius, the general of the Eastern emperor Justinian, who sought to regain Rome for the Eastern Empire. The city changed hands several times, recovering some of its ancient pride by bravely resisting Totilla's forces but eventually being entirely depopulated by the continuing battles.

THE HOLY ROMAN EMPIRE A ravaged Rome entered the Middle Ages with its once-proud population scattered and unrecognizable in rustic exile. A modest population started life again in the swamps of the Campus Martius, while the seven hills, now without water since the aqueducts were cut, stood abandoned and crumbling.

After the fall of the Western Empire, the pope took on more imperial powers, yet there was no political unity. Decades of rule by barbarians and then Goths were followed by takeovers in different parts of the country by various strong warriors, such as the Lombards. Italy was thus divided into several spheres of control. In 731, Pope Gregory II renounced Rome's dependence on Constantinople and thus ended the twilight era of the Greek exarch who had nominally ruled Rome.

Papal Rome turned toward Europe, where the papacy found a powerful ally in Charlemagne, a king of the barbarian Franks. In 800, he was crowned emperor by Pope Leo III. The capital he established at Aachen (*Aix-la-Chapelle* in French) laid deep within territory known to the Romans a half millennium ago as the heart of the barbarian world. Though Charlemagne pledged allegiance to the church and looked to Rome and its pope as the final arbiter in most religious and cultural affairs, he launched northwestern Europe on a course toward bitter political opposition to the meddling of the papacy in temporal affairs.

The successor to Charlemagne's empire was a political entity known as the Holy Roman Empire (962–1806). The new empire defined the end of the Dark Ages but ushered in a period of long, bloody warfare. The Lombard leaders battled the Franks. Magyars from Hungary invaded northeastern Lombardy and were defeated, in turn, by the increasingly powerful Venetians. Normans gained military control of Sicily in the 11th century, divided it from the rest of Italy, and altered forever the island's racial and ethnic makeup and its architecture. As Italy dissolved into a fragmented collection of city-states, the papacy fell under the power of Rome's feudal landowners. Eventually, even the process for choosing popes came into the hands of the increasingly Germanic Holy Roman emperors, although this power balance would very soon shift.

Rome during the Middle Ages was a quaint rural town. Narrow lanes with overhanging buildings filled many areas that had once been showcases of ancient imperial power, such as the Campus Martius. The forums, mercantile exchanges, temples, and theaters of the Imperial Era slowly disintegrated and collapsed. The decay of ancient Rome was assisted by periodic earthquakes, centuries of neglect, and, in particular, the growing need for building materials. Rome receded into a dusty provincialism. As the seat of the Roman Catholic church, the state was almost completely controlled by priests, who had an insatiable need for new churches and convents.

By the end of the 11th century, the popes shook off control of the Roman aristocracy, rid themselves of what they considered the excessive influence of the emperors at Aachen, and began an aggressive expansion of church influence and acquisitions. The deliberate organization of the church into a format modeled on the hierarchies of the ancient Roman Empire put it on a collision course with the Holy Roman Empire and the other temporal leaders of Europe, resulting in an endless series of power struggles.

THE MIDDLE AGES The papacy soon became essentially a feudal state, and the pope became a medieval (later Renaissance) prince engaged in many of the worldly activities that brought criticism on the church in later centuries. The fall of the Holy Land to the Turks in 1065 catapulted the papacy into the forefront of world politics, primarily because of the Crusades, most of which were judged to be military and economic disasters and many of which the popes directly caused or encouraged. During the 12th and 13th centuries, the bitter rivalries that rocked the secular and spiritual bastions of Europe took their toll on the stability of the Holy Roman Empire, which grew weaker as city-states buttressed by mercantile and trade-related prosperity grew stronger. In addition, France emerged as a strong nation in its own right during this period. Each investiture of a new bishop to any influential post became a cause for endless jockeying for power among many political and ecclesiastical factions.

These conflicts achieved their most visible impasse in 1303 with the full-fledged removal of the papacy from Rome to the French city of Avignon. For more than 70 years, until 1377, viciously competing popes (one in Rome, another under the protection of the French kings in Avignon) made simultaneous claims to the legacy of St. Peter, underscoring as never before the degree to which the church was both a victim and a victimizer of European politics.

The seat of the papacy was eventually returned to Rome, where a series of popes proved every bit as fascinating as the Roman emperors they replaced. The great families—Barberini, Medici, Borgia—enhanced their status and fortunes impressively whenever one of their sons was elected pope.

In the mid–14th century, the Black Death ravaged Europe, killing a third of Italy's population. Despite such setbacks, northern Italian city-states grew wealthy from Crusade booty, trade with one another and with the Middle East, and banking. These wealthy principalities and pseudo-republics ruled by the merchant elite flexed their muscles in the absence of a strong central authority.

THE RENAISSANCE The story of Italy from the dawn of the Renaissance in the 15th century to the Age of Enlightenment in the 17th and 18th centuries is as varied and fascinating as that of the rise and fall of the Empire.

Despite the centuries that had passed since the collapse of the Roman Empire, the age of siege wasn't yet over. In 1527, Charles V, king of Spain, carried out the worst sack of Rome ever. To the horror of Pope Clement VII (a Medici), the entire city was brutally pillaged by the man who was crowned Holy Roman Emperor the next year.

During the years of the Renaissance, the Reformation, and the Counter-Reformation, Rome underwent major physical changes. The old centers of culture reverted to pastures and fields, and great churches and palaces were built with the stones of ancient Rome. This construction boom did far more damage to the temples of the Caesars than any barbarian sacking had done. Rare marbles were stripped from the imperial baths and used as altarpieces or sent to limekilns. So enthusiastic was the papal destruction of imperial Rome that it's a miracle anything is left.

This era is best remembered for its art. The great ruling families, especially the Medicis in Florence, the Gonzagas in Mantua, and the Estes in Ferrara, not only reformed law and commerce, but also sparked a renaissance in art. Out of this period arose such towering figures as Leonardo da Vinci and Michelangelo. Many visitors come to Italy to view what's left of the art and glory of that era, including Michelangelo's Sistine Chapel ceiling at the Vatican.

THE MOVE TOWARD A UNITED ITALY During the 17th, 18th, and 19th centuries, the fortunes of Rome rose and fell with the general political and economic situation of the rest of Italy. Since the end of the 13th century, Italy had been divided into a series of regional states, each with mercenary soldiers, its own judicial system, and an interlocking series of alliances and enmities that had created a network of intensely competitive city-states. (Some of these families had attained formidable power under such *signori* as the Este family in Ferrara, the Medici in Florence, and the Sforza in Milan.) Rome, headquarters of the Papal States, maintained its independence and (usually) the integrity of its borders, although some of the city's religious power had been diluted as increasing numbers of Europeans converted to Protestantism.

Napoleon made a bid for power in Italy beginning in 1796, fueling his propaganda machines with what was considered a relatively easy victory. During the 1815 Congress of Vienna, which followed Napoleon's defeat, Italy was once again divided among many different factions: Austria was given Lombardy and Venetia, and the Papal States were returned to the popes. Some duchies were put back into the hands of their hereditary rulers, whereas southern Italy and Sicily went to a newly imported dynasty related to the Bourbons. One historic move, which eventually assisted in the unification of Italy, was the assignment of the former republic of Genoa to Sardinia (which at the time was governed by the House of Savoy).

By now, political unrest had become a fact of Italian (and Roman) life, at least some of it encouraged by the rapid industrialization of the north and the almost total lack of industrialization in the south. Despite these barriers, in 1861 the Kingdom of Italy was proclaimed, and Victor Emmanuel II of the House of Savoy, king of Sardinia, became head of the new monarchy. In 1861 the designated capital of the newly united country, following a 2,000-year-old precedent, became Rome.

Garibaldi, the most respected of all Italian heroes, must be singled out for his efforts, which included taking Sicily, then returning to the mainland and marching north to meet Victor Emmanuel II at Teano, and finally declaring a unified Italy (with the important exception of Rome itself). It must have seemed especially sweet to a man whose efforts at unity had caused him to flee the country fearing for his life on four occasions. It's a tribute to the tenacity of this red-bearded hero that he never gave up, even in the early 1850s, when he was forced to wait out one of his exiles as a candlemaker on Staten Island in New York.

In a controversial move that engendered resentment many decades later, the borders of the Papal States were eradicated from the map as Rome was incorporated into the new nation of Italy. The Vatican, however, did not yield its territory to the new order, despite guarantees of nonintervention proffered by the Italian government, and relations between the pope and the political leaders of Italy remained rocky until 1929.

WORLD WAR II & THE AXIS On October 28, 1922, Benito Mussolini, who had started his Fascist Party in 1919, knew the time was ripe for change. He gathered 50,000 supporters for a march on Rome. Inflation was soaring and workers had just called a general strike, so rather than recognizing a state under siege, King Victor Emmanuel III recognized Mussolini as the new government leader. In 1929, Il Duce defined the divisions between the Italian government and the Vatican by signing a concordat granting political and fiscal autonomy to Vatican City. It also made Roman Catholicism the official state religion—but that designation was removed in 1978 through a revision of the concordat.

During the Spanish Civil War (1936–39), Mussolini's support of Franco's Fascist Party, which staged a coup against the democratically elected government of Spain, helped encourage the formation of the "Axis" alliance between Italy and Nazi Germany. Despite its outdated military equipment, Italy added to the general horror of the era by invading Abyssinia (Ethiopia) in 1935. In 1940, Italy invaded Greece through Albania, and in 1942 it sent thousands of Italian troops to assist Hitler in his disastrous campaign along the Russian front. In 1943, Allied forces, under the command of U.S. Gen. George Patton and British Gen. Bernard Montgomery, landed in Sicily and quickly secured the island as they prepared to move north toward Rome.

In the face of likely defeat and humiliation, Mussolini was overthrown by his own cabinet (Grand Council). The Allies made a separate deal with Victor Emmanuel III, who had collaborated with the fascists during the previous 2 decades and now easily shifted allegiances. A politically divided Italy watched as battalions of fanatical German Nazis released Mussolini from his Italian jail cell to establish the short-lived Republic of Salò, headquartered on the edge of Lake Garda. Mussolini had hoped for a groundswell of popular opinion in favor of Italian fascism, but events quickly proved this nothing more than a futile dream.

In April 1945, with almost half a million Italians rising in a mass demonstration against him and the German war machine, Mussolini was captured by Italian partisans as he fled to Switzerland. Along with his mistress, Claretta Petacci, and several others of his intimates, he was shot and strung upside down from the roof of a Milan gas station.

MODERN ROME Disaffected with the monarchy and its identification with the fallen fascist dictatorship, Italian voters in 1946 voted for the establishment of a republic. The major political party that emerged following World War II was the Christian Democratic Party, a right-of-center group whose leader, Alcide De Gasperi (1881–1954), served as premier until 1953. The second-largest party was the Communist Party; however, by the mid-1970s it had abandoned its revolutionary program in favor of a democratic form of "Eurocommunism" (in 1991, the Communists even changed their name to the Democratic Party of the Left).

Although after the war Italy was stripped of all its overseas colonies, it quickly succeeded in rebuilding its economy, in part because of U.S. aid under the Marshall Plan (1948–52). By the 1960s, as a member of the European Community (founded in Rome in 1957), Italy had become one of the world's leading industrialized nations, prominent in the manufacture of automobiles and office equipment.

But the country continued to be plagued by economic inequities between the prosperous industrialized north and the economically depressed south. It suffered an unprecedented flight of capital (frequently aided by Swiss banks only too willing to accept discreet deposits from wealthy Italians) and an increase in bankruptcies, inflation (almost 20% during much of the 1970s), and unemployment.

During the late 1970s and early 1980s, Italy was rocked by the rise of terrorism, instigated both by neofascists and by left-wing intellectuals from the Socialist-controlled universities of the north.

THE 1990S & INTO THE NEW MILLENNIUM In the 1990s, some 6,000 businesspeople and politicians were implicated in a billion-dollar government graft scandal. Such familiar figures as Bettino Craxi, former head of the Socialist party, and Giulio Andreotti, a seven-time prime minister, were accused of corruption.

Hoping for a renewal after all this exposure of greed, Italian voters in March 1994 turned to the right wing to head their government. In overwhelming numbers, voters elected a former cruise-ship singer turned media billionaire, Silvio Berlusconi, as their new leader. His Forza Italia (Go, Italy) party formed an alliance with the neofascist National Alliance and the secessionist Northern League to sweep to victory. These elections were termed "the most critical" for Italy in 4 decades. The new government was beset with an almost hopeless array of new problems, including destabilization caused by the Mafia and its underground economies. When the Northern League defected from the coalition in December 1994, Berlusconi resigned.

Treasury Minister Lamberto Dini, a nonpolitical international banker, replaced him. Dini signed on merely as a transitional player in Italy's topsy-turvy political game. His austere measures enacted to balance Italy's budget, including cuts in pensions and healthcare, were not popular among the mostly blue-collar Italian workers or the very influential labor unions. Pending a predicted defeat in a no-confidence vote, Dini also stepped down. His resignation in January 1996 left beleaguered Italians shouting "*Basta!*" ("Enough!"). This latest shuffling in Italy's political deck prompted President Oscar Scalfaro to dissolve both houses of the Italian Parliament.

Once again Italians were faced with forming a new government. Elections in April 1996 proved quite a shocker, not only for the defeated politicians but also for the victors. The center-left coalition known as the Olive Tree, led by Romano Prodi, swept both the Senate and the Chamber of Deputies. The Olive Tree, whose roots stem from the old Communist party, achieved victory by shifting toward the center and focusing its campaign on a strong platform protecting social benefits and supporting Italy's bid to become a solid member of the European Union. Prodi followed through on his commitment when he announced a stringent budget for 1997 in a bid to be among the first countries to enter the monetary union.

The year 1997 saw further upheavals as the Prodi government continued to push ahead with cuts to the country's generous social-security system. In the autumn of 1997, Prodi was forced to submit his resignation when he lost critical support in Parliament from the Communist Refounding party, which balked at further pension and welfare cuts in the 1998 budget. The party eventually backed off with its demands, and Prodi was returned to office.

In December 1999, under Prime Minister Massimo D'Alema, Italy received its 57th new government since 1945. But it didn't last long. In April 2000, former Prime Minister Giuliano Amato, a one-time Socialist, returned to power.

As 1999 neared its end, Rome rushed to put the finishing touches on its many monuments, including churches and museums, and everybody was ready for the scaffolding to come down before the arrival of 2000. Italy spent all of 2000 welcoming Jubilee Year visitors from around the world, as its political cauldron bubbled. One particularly notable clash in 2000 pitted the church and social conservatives against more progressive young Italians, as the pope lashed out at the World Gay Pride rally held in the summer of 2000. His condemnation sparked much debate in the media, but the actual event went off without a hitch and, in fact, was labeled as rather tame when compared to more raucous Gay Pride rallies elsewhere around the globe.

In May 2001, with right-wing support, the richest man in Italy, billionaire media tycoon Silvio Berlusconi (owner of three private TV networks) swept to victory as prime minister. Calling for a "revolution" in Italy, Berlusconi promised a million and a half new jobs, pension hikes, epic tax cuts, anticrime bills, and beefed-up public works projects.

In 2002, Italians abandoned their long-beloved lire and began trading in euros along with their neighbors to the north, including France and Germany—a total of 12 countries (but not Britain). As the new currency went into effect, counterfeiters and swindlers had a field day; one elderly woman in Rome who was cashing a benefit check, unwittingly paid the equivalent of 600 U.S. dollars for a cup of cappuccino. But in general, the transition went relatively smoothly, especially among businesses.

Unlike France and Germany, Prime Minister Berlusconi proved to be a valuable ally of the United States when it went to war against Iraq in 2003. Berlusconi has attacked "Saddam apologists" who want to try to regain power through terrorist activity. A great deal of Italy, however, does not take the position of its prime minister and is highly critical of the way the U.S. has handled the war in Iraq.

In the Italian elections in April 2006, Berlusconi was ousted by a narrow vote, losing to Romano Prodi. The new prime minister faced difficult challenges and had a hard time keeping together nine parties that ranged from moderate Catholics to Communists.

In April 2008, Berlusconi made a spectacular comeback, winning a third term as Italy's prime minister. Italian voters gave him a strong mandate to deal with the country's economic and social problems. The media magnate won a big majority in both houses of parliament for his party. The reelection of the conservative leader was the 62nd government Italy has installed since World War II.

Berlusconi, in trying to oversee Italy's woes, in 2010 didn't seem to have his own house in order. As he watched markets plummet and investors panic, the billionaire leader saw shares in some of his own companies nose-dive by 40%.

In his 70s, the leader—nicknamed "Italian Stallion"—continued to be plagued by sex scandals, with the PM admitting, "I'm no saint."

"If I sleep for 3 hours, I still have enough energy to make love for another 3," he told the newspaper *La Repubblica*. "I hope that when you hit 70, you're in as good shape as I am." Berlusconi speaks with such theatrics and locker room humor in public.

The PM has become entangled in various red-hot sex scandals for months over his alleged encounters with young women, often prostitutes. Berlusconi, however, had denied he ever paid any woman for sex. Even while calling the allegations "trash," he candidly admitted, "That's who I am—and that's how the Italians want me to be."

In spite of his problems, his power, at least as we went to press, seemed greater than ever. That's because he controls billions of dollars in public money. He can decide which private companies to bail out, and which to ignore. In spite of its financial woes, Italy remains the seventh largest economy in the world.

Barring an early vote, the next major election is scheduled in 2013. The big political question in Italy is this: Will Berlusconi run again?

ROME'S ART & ARCHITECTURE

The art of Rome ranges from Roman mosaics and Renaissance masterpieces by Michelangelo and Leonardo to baroque statues by Bernini and modern still lifes by Morandi. Its architecture is equally wide ranging, from Roman temples and Byzantine basilicas to Renaissance churches, baroque palaces, and postmodern stadiums that take their cues from the ancient Colosseum.

CLASSICAL: ETRUSCANS & ROMANS (8TH CENTURY B.C. TO 5TH CENTURY A.D.)

The **Etruscans,** who became Rome's pre-Republican Tarquin kings, arrived from Asia Minor with their own styles. By the 6th century B.C., however, they were borrowing heavily from the Greeks in their sculpture and importing thousands of Attic vases, which displayed the most popular and widespread painting style of ancient Greece.

Etruscan artistic remains in Rome are confined to the Villa Giulia and Vatican Museums; the best is the Villa Giulia's terra-cotta sarcophagi covers of reclining figures. Some tomb paintings also survive at Tarquinia.

Painting in ancient **Rome** was used primarily for decorative purposes. Bucolic frescoes (the technique of painting on wet plaster) adorned the walls of the wealthy. Rome's sculptures tended to glorify emperors and the perfect human form, copying ad nauseam from famous Greek originals.

Along with an army of also-ran Roman statues and busts gracing most archaeological collections, you'll find a few standouts: bas-reliefs on the Arch of Constantine; the sculptures, mosaics, and fresco collections at the various branches of the Museo Nazionale Romano; and such sculptures as the gilded equestrian statue of Marcus Aurelius and *The Dying Gaul* at the Capitoline Museum.

BYZANTINE & ROMANESQUE (5TH TO 13TH CENTURIES)

The **Byzantine** style of painting and mosaic was very stylized and static. The oldest Paleochristian mosaics (5th–7th centuries) are in Santa Maria Maggiore, Santa Sabina (which also preserves remarkable 5th-c. wood doors carved with biblical reliefs), and San Giovanni in Laterano's San Venanzio and Santa Rufina chapels (the main church's apse mosaic is 13th c.).

Romanesque sculpture was somewhat more fluid, but still far from naturalistic. San Clemente Basilica's lower church has some of the few remaining early medieval paintings in Rome. At the **National Museum of Palazzo Venezia,** you'll find Rome's best collection of medieval art, including the oldest painted wood statue (13th c.), plus numerous Byzantine crosses.

INTERNATIONAL GOTHIC (LATE 13TH TO EARLY 15TH CENTURIES)

Late medieval Italian art continued to be largely ecclesiastical. In both Gothic painting and sculpture, figures tended to be more natural than in the Romanesque (and the colors in paintings more varied and rich) but remained highly stylized.

The greatest Gothic artist to work in Rome was **Giotto** (1266–1337). The Vatican Pinacoteca owns his *Stefaneschi Triptych* (1315). Arnolfo di Cambio (1245–1302), the Tuscan sculptor, left a venerated bronze *St. Peter* in St. Peter's Basilica.

RENAISSANCE (EARLY 15TH TO MID-17TH CENTURIES)

The painters, sculptors, and architects of the Renaissance experimented with new modes in art and broke with static medieval traditions to pursue a greater degree of expressiveness and naturalism, using such techniques as linear perspective.

Two towering artists left a great legacy in Rome, including **Raphael** (1483–1520) and **Michelangelo** (1475–1564). For Pope Julius II, Michelangelo painted the Sistine Chapel frescoes (1508–12) and the *Last Judgment* (1535–41). He sculpted his world famous *Pietà* in 1500 at the age of 25. It stands in St. Peter's Basilica.

Raphael produced a body of work in his short lifetime (he died at 37) that influenced European painters for generations to come. You'll find his ethereal *Transfiguration* (1520), almost finished when he died, in the Vatican Museums. Also in the Vatican are his greatest works, a series of frescoed rooms (1508–20) including the *School of Athens,* a celebration of Renaissance artistic precepts.

BAROQUE & ROCOCO (LATE 16TH TO 18TH CENTURIES)

The **baroque,** a more theatrical and decorative take on the Renaissance, mixes a kind of super-realism based on using peasants as models and an exaggerated use of light and dark, called *chiaroscuro.*

Caravaggio (1571–1610) reinvented baroque painting, using peasants and commoners as models. Among his masterpieces is the *St. Matthew* (1599) cycle in San Luigi dei Francesi, a series of paintings in the Galleria Borghese and Palazzo Corsini, and the *Deposition* (1604) in the Vatican Museums.

Bernini (1598–1680) was the greatest baroque sculptor. Among his finest sculptures are several in the Galleria Borghese: his youthful *Aeneas and Anchises* (1613), *Apollo and Daphne* (1624), *The Rape of Persephone* (1621), and *David* (1623–24). His other masterpiece is the *Fountain of the Four Rivers* (1651) in Piazza Navona.

LATE 18TH TO 20TH CENTURIES

After carrying the banner of artistic innovation for more than a millennium, Italy ran out of steam with the baroque. Nevertheless, the country did produce a few fine **neoclassical** sculptures in the late 18th century. Italy did not play an important role in 19th- or 20th-century art. Even so, a few great artists arose, notably **Antonio Canova** (1757–1822), the country's top neoclassical sculptor who sculpted both Napoleon and sister Pauline in the nude. His work rests in the Galleria Borghese. **Amadeo Modigliani** (1884–1920) became known for his mysterious, elongated heads and nudes—check them out at the National Gallery of Modern Art.

Giorgio de Chirico (1888–1978) founded freaky ***pittura metafisica*** (metaphysical painting), a forerunner of surrealism wherein figures and objects are stripped of their usual meaning though odd juxtapositions, warped perspective, unnatural shadows, and other bizarre effects. Look for them in the National Gallery of Modern Art and the Collection of Modern Religious Art in the Vatican Museums.

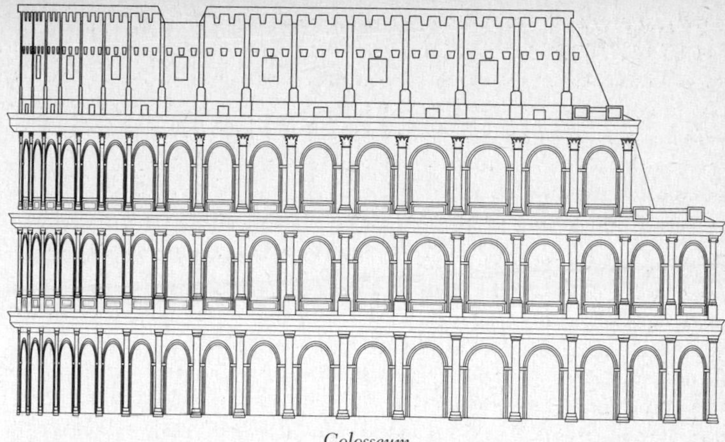
Colosseum

Architecture

Very few buildings (especially churches) were actually built in only one style. Massive, expensive structures often took centuries to complete, during which time tastes changed and plans were altered.

CLASSICAL (6TH CENTURY B.C. TO 4TH CENTURY A.D.)

The **Romans** made use of certain **Greek** innovations, particularly architectural ideas. **Classical orders** (see illustration) are most easily recognized by their column capitals, with the least-ornate capital used on a building's ground level and the most ornate used on the top: Doric (a plain capital), Ionic (a capital with a scroll), and Corinthian (a capital with flowering acanthus leaves).

Although marble is traditionally associated with Roman architecture, Roman engineers could also do wonders with bricks or even simple concrete—concrete seating made possible such enormous theaters as Rome's 2.5-hectare (6-acre), 45,000-seat Colosseum.

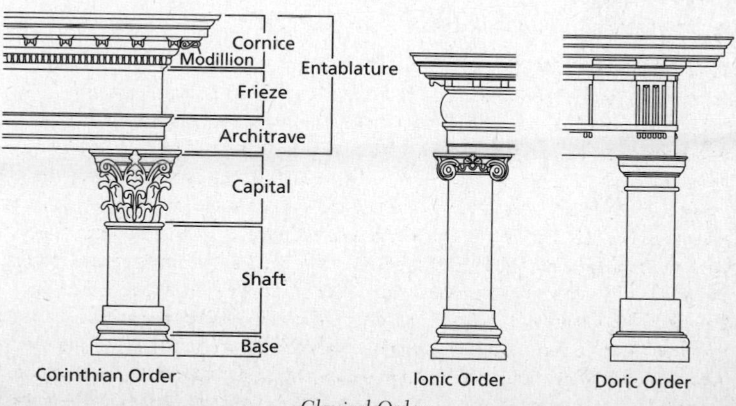

Classical Orders

Roman architecture includes the sports stadium of the **Colosseum** (1st C. A.D.; see illustration), which perfectly displays the use of the classical orders; Hadrian's marvel of engineering, the temple of the **Pantheon** (1st c. A.D.); and the public **Baths of Caracalla** (3rd c. A.D.). Another good example is the **Basilica of Constantine and Maxentius** in the Roman Forum (4th c. A.D.).

ROMANESQUE & GOTHIC (7TH TO 15TH CENTURIES)

The **Romanesque** took its inspiration and rounded arches from ancient Rome (hence the name). The first major churches in Rome were built on the basilica plan of Roman law courts. Architects constructed large churches with wide aisles to accommodate the masses.

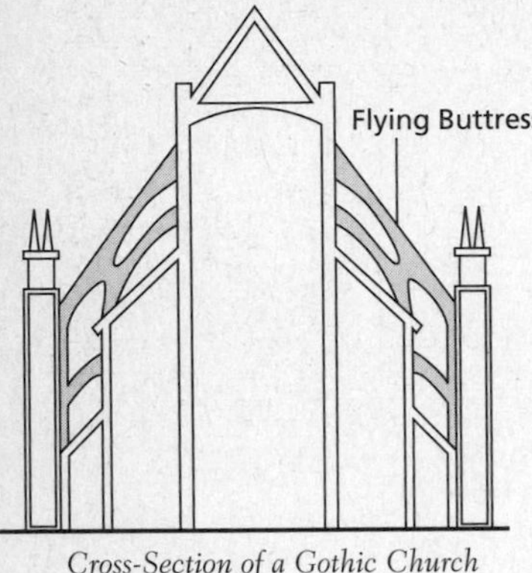

Cross-Section of a Gothic Church

By the late 12th century, the development of the pointed arch and exterior **flying buttress** (see "Cross-Section of Gothic Church" illustration) freed architecture from the heavy, thick walls of Romanesque structures and allowed ceilings to soar, walls to thin, and windows to proliferate in the **Gothic** style.

The great early basilicas, each at least partly altered in decor over the ages, include **Santa Maria Maggiore, San Giovanni in Laterano,** and **San Paolo Fuori le Mure.** Other less grand Romanesque churches include **Santa Maria in Cosmedin** (see illustration) and **Santa Sabina.**

Santa Maria Sopra Minerva is Rome's only **Gothic** church, all pointy arches and soaring ceilings.

RENAISSANCE (15TH TO 17TH CENTURIES)

As in painting, Renaissance architectural rules stressed proportion, order, classical inspiration, and mathematical precision to create unified, balanced structures.

Bramante (1444–1514) was the most mathematical and classically precise of the early High Renaissance architects. This is evident in his (much altered) plans for **St. Peter's Basilica** (his spiral staircase in the Vatican has survived untouched) and his jewel of perfect Renaissance architecture, the textbook **Tempietto** (1502; see illustration) at San Pietro in Montorio on the slopes of Rome's Janiculum Hill.

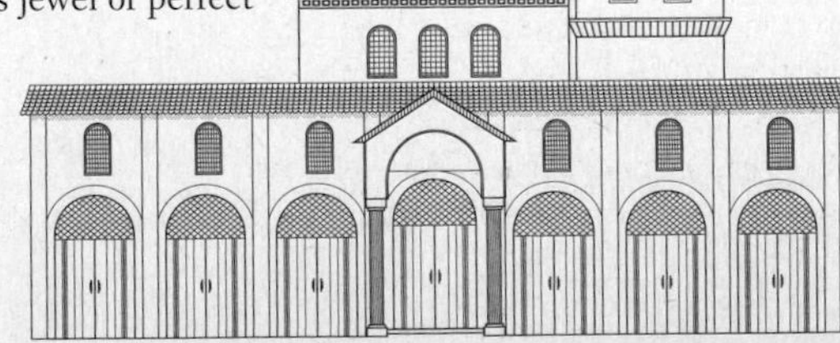
Santa Maria in Cosmedin

Renaissance man **Michelangelo** took up architecture later in life, designing the **dome atop St. Peter's Basilica;** the sloping approach, 12-pointed star courtyard, and trio of palace facades that together make up **Piazza del Campidoglio** atop the Capitoline Hill; and the facade of the **Palazzo Farnese** (1566), which was otherwise built by **Antonio da Sangallo** (1483–1546).

Tempietto

BAROQUE & ROCOCO (17TH TO 18TH CENTURIES)

More than any other movement, the **baroque** aimed toward a seamless meshing of architecture and art. The stuccoes, sculptures, and paintings were all carefully designed to complement one another—and the space itself—to create a unified whole.

Though relatively sedate, **St. Peter's** facade by **Carlo Maderno** (ca. 1556–1629) and sweeping elliptical colonnade by **Bernini** make for one of Italy's most famous baroque assemblages. The two also collaborated (along with Borromini) on the **Palazzo Barberini** (1620–30s). The painter **Pietro da Cortona** designed the distinctive semicircular portico on **Santa Maria della Pace** (1656–57).

For the rococo—more a decorative than architectural movement—look no farther than the **Spanish Steps** (1726), by architect **Francesco de Sanctis** (1693–1740), or the **Trevi Fountain** (1762; see illustration), by **Nicola Salvi** (1697–1751).

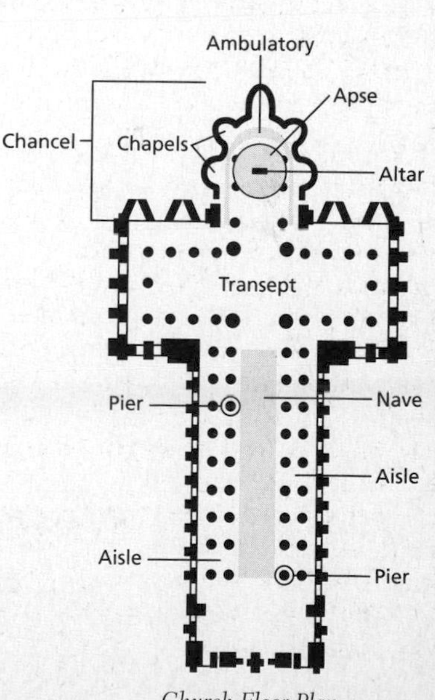

Church Floor Plan

NEOCLASSICAL TO MODERN (18TH TO 20TH CENTURIES)

As a backlash against the excesses of the baroque and rococo, by the middle of the 18th century, Italian architects began turning to the austere simplicity and grandeur of the Classical Age and inaugurated the **neoclassical** style. Neoclassicists reinterpreted ancient temples as buildings with massive colonnaded porticos.

Trevi Fountain

From the 19th century through the 20th century, Italian architects constructed buildings in a variety of styles. Italy's take on the early-20th-century Art Nouveau movement was called **Liberty** style. Mussolini made a spirited attempt to bring back ancient Rome in what can only be called **fascist** architecture. Since then, Italy, like the rest of the world, has mostly erected concrete and glass skyscrapers.

Of the **neoclassical,** the **Vittorio Emanuele Monument** (see illustration), which has been compared to a wedding cake and a Victorian typewriter, was Italy's main monument to reaching its *Risorgimento* goal of a unified Italy.

Liberty style never produced any surpassingly important buildings, although you can glimpse it occasionally in period storefronts.

Fascist architecture still infests all corners of Rome. You can see it at its, er, best in Rome's planned satellite community called **EUR** (including a multistory "square Colosseum" so funky it has been featured in many films and music videos) and the **Stadio Olimpico** complex.

The **mid–20th century** was dominated by **Pier Luigi Nervi** (1891–1979) and his reinforced concrete buildings, including the **Palazzetto dello Sport** stadium (1960).

Vittorio Emanuele Monument

LITERATURE: THE CLASSICS & BEYOND

The passion for empire building spilled over into the development of forms of Roman literature that would affect every literary development in the Western world for the next 2,000 years.

The first true Latin poet was Livius Andronicus (ca. 284–204 B.C.), a Greek slave who translated Homer's *Odyssey* into Latin, but abandoned the poetic rhythms of ancient Greek in favor of Latin's Saturnian rhythm. Quintus Ennius (239–169 B.C.) was the father of Roman epic literature; his *Annales* is permeated with a sense of the divine mission of Rome to civilize the world. Quintus's bitter rival was M. Porcius Cato the Censor (234–149 B.C.), who passionately rejected Rome's dependence on Hellenistic models in favor of a distinctly Latin literary form.

Part of the appeal of Latin literature was in the comedies performed in front of vast audiences. The Latin cadences and rhythms of Plautus (254–184 B.C.) were wholly original, and C. Lucilius (c. 180–102 B.C.) is credited as the first satirist, developing a deliberately casual, sometimes lacerating, method of revealing the shortcomings and foibles of individuals and groups of people (statesmen, poets, gourmands, and the like).

Latin prose and oratory reached their perfect form with the cadences of Marcus Tullius Cicero (106–43 B.C.). A successful and popular general and politician, he is credited with the development of the terms and principles of oratory, which are still used by debating societies everywhere. His speeches and letters are triumphs of diplomacy, and his public policies are credited with binding Rome together during some of its most wrenching civil wars.

Poetry also flourished. The works of Catullus (84–54 B.C.), primarily concerned with the immediacy and strength of his own emotions, presented romantic passion in startlingly vivid ways. Banned by some of the English Victorians, Catullus's works continue to shock anyone who bothers to translate them.

One of the Roman republic's most respected historians was Livy, whose saga of early Rome is more or less the accepted version. Julius Caesar himself (perhaps the most pivotal—and biased—eyewitness to the events he recorded) wrote accounts of his military exploits in Gaul and his transformation of the Roman republic into a dictatorship. Military and political genius combines with literary savvy in his *De Bello Gallica* (Gallic Wars) and *De Bello Civili* (Civil War).

Ancient Roman literature reached its most evocative peak during the Golden Age of Augustus (42 B.C.–A.D. 17). Virgil's (70–19 B.C.) *The Aeneid*, a 12-volume Roman creation myth linking Rome to the demolished city of Troy, has been judged equal to the epics of Homer.

Horace (Quintus Horatius Flaccus; 63–8 B.C.) became a master of satire, as well as the epic "Roman Odes," whose grandeur of style competes with Virgil. Frequently used as an educational text for princes and kings during the Renaissance 1,500 years later, Horace's works often reveal the anxiety he felt about the centralization of unlimited power in Rome after the end of the Republic. Many centuries later some of the themes of Horace were embraced during the Enlightenment of 17th-century Europe, and were even used as ideological buttresses for the tenets that led to the French Revolution.

FAMOUS ROMANS: THE GOOD, THE BAD & THE ugly

St. Alban (3rd or 4th c.) Roman soldier and first British martyr, he was beheaded at Verulamium (now St. Albans), England, for sheltering the Christian priest who had converted him.

Antonioni, Michelangelo (1912–2007) Film director who began his career making documentaries, he is considered one of the best-known cinematists in Italian history. His films deal with the boredom, despair, and alienation of the upper-middle classes in Italy. He is best remembered for a trilogy of film consisting of *La Notte* (1960), *L'Aventura* (1960), and *L'Eclisse* (1961).

Apuleius, Lucius (2nd C. A.D.) The works of this Roman satirist are the only extant examples of Latin-Language prose fiction. His most famous work is *The Golden Ass* (also known as *Metamorphoses*).

Aretino, Pietro (1492–1556) Sponsored and supported by such royal patrons as Emperor Charles V and Francis I of France, he is one of the best-remembered political satirists of the Renaissance. Known as the "scourge of princes," he invariably fell into disgrace as his satirical arrow drove deep.

Augustus (originally Gaius Octavius, later Gaius Julius Caesar Octavianus) (63 B.C.–A.D. 14) Grandnephew of Julius Caesar, who adopted him as his son and heir, he was considered the first Roman emperor, enjoying absolute control of most of the known world after 27 B.C. He defeated Brutus and Cassius, slayers of his mentor, and also Mark Anthony.

Bellini, Vincenzo (1801–35) During his short life, he elevated to a status never before heard the opera form of *bel canto.* Some of the pieces he wrote for coloratura soprano remain among the most sought-after by operatic divas the world over. His operas (*Norma, La Sonnambula,* and *I Puritani*) are noted for their beauty of melody rather than for the complexity of their harmonies, or the dramatic intensities of their plots.

Bernini, Giovanni Lorenzo (1598–1680) This Renaissance sculptor and architect changed forever the architecture of Rome, designing many of its fountains (including those within the Piazza Navona). Even more famous are his designs for the colonnade and piazza in front of St. Peter's, the Vatican, as well as the canopy whose corkscrew columns cover the landmark's principal altar.

Borgia, Cesare (1476–1507) The name of this Italian adventurer and churchman is synonymous with cruelty and treachery, thanks to his ruthlessness in organizing the cities of central Italy under his rule.

Caruso, Enrico (1873–1921) Born in Italy, the most famous operatic tenor of his era achieved his greatest success at New York's Metropolitan Opera. His interpretations of *Rigoletto, Pagliacci,* and *La Bohème* did more than any other singer to spread the allure of opera to the New World.

Cellini, Benvenuto (1500–71) The most famous goldsmith in history, and a notable sculptor *(Perseus with the Head of Medusa)* as well, he was the author of a famous *Autobiography* which, when first published in 1728, established him as one of the greatest rakes of the Renaissance.

Clement Clement was the consistently most popular name of a series of Roman popes and anti-popes who ruled with interruptions—usually more or less despotically—from 88 A.D. (Clement I) to 1774 (Clement XIV). Among the most famous of these not-always-clement princes of the church were Clement V (dubbed the anti-pope by his legions of enemies) and Clement VII (Giulio de Medici).

Donizetti, Gaetano (1797–1848) He was an Italian composer of some of the most famous—and singable—operas anywhere, including *Lucia di Lammermoor, L'Elisir d'Amore,* and *The Daughter of the Regiment.*

Eustachi, Bartolommeo (1520–74) He was an Italian biologist whose painstaking dissections analyzed the ligaments, bones, tendons, nerves, and vessels that compose the human body. Named in his honor were the Eustachian tubes, whose pressure-regulating abilities are vital to the functioning of the human ear. One of his contemporaries and competitors was **Gabrielo Fallopio** (1523–62), who identified and named in his own honor the fallopian tubes.

Fellini, Federico (1920–93) This neorealist film director is known for his zany, visually striking, and sometimes grotesque interpretations of social and psychological dilemmas. Examples of his work include *La Strada, La Dolce Vita* (whose title was adopted by an entire generation of fun-loving Italians as their mode of living), *8½, Juliet of the Spirits,* and his ode to the debaucheries and insanities of Ancient Rome, *Satirycon.*

Fermi, Enrico (1901–54) Rome physicist, and resident of the U.S. from 1939, he postulated the existence of the atomic particle identified as the neutrino, and produced element 93, neptunium. He was awarded the Nobel Prize for physics in 1938, and his work contributed heavily to the later development of the atomic bomb.

Gregory XIII (né Ugo Buoncampagni) (1502–85) Roman pope from 1572 until his death, he launched the Counter-Reformation and departed from the policies of earlier popes by maintaining an unassailable (or at least discreet) personal comportment. One of his accomplishments was to develop a modern calendar, which is today in common usage throughout the Western world.

Machiavelli, Niccoló (1469–1527) Political philosopher and Italian Statesman, he is probably the world's most visible and oft-quoted defender of political conduct with a cynical and deliberate disregard for the moral issues involved. He is best remembered for his treatise on the art of ruling, *Il Principe (The Prince).*

Malpighi, Marcello (1628–94) Personal physician to Pope Innocent XII, he is considered the founder of microscopic anatomy.

Matteotti, Giacomo (1885–1924) He was an Italian socialist whose murder by the Fascists is regarded as the removal of the final obstacle to Mussolini's complete control of Italy.

Menotti, Gian-Carlo (1911–2007) Italian-born, and resident of the U.S. from 1928, he is known as a composer of highly melodic and sometimes satirical operas in the Italian *opera buffa* tradition. These include *The Medium, Amahl and the Night Visitors,* and *The Saint of Bleecker Street.*

Montessori, Maria (1870–1952) Physician and educational theorist, she developed a method of education for young children that directs the child's energies into becoming the adult he or she wants to be within an environment of pedagogical freedom. In 1894, she became the first woman to receive an M.D. in Italy. Her most widely distributed work is *Pedagogical Anthropology.*

Ovid (43 B.C.–A.D. 17), master of the elegy, had an ability to write prose that reflected the traumas and priorities of his own life and emotional involvements. Avoiding references to politics (the growing power of the emperors was becoming increasingly repressive), the elegy grew into a superb form of lyric verse focused on such tenets as love, wit, beauty, pleasure, and amusement. Important works that are read thousands of years later for their charm and mastery of Latin include *Metamorphoses* and *The Art of Love*.

Between A.D. 17 and 170 Roman literature was stifled by a growing fear of such autocrats as Tiberius, Claudius, Nero, and Caligula. An exception is the work of the great Stoic writer Lucius Annaeus Seneca (4 B.C.–A.D. 65), whose work commented directly and sometimes satirically on events of his time and advocated self-sufficiency, moderation, and emotional control.

For several hundred years after the collapse of the Roman Empire very little was written of any enduring merit in Rome. The exceptions include Christian Latin-language writings from such apologists and theologians as St. Jerome (A.D. 340–420) and St. Augustine (354–430), whose works helped bridge the gap to the beginning of the Middle Ages.

From this time onward literature in Rome parallels the development of Italian literature in general. Medieval Italian literature was represented by religious poetry, secular lyric poetry, and sonnets. Although associated with Florence, and not Rome, Dante Alighieri (1265–1321) broke the monotony of a thousand-year literary silence with the difficult-to-translate *terza rima* of *The Divine Comedy.* Called the first masterpiece in Italian—to the detriment of Rome, the Tuscan dialect in which he wrote gradually became accepted as the purest form of Italian—it places Dante, rivaled only by medieval Italian-language poets Petrarch and Boccaccio, in firm control as the founder of both the Italian language and Italian literature.

Rome, however, continued to pulsate with its own distinctive dialect and preoccupations. The imbroglios of the city's power politics during the 1400s and 1500s, and the mores of its ruling aristocracy, were recorded in *The Courtier,* by Baldassare Castiglione (1478–1529), still read as a source of insight into customs, habits, and ambitions during the Renaissance.

From 1600 to around 1850, as the reins of international power and creativity shifted from Italy, literature took a second tier to such other art forms as music, opera, and architecture. The publication of Alessandro Manzoni's (1785–1873) romantic epic *I Promessi Sposi* (the Betrothed) in 1827 signaled the birth of the modern Italian novel.

During the 19th century, Rome's literary voice found its most provocative spokesperson in Giuseppe Gioacchino Belli (1792–1863), who wrote more than 2,000 satirical sonnets (*I Sonetti Romaneschi,* published 1886–96) in Roman dialect rather than academic Italian. A statue in his honor decorates Piazza Belli in Trastevere.

THE ROMANS: FROM MYTH TO LANGUAGE

MYTH Although modern visitors know Rome as the headquarters of Catholicism, the city also developed one of the world's most influential bodies of mythology.

During the days when Rome was little more than a cluster of sheepherder's villages, a body of gods were worshiped whose characters remained basically unchanged throughout the course of Roman history. To this panoply were added and assimilated the deities of other conquered territories (especially Greece) until the roster of Roman gods bristled with imports from around the Mediterranean. In its corrupted (later) version, the list grew impossibly unwieldy as more-or-less demented emperors forced their own deification and worship upon the Roman masses. After the Christianization of Europe, the original and ancient gods retained their astrological significance and provided poetic fodder for endless literary and lyrical comparisons.

A brief understanding of each of the major gods' functions will enhance insights during explorations of the city's museums and excavations.

Apollo was the representative of music, the sun, prophecy, healing, the arts, and philosophy. He was the brother of **Diana** (symbol of chastity and goddess of the hunt, the moon, wild animals, and later, of commerce) and the son of **Jupiter** (king of the gods and god of lightning), by a lesser female deity named **Leto.**

Cupid was the god of falling in love.

Juno, the wife of Jupiter, was attributed with vague but awesome powers and a very human sense of outrage and jealousy. Her main job seemed to be wreaking vengeance against the hundreds of nymphs seduced by Jupiter, and punishment of the thousands of children he supposedly fathered.

Mars, the dignified but bloodthirsty god of war, was reputed to be the father of Romulus and Remus, founders of Rome.

Mercury, symbol of such Geminis (twins) as Romulus and Remus, was one of the most diverse and morally ambiguous of the gods. He served as the guide to the dead as they approached the underworld, and as the patron of eloquence, travel, negotiation, diplomacy, good sense, prudence, and (to a very limited extent) thieving.

Neptune, god of the sea, was attributed with almost no moral implications, but represents solely the watery domains of the earth.

Minerva was the goddess of wisdom, arts and crafts, and (occasionally) of war. A goddess whose allure was cerebral and whose discipline was severe, she wears a helmet and breastplate emblazoned with the head of Medusa (the snake-haired monster whose gaze could turn men into stone). During the Renaissance she became a symbol much associated, oddly enough, with the wisdom and righteousness of the Christian popes.

Venus, whose mythological power grew as the empire expanded, was the goddess of gardens and every conceivable variety of love. She was reportedly the mother of Aeneas, mythical ancestor of the ancient Romans. Both creative and destructive, Venus's appeal and duality are as primeval as the earth itself.

Ceres, goddess of the earth and of the harvest, mourned for half of every year (during winter) when her daughter, Proserpine, abandoned her to live in the house of **Pluto,** god of death and the underworld.

Vulcan was the half-lame god of metallurgy, volcanoes, and furnaces, whose activities at his celestial forge crafted super-weapons for an array of military heroes beloved by the ancient Romans.

Finally, **Bacchus,** the god of wine, undisciplined revelry, drunkenness, and absence of morality, gained an increasing importance in Rome as the city grew decadent and declined.

RELIGION Rome is the world's greatest ecclesiastical center. Few regions on earth have been as religiously prolific—or had such a profound influence on Christianity—as Italy.

Even before the Christianization of the Roman Empire, the ancient Romans artfully (and sometimes haphazardly) mingled their allegiance to the deities of ancient Greece with whatever religious fad happened to be imported at the moment. After its zenith, ancient Rome resembled a theological hodgepodge of dozens of religious and mystical cults, which found fertile soil amid a crumbling empire. Eastern (especially Egyptian) cults became particularly popular, and dozens of emperors showed no aversion to defining themselves as gods and enforcing worship by their subjects.

In A.D. 313 the emperor Constantine, a Christian convert himself, signed the Edict of Milan, stopping the hitherto merciless persecution of Christians. Since then, Italy has adhered, in the main, to Catholicism.

Today the huge majority (99%) of Italians describe themselves as Roman Catholic, although their form of allegiance to Catholicism varies widely according to individual conscience. Despite the fact that only about one-third of the country attends Mass with any regularity, and only about 10% claim to receive the sacrament at Easter, the country is innately—to its very core—favored by the Catholic tradition. That does not always mean that the populace follows the dictates of the Vatican. An example of this is that, despite the pressure by the Holy See against voting in favor of Communist party members (in 1949 the Vatican threatened to excommunicate—ipso facto—any Italian who voted for Communist or Communist-inspired candidates), the Communist platform in Italy used to receive up to 33% of the popular vote in certain elections.

Modern Italy's adherence to Catholicism is legally stressed by a law enacted in 1848 by the Kingdom of Sardinia (later reaffirmed by the Lateran Treaty) which states: "The Catholic apostolic and Roman religion is the sole religion of the [Italian] State." The same treaties, however, give freedom of worship to other religions, but identify Rome as "the center of the Catholic world and a place of pilgrimage," and confer onto the State of Italy the responsibility of safeguarding the security of the pope and his emissaries, and respecting church property and church law in the treatment of certain matters, such as requests for divorces or annulments.

Significantly, throughout history Italy has produced more upper-echelon leaders to staff the Vatican than any other country in the world. Only more recently, beginning with the election of a Polish-born pope (John Paul II), has a pattern of almost complete domination of the papacy by Italian prelates been altered. Because of the sometimes inconvenient juxtaposition of the Vatican inside the administrative capital of Italy, the Lateran Treaty of February 11, 1929, recognized the Vatican City State as an independent and sovereign state and established and defined its relationship to the Italian State. That treaty, originally signed by Mussolini, lasted until 1984.

FOLKLORE The most formal manifestation of folk rituals in all of Rome is the *Commedia dell'Arte*. Although it greatly influenced theatrical styles of France in the 17th century, it is unique to Italy. The plots almost always develop and resolve an imbroglio where the beautiful wife of an older curmudgeon dallies with a handsome swain, against the advice of her maid and much to the amusement of the husband's valet.

Italy, even before the Christian era, was a richly religious land ripe with legends and myths. Modern Italy blends superstition, ancient myths and fables, and Christian symbolism in richly folkloric ways. Throughout Rome, rites of passage—births, first communions, marriages, and deaths—are linked to endless rounds of family celebrations, feasts, and gatherings. Faithful Romans might genuflect when in front of a church, when entering a church, when viewing an object of religious veneration (a relic of a saint, for example), or when hearing a statement that might tempt the Devil to meddle in someone's personal affairs.

LANGUAGE Italian, of course, is the official language of Rome, but it's spoken with a particular dialect that has always given linguistic delight to anyone born in the city. Although the purest form of Italian is said to be spoken in Tuscany (a legacy of medieval author Dante Alighieri, who composed the *Divine Comedy* in the Tuscan dialect), the Romans have always maintained a fierce pride in the particular stresses, intonations, and vocabulary of their own native speech patterns.

Regardless of the dialect, Italian is more directly derived from Latin than any of the other Romance languages. Many older Italians had at least a rudimentary grasp of ecclesiastical (church) Latin because of the role of Latin in the Catholic Mass. Today, however, as the vernacular Italian has replaced the use of Latin in most church services, the ancient tongue can be read and understood only by a diminishing number of academics and priests.

Linguists consider Italian the most "musical" and mellifluous language in the West, and the Italian language easily lends itself to librettos and operas. The language is a phonetic one; this means that you pronounce a word the way it's written, unlike many other languages, including English. It has been said that if an Italian sentence sounds "off-key," it's because the grammar is incorrect.

The Italian alphabet is not as extensive as the English alphabet in that it doesn't normally use such letters as j, k, w, x, and y.

Even as late as World War II, many Italian soldiers couldn't understand each other, as some men spoke only in their local dialects. But with the coming of television, most Italians today speak the language with similarity.

ROME IN POPULAR CULTURE: BOOKS, FILM & MUSIC

General Interest & History

Presenting a "warts and all" view of the Italian character, Luigi Barzini's ***The Italians*** should almost be required reading for anyone contemplating a trip to Rome. It's lively, fun, and not at all academic.

Edward Gibbon's 1776 ***The History of the Decline and Fall of the Roman Empire*** is published in six volumes, but Penguin issues a manageable abridgement. This work has been hailed as one of the greatest histories ever written. No one has ever captured the saga of the glory that was Rome the way Gibbon did.

One of the best books on the long history of the papacy—detailing its excesses, triumphs, defeats, and most vivid characters—is Michael Walsh's ***An Illustrated History of the Popes: Saint Peter to John Paul II***.

In the 20th century, the most fascinating period in Italian history was the rise and fall of fascism, as detailed in countless works. One of the best biographies of Il Duce is Denis M. Smith's ***Mussolini: A Biography***. Another subject that's always engrossing is the Mafia, which is detailed, godfathers and all, in Pino Arlacchi's ***Mafia Business: The Mafia Ethic and the Spirit of Capitalism.***

William Murray's ***The Last Italian: Portrait of a People*** is his second volume of essays on his favorite subject—Italy, its warm people, and its astonishing civilization. The *New York Times* called it "a lover's keen, observant diary of his affair."

Once Upon a Time in Italy: The Vita Italiana of an American Journalist, by Jack Casserly, is the entertaining and affectionate memoir of a former bureau chief in Rome from 1957 to 1964. He captures the spirit of *Italia sparita* (bygone Italy) with such celebrity cameos as Maria Callas and the American expatriate singer Bricktop.

Art & Architecture

From the Colosseum to Michelangelo, T. W. Potter provides one of the best accounts of the art and architecture of Rome in ***Roman Italy,*** which is also illustrated. Another good book on the same subject is ***Roman Art and Architecture,*** by Mortimer Wheeler.

The Sistine Chapel: A Glorious Restoration, by Michael Hirst and others, uses nearly 300 color photographs to illustrate the lengthy and painstaking restoration of Michelangelo's 16th-century frescoes in the Vatican.

Giorgio Vasari's ***Lives of the Artists* Vols. I and II** is a collection of biographies of the great artists from Cimabue up to Vasari's 16th-century contemporaries. It's an interesting read, full of anecdotes and Vasari's theories on art practice. For a more modern art history take, the indispensable tome is Frederick Hartt's ***History of Italian Renaissance Art.*** For an easier and more colorful introduction, get Michael Levey's ***Early Renaissance*** and ***High Renaissance.***

Fiction & Biography

No one does it better than John Hersey in his Pulitzer Prize–winning ***A Bell for Adano,*** a frequently reprinted classic. It's a well-written and disturbing story of the American invasion of Italy.

One of the best-known Italian writers published in England is Alberto Moravia, born in 1907. His neorealistic novels are immensely entertaining and are read around the world. Notable works include ***Roman Tales, The Woman of Rome,*** and ***The Conformist.***

For the wildly entertaining books on ancient Rome, detailing its most flamboyant personalities and excesses, read ***I, Claudius*** and ***Claudius the God,*** both by Robert Graves. Borrowing from the histories of Tacitus and Suetonius, the series begins at the end of the Emperor Augustus's reign and ends with the death of Claudius in the 1st century A.D. In 1998, the Modern Library placed *I, Claudius* at no. 14 on its list of the 100 finest English-language novels published last century.

Colleen McCullough's "Masters of Rome" series is rich, fascinating, and historically detailed, bringing to vivid life such greats as Gaius Marius ***(The First Man in Rome),*** Lucius Cornelius Sulla ***(The Grass Crown),*** and Julius Caesar (***Fortune's Favorites*** and ***Caesar's Women***).

Michelangelo: a Biography, by George Bull, is a well-written scholarly take on the life of the artist, penned by a Renaissance expert and one of the most respected translators of Italian classic literature.

Irving Stone's ***The Agony and the Ecstasy,*** filmed with Charlton Heston playing Michelangelo, is the easiest to read and the most pop version of the life of this great artist. Heston viewed it as his greatest role and never ceased trying to keep Michelangelo from coming out of the closet.

Many other writers have tried to capture the peculiar nature of Italy. Notable works include Italo Calvino's ***The Baron in the Trees,*** Umberto Eco's ***The Name of the Rose,*** E. M. Forster's ***Where Angels Fear to Tread*** and ***A Room with a View,*** Henry James's ***The Aspern Papers,*** Giuseppe di Lampedusa's ***The Leopard,*** Carlo Levi's ***Christ Stopped at Eboli,*** Susan Sontag's ***The Volcano Lover,*** and Mark Helprin's underappreciated masterwork, ***A Soldier of the Great War.***

Films

Italian films have never regained the glory they enjoyed in the postwar era. Roberto Rossellini's *Rome, Open City* (1946) influenced Hollywood's films noirof the late 1940s and Vittorio De Sica's *Bicycle Thief* (1948) achieved world renown.

The late Federico Fellini burst into Italian cinema with his highly individual style, beginning with *La Strada* (1954) and going on to such classics as *Juliet of the Spirits* (1965), *Amarcord* (1974), *Roma* (1972), and *The City of Women* (1980). *La Dolce Vita* (1961) helped to define an era.

Marxist, homosexual, and practicing Catholic, Pier Paolo Pasolini was the most controversial of Roman filmmakers until his mysterious murder in 1975. Explicit sex scenes in *Decameron* (1971) made it a world box-office hit.

Bernardo Bertolucci, once an assistant to Pasolini, achieved fame with such films as *The Conformist* (1970), based on the novel by Moravia. His *1900* is an epic spanning 20th-century Italian history and politics.

Michelangelo Antonioni swept across the screens of the world with his films of psychological anguish, including *La Notte* (1961), *L'Avventura* (1964), and *The Red Desert* (1964).

Mediterraneo, directed by Gabriele Salvatores, was a whimsical comedy that won an Oscar for best foreign-language film in 1991. It tells the story of eight Italian soldiers stranded on a Greek island in World War II.

Giuseppe Tornatore, who achieved such fame with *Cinema Paradiso,* which won the Academy Award for best foreign-language film of 1989, directed one of three vignettes in the 1992 film *Especially on Sunday.* The Taviani brothers, Paolo and Vittorio, both directors, created a stir in 1994 with the release of their film *Fiorile.*

Caro Diario (1994), starring and directed by Nanni Moretti, is a three-part traipse through modern-day Italy. Moretti, a cult figure in Italy, is noted for his prickly personality, quirky sense of humor, and deadpan tone.

The Flight of the Innocent (1995) is one of the finest films to come out of Italy in recent times—and one that quickly gained an international audience. The director, Carlo Carlei, takes us inside the world of a 10-year-old boy fleeing for his life. It's one of the best depictions ever of a child alone who must improvise and cope with a world he doesn't understand.

Although directors more than stars have dominated Italian cinema, three actors have emerged to gain worldwide fame, including Marcello Mastroianni, star of such hits as *La Dolce Vita* (1961), and Sophia Loren, whose best film is considered *Two Women* (1961). Mastroianni was Fellini's favorite male actor and he starred him once again in 8½. Anna Magnani not only starred in Italian films but also made many American films as well, including *The Rose Tattoo* (1955), with Burt Lancaster, and *The Fugitive Kind* (1960), with Marlon Brando.

Many 20th-century film classics with Roman backgrounds are available in DVD, including *Roman Holiday* (1953), starring Gregory Peck and Audrey Hepburn. Basically a travelogue of Rome, *Three Coins in the Fountain* (1954) launched the tradition of tossing coins in the Trevi Fountain.

Rome came in for its greatest attention in recent years in the hit TV series *Rome* (2005–07), a saga centering on the last years of the reign of Julius Caesar and the founding of the empire. The series combined historical figures with equally compelling fictional side characters.

Recordings

MEDIEVAL & RENAISSANCE MUSIC

An excellent collection of the late Renaissance's sonatas, canzonettas, and madrigals, played on original Renaissance instruments, is entitled *Music from the Time of Guido Reni.* (Guido Reni, born 1575 and died 1642, was a Renaissance painter who probably caused more public discord because of his philandering and political intrigues than any other in Italian history. He was eventually exiled from Rome in 1622.) This particular collection of works by this artist's musical contemporaries was recorded by the Aurora Ensemble.

ORCHESTRAL & OPERATIC WORKS

The best way for most novices to begin an appreciation of opera is to hear an assemblage of great moments of opera accumulated onto one record. A good example contains works by the most evocative and dramatic singer who ever hit a high "C" on the operatic stage, Maria Callas. *La Voce: Historic Recordings of the Great Diva* brings together "La Callas'" spectacular arias from *Lucia di Lammermoor, La Traviata, Norma,* and *The Barber of Seville.*

Recordings of complete and unedited operas are even more rewarding. Excellent examples include the following: Bellini's *Norma,* featuring the divine and legendary Maria Callas, accompanied by the orchestra and the chorus of Milan's La Scala, is one of the world's great operatic events; Tullio Serafin conducts. Giuseppe Verdi's genius can be appreciated through *Nabucco,* performed with Plácido Domingo by the Rydl Choir and Orchestra of the Dutch National Opera, conducted by Giuseppe Sinopoli. Also insightful for the vocal techniques of Verdi, his *Complete Songs* is recorded by Renata Scotto (soprano) and Paolo Washington (bass), accompanied by Vincenzo Scalera (piano). Rossini's great opera *Il Barbiere di Siviglia* and Puccini's *Tosca,* both recorded in their complete versions by the Turin Opera Orchestra and Chorus, are both conducted by Bruno Campanella.

And no compendium of Italian opera would be complete without including the immortal tenor Luciano Pavarotti, whose interpretations of Verdi's idealistic heroes have become almost definitive. His *La Traviata* is particularly memorable and passionate.

The music of Rome continues to enjoy brisk sales, and recordings are available on such sites as Amazon.com. An unusual offering is "Synaulia—Music from Ancient Rome," Vol. 1, devoted to wind instruments. "Night in Rome" features music played by the London Philharmonic, and another DVD audio, also called "Night in Rome," stars Italian musicians. "Rome: A Musical Journey" takes you on a musical tour of Rome in DVD. "Respighi: Pines of Rome/Roman Festivals" is an audio CD featuring such conductors as Leonard Bernstein.

EATING & DRINKING IN ROME

You'll find restaurants of international renown here and an infinite number of trattorie and *rosticcerie* that offer good meals at moderate prices. The main meals are from noon to 3pm and 8 to 11pm, but you can get food at other hours at the more informal trattorie and rosticcerie. Many restaurants throughout Rome offer fixed-price meals that include two courses, a dessert, a house wine, and service. For more details, see chapter 6, "Where to Dine in Rome."

Rome also has many specialty restaurants that represent every major region of the country. The dishes they serve carry such designations as *alla genovese* (Genoa), *alla milanese* (Milan), *alla napolitana* (Naples), *alla fiorentina* (Florence), and *alla bolognese* (Bologna).

For a quick bite, go to a **bar.** Although bars in Rome do serve alcohol, they function mainly as cafes. Prices have a split personality: *al banco* is standing at the bar, while *à tavola* means sitting at a table where you'll be waited on and charged two to four times as much. In bars you can find panino sandwiches on various kinds of rolls and *tramezzini* (giant triangles of white bread sandwiches with the crusts cut off). They are traditionally put in a kind of tiny press to flatten and toast them so the crust is crispy and the filling is hot and gooey; microwave ovens have unfortunately invaded and are everywhere, turning panini into something resembling a soggy hot tissue.

Pizza a taglio or *pizza rustica* indicates a place where you can order pizza by the slice. *Pizzerie* are casual sit-down restaurants that cook large, round pizzas with very thin crusts in wood-burning ovens. A *tavola calda* (literally "hot table") serves ready-made hot foods you can take away or eat at one of the few small tables often available. The food is usually very good. A *rosticceria* is the same type of place, and you'll often see chickens roasting on a spit in the window.

A full-fledged restaurant will go by the name *osteria,* trattoria, or ristorante. Once upon a time, these terms meant something—osterie were basic places where you could get a plate of spaghetti and a glass of wine; trattorie were casual places serving full meals of filling peasant fare; and ristoranti were fancier places with waiters in bow ties, printed menus, wine lists, and hefty prices. Nowadays, fancy restaurants often go by the name of trattoria to cash in on the associated charm factor; trendy spots use osteria to show they're hip; and simple, inexpensive places sometimes tack on ristorante to ennoble themselves.

The *pane e coperto* (bread and cover) is a 1€ to 3€ cover charge that you must pay at most restaurants for the mere privilege of sitting at the table. Most Romans eat a leisurely full meal—appetizer and first and second courses—at lunch and dinner and expect you to do the same, or at least a first and second course. To request the bill, say "*Il conto, per favore*" (eel *con*-toh, pore fah-*vohr*-ay). A tip of 15% is usually included in the bill these days, but if you're unsure, ask "*È incluso il servizio?*" (ay een-*cloo*-soh eel sair-*vee*-tsoh?)

You'll find at many restaurants, especially larger ones, a *menu turistico* (tourist's menu), sometimes called *menu del giorno* (menu of the day). This set-price menu usually covers all meal incidentals—including table wine, cover charge, and 15% service charge—along with a first course *(primo)* and second course *(secondo),* but it almost always offers an abbreviated selection of pretty bland dishes: spaghetti in tomato sauce and slices of pork. Sometimes a better choice is a *menu à prezzo fisso* (fixed-price menu). It usually doesn't include wine but sometimes covers the service and often offers a wider selection of better dishes, occasionally house specialties and local foods. Ordering a la carte, however, offers you the best chance for a memorable meal. Even better, forego the menu entirely and put yourself in the capable hands of your waiter.

The *enoteche* (wine bar) is a popular marriage of a wine bar and an osteria, where you can sit and order from a host of local and regional wines by the glass while snacking on finger foods (and usually a number of simple first-course possibilities) that reflect Rome's fare. Relaxed and full of ambience and good wine, these are great spots for light and inexpensive lunches—perfect to educate your palate and recharge your batteries.

Further, we recommend that you go to a different part of town for dinner each night. It's a great way to see Rome.

A final word: All Roman restaurants are closed at least 1 day a week (usually Sunday or Monday, but it varies). Also, beware of August, the month when most Romans go on their holidays. Scores of restaurants close down, displaying only a lonely *chiuso per ferie* sign.

PLANNING YOUR TRIP TO ROME

3

This chapter is devoted to the where, when, and how of your trip—the advance planning required to get it together and take it on the road.

WHEN TO GO

April to June and **late September to October** are the best months for traveling in Italy—temperatures are usually mild and the crowds aren't quite so intense. Starting in mid-June, the summer rush really picks up, and from **July to mid-September** the country teems with visitors. **August** is the worst month: Not only does it get uncomfortably hot, muggy, and crowded, but the entire country goes on vacation at least from August 15 to the end of the month—and many Italians take off the entire month. Many hotels, restaurants, and shops are closed (except at the spas, beaches, and islands, which are where 70% of the Italians head). From **late October to Easter,** most attractions go on shorter winter hours or are closed for renovation. Many hotels and restaurants take a month or two off between **November and February,** and it can get much colder than you'd expect (it might even snow).

Weather

It's warm all over Italy in summer; it can be very hot in Rome. The high temperatures begin in Rome in May, often lasting until sometime in October. In Rome the weather is warm year-round, averaging 50°F (10°C) in winter.

For the most part, it's drier in Italy than in North America, so high temperatures don't seem as bad because the humidity is lower. In Rome, temperatures can stay in the 90s for days, but nights are usually cooler and more comfortable.

The average high temperatures in central Italy and Rome are 82°F (28°C) in June, 87°F (31°C) in July, and 86°F (30°C) in August; the average lows are 63°F (17°C) in June and 67°F (19°C) in July and August.

Rome's Average Daily Temperature & Monthly Rainfall

	JAN	FEB	MAR	APR	MAY	JUNE	JULY	AUG	SEPT	OCT	NOV	DEC
TEMP. (°F)	49	52	57	62	72	82	87	86	73	65	56	47
TEMP. (°C)	9	11	14	17	22	28	31	30	23	20	13	8
RAINFALL (IN.)	2.3	1.5	2.9	3.0	2.8	2.9	1.5	1.9	2.8	2.6	3.0	2.1

Rome Calendar of Events

For major events in which tickets should be procured well before arriving, check with **Keith Prowse** in the United States at ✆ **800/669-8687;** www.keithprowse.com.

JANUARY

Epiphany celebrations, nationwide. All cities, towns, and villages in Italy stage Roman Catholic Epiphany observances. One of the most festive celebrations is the Epiphany Fair at Rome's Piazza Navona. Usually January 5 to January 6.

Festa di Sant'Agnese, Sant'Agnese Fuori le Mura. During this ancient ceremony, two lambs are blessed and shorn, and their wool is used later for palliums (Roman Catholic vestments). Usually January 21.

FEBRUARY

Carnevale, Piazza Navona, Rome. This festival marks the last day of the children's market and lasts until dawn of the following day. Usually 3 days before Ash Wednesday.

MARCH

Festa di Santa Francesca Romana, Piazzale del Colosseo near Santa Francesca Romana in the Roman Forum. A blessing of cars is performed at this festival. Usually March 9.

Festa di San Giuseppe, the Trionfale Quarter, north of the Vatican. The heavily decorated statue of the saint is brought out at a fair with food stalls, concerts, and sporting events. Usually March 19.

APRIL

Holy Week observances. Processions and age-old ceremonies—some from pagan days, some from the Middle Ages—are staged throughout the country. The most notable procession is led by the pope, passing the Colosseum and the Roman Forum up to Palatine Hill; a torch-lit parade caps the observance. Beginning 4 days before Easter Sunday.

Easter Sunday (Pasqua). In an event broadcast around the world, the pope gives his blessing from the balcony of St. Peter's.

Festa della Primavera, Rome. The Spanish Steps are decked out with banks of azaleas and other flowers; later, orchestral and choral concerts are presented in Trinità dei Monti. Dates vary.

MAY

Concorso Ippico Internazionale (International Horse Show), Piazza di Siena in the Villa Borghese. Usually May. Call tourist office for information.

JUNE

Son et Lumière. The Colosseum, the Roman Forum, and Tivoli areas are dramatically lit at night. Early June to end of September.

Festa di San Pietro, St. Peter's Basilica, Rome. This most significant Roman religious festival is observed with solemn rites. Usually around June 29.

Estate Romana. The Rome Summer Festival lasts for 6 weeks of mostly outdoor shows, with an emphasis on music—from rock to opera, from reggae to jazz. Late June to early August. For more information, check www.estateromana.comune.roma.it.

JULY

Festa di Noantri, Trastevere. In July, Rome's most colorful neighborhood becomes a gigantic outdoor restaurant, with tables lining the streets, and musicians providing the entertainment. Find the first empty table and try to get a waiter—but keep an eye on your valuables. For details, contact the tourist information service run by the commune di Roma (✆ **06-0608**).

The White Night of Rome

Rome rocks around the clock for the 8th edition of *La Notte Bianca* or "White Night," scheduled for September 7, 2011 (the date could change). Seemingly half of Rome from the imperial center to the suburbs takes to the streets for open-air events that include street dances, food stands, wine tastings, pyrotechnic displays, concerts, and children's activities.

Museums stay open until dawn, as do shops. Floodlit churches and monuments are also open to the public, and special artistic presentations are held throughout the city. Voices of famous Italian actors give life to readings and short plays all over the city. The sound of music fills the night—rock, jazz, opera arias, even music from North Africa. The center of Rome becomes one great pedestrian mall from Lungotevere to Piazza del Popolo, from Stazione Termini to the Colosseum.

AUGUST

Festa delle Catene, San Pietro in Vincoli. The chains of St. Peter are shown to the faithful during prayer. August 1.

Ferragosto. Beginning on August 15, most city residents not directly involved with the tourist trade take a 2-week vacation (many restaurants are closed as well). This is a good time *not* to be in Rome.

SEPTEMBER

Sagra dell'Uva, Basilica of Maxentius, the Roman Forum. At this harvest festival, musicians in ancient costumes entertain, and grapes are sold at reduced prices. Dates vary, usually early September.

DECEMBER

Christmas Blessing of the Pope. Delivered at noon from the balcony of St. Peter's Basilica, the pope's words are broadcast around the world. December 25.

ENTRY REQUIREMENTS

Passports

U.S., Canadian, U.K., Irish, Australian, and New Zealand citizens with a **valid passport** don't need a visa to enter Italy if they don't expect to stay more than 90 days and don't expect to work there. If after entering Italy you want to stay more than 90 days, you can apply for a permit for an extra 90 days, which, as a rule, is granted immediately. Go to the nearest *questura* (police headquarters) or to your home country's consulate. If your passport is lost or stolen, head to your consulate as soon as possible for a replacement.

For information on how to get a passport, go to the "Fast Facts" section—the websites listed provide downloadable passport applications as well as the current fees for processing passport applications. For an up-to-date country-by-country listing of passport requirements around the world, go to the "Foreign Entry Requirement" Web page of the U.S. State Department at **http://travel.state.gov**.

Traveling with Minors

It's always wise to have plenty of documentation when traveling in today's world with children. For changing details on entry requirements for children traveling abroad, keep up to date by going to the U.S. State Department website: http://travel.state.gov/travel-1744.html.

To prevent international child abduction, E.U. governments have initiated procedures at entry and exit points. These often (but not always) include requiring documentary evidence of your relationship with your child and permission for the child's travel from the parent or legal guardian not present. Having such documentation on hand, even if not required, facilitates entries and exits. All children must have their own passports. To obtain a passport, the child must be present—that is, in person—at the center issuing the passport. Both parents must be present as well. If not, then a notarized statement from the parents is required.

Any questions parents or guardians might have can be answered by calling the National Passport Information Center at ✆ **877/487-6868** Monday to Friday 8am to 8pm Eastern Standard Time.

Customs Regulations

WHAT YOU CAN BRING INTO ITALY Foreign visitors can bring along most items for personal use duty-free, including fishing tackle, a pair of skis, two tennis racquets, a baby carriage, two hand cameras with 10 rolls of film, and 400 cigarettes or a quantity of cigars or pipe tobacco not exceeding 500 grams (1.1 lb.). There are strict limits on importing alcoholic beverages. However, for alcohol bought tax-paid, limits are much more liberal than in other countries of the European Union.

There are no restrictions on the amount of local currency you can bring into Italy, although you should declare the amount. Your declaration proves to the Italian Customs office that the currency came from outside the country, and, therefore, you can take out the same amount or less. Foreign currency taken into or out of Italy may not exceed 12,500€. No declaration is needed up to this amount.

WHAT YOU CAN TAKE HOME FROM ITALY Rules governing what you can bring back duty-free vary from country to country and are subject to change, but they're generally posted on the Web. Anyone caught buying counterfeit products can be fined up to 10,000€.

U.S. Citizens: For specifics on what you can bring back, download the invaluable free pamphlet *Know Before You Go* online at **www.cbp.gov**. (Click on "Travel," and then click on "Know Before You Go.") Or contact the **U.S. Customs & Border Protection (CBP),** 1300 Pennsylvania Ave. NW, Washington, DC 20229 (✆ **877/227-5511;** www.cbp.gov) and request the pamphlet.

Canadian Citizens: For a clear summary of **Canadian** rules, write for the booklet *I Declare,* issued by the **Canada Border Services Agency** (✆ **800/461-9999** in Canada, or 204/983-3500; www.cbsa-asfc.gc.ca).

U.K. Citizens: For information, contact **HM Revenue & Customs** at ✆ **0845/010-9000** (from outside the U.K., 02920/501-261), or consult at www.hmrc.gov.uk.

Australian Citizens: A helpful brochure available from Australian consulates or Customs offices is *Know Before You Go.* For more information, call the **Australian Customs Service** at ✆ **1300/363-263,** or log on to www.customs.gov.au.

New Zealand Citizens: Most questions are answered in a free pamphlet available at New Zealand consulates and Customs offices: *New Zealand Customs Guide for Travellers, Notice no. 4.* For more information, contact **New Zealand Customs Service,** the Customhouse, 17–21 Whitmore St., Box 2218, Wellington (✆ **04/473-6099** or 0800/428-786; www.customs.govt.nz).

GETTING THERE & GETTING AROUND

By Plane

High season on most airlines' routes to Rome is usually June to the beginning of September. This is the most expensive and crowded time to travel. **Shoulder season** is April and May, early September to October, and December 15 to December 24. **Low season** is November 1 to December 14 and December 25 to March 31.

FROM NORTH AMERICA Fares to Italy are constantly changing, but you can expect to pay somewhere in the range of $550 to $1,980 for a direct round-trip ticket from New York to Rome in coach class.

Flying time to Rome from New York, Newark, and Boston is 8 hours; from Chicago, 10 hours; and from Los Angeles, 12½ hours. Flying time to Milan from New York, Newark, and Boston is 8 hours; from Chicago, 9¼ hours; and from Los Angeles, 11½ hours.

Note: For all airline phone numbers and websites, see Chapter 12 of this book.

American Airlines offers daily nonstop flights to Rome from Chicago's O'Hare, with flights from all parts of American's vast network making connections into Chicago. **Delta** flies from New York's JFK to Milan, Venice, and Rome, and from Atlanta to Rome and Milan. **AmericaWest/US Airways** offers one flight daily to Rome out of Philadelphia. And **Continental** flies five times a week to Rome and Milan from its hub in Newark.

Air Canada flies daily from Toronto to Rome. Two of the flights are nonstop; the others touch down en route in Montreal, depending on the schedule.

British Airways, Virgin Atlantic Airways, Air France, Northwest/KLM, and **Lufthansa** offer some attractive deals for anyone interested in combining a trip to Italy with a stopover in, say, Britain, Paris, Amsterdam, or Germany.

Alitalia is the Italian national airline, with nonstop flights to Rome from different North American cities, including New York (JFK), Newark, Boston, Chicago, Miami, Washington, and Toronto. Nonstop flights into Milan are from New York (JFK) and Newark. From Milan or Rome, Alitalia can easily book connecting domestic flights if your final destination is elsewhere in Italy. Alitalia participates in the frequent-flier programs of other airlines, including Continental and US Airways.

FROM THE UNITED KINGDOM Operated by the European Travel Network, **www.discount-tickets.com** is a great online source for regular and discounted airfares to destinations around the world. You can also use this site to compare rates and book accommodations, car rentals, and tours. Click on "Special Offers" for the latest package deals.

British newspapers are always full of classified ads touting slashed fares to Italy. One good source is ***Time Out.*** London's ***Evening Standard*** has a daily travel section, and the Sunday editions of almost any newspaper run many ads. Although competition is fierce, one well-recommended company that consolidates bulk ticket purchases and then passes the savings on to its consumers is **Trailfinders** (✆ **0845/058-5858;** www.trailfinders.com). It offers access to tickets on such carriers as SAS, British Airways, and KLM.

Both **British Airways** and **Alitalia** have frequent flights from London's Heathrow to Rome. British Airways also has one direct flight a day from Manchester to Rome. Bargain fares are offered by smaller carriers flying from the British Isles to Italy. **Easyjet** (✆ **08712/442366;** www.easyjet.com) flies into Rome from London, as does **Ryanair** (✆ **0899/289993;** www.ryanair.com).

GETTING THROUGH THE AIRPORT

With the federalization of airport security, security procedures at U.S. airports are more stable and consistent than ever. Generally, you'll be fine if you arrive at the airport **2 hours** before a domestic flight and **3 hours** before an international flight; if you show up late, tell an airline employee so you can be whisked to the front of the line.

You'll need a current passport for international flights. Keep your ID at the ready to show at check-in, the security checkpoint, and sometimes even the gate. (Children 17 and under do not need government-issued photo IDs for domestic flights, but they do for international flights to most countries.)

E-tickets have made paper tickets nearly obsolete. Passengers with e-tickets can still beat the ticket-counter lines by using airport **electronic kiosks** or even **online check-in** from your home computer. Online check-in involves logging on to your airline's website, accessing your reservation, and printing out your boarding pass—and the airline may even offer you bonus miles to do so. If you're using a kiosk at the airport, bring the credit card you used to book the ticket or your frequent-flier card. Print out your boarding pass from the kiosk and simply proceed to the security checkpoint with your pass and a photo ID. If you're checking bags or looking to snag an exit-row seat, you will be able to do so using most airlines' kiosks. Even the smaller airlines are employing the kiosk system, but always call your airline to make sure these alternatives are available. **Curbside check-in** is also a good way to avoid lines, although a few airlines still ban curbside check-in; call before you go.

Security checkpoint lines are getting shorter, but some doozies remain. If you have trouble standing for long periods of time, tell an airline employee; the airline will provide a wheelchair. Speed up security by **not wearing metal objects** such as big belt buckles or carrying banned liquids. If you've got metallic body parts, a note from your doctor can prevent a long chat with the security screeners. Keep in mind that only **ticketed passengers** are allowed past security, except for folks escorting children or passengers with disabilities.

Federalization has stabilized **what you can carry on** and **what you can't.** The general rule is that sharp things are out, nail clippers are okay, and many foods and beverages are banned. Bring food in your carry-on rather than checking it, as explosive-detection machines used on checked luggage have been known to mistake food (especially chocolate, for some reason) for bombs. Travelers in the U.S. are allowed one carry-on bag, plus a "personal item" such as a purse, briefcase, or laptop bag.

Carry-on hoarders can stuff all sorts of things into a laptop bag; as long as it has a laptop in it, it's still considered a personal item. The Transportation Security Administration (TSA) has issued a list of restricted items; check its website (www.tsa.gov) for details.

Airport screeners may decide that your checked luggage needs to be searched by hand. You can now purchase luggage locks that allow screeners to open and relock a checked bag if hand searching is necessary. Look for Travel Sentry certified locks at luggage or travel shops and Brookstone stores (you can buy them online at www.brookstone.com). These locks, approved by the TSA, can be opened by luggage inspectors with a special code or key. For more information on the locks, visit www.travelsentry.org. If you use something other than TSA-approved locks, your lock will be cut off your suitcase if a TSA agent needs to hand-search your luggage.

Chances are, you'll arrive at Rome's **Leonardo da Vinci International Airport** (✆ **06-65951**), popularly known as **Fiumicino,** 30km (19 miles) from the city center. (If you're flying by charter, you might land at Ciampino Airport, discussed below.)

In 2008 a Terminal 5 opened at Fiumicino for departing passengers of American Airlines, Continental Airlines, Delta, United Airlines, and US Airways. The terminal is connected to other parts of the airport by shuttle bus.

Arriving passengers at Fiumicino must clear Passport Control. After that, you'll see an **information desk** (✆ **06-0608**). You can pick up a general map and some pamphlets daily from 8:15am to 7pm; the staff can also help you find a hotel room if you haven't reserved ahead. A ***cambio*** (money exchange) operates daily from 7:30am to 11pm, offering surprisingly good rates.

There's a **train station** in the airport. To get into the city, follow the signs marked TRENI for the 30-minute shuttle to Rome's main station, **Stazione Termini** (arriving on Track 22). The shuttle runs from 6:36am to 11:36pm for 9.50€ one-way. On the way, you'll pass a machine dispensing tickets, or you can buy them in person near the tracks if you don't have small bills on you. When you arrive at Termini, quickly get out of the train, and grab a baggage cart. (It's a long schlep from the track to the exit or to the other train connections, and baggage carts can be scarce.)

A **taxi** from da Vinci airport to the city costs 45€ and up for the 1-hour trip, depending on traffic. The expense might be worth it if you have a lot of luggage or just don't want to bother taking a train. Call ✆ **06-6645,** 06-3570, or 06-4994 for information.

If you arrive on a charter flight at **Ciampino Airport** (14km/9 miles south of Rome; ✆ **06-65951**), you can take a CoTral bus (✆ **800-150008** within Italy), which departs every 30 minutes or so for the Anagnina stop of Metropolitana (subway) Line A. Take Line A to Stazione Termini, where you can make your final connections. Trip time is about 45 minutes and costs 1€. A **taxi** from this airport to Rome costs about 30€ as does one from the da Vinci Airport (see above), but the trip is shorter (about 40 min.).

BY TRAIN OR BUS Trains and buses (including trains from the airport) arrive in the center of old Rome at the silver **Stazione Termini,** Piazza dei Cinquecento (✆ **06-478411**); this is the train, bus, and subway transportation hub for all of Rome and is surrounded by many hotels (especially cheaper ones).

If you're taking the **Metropolitana** (subway), follow the illuminated red-and-white M signs. To catch a bus, go straight through the outer hall and enter the sprawling bus lot of Piazza dei Cinquecento. You'll also find **taxis** there.

The station is filled with services. At a branch of the Banca San Paolo IMI (at tracks 1 and 24), you can exchange money. **Informazioni Ferroviarie** (in the outer hall) dispenses information on rail travel to other parts of Italy. There's also a **tourist information booth** here, along with baggage services, newsstands, and snack bars.

By Train

Trains provide a medium-priced means of transport, even if you don't buy the Eurailpass or one of the special Italian Railway tickets (below). As a rule of thumb, second-class travel usually costs about two-thirds the price of an equivalent first-class trip. The relatively new **InterCity trains** (IC on train schedules) are modern, air-conditioned trains that make limited stops; compared to the slower direct or regional trains, the supplement can be steep, but a second-class IC ticket will provide a first-class experience.

A couchette (a private fold-down bed in a communal cabin) requires a supplement above the price of first-class travel. Children 4 to 11 receive a discount of 50% off the adult fare, and children 3 and under travel free with their parents. Seniors and travelers 25 and under can also purchase discount cards. Seat reservations are highly recommended during peak season and on weekends or holidays; they must be booked in advance.

Trenitalia Pass for Italy covers 4 to 10 days of travel within 2 months. Price for 4 days is 217€ first class, 174€ second class. Additional days cost 22€ first class, 18€ second class.

Discounts and bonuses include ferries to Sicily; they do not include international Artesia, France-Italy Night, and Elipsos trains, but they do offer passholder fares on those trains.

You can buy these passes from any travel agent or by calling © **800/848-7245.** You can also call © 800/4-EURAIL (800/438-7245) or 800/EUROSTAR (800/387-6782).

Travel Times between the Major Cities

CITIES	DISTANCE	AIR TRAVEL TIME	TRAIN TRAVEL TIME	DRIVING TIME
Rome to Florence	277km/ 172 miles	1 hr., 10 min.	2½ hr.	3 hr., 20 min.
Rome to Milan	572km/ 355 miles	1 hr., 5 min.	5 hr.	6½ hr.
Rome to Naples	219km/ 136 miles	50 min.	2½ hr.	2½ hr.
Rome to Venice	528km/ 327 miles	1 hr., 5 min.	5¼ hr.	6 hr.
Rome to Genoa	501km/ 311 miles	1 hr.	6 hr.	5¾ hr.
Rome to Torino	669km/ 415 miles	1 hr., 5 min.	9–11 hr.	7¾ hr.

By Bus

We don't recommend traveling to Rome by bus from some other Italian city. All the major cities are connected by rail, which is the fast, efficient, and affordable way to go.

By Car

From the north, the main access route is the **Autostrada del Sole (A1),** which cuts through Milan and Florence, or you can take the coastal route, **SSI Aurelia,** from Genoa. If you're driving north from Naples, you take the southern lap of the **Autostrada del Sole (A1).** All the autostrade join with the **Grande Raccordo Anulare,** a ring road encircling Rome, channeling traffic into the congested city. Long before you reach this road, you should carefully study a map to see what part of Rome you plan to enter and mark your route accordingly. Route markings along the ring road tend to be confusing.

Important advice: Return your rental car immediately, or at least get yourself to a hotel, park your car, and leave it there until you leave Rome. Don't even try to drive in Rome—the traffic and parking are just too nightmarish. Many hotels do not have their own parking lots, and the closest paid parking garage may be blocks away.

GASOLINE Gasoline, or petrol (known as *benzina*) is very expensive in Italy. Be prepared for sticker shock every time you fill up even a medium-size car. Only unleaded gasoline is available in Italy. It has often (but not always) a greenish color and is also called "benzina verde" (green) or "benzina senza piombo" (unleaded) to distinguish it from "benzina super" (not available anymore). Benzina super was banned years ago as it was considered polluted. Many cars have diesel powered engines. Gas stations on the autostrade are open 24 hours, but on regular roads gas stations are rarely open on Sunday; also, many close from noon to 3pm for lunch, and most shut down after 7pm. Make sure the pump registers zero before an attendant starts filling your tank. A popular scam, particularly in the south, is to fill your tank before resetting the meter, so you pay not only your bill but also the charges run up by the previous motorist.

DRIVING RULES Driving is on the right; passing is on the left. Violators of the highway code are fined; serious violations might also be punished by imprisonment. In cities and towns, the speed limit is 50kmph (31 mph). For all cars and motor vehicles on main roads and local roads, the limit is 90kmph (56 mph). For the autostrade, the limit is 130kmph (81 mph). Use the left lane only for passing. If a driver zooms up behind you on the autostrade with his or her lights on, that's your sign to get out of the way! Use of seat belts is compulsory.

BREAKDOWNS & ASSISTANCE In case of car breakdown or for any tourist information, foreign motorists can call ✆ **803-116** (24-hr. nationwide telephone service).

Getting Around

Rome is excellent for walking, with sites of interest often clustered together. Much of the inner core is traffic-free, so you'll need to walk whether you like it or not. However, in many parts of the city, it's hazardous and uncomfortable because of the crowds, heavy traffic, and narrow sidewalks. Sometimes sidewalks don't exist at all, and it becomes a sort of free-for-all with pedestrians competing for space against vehicular traffic. Always be on your guard. The hectic crush of urban Rome is considerably less during August, when many Romans leave town for vacation.

By Subway

The **Metropolitana,** or **Metro,** for short, is the fastest means of transportation, operating daily from 5:30am to 11:30pm. A big red M indicates the entrance to the subway.

Tickets are 1€ and are available from *tabacchi* (tobacco shops, most of which display a sign with a white T on a brown background), many newsstands, and vending machines at all stations. Some stations have managers, but they won't make change. Booklets of tickets are available at tabacchi and in some terminals. You can also buy **passes** for 1 to 7 days (see "By Bus & Tram," below).

By Bus & Tram

Roman buses and trams are operated by an organization known as **ATAC** (Azienda Tramvie e Autobus del Comune di Roma), Via Ostiense 131L (© **800-431784** for information).

For 1€ you can ride to most parts of Rome, although it can be slow going in all that traffic, and the buses are often very crowded. Your ticket is valid for 75 minutes, and you can get on many buses and trams (and the subway) during that time by using the same ticket. Ask where to buy bus tickets, or buy them in tabacchi or bus terminals. You must have your ticket before boarding because there are no ticket-issuing machines on the vehicles.

At Stazione Termini, you can buy a **1-day ticket** *(biglietto giornaliero),* which costs 4€, or a **weekly ticket** *(biglietto settimanale "carta"),* which costs 16€. These passes allow you to ride the ATAC network without buying individual tickets. A **tourist pass** costs 11€ and is valid for 3 days. The tourist pass, the biglietto giornaliero, and the biglietto settimanale tickets are valid on buses, trams, and the subway—but never ride the trains when the Romans are going to or from work, or you'll be smashed flatter than fettuccine. On the first bus you board, you place your

A Few Train Station Warnings

In Stazione Termini, you'll almost certainly be approached by touts claiming to work for a tourist organization. They really work for individual hotels (not always the nicest) and will say almost anything to sell you a room. Unless you know something about Rome's layout and are savvy, it's best to ignore them.

Be aware of all your belongings at all times, and keep your wallet and purse away from professionally experienced fingers. Never ever leave your bags unattended for even a second, and while making phone calls or waiting in line, make sure that your attention doesn't wander from any bags you've set by your side or on the ground. Be aware if someone asks you for directions or information—it's likely meant to distract you and easily will.

Ignore the taxi drivers soliciting passengers right outside the terminal; they can charge as much as triple the normal amount. Instead, line up in the official taxi stand in Piazza dei Cinquecento.

Rome Metropolitana

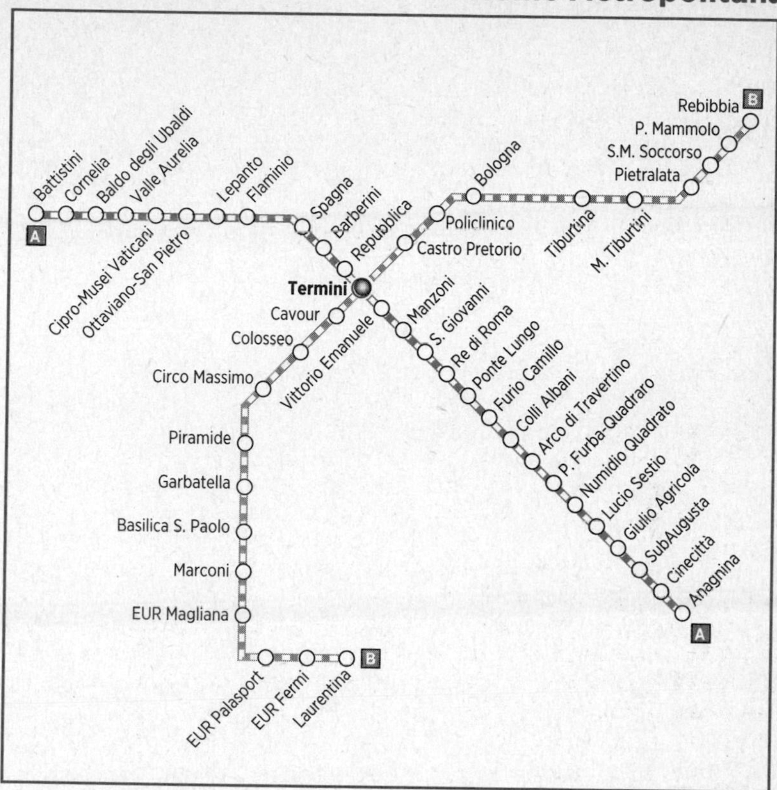

ticket in a small machine, which prints the day and hour you boarded, and then you withdraw it.

Buses and trams stop at areas marked FERMATA. At most of these, a yellow sign displays the numbers of the buses that stop there and a list of all the stops along each bus's route in order, so you can easily search out your destination. In general, they're in service daily from 6am to midnight. After that and until dawn, you can ride on special night buses (they have an N in front of their bus numbers), which run only on main routes. It's best to take a taxi in the wee hours—if you can find one.

At the **bus information booth** at Piazza dei Cinquecento, in front of the Stazione Termini, you can purchase a directory complete with maps summarizing the routes.

Although routes change often, a few reliable routes have remained valid for years, such as **no. 75** from Stazione Termini to the Colosseum, **H** from Stazione Termini to Trastevere, and **no. 40** from Stazione Termini to the Vatican. But if you're going somewhere and are dependent on the bus, be sure to carefully check where the bus stop is and exactly which bus goes there—don't assume that it'll be the same bus the next day.

Two Bus Warnings

Any map of the Roman bus system will likely be outdated before it's printed. Many buses listed on the "latest" map no longer exist; others are enjoying a much-needed rest, and new buses suddenly appear without warning. There's also talk of completely renumbering the whole system soon, so be aware that the route numbers we've listed might have changed by the time you travel.

Take extreme caution when riding Rome's overcrowded buses—pickpockets abound! This is particularly true on bus no. 64, a favorite of visitors because of its route through the historic districts and thus also a favorite of Rome's vast pickpocketing community. This bus has earned various nicknames, including the "Pickpocket Express" and "Wallet Eater."

By Taxi

Don't count on hailing a taxi on the street or even getting one at a stand. If you're going out, have your hotel call one. At a restaurant, ask the waiter or cashier to dial for you. If you want to phone for yourself, try one of these numbers: ✆ **06-6645,** 06-3570, or 06-4994.

The meter begins at 2.80€ for the first 3km (1¾ miles) and then rises .92€ per kilometer. Every suitcase costs 1€, and on Sunday, a 4€ supplement is assessed. There's another 5.80€ supplement from 10pm to 7am. Avoid paying your fare with large bills—invariably, taxi drivers claim that they don't have change, hoping for a bigger tip (stick to your guns and give only about 10%).

By Car

All roads might lead to Rome, but you don't want to drive once you get here. Because the reception desks of most Roman hotels have at least one English-speaking person, call ahead to find out the best route into Rome from wherever you're starting out. You're usually allowed to park in front of the hotel long enough to unload your bags. You'll want to get rid of your rental car as soon as possible or park in a garage.

By Bike

Other than walking, the best way to get through the medieval alleys and small piazzas of Rome is perched on the seat of a bicycle. The heart of ancient Rome is riddled with bicycle lanes to get you through the murderous traffic. The most convenient place to rent bikes is **Bici & Baci,** Via del Viminale 5 (✆ **06-4828443;** www.bicibaci.com), lying 2 blocks west of Stazione Termini, the main rail station. Prices start at 3€ per hour or 11€ per day.

MONEY

Currency

The Italian lire disappeared into history on March 1, 2002, replaced by the **euro,** the single European currency, whose official abbreviation is "EUR." Exchange rates of participating countries are locked into a common currency fluctuating against the dollar. For more details on the euro, check out **www.ec.europa.eu./economy_finance/euro**.

THE VALUE OF THE EURO VS. OTHER POPULAR CURRENCIES

Euro	US$	UK £	C$	A$	NZ$
1.00	1.20	0.83	1.25	1.43	1.75

Frommer's lists prices in local currency. The currency conversions quoted above were correct at press time. However, rates fluctuate, so before departing consult a currency exchange website such as www.oanca.com/convert/classic to check up-to-the-minute rates.

Exchanging Money

Exchange rates are more favorable at the point of arrival. Nevertheless, it's often helpful to exchange at least some money before going abroad (standing in line at the ***cambio*** [exchange bureau] in the Rome airport could make you miss the next bus leaving for downtown). Check with any of your local American Express or Thomas Cook offices or major banks. Or, order euros in advance from **American Express** (**© 800/492-3344;** http://home.americanexpress.com).

It's best to exchange currency or traveler's checks at a bank, not a *cambio,* hotel, or shop. Currency and traveler's checks (for which you'll receive a better rate than cash) can be changed at all principal airports and at some travel agencies, such as American Express and Thomas Cook. Note the rates and inquire about commission fees; it can sometimes pay to shop around.

ATMs

The easiest and best way to get cash away from home is from an ATM (automated teller machine), called a Bancomat in Italy. The **Cirrus** (**© 800/424-7787;** www.mastercard.com) and **PLUS** (www.visa.com) networks span the globe; look at the back of your bank card to see which network you're on; then call or check online for ATM locations at your destination. Be sure you know your personal identification number (PIN) before you leave home and be sure to find out your daily withdrawal limit before you depart. Also keep in mind that many banks impose a fee every time a card is used at a different bank's ATM, and that fee can be higher for international transactions (up to $5 or more) than for domestic ones (where they're rarely more than $1.50). On top of this, the bank from which you withdraw cash may charge its own fee. To compare banks' ATM fees within the U.S., use www.bankrate.com. For international withdrawal fees, ask your bank.

You can also get cash advances on your credit card at an ATM. Keep in mind that credit card companies try to protect themselves from theft by limiting the funds someone can withdraw outside the home country, so call your credit card company before you leave home. And keep in mind that you'll pay interest from the moment of your withdrawal, even if you pay your monthly bills on time.

Traveler's Checks

Traveler's checks seem less necessary these days because most Italian cities and towns have 24-hour ATMs, allowing you to withdraw small amounts of cash as needed. But if you prefer the security of the tried-and-true, you might want to stick

WHAT THINGS COST IN ROME	EUROS
Taxi from airport to city center	45.00
Bus fare from central rail station to Piazza di Spagna	1.00
Subway or public bus (to any destination)	1.00
Double room at the Hassler (very expensive)	350.00
Double room at Hotel Columbus (moderate)	180.00
Double room at Nicolas Inn (inexpensive)	100.00
Lunch for one at Aurora 10 da Pin il Sommelier (moderate)	28.00
Lunch for one at Césarina (inexpensive)	18.00
Dinner for one, without wine, at Il Drappo (expensive)	50.00
Dinner for one, without wine, at Ristorante del Pallaro (moderate)	25.00
Dinner for one, without wine, at Osteria del Gallo (inexpensive)	14.00
Pint of beer	8.00
Glass of wine	5.00–12.00
Coca-Cola	2.50–3.50
Cup of coffee	1.50
Admission to the Vatican museums and Sistine Chapel	14.00

with traveler's checks—provided that you don't mind showing an ID every time you want to cash a check.

You can buy traveler's checks at most banks. They are offered in denominations of $20, $50, $100, $500, and sometimes $1,000. Generally, you'll pay a service charge ranging from 1% to 4%.

The most popular traveler's checks are offered by **American Express** (✆ **800/221-7282** for cardholders—this number accepts collect calls, offers service in several foreign languages, and exempts Amex gold and platinum cardholders from the 1% fee). AAA members can obtain Visa checks free; nonmembers pay a $4.95 fee for checks up to $1,500. Checks are available at most AAA offices or by calling ✆ **866/339-3378. For Visa** checks call ✆ **800/732-1322,** or for **MasterCard** checks call ✆ **800/223-9920.**

American Express, Visa, and **MasterCard** offer **foreign currency traveler's checks,** which are useful if you're traveling to one country, or to the Euro zone; they're accepted at locations where dollar checks may not be.

If you carry traveler's checks, keep a record of their serial numbers separate from your checks in the event that they are stolen or lost. You'll get a refund faster if you know the numbers.

Dear Visa: I'm off to Rome!

Some credit card companies recommend that you notify them of any impending trip abroad so that they don't become suspicious when the card is used numerous times in a foreign destination and block your charges. Even if you don't call your credit card company in advance, you can always call the card's toll-free emergency number if a charge is refused—a good reason to carry the phone number with you. But perhaps the most important lesson here is to carry more than one card with you on your trip; a card might not work for any number of reasons, so having a backup is the smart way to go.

Credit Cards

Credit cards are a safe way to carry money. They also provide a convenient record of all your expenses, and they generally offer relatively good exchange rates. You can also withdraw cash advances from your credit cards at banks or ATMs, provided you know your PIN. If you've forgotten yours, or didn't even know you had one, call the number on the back of your credit card and ask the bank to send it to you. It usually takes 5 to 7 business days, though some banks will provide the number over the phone if you tell them your mother's maiden name or some other personal information. Keep in mind that when you use your credit card abroad, most banks assess a 2% fee above the 1% fee charged by Visa, MasterCard, or American Express for currency conversion on credit charges. But credit cards still may be the smart way to go when you factor in things such as exorbitant ATM fees and higher traveler's check exchange rates (and service fees).

HEALTH

Staying Healthy

In general, Rome is viewed as a fairly "safe" destination, although problems, of course, can and do occur anywhere. You don't need to get shots, most foods are safe, and the water in Rome is potable. If you're concerned, just order bottled water. It is easy to get a prescription filled, and Rome has English-speaking doctors at hospitals with well-trained medical staffs.

Vegetarians can go into almost any restaurant in Rome, even those specializing in meat and fish, and order a heaping plate of fresh antipasti made with fresh vegetables.

WHAT TO DO IF YOU GET SICK AWAY FROM HOME

If you worry about getting sick away from home, consider purchasing **medical travel insurance** and carry your ID card in your purse or wallet. In most cases, your existing health plan will provide the coverage you need.

Any foreign consulate can provide a list of area doctors who speak English. If you get sick, consider asking your hotel concierge to recommend a local doctor—even his or her own. You can also try the emergency room at a local hospital; many have walk-in clinics for emergency cases that are not life-threatening. You may not get immediate attention, but you won't pay the high price of an emergency room visit. We list hospitals and emergency numbers under "Fast Facts" in Chapter 12.

If you suffer from a chronic illness, consult your doctor before your departure. For conditions such as epilepsy, diabetes, or heart problems, wear a **Medic Alert Identification Tag** (✆ **888/633-4298;** www.medicalert.org), which will immediately alert doctors to your condition and give them access to your records through Medic Alert's 24-hour hot line.

Keep **prescription medications** in their original containers, and pack them in your carry-on luggage. Also bring along copies of your prescriptions in case you lose your pills or run out. Carry the generic name of prescription medicines, in case a local pharmacist is unfamiliar with the brand name.

And don't forget sunglasses and an extra pair of contact lenses or prescription glasses.

Contact the **International Association for Medical Assistance to Travelers** (**IAMAT;** ✆ **716/754-4883** or, in Canada, 416/652-0137; www.iamat.org) for tips on travel and health concerns in the countries you're visiting, and for lists of local, English-speaking doctors. The United States **Centers for Disease Control and Prevention** (✆ **800/311-3435;** www.cdc.gov) provides up-to-date information on health hazards by region or country and offers tips on food safety. The website **www.tripprep.com**, sponsored by a consortium of travel medicine practitioners, may also offer helpful advice on traveling abroad. You can find listings of reliable clinics overseas at the **International Society of Travel Medicine** (✆ **404/373-8280;** www.istm.org).

The following government websites offer up-to-date health-related travel advice.

- **Australia:** www.smartraveller.gov.au
- **Canada:** www.phac-aspc.gc.ca/tmp-pmv
- **U.K.:** www.nhs.uk/nhsengland/healthcareabroad/pages/healthcareabroad.aspx
- **U.S.:** wwwnc.cdc.gov/travel

SAFETY

The most common menace, especially in large cities, particularly Rome, is the plague of pickpockets and roving gangs of Gypsy children who surround you, distract you in all the confusion, and steal your purse or wallet. If accosted by a group of children, even though they're children, don't be polite. Never leave valuables in a car, and never travel with your car unlocked. A U.S. State Department travel advisory warns that every car (whether parked, stopped at a traffic light, or even moving) can be a potential target for armed robbery. In these uncertain times, it is always prudent to check the U.S. State Department's travel advisories at http://travel.state.gov.

SPECIALIZED TRAVEL RESOURCES

Gay & Lesbian Travelers

Since 1861, Italy has had liberal legislation regarding homosexuality, but that doesn't mean it has always been looked on favorably in a Catholic country. Homosexuality is much more accepted in Rome than in the south, especially in Sicily, although Taormina has long been a gay mecca.

The **International Gay and Lesbian Travel Association** (**IGLTA;** ✆ **800/448-8550** or 954/776-2626; www.iglta.org) links travelers up with gay-friendly hoteliers, tour operators, and airline and cruise-line representatives. It offers monthly newsletters, marketing mailings, and a membership directory that's updated once a year.

Many agencies offer tours and travel itineraries specifically for gay and lesbian travelers. **Above and Beyond Tours** (✆ **800/397-2681;** www.abovebeyondtours.com) is the exclusive gay and lesbian tour operator for United Airlines. **Now, Voyager** (✆ **800/255-6951;** www.nowvoyager.com) is a well-known San Francisco–based gay-owned and -operated travel service. **Olivia Cruises & Resorts** (✆ **800/631-6277;** www.olivia.com) charters entire resorts and ships for exclusive lesbian vacations and offers smaller group experiences for both gay and lesbian travelers.

Gay.com Travel (✆ **415/834-6500;** www.gay.com) is an excellent online successor to the popular ***Out & About*** print magazine. It provides regularly updated information about gay-owned, gay-oriented, and gay-friendly lodging, dining, sightseeing, nightlife, and shopping establishments in every important destination worldwide. It also offers trip-planning information for gay and lesbian travelers for more than 50 destinations, along various themes, ranging from Sex & Travel to Vacations for Couples.

Travelers with Disabilities

Laws in Italy have compelled rail stations, airports, hotels, and most restaurants to follow a stricter set of regulations about **wheelchair accessibility** to restrooms, ticket counters, and the like. Even museums and other attractions have conformed to the regulations, which mimic many presently in effect in the United States. Always call ahead to check on the accessibility in hotels, restaurants, and sights you want to visit.

Many travel agencies offer customized tours and itineraries for travelers with disabilities. **Flying Wheels Travel** (✆ **877/451-5006;** www.flyingwheelstravel.com) offers escorted tours and cruises that emphasize sports and private tours in minivans with lifts. **Access-Able Travel Source** (www.access-able.com) offers extensive access information and advice for traveling around the world with disabilities. **Accessible Journeys** (✆ **800/846-4537** or 610/521-0339; www.disabilitytravel.com) caters specifically to slow walkers and wheelchair travelers and their families and friends.

Senior Travel

Mention the fact that you're a senior when you make your travel reservations. Although all of the major U.S. airlines except America West have canceled their senior discount and coupon book programs, many hotels still offer discounts for seniors. In most cities, people 60 and over qualify for reduced admission to theaters, museums, and other attractions, as well as discounted fares on public transportation.

Members of **AARP** (formerly known as the American Association of Retired Persons), 601 E St. NW, Washington, DC 10049 (✆ **888/687-2277;** www.aarp.org), get discounts on hotels, airfares, and car rentals. AARP offers members a wide range of benefits, including *AARP The Magazine* and a monthly newsletter. Anyone 50 and over can join.

FROMMERS.COM: THE complete TRAVEL RESOURCE

Planning a trip or just returned? Head to **Frommers.com,** voted Best Travel Site by *PC Magazine.* We think you'll find our site indispensable before, during, and after your travels—with expert advice and tips; independent reviews of hotels, restaurants, attractions, and preferred shopping and nightlife venues; vacation giveaways; and an online booking tool. We publish the complete contents of over 135 travel guides in our **Destinations** section, covering over 4,000 places worldwide. Each weekday, we publish original articles that report on **Deals and News** via our free **Frommers.com Newsletters.** What's more, **Arthur Frommer** himself blogs five days a week, with cutting opinions about the state of travel in the modern world. We're betting you'll find our **Events** listings an invaluable resource; it's an up-to-the-minute roster of what's happening in cities everywhere—including concerts, festivals, lectures, and more. We've also added weekly **podcasts, interactive maps,** and hundreds of new images across the site. Finally, don't forget to visit our **Message Boards,** where you can join in conversations with thousands of fellow Frommer's travelers and post your trip report once you return.

SUSTAINABLE TOURISM

Sustainable tourism is conscientious travel. It means being careful with the environments you explore and respecting the communities you visit—in this case Rome. Two overlapping components of sustainable travel are **eco-tourism** and **ethical tourism.** The **International Ecotourism Society (TIES)** defines eco-tourism as responsible travel to natural areas that conserves the environment and improves the well-being of local people, the Romans themselves. TIES suggests that eco-tourists follow these principles:

- If all roads lead to Rome, why not take the green one?
- Minimize environmental impact.
- Build environmental and cultural awareness and respect.
- Provide positive experiences for both visitors and hosts.
- Provide direct financial benefits for conservation and for local people.
- Raise sensitivity to host countries' political, environmental, and social climates.
- Support international human rights and labor agreements.

In 2010, the mayor of Rome unveiled a master plan to turn the Eternal City into a green, low-carbon, post-petroleum capital. His attempt was to bolster the city's standing in its bid for the 2020 Olympics, but the impact of certain moves will have far-reaching consequences for "Green Rome" overall.

The plan, one of the most ambitious ever for the city, calls for Rome to invest more than $615 million (U.S.) over the next 2 decades in new business and clean industries. This move, when carried out, will result in thousands of new jobs and also make the capital more independent of fossil fuels.

"This is a complete plan to transform Rome," said Mayor Gianni Alemanno. "It's more than an energy plan. It is also an environmental, urban, and economic one."

Plans call for three main areas of development:

1. Turning the congested historic core of Rome into a greener, pedestrian-friendly space;
2. Developing the commercial and industrial "ring" around Rome; and
3. Improving the agriculture districts outside Rome to reduce carbon imprint.

Rome also has a new event on its calendar every September known as **Zeromission Rome,** an event dedicated to promoting renewable energies in the Mediterranean area.

Speakers from all over the world fly into Rome at this time for numerous conferences, workshops, and meetings, each dedicated to renewable energy and global warming.

In this ever-changing world, highlights of the upcoming convention will focus on electricity from wind energy, photovoltaic technologies, solar power plants, geothermal energy, energy saving, the carbon credit market, and other 21st-century technologies to save not only Rome, but the planet itself.

The new emphasis on Green Rome is seen in modern developments such as the new stadium of the **Rome Soccer Club** launched in 2009. The stadium has become energy self-sufficient thanks to the use of a photovoltaic system and to micro-generation. The designers of the stadium implemented plans that eliminate greenhouse gases at the rate of 3,000 tons a year, an amazing figure.

Even Rome's largest public hospital, **Policlinico Umberto I,** has become more eco- and user-friendly by installing a solar-powered recreational pavilion that was formerly the waiting room. Today, the pavilion has been called a place where the "Alice in Wonderland mushroom meets solar-ray chomping Pac-Man."

Eden Walks (**© 039/338-596-1622;** www.edenwalks.com) is a pioneer of eco-conscious walking tours through both historical Rome and the Vatican. It offers three "low-impact" tours of Rome. Well-trained English-speaking guides take you on tours through history. Although group tours are offered, the Eden walks also features a number of 2-hour tours (maximum 4 people), costing 200€.

If you'd like to stay green while in Rome, you can book rooms at the **Ecohotel,** Via Di Bravetta 91, 00164 Roma (**© 06-66156920;** www.ecohotelroma.com). The government-rated, three-star hotel lies right outside the city center, within an easy commute by bus. It offers modern, comfortable bedrooms that the owners define as "a regenerating organic-style stay." The location is in the Valle dei Casali, a nature preserve. Verandas overlook the greenery and the garden. Breakfast is a selection of organic products. Even the cleaning products are environmentally friendly, and recycled paper is used. Free bikes are also available.

Several types of rooms are available, all nonsmoking, airy, and simply yet comfortably decorated, containing Wi-Fi, plus an adjustable heating and cooling system. Prices are economical, ranging from 80€ to 115€ in a double.

You can find some eco-friendly travel tips and statistics, as well as touring companies and associations—listed by destination under "Travel Choice"—at the **TIES** website, www.ecotourism.org. Also check out **Ecotravel.com,** which lets you search for sustainable touring companies in several categories (water-based, land-based, spiritually oriented, and so on).

While much of the focus of eco-tourism is about reducing impacts on the natural environment, ethical tourism concentrates on ways to preserve and enhance local

IT'S EASY BEING green

Here are a few simple ways you can help conserve fuel and energy when you travel to Rome:

- Each time you take a flight or drive a car greenhouse gases release into the atmosphere. You can help neutralize this danger to the planet through "carbon offsetting"—paying someone to invest your money in programs that reduce your greenhouse gas emissions by the same amount you've added. Before buying carbon offset credits, just make sure that you're using a reputable company, one with a proven program that invests in renewable energy. Reliable carbon offset companies include **Carbonfund** (www.carbonfund.org), **TerraPass** (www.terrapass.org), and **Carbon Neutral** (http://coolclimate.berkeley.edu).
- Whenever possible, choose nonstop flights; they generally require less fuel than indirect flights that stop and take off again. Try to fly during the day—some scientists estimate that nighttime flights are twice as harmful to the environment. And pack light—each 15 pounds of luggage on a 5,000-mile flight adds up to 50 pounds of carbon dioxide emitted.
- Where you stay during your travels can have a major environmental impact. To determine the green credentials of a property, ask about trash disposal

economies and communities, regardless of location. You can embrace ethical tourism by staying at a locally owned hotel in Rome or shopping at a store that employs local workers and sells locally produced goods.

Responsible Travel (www.responsibletravel.com) is a great source of sustainable travel ideas; the site is run by a spokesperson for ethical tourism in the travel industry. **Sustainable Travel International** (www.sustainabletravelinternational.org) promotes ethical tourism practices, and manages an extensive directory of sustainable properties and tour operators in Rome.

In the U.K., **Tourism Concern** (www.tourismconcern.org.uk) works to reduce social and environmental problems connected to tourism. The **Association of Independent Tour Operators** (**AITO;** www.aito.co.uk) is a group of specialist operators leading the field in making holidays sustainable, including jaunts to Rome.

SPECIAL INTEREST TRIPS & ESCORTED GENERAL INTEREST TOURS

Escorted General Interest Tours

Escorted tours are structured group tours, with a group leader. The price usually includes everything from airfare to hotels, meals, tours, admission costs, and local transportation.

and recycling, water conservation, and energy use; also question whether sustainable materials were used in the construction of the property. The website **www.greenhotels.com** recommends green-rated member hotels around the world that fulfill the company's stringent environmental requirements. Also consult **www.environmentally friendlyhotels.com** for more green accommodations ratings.

- At hotels in Rome, request that your sheets and towels not be changed daily. (Many hotels already have programs like this in place.) Turn off the lights and air conditioner (or heater) when you leave your room.
- Use public transport where possible—trains, buses, and even taxis are more energy-efficient forms of transport than driving. Even better is to walk or cycle; you'll produce zero emissions and stay fit and healthy on your travels.
- If renting a car is necessary, ask the rental agent for a hybrid, or rent the most fuel-efficient car available. You'll use less gas and save money at the tank.
- Eat at Roman owned and operated restaurants that use produce grown in the area. This contributes to the local economy and cuts down on greenhouse gas emissions by supporting restaurants where the food is not flown or trucked in across long distances.

The biggest operator of escorted tours to Italy is **Perillo Tours** (✆ **800/431-1515;** www.perillotours.com), family operated for three generations. Since it was founded in 1945, it has sent more than a million travelers to Italy on guided tours. Perillo's tours cost much less than you'd spend if you arranged a comparable trip yourself. Accommodations are in first-class hotels, and guides are well qualified.

Trafalgar Tours (✆ **866/544-4434;** www.trafalgartours.com) is one of Europe's largest tour operators, offering affordable guided tours with lodgings in unpretentious hotels. Check with your travel agent for more information on these tours (Trafalgar takes calls only from agents).

One of Trafalgar's leading competitors is **Globus+Cosmos Tours** (✆ **866/755-8581;** www.globusandcosmos.com). Globus has first-class escorted coach tours of various regions lasting from 8 to 16 days. Cosmos, a budget branch of Globus, sells escorted tours of about the same length. Tours must be booked through a travel agent, but you can call the 800 number for brochures. Another competitor is **Insight Vacations** (✆ **888/680-1241;** www.insightvacations.com), which books superior first-class, fully escorted motorcoach tours lasting from 1 week to a 36-day grand tour.

Special-Interest Trips

For special-interest travel, a good overview of what's out there is available from **Specialty Travel** (www.specialtytravel.com), which issues a biannual magazine devoted to special-interest tours. Contact information is provided for some 400 tour operators, including those operating in Rome. Everything is covered, from details on art classes to how to explore the history of Rome. Contact them at P.O. Box 458, San Anselmo, CA 94979 (© **888/624-4030**).

Tennis fans set their calendars by the events that transpire every year at the Italian Open, which is held in mid-May at the Foro Italica, near Mussolini's Olympic site in Rome. A California-based company, **Advantage Tennis Tours,** 33 White Sail Dr., Ste. 100, Laguna Niguel, CA 92677 (© **800/341-8687** or 949/661-7331; fax 949/489-2837; www.advantagetennistours.com), conducts tours to the Open that include 6 nights' accommodations in a deluxe Roman hotel, Center Court seats at three sessions of the tournament, city tours of ancient Rome, a farewell dinner, the organizational and communications skill of a tour hostess, and the opportunity to play tennis.

STAYING CONNECTED

Telephones

To call Italy from the United States, dial the **international prefix, 011;** then Italy's **country code, 39;** and then the city code (for example, **06** for Rome and **055** for Florence), which is now built into every number. Then dial the actual **phone number.**

A **local phone call** in Italy costs around .20€ (30¢). **Public phones** accept coins, precharged phone cards (*scheda* or *carta telefonica*), or both. You can buy a *carta telefonica* at any *tabacchi* (tobacconists; look for a white T on a brown background) in increments of 5€ ($8), 10€ ($16), and 20€ ($32). To make a call, pick up the receiver and insert .10€ (15¢) or your card (break off the corner first). Most phones have a digital display to tell you how much money you inserted (or how much is left). Dial the number, and don't forget to take the card with you.

To **call from one city code to another,** dial the city code, complete with initial 0, and then dial the number. (Numbers in Italy range from four to eight digits. Even when you're calling within the same city, you must dial that city's area code—including the zero. A Roman calling another Rome number must dial 06 before the local number.)

To **dial direct internationally,** dial **00** and then the country code, the area code, and the number. **Country codes** are as follows: the United States and Canada, 1; the United Kingdom, 44; Ireland, 353; Australia, 61; New Zealand, 64. Make international calls from a public phone, if possible, because hotels charge inflated rates for direct dial—but bring plenty of *schede* (change). A reduced rate is applied from 11pm to 8am on Monday through Saturday and all day Sunday. Direct-dial calls from the United States to Italy are much cheaper, so arrange for whomever to call you at your hotel.

Purchase **international phone cards** in Italy at a tabacchi (tobacco) store. These cards give you very good rates for calling long distance within Europe or to the US/Canada. On the back of the card you will find the access number to call and, under a "scratch off" area, your PIN for the card. You do not need to have the actual card with you—just the access number and PIN—so you can share one card if you want to.

Use these international phone cards from public phones, from your cellphone, or from your vacation rental or hotel phone. The prices vary and some cards have very cheap per minute rates.

The back of the card gives you local numbers to dial from several Italian cities, plus the numbers to use from public phones, cellphones, and for instructions in English.

When you are dialing a toll-free number, there is no extra charge for the call from a land line, public phone, or cellphone. But if you are calling from a cellphone, you do not get as good per minute rates using the card as you would from a land line.

To call the **national or international telephone information** (in Italian) in Italy, dial ✆ **1254.** It costs .40€ a call plus .10€ per 2 seconds.

To make **collect or calling-card calls,** drop in .10€ (15¢) or insert your card and dial one of the numbers here; an American operator will come on to assist you (because Italy has yet to discover the joys of the touch-tone phone). The following calling-card numbers work all over Italy: **AT&T** ✆ 172-1011, **MCI** ✆ 172-1022, and **Sprint** ✆ 172-1877. To make collect calls to a country besides the United States, dial ✆ **170** (.31€), and practice your Italian counting in order to relay the number to the Italian operator. Tell him or her that you want it *a carico del destinatario* (charged to the destination, or collect).

For calls to the United States, the U.K., or Canada, there is a surcharge of .18€ per minute.

Cellphones

The three letters that define much of the world's wireless capabilities are GSM (Global System for Mobiles), a big, seamless network that makes for easy cross-border cellphone use. In general, reception is good. In Canada, Microcell and some Rogers customers are GSM, and all Europeans and most Australians use GSM. Per-minute charges are usually .10€ to .40€ per minute.

For many, **renting** a phone is a good idea. While you can rent a phone from any number of overseas sites, including kiosks at airports and at car-rental agencies, we suggest renting the phone before you leave home. North Americans can rent one before leaving home from **InTouch USA** (✆ **800/872-7626** or 703/222-7161; www.intouchglobal.com) or **RoadPost** (✆ **888/290-1616** or 905/272-5665; www.roadpost.com). InTouch will also, for free, advise you on whether your existing phone will work overseas.

Buying a phone can be economically attractive, as many nations have cheap prepaid phone systems. Once you arrive at your destination, stop by a local cellphone shop and get the cheapest package; you'll probably pay less than 62€ ($100) for a phone and a starter calling card. Local calls may be as low as .05€ (10¢) per minute, and in E.U. countries incoming calls are free.

Internet & E-Mail

WITH YOUR OWN COMPUTER

More and more hotels, cafes, and retailers are signing on as Wi-Fi (wireless fidelity) "hot spots." Mac owners have their own networking technology: Apple AirPort. **T-Mobile Hotspot** (http://content.hotspot.t-mobile.com/AssetProcess.asp?asset=com.default.main.001) serves up wireless connections at coffee shops nationwide. **Boingo** (www.boingo.com) and **Wayport** (http://aws.wayport.net) have set up networks in airports and high-class hotel lobbies. IPass providers (see below) also give you access to a few hundred wireless hotel lobby setups. To locate other hot spots that provide **free wireless networks,** go to **www.jiwire.com**.

For dial-up access, most business-class hotels offer dataports for laptop modems, and a few thousand hotels in Italy now offer free high-speed Internet access. In addition, major Internet service providers (ISPs) have **local access numbers** around the world, allowing you to go online by placing a local call. The **iPass** network also has dial-up numbers around the world. You'll have to sign up with an iPass provider, who will then tell you how to set up your computer for your destination(s). For a list of iPass providers, go to www3.ipass.com and click on "Individuals Buy Now." One solid provider is **i2roam** (✆ **866/811-6209** or 920/233-5863; www.i2roam.com).

Wherever you go, bring a **connection kit** of the right power and phone adapters, a spare phone cord, and a spare Ethernet network cable—or find out whether your hotel supplies them to guests.

WITHOUT YOUR OWN COMPUTER

To find cybercafes check **www.cybercaptive.com** and **www.cybercafe.com**. Cybercafes are found in all large cities. But they do not tend to cluster in any particular neighborhoods because of competition. They are spread out.

Aside from formal cybercafes, most **public libraries** have Internet access. Avoid **hotel business centers** unless you're willing to pay exorbitant rates.

Most major airports now have **Internet kiosks** scattered throughout their gates. These give you basic Web access for a per-minute fee that's usually higher than cybercafe prices.

TIPS ON ACCOMMODATIONS

If you're looking to rent a villa or an apartment, one of the best agencies to call is **Rent Villas** (✆ **800/920-3136;** www.rentvillas.com). It's the representative for the Cuendet properties, some of the best in Italy, and its agents are very helpful in tracking down the perfect place to suit your needs. **Insider's Italy** (✆/fax **914/470-1612;** www.insidersitaly.com) is a small, upscale outfit run by a personable agent who's familiar with all her properties and Italy in general.

For some of the top properties, call the **Parker Company, Ltd.** (✆ **800/280-2811** or 781/596-8282; fax 781/596-3125; www.theparkercompany.com). This agency rents apartments, villas, restored farmhouses, and even castles, throughout Italy in almost every region from the Veneto in the northeast to remote Sicily in the southwest. In the U.K., contact **Cottages to Castles** (✆ **1622/775-217;** www.cottagestocastles.com); in the U.S. the agent to contact is **Italy My Dream** (✆ **866/687-7700;** www.italymydream.com). One of the most reasonably priced agencies is **Villas and Apartments Abroad, Ltd.** (✆ **212/213-6435;** fax 212/213-8252; www.ideal-villas.com). **Vacanze in Italia** (✆ **413/528-6610;** fax 413/528-6222; www.homeabroad.com) handles hundreds of rather upscale rentals. A popular but very pricey agency is **Villas International** (✆ **800/221-2260** or 415/499-9490; www.villasintl.com).

If you want to stay in a historic palazzo, contact **Abitare la Storia,** Villa Dal Pozzo D'Annone, St. Le Del Sempione 5, 28832 Belgirate-Lago Maggiore (✆ **0322-772156;** fax 0332-292678; www.abitarelastoria.it).

For apartment, farmhouse, or cottage stays of 2 weeks or more, **Untours** (✆ **888/868-6871;** www.untours.com) provides exceptional lodgings for a reasonable price, which includes air/ground transportation, cooking facilities, and on-call

House-Swapping

House-swapping is becoming a more popular and viable means of travel; you stay in their place, they stay in yours, and you both get a more authentic and personal view of a destination, the opposite of the escapist retreat many hotels offer. Try **HomeLink International** (www.homelink.org), the largest and oldest home-swapping organization, founded in 1952, with more than 11,000 listings worldwide ($90 yearly membership). **HomeExchange.com** ($100 for 6,000 listings) and **InterVac.com** ($95 for over 10,000 listings) are also reliable.

support from a local resident. Best of all: Untours—named the "Most Generous Company in America" by Newman's Own—donates most profits to provide low-interest loans to underprivileged entrepreneurs around the world (see website for details).

Also try **www.venere.com** (✆ **877/214-4288**) for everything from Roman hotels and suites to Tuscan farmhouses and B&Bs.

SUGGESTED ITINERARIES

For visitors on the run, who are forced by their tight schedules to see Rome in anywhere from 1 to 3 days, we've devised a trio of self-guided tours, presented as three 1-day itineraries. With these ready-made itineraries, you can have a complete, unforgettable trip, even though the clock is ticking away.

4

"It's not possible!" a Roman might warn you. If such an idea, especially Rome in 1 day, were presented to the pope, he might say, "I'll pray for you, dear child. Godspeed will be needed."

Actually, seeing Rome in 1 to 3 days is possible, but it calls for some discipline and fast moving on your part.

It's only fair to warn you that as we present these itineraries for "conquering" Rome in a nutshell, you'll actually need a month to develop a passing acquaintance with Rome. Save that for another trip, when perhaps you'll have more time.

Start your voyage of discovery right outside your hotel door. We offer bus and Metro routes from place to place, but you'll find that many of the major sites in Rome are a short walk from one another.

City Layout

Arm yourself with a detailed street map, not the general overview handed out free at tourist offices. Most hotels provide a pretty good version at their front desks.

The bulk of ancient, Renaissance, and baroque Rome (as well as the train station) lies on the east side of the **Tiber River (Fiume Tevere),** which meanders through town. However, several important landmarks are on the other side: **St. Peter's Basilica** and the **Vatican,** the **Castel Sant'Angelo,** and the colorful **Trastevere** neighborhood.

The city's various quarters are linked by large boulevards (large, at least, in some places) that have mostly been laid out since the late 19th century. Starting from the **Vittorio Emanuele Monument,** a controversial pile of snow-white Brescian marble that's often compared to a wedding cake, there's a street running practically due north to **Piazza del Popolo** and the city wall. This is **Via del Corso,** one of the main streets of Rome—noisy, congested, always crowded with buses and shoppers, and called simply "Il Corso." To its left (west) lie the Pantheon,

Piazza Navona, Campo de' Fiori, and the Tiber. To its right (east) you'll find the Spanish Steps, the Trevi Fountain, the Borghese Gardens, and Via Veneto.

Back at the Vittorio Emanuele Monument, the major artery going west (and ultimately across the Tiber to St. Peter's) is **Corso Vittorio Emanuele.** Behind you to your right, heading toward the Colosseum, is **Via del Fori Imperiali,** laid out in the 1930s by Mussolini to show off the ruins of the Imperial Forums he had excavated, which line it on either side. Yet another central conduit is **Via Nazionale,** running from **Piazza Venezia** (just in front of the Vittorio Emanuele Monument) east to **Piazza della Repubblica** (near Stazione Termini). The final lap of Via Nazionale is called **Via Quattro Novembre.**

Finding an address in Rome can be a problem because of the narrow streets of old Rome and the little, sometimes hidden *piazze* (squares). Numbers usually run consecutively, with odd numbers on one side of the street and even numbers on the other. However, in the old districts, the numbers will sometimes run consecutively up one side of the street to the end, and then back in the opposite direction on the other side. Therefore, no. 50 could be opposite no. 308.

The Neighborhoods in Brief

This section will give you some idea of where you might want to stay and where the major attractions are located.

Near Stazione Termini The main train station, **Stazione Termini,** adjoins **Piazza della Repubblica,** and most likely this will be your introduction to Rome. Much of the area is seedy and filled with gas fumes from all the buses and cars, but it has been improving. If you stay here, you might not get a lot of atmosphere, but you'll have a lot of affordable options and a very convenient location, near the transportation hub of the city and not too far from ancient Rome. There's a lot to see here, including the **Basilica di Santa Maria Maggiore** and the **Baths of Diocletian.** Some high-class hotels are sprinkled in the area, including the **Grand,** but many are long past their heyday.

The neighborhoods on either side of Termini have been improving greatly, and some streets are now attractive. The best-looking area is ahead and to your right as you exit the station on the Via Marsala side. Most budget hotels here occupy a floor or more of a palazzo; many of their entryways are drab, although upstairs they're often charming or at least clean and livable. In the area to the left of the station as you exit, the streets are wider, the traffic is heavier, and the noise level is higher. This area off Via Giolitti is being redeveloped, and most streets are in good condition. A few still need improving; be careful at night.

Via Veneto & Piazza Barberini In the 1950s and early 1960s, **Via Veneto** was the swinging place to be, as the likes of King Farouk, Frank Sinatra, and Swedish actress Anita Ekberg paraded up and down the boulevard to the delight of the paparazzi. The street is still here and is still the site of luxury hotels and elegant cafes and restaurants, although it's no longer a hot spot. It's lined with restaurants catering to those visitors who've heard of this famous boulevard from decades past, but the restaurants are mostly overpriced and overcrowded tourist traps. City authorities have tried to restore this legendary street to some of its former glory by banning vehicular traffic on the top half. It makes for a pleasant stroll, in any case.

To the south, Via Veneto comes to an end at **Piazza Barberini,** dominated by the 1642 **Triton Fountain (Fontana del Tritone),** a baroque celebration with four dolphins holding up an open scallop shell in which a triton sits blowing into a conch. Overlooking the square is the **Palazzo Barberini.** In 1623, when Cardinal Maffeo Barberini became Pope Urban VIII, he ordered Carlo Maderno to build a palace here; it was later completed by Bernini and Borromini.

Ancient Rome Most visitors explore this area first, taking in the **Colosseum, Palatine Hill, Roman Forum, Imperial Forums,** and **Circus Maximus.** The area forms part of the *centro storico* (historic district), along with **Campo de' Fiori, Piazza Navona,** and the **Pantheon,** which are described below (we've considered them separately for the purposes of helping you locate hotels and restaurants). Because of its ancient streets, airy piazzas, classical atmosphere, and heartland location, this is a good place to stay. If you base yourself here, you can walk to the monuments and avoid the hassle of Rome's inadequate public transportation.

This area offers only a few hotels—most of them inexpensive to moderate in price—and not a lot of great restaurants. Many restaurant owners have their eyes on the cash register and the tour bus crowd, whose passengers are often hustled in and out of these restaurants so fast that they don't know whether the food is any good.

Campo de' Fiori & the Jewish Ghetto South of Corso Vittorio Emanuele and centered on **Piazza Farnese** and the market square of **Campo de' Fiori,** this area includes many buildings that were constructed in Renaissance times as private homes. Stroll along **Via Giulia**—Rome's most fashionable street in the 16th century—with its antiques stores, interesting hotels, and modern art galleries.

West of Via Arenula lies one of the city's most intriguing districts, the old **Jewish Ghetto,** where restaurants far outnumber hotels. In 1556, Pope Paul IV ordered the Jews, about 8,000 at the time, to move into this area. The walls weren't torn down until 1849. Although ancient and medieval Rome has a lot more atmosphere, this working-class neighborhood is close to many attractions. You're more likely to want to dine here than to stay here.

Piazza Navona & the Pantheon One of the most desirable areas of Rome, this district is a maze of narrow streets and alleys dating from the Middle Ages. It is filled with churches and palaces built during the Renaissance and baroque eras, often with rare marble and other materials stripped from ancient Rome. The only way to explore it is on foot. Its heart is **Piazza Navona,** built over Emperor Domitian's stadium and bustling with sidewalk cafes, palazzi, street artists, musicians, and pickpockets. There are several hotels in the area and plenty of trattorie.

Rivaling Piazza Navona—in general activity, the cafe scene, and nightlife—is the area around the **Pantheon,** which remains from ancient Roman times and is surrounded by a district built much later (this "pagan" temple was turned into a church and rescued, but the buildings that once surrounded it are long gone).

Piazza del Popolo & the Spanish Steps **Piazza del Popolo** was laid out by Giuseppe Valadier and is one of Rome's largest squares. It's characterized by an obelisk brought from Heliopolis in lower Egypt during the reign of Augustus. At the end of the square is the **Porta del Popolo,** the gateway in the 3rd-century Aurelian wall. In the mid-16th century, this was one of the major gateways into the old city. If you enter the piazza along Via del Corso from the south, you'll see twin churches, **Santa Maria del Miracoli** and **Santa Maria di Montesanto,** flanking the street. But the square's major church is **Santa Maria del Popolo** (1442–47), one of the best examples of a Renaissance church in Rome.

Since the 17th century, the **Spanish Steps** (the former site of the Spanish ambassador's residence) have been a meeting place for visitors. Some of Rome's most upscale shopping streets, including **Via Condotti,** fan out from here. The elegant **Hassler,** one of Rome's grandest hotels, lies at the top of the steps. This is Rome at its most upscale, full of $500-a-night hotels, designer boutiques, and high-end restaurants.

Around Vatican City Across the Tiber, **Vatican City** is a small city-state whose influence extends around the world. The **Vatican Museums, St. Peter's,** and the **Vatican Gardens** take up most of the land area, and the popes have lived here for 6 centuries. The neighborhood around the Vatican—called the "Borgo"—contains some good hotels (and several bad ones), but it's removed from the more happening scene of ancient and Renaissance Rome, and getting to and from it can be time-consuming. The area is rather dull at night and contains few, if any, of Rome's finest restaurants. For the average visitor, Vatican City and its surrounding area are best for exploring during the day. Nonetheless, the area is very popular for those whose sightseeing or even business interests center on the Vatican.

Trastevere In Roman dialect, *Trastevere* means "across the Tiber." For visitors arriving in Rome decades ago, it might as well have meant Siberia. All that has changed now: This once medieval working-class district has been gentrified and overrun with visitors from all over the world. It started to change in the 1970s when expats and others discovered its rough charm. Since then, Trastevere has been filling up with tour buses, dance clubs, offbeat shops, sidewalk vendors, pubs, and little trattorie with menus printed in English. There are even places to stay here, but as of yet, it hasn't burgeoned into a major hotel district. There are some excellent restaurants here as well.

The original people of the district, and there are still some of them left, are of mixed ancestry—mainly Jewish, Roman, and Greek. For decades they were known for speaking their own dialect in a language rougher than that spoken in central Rome. Even their cuisine was spicier.

The area still centers on the ancient churches of **Santa Cecilia** and **Santa Maria** in Trastevere. Trastevere remains one of Rome's most colorful quarters, even if it is a bit overrun. Known as a "city within a city," it is at least a village within a city.

Testaccio & the Aventine In A.D. 55, Nero ordered that Rome's thousands of broken amphorae and terra-cotta roof tiles be stacked in a carefully designated pile to the east of the Tiber, just west of Pyramide and today's Ostia Railway Station. Over the centuries, the mound grew to a height of around 200 feet and then was compacted to form the centerpiece for one of the city's most unusual working-class neighborhoods, **Testaccio.** Eventually, houses were built on the terra-cotta mound, and caves were dug into its mass to store wine and foodstuffs. Once home to the slaughterhouses of Rome and its former port on the Tiber, *Testaccio* means "ugly head" in Roman dialect. Bordered by the Protestant cemetery, Testaccio is known for its authentic Roman restaurants. Chefs here still cook traditionally, satisfying local—not tourist—palates. Change is on the way, however, and this is a neighborhood on its way up. Nightclubs have sprung up in the old warehouses, although they come and go rather quickly.

Another offbeat section of Rome is **Aventine Hill,** south of the Palatine and close to the Tiber. In 186 B.C., thousands of residents of the area were executed for joining in "midnight rituals of Dionysos and Bacchus." These bloody orgies are a thing of the past, and the Aventine area is now a leafy and rather posh residential quarter.

The Appian Way Via Appia Antica is a 2,300-year-old road that has witnessed much of the history of the ancient world. By 190 B.C., it extended from Rome to Brindisi on the southeast coast. Its most famous sights today are the **catacombs,** the graveyards of patrician families (despite what it says in *Quo Vadis?,* they weren't used as a place for Christians to hide out while fleeing persecution). This is one of the most historically rich areas of Rome to explore, but it's not a viable place to stay. It does contain some restaurants, however, where you can order lunch on your visit to the catacombs.

Prati The little-known **Prati** district is a middle-class suburb north of the Vatican. It has been discovered by budget travelers because of its affordable *pensioni*, although it's not conveniently located for much of the sightseeing you'll want to do. The **Trionfale flower-and-food market** itself is worth the trip. The area also abounds in shopping streets less expensive than those found in central Rome, and street crime isn't much of a problem.

Parioli Rome's most elegant residential section, Parioli, is framed by the green spaces of the **Villa Borghese** to the south and the **Villa Glori** and **Villa Ada** to the north. It's a setting for some of the city's finest restaurants, hotels, and nightclubs. It's not exactly central, however, and it can be a hassle if you're dependent on public transportation. Parioli lies adjacent to Prati but across the Tiber to the east; like Prati, this is one of the safer districts. We'd call Parioli an area for connoisseurs, attracting those who shun the overrun Spanish Steps and the overly commercialized Via Veneto, and those who'd never admit to having been in the Termini area.

Monte Mario On the northwestern precincts of Rome, **Monte Mario** is the site of the deluxe **Cavalieri Hilton,** an excellent stop to take in a drink and the panorama of Rome. If you plan to spend a lot of time shopping and sightseeing in the heart of Rome, it's a difficult and often expensive commute. The area lies north of Prati, away from the hustle and bustle of central Rome. Bus no. 913 runs from Piazza Augusto Imperator near Piazza del Popolo to Monte Mario.

THE BEST OF ROME IN 1 DAY

Since time is wasting, arise early and begin your day with some "live theater" by walking the streets of the Eternal City around your hotel, as Rome awakens to another day. Deliveries are being made; Romans with early calls are reporting to work, and the famous cats of the city are out looking for a fish head. This walk can acclimatize you faster than anything else to the sights, sounds, and smells of this ancient capital, once the seat of one of the world's most powerful kingdoms, with many reminders of its heyday. This walk will get you centered before you catch a taxi, hop a bus, or board the Metro for a ride to the first attraction on our tour.

Rush Hour(s)

Rome has *four* daily rush hours: to work (8–9am), to home for lunch (1pm), back to work (3:30pm), and to home in the evening (6–7pm).

But first, we suggest that you duck into a Roman cafe for breakfast. It doesn't matter which one. On virtually every street of Rome, you'll find one. If it's your desire, begin your day with a cup of coffee, a glass of blood-red orange juice, and one of those delicious Italian pastries.

Sit back and people-watch as patrons go through the same ritual as you, fortifying themselves for another day.

A lot of the museums, piazzas, and other attractions will have to wait for another day, if you have one. The "Rome in 1 Day" crowd will want to concentrate on the "greatest hits" itinerary by taking in the monuments that made Imperial Rome revered throughout the known world.

If you have just 1 day, consider rejecting Imperial Rome (as hard as this is to do) and opt instead to explore St. Peter's and the Vatican. The choice is yours. We'll lead off Day 1 with Imperial Rome, saving Day 2 for the Vatican and St. Peter's. But, if it's your wish, you can reverse these itineraries, of course.

One day is far too brief—after all, Rome wasn't built in a day, and you can't see it in one—but you can make the most of your limited time.

If you're in Rome for at least 3 days, stop by or call the ticket office of Galleria Borghese (p. 179) and secure a reservation for a visit on Day 2.

Start: Take bus no. 30, 40, 62, 64, 70, 87, 95, 170, 492, or 628 to Piazza dell'Ara Coeli and climb the stairs to Piazza del Campidoglio.

1 Piazza del Campidoglio ★★

The Campidoglio stands on the summit of Capitoline Hill, the most sacred of ancient Rome, where the Temples of Jupiter and Juno once stood. This was the spiritual heart of ancient Rome, where triumphant generals made sacrifices to the gods for giving them victories.

At the top of the graceful steps leading to the Campidoglio is the fabled equestrian statue of the emperor Marcus Aurelius. Actually, it's a copy; the original is in the Capitoline Museum on your left. Across the piazza is the Palace of the Conservatori based on an architectural plan of Michelangelo. Save these museums for a future visit.

Walk around the corner (as you face it) of the Senatorium (Town Council) for a panoramic view of the Roman Forum, which we'll visit later. In the distance you can see the Colosseum, also coming up later in our itinerary. The decaying columns and crumbling temples of Imperial Rome rank as one of the grandest man-made views you'll see in Europe. Allow at least 30 minutes or more to walk up and down the steps leading to Capitoline Hill taking in the view.

After Capitoline Hill, head east following our map for a walk along Via dei Fori Imperiali, taking in:

2 Fori Imperiali (Imperial Forums) ★★

From the railing that skirts Via dei Fori Imperiali, you can take in the view of the famous forums of Imperial Rome in about 30 minutes. Arm yourself with a trusty map so you'll know which ruins you're viewing. Right off Piazza Venezia stands **Trajan's Column,** with its intricate bas-relief sculpture depicting Trajan's victorious campaign against Dacia at the dawn of the 2nd century. Immediately east of the column is **Basilica Ulpia,** whose gray marble columns rise roofless into the sky. Moving east you come to the **Forum of Julius Caesar,** the site of the ancient Roman stock exchange and the Temple of Venus. Next you'll pass on your left the **Forum of Augustus,** built before the birth of Christ and once home to a mammoth statue of Augustus. On your right is the **Forum of Nerva,** honoring an emperor with a 2-year reign (A.D. 96–98). Directly east of Nerva is the **Forum of Vespasian** begun by the emperor after the capture of Jerusalem in A.D. 71. Immediately following that is the **Temple of Venus and Roma,** or what little is left of it.

At this point you'll be at the doorway to the Colosseum.

Rome in 1 Day

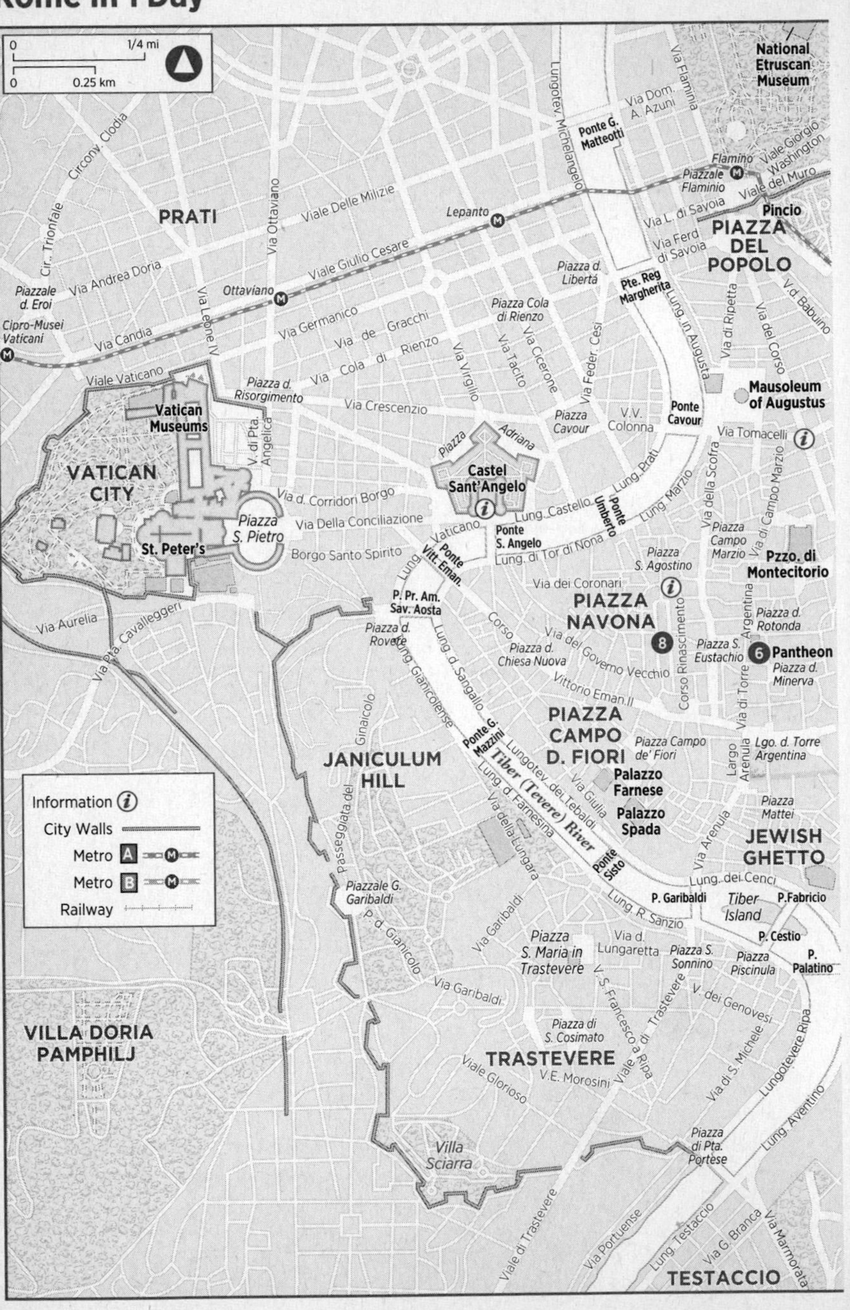

0
1/4 mi
0
0.25 km
National Etruscan Museum
Via Flaminia
Via Dom. A. Azuni
Lungotev. Michelangelo
Ponte G. Matteotti
Circonv. Clodia
Flaminio
Piazzale Flaminio
Viale Giorgio Washington
Viale del Muro
Via Ottaviano
Viale Delle Milizie
Lepanto
PRATI
Cir. Trionfale
Viale Giulio Cesare
Via L. di Savoia
Pincio
Via Ferd di Savoia
PIAZZA DEL POPOLO
Piazza d. Libertà
Pte. Reg Margherita
Piazzale d. Eroi
Via Andrea Doria
Via Leone IV
Ottaviano
Piazza Cola di Rienzo
Lung. in Augusta
Via di Ripetta
Via del Corso
V.d. Babuino
Cipro-Musei Vaticani
Via Candia
Via Germanico
Via de Gracchi
Via Cola di Rienzo
Via Virgilio
Via Tacito
Via Cicerone
Via Feder. Cesi
Viale Vaticano
Piazza d. Risorgimento
Via Crescenzio
Mausoleum of Augustus
Vatican Museums
Piazza Cavour
V.V. Colonna
Ponte Cavour
Via Tomacelli
V. di Pta. Angelica
Piazza Adriana
VATICAN CITY
Castel Sant'Angelo
Lung. Prati
Via della Scrofa
Via di Campo Marzio
Via d. Corridori Borgo
Lung. Castello
Ponte Umberto
Lung. Marzio
Piazza S. Pietro
Via Della Conciliazione
Lung. Vaticano
Ponte S. Angelo
Piazza Campo Marzio
St. Peter's
Borgo Santo Spirito
Ponte Vitt. Eman.
Lung. di Tor di Nona
Piazza S. Agostino
Pzzo. di Montecitorio
Via dei Coronari
PIAZZA NAVONA
P. Pr. Am. Sav. Aosta
Via Aurelia
Via Pta. Cavalleggeri
Piazza d. Rovere
Corso
Piazza d. Rotonda
Via del Governo Vecchio
Piazza S. Eustachio
Pantheon
Piazza d. Chiesa Nuova
Corso Rinascimento
Via di Torre Argentina
Piazza d. Minerva
Vittorio Eman.II
Lung. Gianicolense
Lung. d. Sangallo
PIAZZA CAMPO D. FIORI
Piazza Campo de' Fiori
Lgo. d. Torre Argentina
Ginaicolo
Ponte G. Mazzini
Largo Arenula
JANICULUM HILL
Lungotev. dei Tebaldi
Tiber (Tevere) River
Palazzo Farnese
Information
City Walls
Metro A
Metro B
Railway
Lung. d. Farnesina
Via Giulia
Palazzo Spada
Piazza Mattei
Passeggiata del
Via della Lungara
JEWISH GHETTO
Via Arenula
Ponte Sisto
Lung. dei Cenci
Piazzale G. Garibaldi
P. Garibaldi
Tiber Island
P.Fabricio
Lung. R. Sanzio
P. d. Gianicolo
Via Garibaldi
Piazza S. Maria in Trastevere
Via d. Lungaretta
Piazza S. Sonnino
Piazza Piscinula
P. Cestio
P. Palatino
V. dei Genovesi
V.S. Francesco a Ripa
Viale di Trastevere
Via Garibaldi
Piazza di S. Cosimato
Via di S. Michele
Lungotevere Ripa
VILLA DORIA PAMPHILJ
TRASTEVERE
Viale Glorioso
V.E. Morosini
Lung. Aventino
Piazza di Pta. Portese
Villa Sciarra
Viale di Trastevere
Via Portuense
Lung. Testaccio
Via G. Branca
Via Marmorata
TESTACCIO

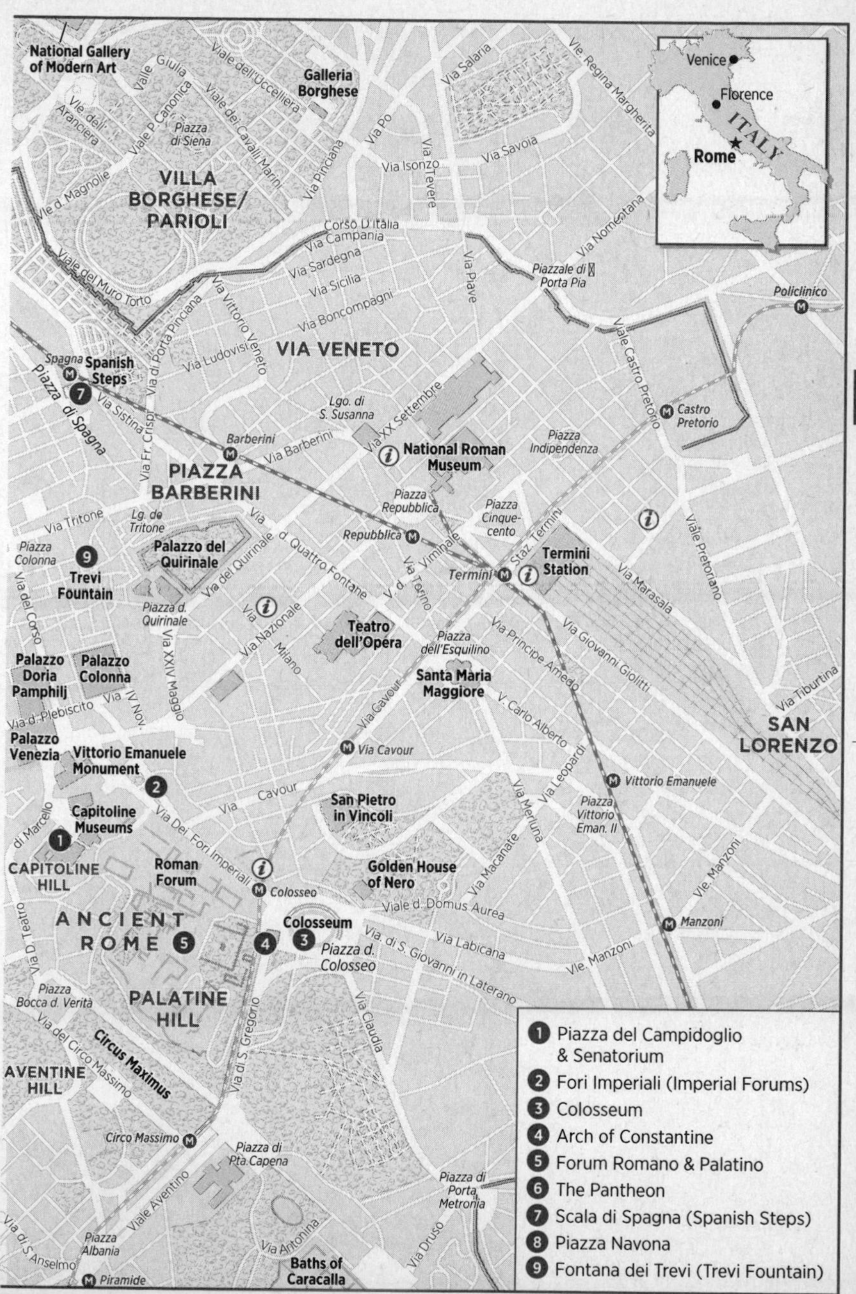

National Gallery of Modern Art
Galleria Borghese
VILLA BORGHESE/ PARIOLI
VIA VENETO
Spanish Steps
PIAZZA BARBERINI
National Roman Museum
Palazzo del Quirinale
Trevi Fountain
Termini Station
Teatro dell'Opera
Santa Maria Maggiore
Palazzo Doria Pamphilj
Palazzo Colonna
Palazzo Venezia
Vittorio Emanuele Monument
Capitoline Museums
CAPITOLINE HILL
Roman Forum
San Pietro in Vincoli
Golden House of Nero
Colosseum
ANCIENT ROME
PALATINE HILL
Circus Maximus
AVENTINE HILL
Baths of Caracalla
SAN LORENZO
Venice
Florence
Rome
ITALY
1 Piazza del Campidoglio & Senatorium
2 Fori Imperiali (Imperial Forums)
3 Colosseum
4 Arch of Constantine
5 Forum Romano & Palatino
6 The Pantheon
7 Scala di Spagna (Spanish Steps)
8 Piazza Navona
9 Fontana dei Trevi (Trevi Fountain)

3 Colosseum ★★★

Construction on this amphitheater began in A.D. 72, and it was a marvel of engineering since its enormous weight rested in a swamp (Nero's former lake) on artificial supports. The completed stadium was dedicated by Titus in A.D. 80. Covered with marble, it could hold 80,000 spectators who watched games that nearly rendered extinct many species of animals from the Roman Empire. Allow at least 1½ hours to explore it; for more information, see p. 158.

Next to the Colosseum is the:

4 Arch of Constantine ★★

This spectacular arch was erected in honor of Constantine's defeat of the pagan Maxentius in A.D. 312. You can gaze in awe at this remarkable arch with its intricate carving for at least 15 minutes before pressing on. Before tackling the Roman Forum and the Palatine Hill, we suggest a luncheon break in the area of the Colosseum. If you don't want to waste precious time, you can avail yourself of food on the run at a street vendor, or else patronize one of the trattorie in the vicinity, if you're seeking a sit-down meal.

Within a short walk of the Colosseum you can take in the glories of:

5 Forum Romano (Roman Forum), Palatino (Palatine Hill), and Museo Palatino (Palatine Museum) ★★★

The Roman Forum was the literal heart of ancient Rome, a center for trade, religion, and politics. The entrance is off Via dei Fori Imperiali, right at the intersection with Via Cavour. For more detailed information, refer to p. 160. There is also a walking tour of the area (p. 194) if you need more guidance.

After you view the Roman Forum, you can explore Palatine Hill, which was once covered with the palaces of patrician families and early emperors. Today it's a tree-shaded hilltop of gardens and fragments of ancient villas. Allow at least 3 hours to take in these attractions and the Palatine Museum.

To reach our next attraction, pick up bus no. 46, 62, 64, 170, or 492 at Arco di Costantino to Largo di Torre, or Metro to Barberini.

6 The Pantheon ★★★

This fabulous ancient monument was built and rebuilt several times, first by Agrippa who began it in 27 B.C. The present structure is the result of an early 2nd century A.D. reconstruction by the Emperor Hadrian. The Pantheon stands on Piazza della Rotonda, which is complete with obelisk and baroque fountain. It is in an astonishing state of preservation, considering nearly 2 millennia of vandalism. Allow 45 minutes for a visit. For more information refer to p. 169.

Take the Metro to Spagna for our next stop.

7 Caffe Sant'Eustachio

For a break, head nearby to this cafe, which Romans claim serves the most superior coffee in Rome. What's the secret? The pure water used in the brew is funneled into the city by an aqueduct built in 19 B.C. Piazza Sant'Eustachio 82 (✆ 06-97618552).

8 Scala di Spagna (Spanish Steps) ★★

Rising over the Piazza di Spagna in the very heart of Rome is a monumental baroque staircase—best viewed in spring when the flowers are in full bloom. It was the work of Francesco de Sanctis in the 18th century. The stairs lead to the Trinità dei Monti Church. At no. 26 on the piazza is the Keats-Shelley House where Keats died of tuberculosis at the age of 25.

It's a rare visitor who hasn't sat for a while on one of the landings—there's one every 12 steps—perhaps to download an e-mail from home on a laptop or observe the other sitters, most often young. The fountain at the foot of the steps was designed by Bernini's father at the end of the 16th century, and it's reputed to have the sweetest water in Rome. Allow at least 30 minutes for a visit. For more information, see p. 175.

After perhaps a shower and rest at your hotel, take bus no. 30, 40, 62, 64, 70, 87, 116, or 492 to reach the:

9 Piazza Navona ★★★

The most beautiful square in all of Rome—and best seen at night—is like an ocher-colored gem, unspoiled by new buildings, or even by traffic. The shape stems from the Stadium of Domitian, whose ruins lie underneath. Great chariot races were once held here. In the center is Bernini's Fountain of the Four Rivers, floodlit at night. During summer evenings there are outdoor art shows. Some of the oldest streets in Rome surround Piazza Navona. There is no more romantic place to dine in all the city; our selections of restaurants begins on p. 170.

For your *arrivederci* to Roma, take bus no. 62, 95, 175, or 492.

10 Fontana dei Trevi (Trevi Fountain) ★★

This is an 18th-century extravaganza of baroque stonework ruled over by a large statue of Neptune. Visitors come here at night for 20 minutes or so to toss a coin into the fountain, which is said to ensure that you will some day return to Rome.

THE BEST OF ROME IN 2 DAYS

If you thought Day 1 was hectic, wait until you sample our agenda for Day 2. Fortify yourself with a good breakfast and wear a pair of sturdy walking shoes. The great challenge of **St. Peter's Basilica,** followed by the dazzling treasures of the **Vatican Museums,** await you on this day. And, if you're lucky, you can also take in some of the wonder of the **Castel Sant'Angelo,** that mausoleum-turned-fortress, and even the best of the masterpieces of the **Galleria Borghese** if you can get in. Since it opens early (8am), get an early jump on the day by heading first for the **Basilica di San Pietro** (St. Peter's Basilica). ***Start:*** Metro to Ottaviano–San Pietro.

---

1 Piazza San Pietro ★★★

You can even arrive here early—perhaps 7:30am—for a 30-minute walk around before the basilica opens. This is one of the world's most famous squares, designed by Bernini in 1656–1667. It is the gateway to the largest church in the world (see below). For more on this square, see p. 150.

Rome in 2 Days

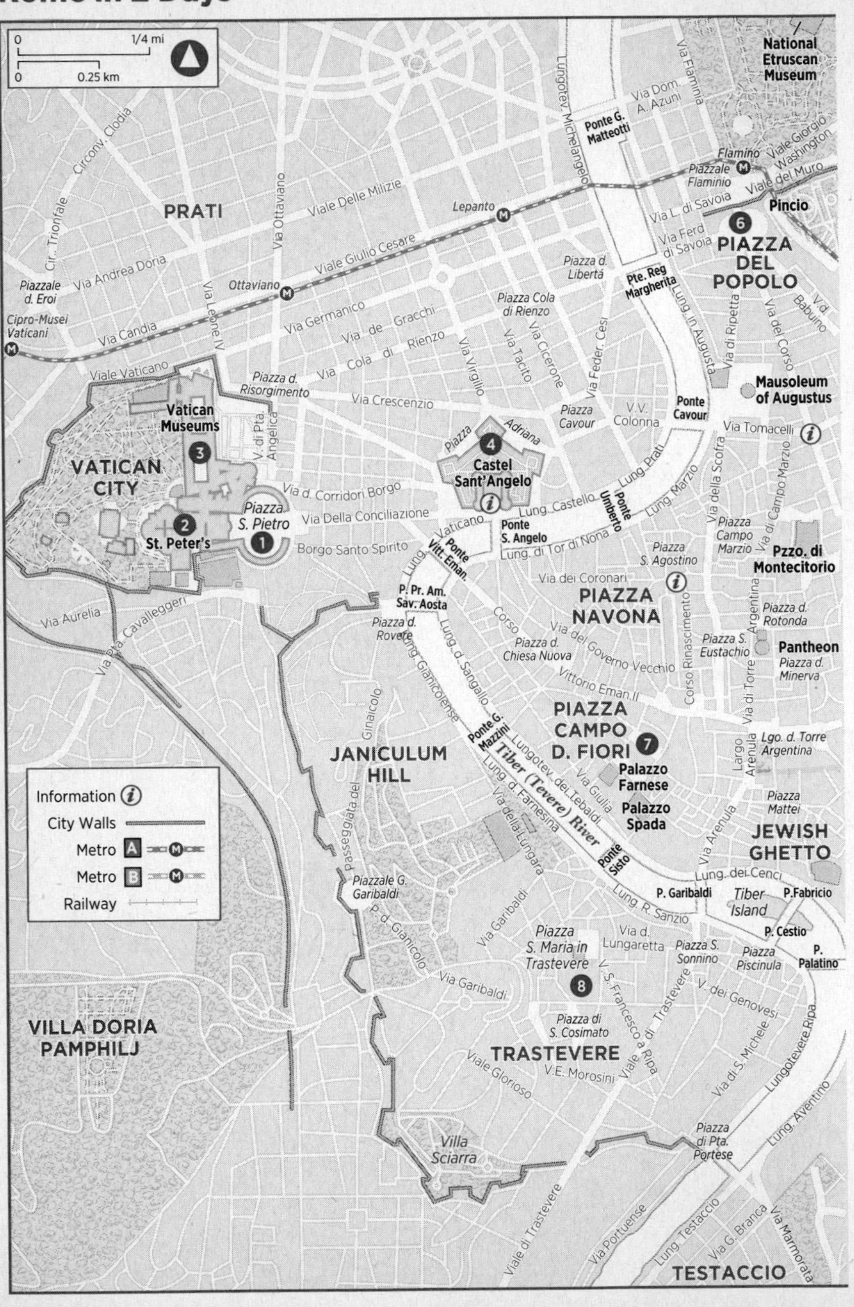

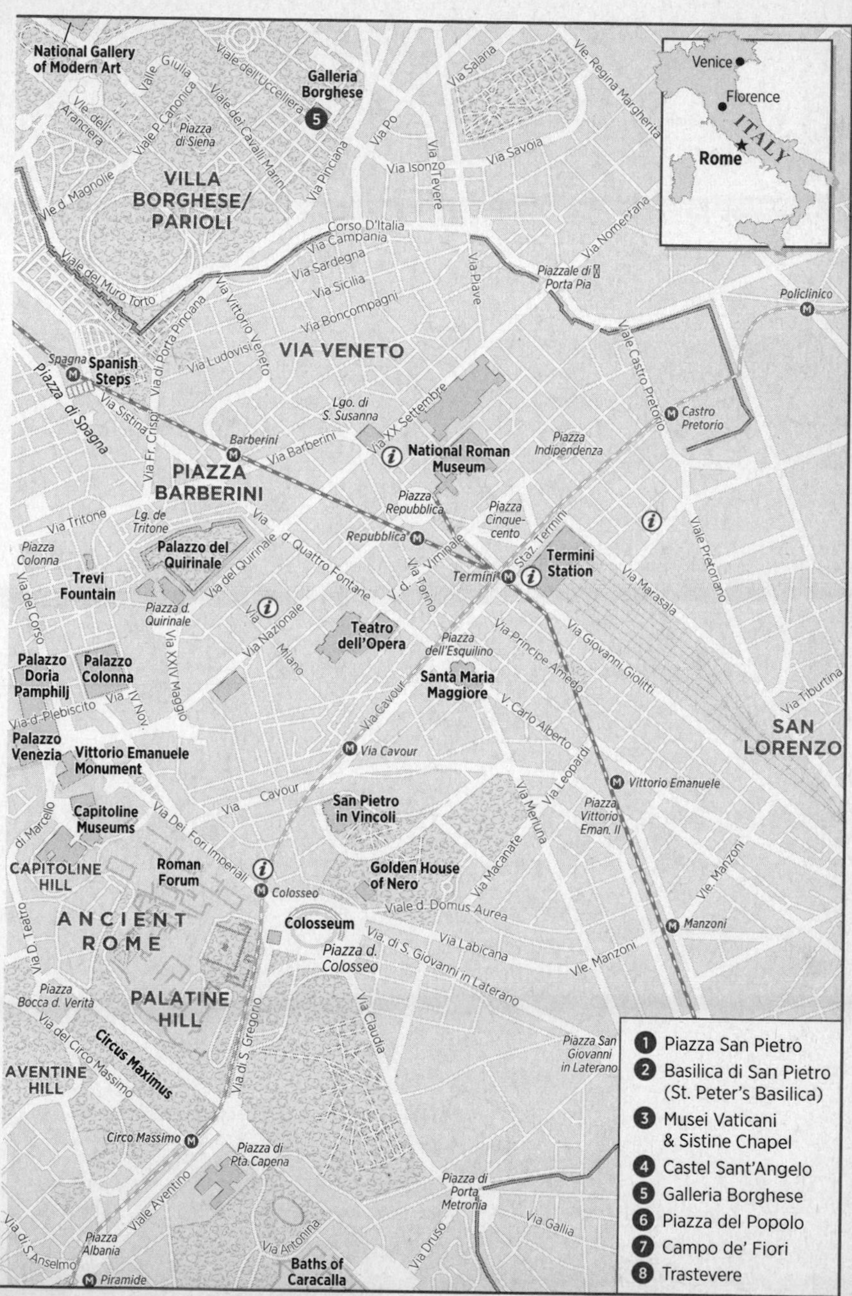
National Gallery of Modern Art
Galleria Borghese
5
VILLA BORGHESE/ PARIOLI
Venice
Florence
ITALY
Rome
VIA VENETO
Spanish Steps
Spagna
Piazza di Spagna
Barberini
PIAZZA BARBERINI
Lgo. di S. Susanna
National Roman Museum
Piazza Repubblica
Repubblica
Piazza Cinque-cento
Termini
Termini Station
Castro Pretorio
Piazza Indipendenza
Policlinico
Piazzale di Porta Pia
Palazzo del Quirinale
Piazza d. Quirinale
Trevi Fountain
Piazza Colonna
Lg. de Tritone
Teatro dell'Opera
Piazza dell'Esquilino
Santa Maria Maggiore
Palazzo Doria Pamphilj
Palazzo Colonna
Palazzo Venezia
Vittorio Emanuele Monument
Via Cavour
SAN LORENZO
Vittorio Emanuele
Piazza Vittorio Eman. II
San Pietro in Vincoli
Capitoline Museums
CAPITOLINE HILL
Roman Forum
Golden House of Nero
Colosseo
Colosseum
Piazza d. Colosseo
Manzoni
ANCIENT ROME
PALATINE HILL
Piazza Bocca d. Verità
Circus Maximus
AVENTINE HILL
Circo Massimo
Piazza di Pta.Capena
Piazza San Giovanni in Laterano
Piazza di Porta Metronia
Piazza Albania
Piramide
Baths of Caracalla
Via Salaria
Vle. Regina Margherita
Via Po
Via Isonzo
Via Tevere
Via Savoia
Via Pinciana
Viale dell'Uccelliera
Viale dei Cavalli Marini
Viale P. Canonica
Valle Giulia
Piazza di Siena
Vle. degli Aranciera
Vle.d. Magnolie
Corso D'Italia
Via Campania
Via Sardegna
Via Sicilia
Via Boncompagni
Via Piave
Via Nomentana
Viale del Muro Torto
Via di Porta Pinciana
Via Vittorio Veneto
Via Ludovisi
Via Sistina
Via Fr. Crispi
Via Barberini
Via XX Settembre
Viale Castro Pretorio
Via Tritone
Via del Corso
Via d. Quattro Fontane
Via del Quirinale
Via Nazionale
Via XXIV Maggio
Via IV Nov.
Via d. Plebiscito
Via Milano
Via Torino
V. d. Viminale
Staz. Termini
Via Marsala
Viale Pretoriano
Via Principe Amedeo
Via Giovanni Giolitti
Via Tiburtina
V. Carlo Alberto
Via Leopardi
Via Merulana
Via Macanate
Vle. Manzoni
Via Dei Fori Imperiali
di Marcello
Via D. Teatro
Viale d. Domus Aurea
Via Labicana
Via. di S. Giovanni in Laterano
Via Claudia
Via di S. Gregorio
Via del Circo Massimo
Viale Aventino
Via di S. Anselmo
Via Antonina
Via Druso
Via Gallia
1 Piazza San Pietro
2 Basilica di San Pietro (St. Peter's Basilica)
3 Musei Vaticani & Sistine Chapel
4 Castel Sant'Angelo
5 Galleria Borghese
6 Piazza del Popolo
7 Campo de' Fiori
8 Trastevere

2 Basilica di San Pietro (St. Peter's Basilica) ★★★

When the church doors open, rush in. Once here, it's hard to do anything but gasp at the size and the magnificence. The cupola was designed by Michelangelo, and the artist also created the most famous *Pietà* in the world. There is so much to see here that you should allow at least 1½ hours. See p. 150 for more details on the best of its treasures.

With what time remains in the morning, explore the:

3 Musei Vaticani (the Vatican Museums) & the Cappella Sistina (Sistine Chapel) ★★★

These museums are the richest in the world, and will take up the better part of your day—allow at least 3 hours for a cursory visit. They are well worth your valuable time. There are so many museums here in addition to Michelangelo's Sistine Chapel, plus several papal apartments. A full day is actually needed, but you can cut your visit to a fraction of that by previewing the attractions on p. 152 and deciding in advance what you want to see. If you took our advice and had a large breakfast, you can hold out for a late lunch. For a list of restaurants in the area, see our selections on p. 155.

After lunch, take bus no. 40, 62, or 74 to Castel Sant'Angelo/Piazza Pia.

4 Castel Sant'Angelo ★

Built in A.D. 135, this imposing fortress was originally constructed as a mausoleum for the Emperor Hadrian and his family. The entrance is across from the Ponte Sant'Angelo, the bridge across the Tiber. Inside, you can visit the Popes' Apartments and from the terraces enjoy one of the great panoramic views in all of Rome. Allow at least 30 minutes (more if you can spare it) to look around.

If you've made an advance reservation, take bus no. 116 or 910 to:

5 Galleria Borghese ★★★

Only if you can fit it into your busy schedule, and have gone through the red tape of making a reservation, should you even attempt to see one of Italy's greatest art museums. See p. 179 for more details. Sculptures by Canova and Bernini and paintings by Raphael, Correggio, Titian, and Caravaggio are awaiting your viewing pleasure. Allow at least an hour. After you leave, you can stroll in the **Villa Borghese ★★** gardens, one of the most beautiful in all of Italy. See p. 179 for more information.

After all this touring, wind down at the Piazza del Popolo (Metro: Flaminia).

6 Piazza del Popolo ★★

With its Egyptian obelisk from the 13th century B.C. and lovely Santa Maria del Popolo church, this is our favorite place to head to for a drink in the late afternoon as the sun begins its descent over Rome. The square is also one of the great places in all of Rome for people-watching. Our two favorite cafes here are **Café Rosati** (p. 135) and **Canova Café** (p. 136), both in chapter 10.

After refreshing yourself, head back to your hotel for a rest and a shower before setting out for another night in Rome.

Take bus no. 23, 30, 40, 62, 64, 70, 87, 116, or 492 to:

7 Campo de' Fiori ★

This is not only the geographic center of Rome but a cultural center as well and the site of an open-air food market. After the vendors have left for the day, the cafes and the square come alive. It's our favorite place in Rome for an evening *apertivo* at one of the piazza's cafes and wine bars. Try for a table at **Grappolo d'Oro Zampanò** at Piazza della Concalleria (✆ **06-6897080**), which has 200 types of wine. It's found between V. Emanuele II and the Campo.

To cap a long day of sightseeing, hop on bus no. 56, 60, or 97 and pick a restaurant in:

8 Trastevere ★★★

We always like to end our final night in Rome by a visit to one of the characteristic trattorie of Trastevere, where locals tell you that you can experience the "real" Rome (as opposed to tourist Rome). Our selection of restaurants begins on p. 141.

The district is separated from the heart of ancient Rome by the River Tiber. It still has much of the look of medieval Rome and remains the city's most "authentic" neighborhood. In one of its bustling restaurants, you can have a good and perhaps affordable meal to end a full day—unless you plan to hang with us for yet another busy day of touring.

THE BEST OF ROME IN 3 DAYS

On your final day, head outside of Rome to explore the attractions of the Appian Way, the hill town of Tivoli, the ruins of Hadrian's Villa, and the Villa d'Este gardens.

Start: Take bus no. 118 or a taxi to the Catacombe di San Callisto on the Appian Way. The entrance is 3.2km (2 miles) south of Porta San Sebastiano Gate.

---

1 Catacombe di San Callisto ★★

Perhaps no one has ever explored all 19km (12 miles) of these catacombs, where some half a million Christians were buried from the 1st to the 4th centuries. The catacombs are webbed with 9m (30-ft.) tunnels containing these impressive tombs. After about an hour, you'll get the picture of what it's about. See p. 181 for more information.

Before leaving the Appian Way, we'd recommend a visit to another important catacomb:

2 Catacombe di San Domitilla ★★★

Also reached by bus no. 218, and entered at Via d. Sette Chiese 282, this is the oldest of the catacombs, containing a 3rd-century portrait of Christ and the Apostles. You enter through a sunken 4th-century church. Allow 45 minutes for a visit. For more information, see p. 182.

Rome in 3 Days

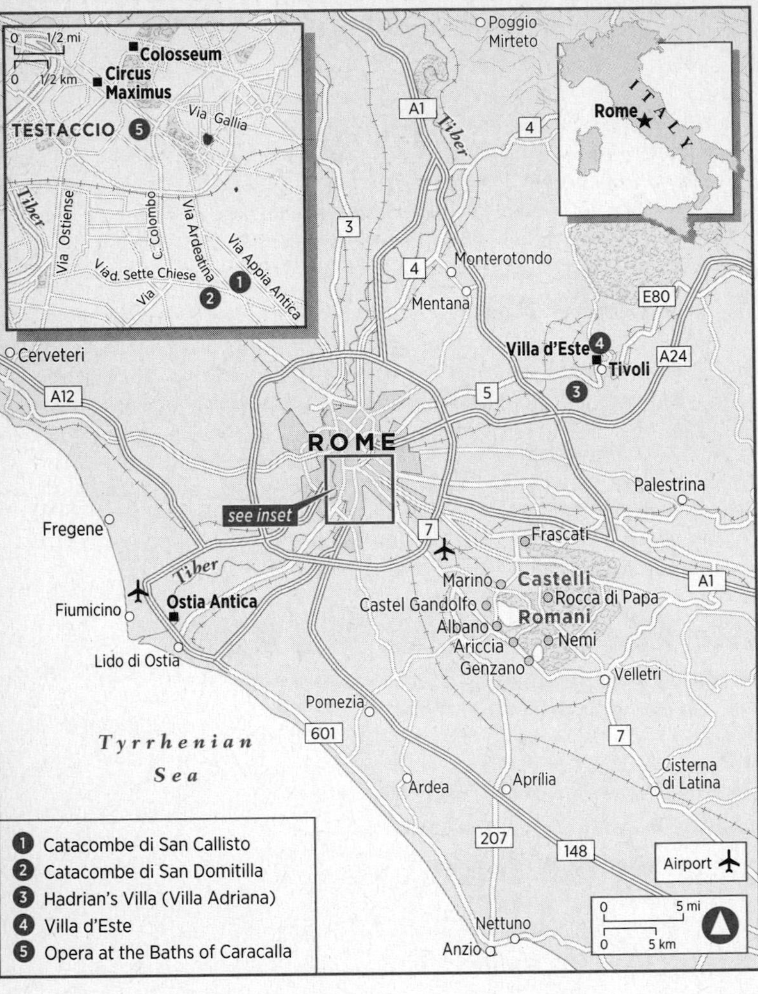

For our next attraction, we leave the city of Rome altogether, heading for the hill town of Tivoli, 32km (20 miles) east of Rome. For bus directions, see "Tivoli & the Villas" beginning on p. 248. We recommend a luncheon stopover here, preferably at a restaurant with a view over the countryside.

After lunch, head for the town's major attraction:

3 Hadrian's Villa (Villa Adriana) ★★★

The ancient ruins of the Villa of Hadrian (A.D. 135) are among the most impressive in Italy, lying some 6.5km (4 miles) from the center of Tivoli and reached by bus no. 4 or 4X from Tivoli. Allow at least 1½ hours to take in the major attractions here, including the Teatro Marittimo, a circular maritime theater. Hadrian was an amateur architect, and much of the villa was designed by him. For more details about the highlights to see, refer to p. 248.

With the time remaining, return to the center of Tivoli and for a call on the spectacular:

4 Villa d'Este ★★

The villa, built by a cardinal in the mid–16th century, is an afterthought to the hillside gardens, among the most beautiful in Greater Rome. The gardens appear like a fairy tale of the Renaissance, using water as a medium of sculpture. There are fountains in every imaginable shape and size, the pathways lined with some 100 fountains, the stairs flanked with cascades on either side. Allow at least an hour for exploration; see p. 250 for more information.

Return to Rome for the evening. If you made reservations in advance and it's summer, you can attend an:

5 Opera at the Baths of Caracalla

You can head out for an opera at these ancient baths, entered along Villa della Terme di Caracalla. See p. 165 for more details. Take the Metro to Circo Massimo.

WHERE TO STAY IN ROME

5

The good news is that Rome's hotels are in better shape than they've ever been. Dozens upon dozens of properties have undergone major renovations.

The bad news is that Rome has experienced a huge surge in tourism in recent years, and finding a reasonably priced hotel room at any time of the year is harder than ever. ***Make your reservations as far ahead as possible.*** If you arrive without a reservation, head quickly to the **airport information desk** or, once you get into town, to the offices of **Enjoy Rome** (p. 266)—its staff can help reserve you a room, if any are available.

Rome's high-end hotels are among the most luxurious in Europe. In addition to reviewing the best of the upscale hotels, we've tried to give you a good selection of moderately priced hotels, where you'll find comfortable, charming lodgings with private bathrooms. Even our inexpensive choices are clean and cheerful, and they offer more in services and facilities than you might expect. In the less-expensive categories, you'll find a few pensioni, the Roman equivalent of a boardinghouse.

The Italian government controls the prices of its hotels, designating a minimum and a maximum rate. The difference between the two might depend on the season, the location of the room, and even its size. The government also classifies hotels with star ratings that indicate their category of comfort: five stars for deluxe, four for first class, three for second class, two for third class, and one for fourth class. Most former pensioni are now rated as one- or two-star hotels.

The distinction between a pensione hotel (where some degree of board was once required along with the room) and a regular hotel is no longer officially made, although many smaller, family-run establishments still call themselves pensioni. Government ratings don't depend on sensitivity of decoration or frescoed ceilings, but they're based on facilities, such as elevators and the like. Many of the finest hotels in Rome have a lower rating because they serve only breakfast.

Almost all the hotels listed serve breakfast (often a buffet with coffee, fruit, rolls, and cheese), but you can't take for granted that it's included in the room rate. That used to be universal, but it's not anymore, so check the listing carefully and ask the hotel to confirm what's included.

Nearly all hotels are heated in the cooler months, but not all are air-conditioned in summer, which can be vitally important during a stifling July or August. The deluxe and first-class ones are, but after that, it's a tossup. Be sure to check the listing carefully before you book a stay in the dog days of summer.

All Italian hotels impose an **IVA** (Imposta sul Valore Aggiunto), or value-added tax. This tax is in effect throughout the European Union countries. It replaces some 20 other taxes and is an effort to streamline the tax structure. What does this mean for you? A higher hotel bill. All hotels impose a 10% tax. In deluxe establishments, there is a 20% tax on in-room services such as Wi-Fi and minibar charges. Most hotels quote a rate inclusive of this tax, but others prefer to add it on when you go to pay the bill. To avoid unpleasant surprises, ask to be quoted an all-inclusive rate—that is, with service, even a continental breakfast (which is often obligatory)—when you check in.

See "Best Hotel Bets," in chapter 1, for a quick-reference list of our favorite hotels in a variety of categories. See also "The Neighborhoods in Brief," in chapter 4, for a quick summary of each area that will help you decide if you'd like to stay there.

NEAR STAZIONE TERMINI

Despite a handful of pricey choices, this area is most notable for its concentration of cheap hotels. It's not the most picturesque location, and parts of the neighborhood are still transitional and edgy, but it's certainly convenient in terms of transportation and easy access to many of Rome's top sights.

Very Expensive

Hotel Artemide ★★ This boutique hotel, situated near the train station, combines stylish simplicity with modern comforts against a backdrop of Art Nouveau motifs. The original stained-glass skylight dome was retained in the lobby. The midsize to spacious guest rooms are furnished in natural colors and have tasteful furnishings, including elegantly comfortable beds. For those who want to pay more, a series of deluxe rooms offers extras such as DVD players, battery chargers for cellular phones, and more deluxe bedding.

Via Nazionale 22, 00184 Roma. ✆ **06-489911.** Fax 06-48991700. www.hotelartemide.it. 85 units. 189€–364€ double; 349€–480€ suite. Rates include buffet breakfast. AE, DC, MC, V. Parking 25€–30€. Metro: Piazza Repubblica. **Amenities:** 2 restaurants; bar; airport transfers (60€); concierge; exercise room; room service; sauna. *In room:* A/C, TV, hair dryer, minibar (in some), Wi-Fi (12€ per day).

Radisson Blu Es. Hotel ★★ 🎁 If you want 19th-century Rome, look elsewhere: If you prefer a hyper-modern atmosphere, the Es. Hotel is for you. This hotel is so dramatic, innovative, and high-tech that its opening sparked a bit of environmental recovery in the old but decaying Esquilino quarter on the fringe of the Termini. A government-rated five-star *luxe* hotel, it is posh and severe, yet comfortably modern.

Don't judge the hotel by its rather dull seven-story exterior, which resembles an office building. Inside, the lobby showcases the ruins of a 2nd-century-A.D. Roman road. The midsize to spacious bedrooms emphasize minimalist Japanese designs, with wool rugs, glass desks, and plastic chairs in either orange or pea green. Rooms are soundproof; some open onto balconies with city views. In summer, a sun deck and pool are available. Especially alluring is the top-floor fitness center and the on-site spa.

Via Turati 171, 00185 Roma. ✆ **06-444841.** Fax 06-44341396. www.eshotel.it. 232 units. 210€–296€ double; from 310€ suite. AE, DC, MC, V. Parking 15€. Metro: Vittoria. Bus: 70 or 71. **Amenities:** 2 restaurants; bar; babysitting; concierge; exercise room; outdoor pool; room service; spa. *In room:* A/C, TV, hair dryer, minibar, Wi-Fi (free).

St. Regis Grand ★★★ This restored landmark is more plush and upscale than any hotel in the area—not even the comparable Excelsior or the Eden across town can match its sheer opulence. Its drawback is its location at the dreary Stazione Termini, but once you're inside its splendid shell, all thoughts of railway stations vanish. When Ceásar Ritz founded this outrageously expensive hotel in 1894, it was the first to offer a private bathroom and two electric lights in every room. Today it is a magnificent Roman palazzo, combining Italian and French styles in decoration and furnishings. The lobby is decked out with Murano chandeliers, columns, marble busts, and cherubs. The guest rooms are exceedingly spacious and luxuriously furnished with hand-painted frescoes installed above each headboard. For the best rooms and the finest service, ask to be booked on the St. Regis floor.

Via Vittorio Emanuele Orlando 3, 00185 Roma. ✆ **06-47091.** Fax 06-4747307. www.starwoodhotels.com. 161 units. 632€–990€ double; from 1,000€ suite. AE, DC, MC, V. Parking 40€. Metro: Repubblica. **Amenities:** Restaurant; bar; babysitting; concierge; exercise room; room service; sauna. *In room:* A/C, TV, hair dryer, minibar, Wi-Fi (15€ per day).

Expensive

Empire Palace Hotel ★★ This hotel combines a historic core (in this case, a palazzo built around 1870) with modern luxuries; together these elements create a very comfortable and appealing ambience. The original builders, an aristocratic Venetian family, installed ceiling frescoes showing the heavens in azure blue on some of the ceilings. Some of the striking combinations of the original core with unusual modern paintings are showstoppers. Opened as a hotel in 1999, the Empire Palace is classified four stars by the Italian government. Most bedrooms are quite large. The building's courtyard is outfitted with a splashing fountain and a verdant garden.

Via Aureliana 39, 00187 Roma. ✆ **06-421281.** Fax 06-42128400. www.empirepalacehotel.com. 113 units. 250€–586€ double; 450€–887€ suite. Rates include breakfast. AE, DC, MC, V. Parking 40€. Metro: Repubblica or Termini. **Amenities:** Restaurant; bar; babysitting; concierge; exercise room; room service. *In room:* A/C, TV, hair dryer, minibar, Wi-Fi (5€ per hour).

Exedra ★★ This neoclassical palace overlooking the Piazza della Repubblica at the rail terminal also fronts the Baths of Diocletian and Michelangelo's Basilica degli Angeli. One of Rome's latest government-rated five-star luxury hotels, the Exedra is a study in modern elegance combined with the romance of the past. Our favorite rooms are the top-floor accommodations in the Clementino Wing, each with bare brick walls and the original ceiling beams. You'll find creamy marble, lush carpeting, discreet lighting, and high ceilings throughout the building, while rooms feature such decorative notes as leather headboards and silk wallcoverings. You can take morning coffee on the rooftop garden terrace overlooking the Fountain of the

Accommodations near Stazione Termini, Via Veneto & Piazza Barberini

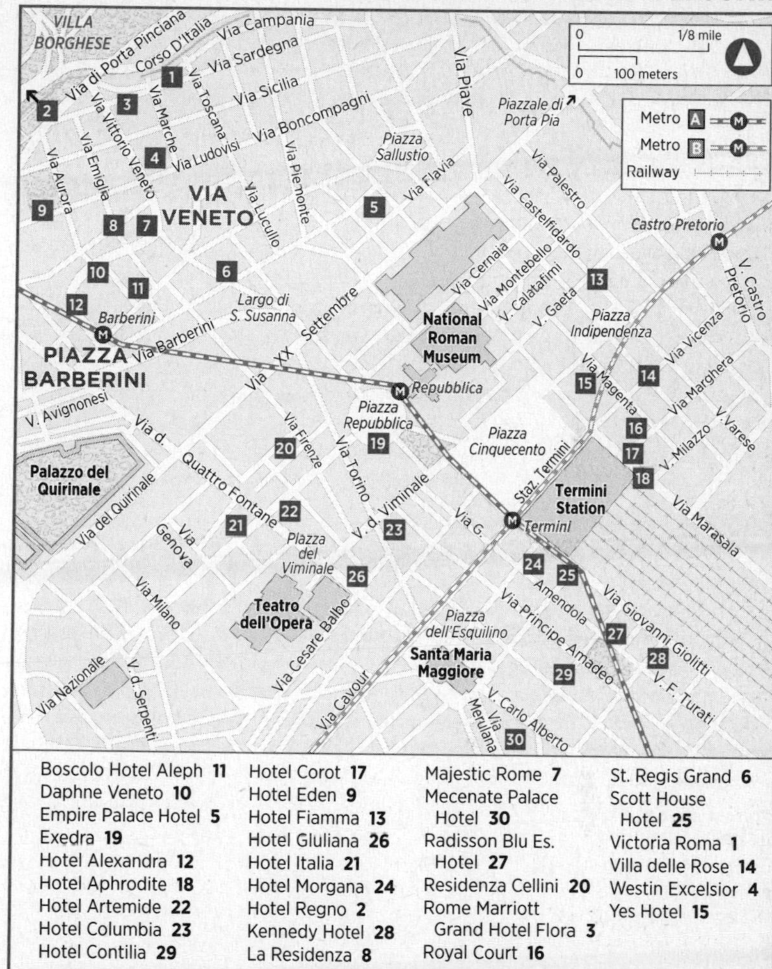

Naiads. Later you can retreat to one of Rome's best hotel spas. The restaurants celebrate Rome in the 1950s and 1960s—for example, La Frustra was inspired by Fellini's Oscar-winning film 8½.

Piazza della Repubblica 47, 00185 Roma. ✆ **06-489381.** Fax 06-48938000. www.boscolohotels.com. 240 units. 314€–539€ double; from 680€ suite. AE, DC, MC, V. Parking 35€. Metro: Repubblica. **Amenities:** 3 restaurants; 2 bars; babysitting; concierge; rooftop heated pool; room service; spa. *In room:* A/C, TV, hair dryer, minibar.

Hotel Columbia ★★ This is one of the best hotels in the neighborhood, with a hardworking multilingual staff. A government-rated three-star choice, originally built around 1900, it underwent a well-done radical renovation in 1997. The interior contains Murano chandeliers and conservatively modern furniture. The compact, cozy guest rooms compare well with the accommodations in the best hotels nearby. The appealing rooftop garden has a view of the surrounding rooftops.

Via del Viminale 15, 00184 Roma. ✆ **06-4883509.** Fax 06-4740209. www.hotelcolumbia.com. 45 units. 250€ double; 434€ suite. Rates include buffet breakfast. AE, DC, MC, V. Parking nearby 35€. Metro: Repubblica. **Amenities:** Bar; room service. *In room:* A/C, TV, hair dryer, minibar, Wi-Fi (13€ per day).

Moderate

Hotel Fiamma Near the Baths of Diocletian, the Fiamma is in a renovated building, with five floors of bedrooms and a ground floor faced with marble and plate-glass windows. It's an old favorite, if a bit past its prime. The lobby is long and bright, filled with a varied collection of furnishings, including overstuffed chairs and blue enamel railings. On the same floor is an austere marble breakfast room. The comfortably furnished guest rooms range from small to medium.

Via Gaeta 61, 00185 Roma. ✆ **06-4818436.** Fax 06-4883511. www.leonardihotels.com. 79 units (shower only). 120€–135€ double; 160€–196€ triple. Rates include buffet breakfast. AE, DC, MC, V. Parking 30€. Metro: Termini. **Amenities:** Bar; room service. *In room:* A/C, TV, hair dryer, minibar.

Mecenate Palace Hotel ★★ 🎁 A real gem, this little charmer lies 5 blocks south of Termini. It's even more intimate and more professionally run than its closest competitor, the Artemide (although it's also pricier). Its downside is a location that's inconvenient for those wanting to spend a lot of time visiting the Vatican or classical Rome. The hotel is composed of two adjacent buildings. One of them was designed by Rinaldi in 1887; the second one (on Via Carlo Alberto) was designed a few years later. The guest rooms, where traces of the original detailing mix with contemporary furnishings, overlook the city rooftops or Santa Maria Maggiore. They range from small to medium but boast high ceilings and extras such as luxury mattresses. Three suites offer superior comfort, authentic 19th-century antiques, and a fireplace.

Via Carlo Alberto 3, 00185 Roma. ✆ **06-44702024.** Fax 06-4461354. www.mecenatepalace.com. 62 units. 145€–300€ double; from 200€ suite. Rates include buffet breakfast. AE, DC, MC, V. Parking 30€. Metro: Termini or Vittorio Emanuele. **Amenities:** Restaurant; bar; airport transfers (55€); babysitting; concierge; Internet (10€ per day); room service. *In room:* A/C, TV, hair dryer, minibar, Wi-Fi (10€ per day).

Hotel Morgana Between Santa Maria Maggiore and Stazione Termini, this hotel was last renovated in 2001 and is completely up to date. Bedrooms are comfortable and furnished in a vaguely English-style decor. The English-speaking staff is pleasant and will help guide you to some of the city's most important attractions, many of which lay only a short walk from the hotel. Because this hotel lies in a noisy area, all of the bedrooms are soundproof.

Via F. Turati 33–37, 00185 Roma. ✆ **06-4467230.** Fax 06-4469142. www.hotelmorgana.com. 106 units. 165€ double; 220€ suite. Rates include buffet breakfast. AE, DC, MC, V. Parking 14€. Metro: Termini. **Amenities:** Bar; airport transfers (55€); babysitting; concierge; room service. *In room:* A/C, TV, hair dryer, minibar, Wi-Fi (10€ per day).

Kennedy Hotel A 5-minute walk from the Termini Station, this completely restored hotel is one of the best bets for those who want to stay in the rail station area. The hotel, launched in 1963 when President Kennedy died, was named to honor his memory. The building itself is from the late 19th century, although it has been much restored and modernized over the years. The hotel is within an easy walk to many of the historical monuments of Rome, including the Basilica of S. Maria Maggiore, the Opera House, the Colosseum, and the Roman Forum. Bedrooms are renovated, with tasteful furnishings and double-glass soundproofing. Many rooms open to views of the antique Roman wall of Servio Tullio.

Via Filippo Turati 62–64, 00185 Roma. ✆ **06-4465373.** Fax 06-4465417. www.hotelkennedy.net. 52 units. 69€–160€ double; 125€–260€ suite. Rates include buffet breakfast. AE, DC, MC, V. Bus: 71. **Amenities:** Bar; bikes; exercise room; room service. *In room:* A/C, TV, hair dryer, Wi-Fi (18€ per day).

Residenza Cellini ★ 🎁 This small hotel is run by the English-speaking De Palais family, who welcome guests with warm hospitality. In the heart of Rome, Cellini lies near the Termini rail station. Gaetano and Barbara De Palais have lavished attention on their small number of bedrooms, and the results are comfortable and stylish. Rooms are midsize and traditionally furnished, with polished wood pieces and Oriental carpets on the hardwood floors. The king-size beds have anti-allergic orthopedic mattresses, and the bathrooms come with hydrojet showers or Jacuzzi.

Via Modena 5, 00184 Roma. ✆ **06-47825204.** Fax 06-47881806. www.residenzacellini.it. 6 units. 145€–240€ double; 165€–280€ junior suite. Rates include buffet breakfast. AE, DC, MC, V. Parking 35€. Metro: Repubblica. **Amenities:** Bar; airport transfers (55€); concierge; room service. *In room:* A/C, TV, hair dryer, minibar, Wi-Fi.

Royal Court ★ 🎁 This winner lies in a recently restored Liberty-style palace a short walk from the Termini. The hotel evokes a tranquil, elegantly decorated private town house. Some of the superior rooms offer Jacuzzis in their bathrooms, and all units feature well-maintained bathrooms with shower/tub combinations. The superior rooms also come with small balconies opening onto cityscapes. Even the standard doubles are comfortable, but if you're willing to pay the price, you can stay in the deluxe doubles, which are like junior suites in most Rome hotels. Some of the bedrooms are large enough to sleep three or four guests comfortably.

Via Marghera 51, 00185 Roma. ✆ **06-44340364.** Fax 06-4469121. www.morganaroyalcourt.com. 24 units. 143€–250€ double. Rates include buffet breakfast. AE, DC, MC, V. Parking 24€. Metro: Termini. **Amenities:** Bar; airport transfers (55€); babysitting; concierge; room service. *In room:* A/C, TV, hair dryer (in some), minibar, Wi-Fi (10€ per day).

Villa delle Rose ☺ Located less than 2 blocks north of the rail station, this hotel is an acceptable, if unexciting, choice. In the late 1800s, it was a villa with a dignified cut-stone facade inspired by the Renaissance. Despite many renovations, the ornate trappings of the original are still visible, including the lobby's Corinthian-capped marble columns and the flagstone-covered terrace that is part of the verdant back garden. Much of the interior has been redecorated and upgraded with traditional wallcoverings, carpets, and tiled bathrooms. Breakfasts in the garden do a lot to add country flavor to an otherwise very urban setting. Families often book here asking for one of the three rooms with lofts that can sleep up to five.

Via Vicenza 5, 00185 Roma. ✆ **06-4451788.** Fax 06-4451639. www.villadellerose.it. 38 units (some with shower only). 105€–180€ double. Rates include buffet breakfast. AE, DC, MC, V. Free parking (only 4 cars). Metro: Termini or Castro Pretorio. **Amenities:** Bar. *In room:* A/C (30 rooms), TV, hair dryer, minibar (in some).

Inexpensive

Hotel Aphrodite Completely renovated, this new government-rated three-star hotel in the heart of Rome is a good deal. Directly next to Stazione Termini, this four-story hotel is a reliable and well-run choice, although the surrounding area is a little seedy at night. For rail passengers who want quick check-ins and fast getaways, it's the most convenient choice there is. Bedrooms are attractively and comfortably furnished with modern pieces and parquet floors. Ask at the desk about walking tours through the historic districts. A special feature here is the sunny rooftop terrace.

Via Marsala 90, 00185 Roma. ✆ **06-491096.** Fax 06-491579. www.accommodationinrome.com. 50 units. 80€–145€ double; 95€–165€ triple. Rates include continental breakfast. AE, DC, MC, V. Parking 15€. Metro: Termini. **Amenities:** Exercise room. *In room:* A/C, TV, hair dryer, minibar, Wi-Fi (in some; free).

Hotel Contilia As the automatic doors part to reveal a stylish marble lobby with Persian rugs and antiques, you might step back to double-check the address. The former *pensione* Tony Contilia has become one of the neighborhood's best choices. The guest rooms have firm beds and built-in shelving units. Rooms overlooking the cobblestone courtyard are the most tranquil.

Via Principe Amadeo 81, 00185 Roma. ✆ **06-4466875.** Fax 06-4466904. www.hotelcontilia.com. 42 units. 60€–170€ double; 120€–250€ triple. AE, DC, MC, V. Parking 25€; free on street. Metro: Termini. **Amenities:** Bar; room service. *In room:* A/C, TV, hair dryer, Wi-Fi (free).

Hotel Corot North of the train station, this simple haven occupies the second and third floors of an early 1900s building that contains a handful of apartments and another inferior hotel. Each high-ceilinged guest room is soundproof and has simple but traditional furniture. Superior rooms have a bathtub Jacuzzi.

Via Marghera 15–17, 00185 Roma. ✆ **06-44700900.** Fax 06-44700905. www.hotelcorot.it. 28 units. 110€–180€ double; 130€–220€ triple; 150€–250€ quad. Rates include continental breakfast. AE, MC, V. Parking 26€. Metro: Termini. **Amenities:** Bar; room service; Wi-Fi (free, in lobby). *In room:* A/C, TV, hair dryer, minibar.

Hotel Giuliana Close to the landmark Opera House deep in the heart of Rome, this is a well-maintained, neat little family-run hotel facing the Basilica Santa Maria Maggiore. Personal service is a hallmark. Although not grandly stylish, bedrooms are exceedingly comfortable and of good size, with up-to-date bathrooms. A generous breakfast is served every morning in a cozy room.

Via Agostino Depretis 70, 00184 Roma. ✆ **06-4880795.** Fax 06-4824287. www.hotelgiuliana.com. 11 units. 90€–180€ double; 110€–240€ triple. Rates include buffet breakfast. AE, DC, MC, V. Parking 25€. Metro: Repubblica. **Amenities:** Bar; room service. *In room:* A/C (some units), TV, hair dryer.

Hotel Italia This is a turn-of-the-20th-century building with an eight-room annex across the street. It's been a hotel for 20 years, but it has never been as well managed as it is now under the stewardship of the Valentini family. Both buildings employ a night porter/security guard, and both offer their guests a breakfast buffet that's one of the most appealing in the neighborhood. Midsize bedrooms are well maintained and conservatively decorated with comfortable yet simple furniture. Most units have parquet floors, and all rooms have private bathrooms, although the facilities for room no. 6 are across the hallway.

Via Venezia 18, 00184 Roma. ✆ **06-4828355.** Fax 06-4745550. www.hotelitaliaroma.com. 31 units. 70€–130€ double; 115€–170€ triple. Rates include buffet breakfast. AE, DC, MC, V. Parking nearby 15€–20€. Metro: Repubblica. Bus: 64. **Amenities:** Bar; babysitting; Internet (free, in lobby). *In room:* A/C, TV, hair dryer, Wi-Fi (free).

Scott House Hotel Simple but adequate for low-maintenance travelers on tight budgets, this hotel occupies the fourth and fifth floors of a building originally constructed in the 18th century. Bedrooms are high-ceilinged, freshly painted, and compact; most have comfortable beds and at least one upholstered armchair.

Via Gioberti 30, 00185 Roma. ✆ **06-4465379.** Fax 06-45438780. www.scotthouse.com. 36 units (with shower only). 65€–98€ double. Rates include continental breakfast. AE, DC, MC, V. Metro: Termini. **Amenities:** Bar. *In room:* A/C, TV.

Yes Hotel We'd definitely say yes to this hotel which lies only 100m (328 ft.) from Stazione Termini. Opened in 2007, it was quickly discovered by frugal-minded travelers who want a good bed and comfortable surroundings for the night. It's a two-story hotel housed in a restored 19th-century building with simple, though well-chosen furnishings resting on tiled floors. There is a sleek, modern look to both the bedrooms and public areas, and the staff is helpful but not effusive.

Via Magenta 15, 00185 Roma. ✆ **06-44363836.** Fax 06-44363829. www.yeshotelrome.com. 29 units. 79€–199€ double. DC, MC, V. Parking 20€. Metro: Termini. **Amenities:** Bar; babysitting; room service. *In room:* A/C, TV, hair dryer, Wi-Fi (20€ per day).

NEAR VIA VENETO & PIAZZA BARBERINI

If you stay in this area, you definitely won't be on the wrong side of the tracks. Unlike the area around the dreary rail station, this is a beautiful and upscale commercial section, near some of Rome's best shopping.

To locate the hotels listed below, see the "Accommodations near Stazione Termini, Via Veneto & Piazza Barberini" map on p. 89.

Very Expensive

Hotel Eden ★★★ It's not as grand architecturally as the Westin Excelsior, it doesn't have the views of the Hassler, and it's certainly not a stunner like the Hilton. However, the Eden is Rome's top choice for discerning travelers who like their comforts striking but not ostentatious.

Since its 1889 opening, this hotel, about a 10-minute walk east of the Spanish Steps, has reigned over one of the world's most stylish shopping neighborhoods. Hemingway, Callas, Ingrid Bergman, Fellini—all checked in during its heyday, and the hotel still retains its former grandeur, coupled with the new amenities that its government-rated five-star status calls for. The Eden's hilltop position guarantees a panoramic view from most guest rooms; all are spacious and elegantly appointed. Try to get one of the front rooms with a balcony boasting views over Rome. The hotel's restaurant, **La Terrazza,** is one of Rome's best (see chapter 6).

Via Ludovisi 49, 00187 Roma. ✆ **06-478121.** Fax 06-4821584. www.starwoodhotels.com. 121 units. 315€–830€ double; from 1,100€ suite. AE, DC, DISC, MC, V. Parking 30€. Metro: Piazza Barberini. **Amenities:** Restaurant (La Terrazza; see chapter 6); bar; airport transfers (85€); babysitting; concierge; health club; Jacuzzi; room service. *In room:* A/C, TV/DVD, CD player, hair dryer, minibar, Wi-Fi (19€ per day).

Majestic Rome ★★ Built in 1889 in the center of Rome, this government-rated five-star hotel is one of the grandest addresses of Rome, standing on the street that enjoyed its *La Dolce Vita* heyday in the 1950s. Still a home for many celebrities and political figures, the hotel is a member of one of the Leading Small Hotels of the World. Although completely modernized and up to date, the Majestic was the center of high society life in Rome in the 1920s when movie stars and royalty paraded through its lobby. The bedrooms are often filled with antiques, including tapestries and frescoes. Much of the past splendor has been regained in a sensitive restoration. The spacious rooms are beautifully appointed, and many accommodations open onto private balconies. The on-site restaurant Filippo La Mantia specializes in discovering ancient Roman recipes.

Via Vittorio Veneto 50, 00187 Roma. ✆ **06-421441.** Fax 06-4885657. www.rome-hotels-majestic.com. 98 units. 640€–720€ double; from 1,620€ suite. AE, DC, MC, V. Parking 70€. Metro: Piazza Barberini. **Amenities:** Restaurant; bar; airport transfers (82€); babysitting; concierge; exercise room; room service. *In room:* A/C, TV/DVD, CD player, hair dryer, minibar, Wi-Fi (free).

Rome Marriott Grand Hotel Flora ★★ This long-standing monument at the top of the Via Veneto has been restored for its new life in the 21st century. One of the grand stopovers in the heyday of *La Dolce Vita,* the hotel offers spacious, beautifully furnished bedrooms overlooking the Villa Borghese gardens. Its only drawback, as we see it, is that the individual visitor to Rome might get lost in a sea of businesspeople and tour groups. The bedrooms are supremely comfortable, although they evoke those found in a large American city more than the typical offerings in the Eternal City. The suites are some of the grandest in Rome.

Via Vittorio Veneto 191, 00187 Roma. ✆ **800/228-9290** in the U.S., or 06-489929. Fax 06-4820359. www.marriott.com. 155 units. 379€–599€ double; from 669€ suite. AE, DC, MC, V. Parking 50€. Metro: Barberini. **Amenities:** Restaurant; bar; airport transfers (88€); babysitting; concierge; room service. *In room:* A/C, TV, hair dryer, minibar, Wi-Fi (free).

Westin Excelsior ★ If money is no object, here's a good place to spend it. The Excelsior is more grandiose architecturally than either the Eden or the Hassler, but it is not as up to date or as beautifully renovated as the Eden or the St. Regis Grand. Everything looks just a tad dowdy today, but the Excelsior endures, in no small part because of the hospitable staff. The baroque corner tower of this limestone palace, overlooking the U.S. Embassy, is a landmark in Rome. Cavernous reception rooms are adorned with thick rugs, marble floors, gilded garlands decorating the walls, and Empire furniture. The guest rooms come in two varieties: new (the result of a major renovation) and traditional. The older ones are a bit worn, while the newer ones have more imaginative color schemes and plush carpeting. All are spacious and elegantly furnished, with antiques and silk curtains.

Via Vittorio Veneto 125, 00187 Roma. ✆ **800/325-3589** in the U.S., or 06-47081. Fax 06-4826205. www.westin.com/excelsiorrome. 316 units. 310€–780€ double; from 1,100€ junior suite; from 2,300€ suite. AE, DC, DISC, MC, V. Parking 42€. Metro: Barberini. **Amenities:** Restaurant; bar; babysitting; concierge; health club; Jacuzzi; indoor heated pool; room service; sauna. *In room:* A/C, TV, hair dryer, minibar, Wi-Fi (15€ per day).

Expensive

Boscolo Hotel Aleph ★★ Called "sexy and decadent" by some hotel critics when it opened, this winning choice leads the pack among "new wave" Italian hotels. The Aleph was designed by Adam Tihany, who said he wanted to "humanize the rooms with indulgent details." Only a minute's walk from the Via Veneto, the hotel offers spacious guest rooms adorned with elegant Italian fabrics, a tasteful decor, and all the latest technology. Murano chandeliers, window blinds made of strings of metal beads, a dramatic roof terrace overlooking the heart of Rome, and an indoor swimming pool are just some of the features of this hotel. Tihany wanted something eccentric and intriguing, exclusive yet provocative—and his creation is all that and vastly comfortable as well, with its 1930s- and 1940s-inspired style. Large black-and-white photos of New York by (father of the designer) Bram Tihany adorn the walls.

Via San Basilio 15, 00187 Roma. ✆ **06-422901.** Fax 06-42290000. www.boscolohotels.com. 96 units. 195€–430€ double; from 460€ junior suite; from 800€ suite. AE, DC, MC, V. Parking 35€. Metro: Barberini. **Amenities:** Restaurant; 2 bars; babysitting; concierge; exercise room; indoor heated pool; room service; spa. *In room:* A/C, TV, hair dryer, minibar.

Daphne Veneto ★ In a restored building from the 19th century deep in the heart of Rome, this is a top-notch B&B, just minutes on foot from the Trevi Fountain. The midsize guest rooms have an understated elegance, with crisp linens and fluffy comforters on the beds. The public rooms contain sitting areas, cozy reading sections, a lending library, and high-speed Internet access. Floors are reached by elevator, and two of the units are two-bedroom, two-bathroom suites. Fresh fruit and freshly baked pastries are served with your morning coffee.

Via di San Basilio 55, 00187 Roma. ✆ **06-87450086.** Fax 06-23324-967. www.daphne-rome.com. 8 units. 140€–220€ double; 320€–460€ suite. Rates include buffet breakfast. AE, MC, V. Parking nearby 30€. Metro: Piazza Barberini. **Amenities:** Airport transfers 55€. *In room:* A/C, hair dryer, Wi-Fi (free).

Hotel Alexandra ★ This is one of the few places you can stay on Via Veneto without going broke (although it's not exactly cheap). Set behind the dignified stone facade of what was a 19th-century mansion, the Alexandra offers immaculate guest rooms. Those facing the front are exposed to roaring traffic and street noise; those in back are quieter but have lesser views. The rooms range from rather cramped to medium size, but each has been recently redecorated and filled with antiques or tasteful contemporary pieces. Among the extras are swing-mirror vanities and brass or wood bedsteads. The breakfast room is especially appealing: Inspired by an Italian garden, it was designed by noted architect Paolo Portoghesi.

Via Vittorio Veneto 18, 00187 Roma. ✆ **06-4881943.** Fax 06-4871804. www.hotelalexandraroma.com. 60 units (some with shower only). 220€–280€ double; 350€–800€ junior suite. Rates include buffet breakfast. AE, DC, MC, V. Parking 26€–36€. Metro: Barberini. **Amenities:** Room service; Wi-Fi (4€ per hour). *In room:* A/C, TV, hair dryer, minibar.

Victoria Roma ★ The Victoria Roma's great location overlooking the Borghese Gardens remains one of its most desirable assets; you can sit in the rooftop garden drinking your cocktail amid palm trees and potted plants, imagining that you're in a country villa. The lounges and living rooms retain a country-house decor, with soft touches that include high-backed chairs, large oil paintings, bowls of freshly cut flowers, provincial tables, and Oriental rugs. You don't get opulence, but you do get a sort of dowdy charm and good maintenance. Rooms range from standard to spacious; each is comfortably equipped with good beds. Furnishings such as Oriental carpets are common. Floor no. 5 has the best views of the Villa Borghese.

Via Campania 41, 00187 Roma. ✆ **06-473931.** Fax 06-4871890. www.hotelvictoriaroma.com. 108 units. 220€–350€ double; 270€–410€ triple. Rates include buffet breakfast. AE, DC, MC, V. Parking 35€. Metro: Barberini. Bus: 95 or 116. **Amenities:** Restaurant; bar; airport transfers (50€); babysitting; room service. *In room:* A/C, TV, hair dryer, minibar.

Moderate

Hotel Regno Set in a great shopping area, this six-story hotel stands behind a severe stone facade. It was originally a library in the 1600s. In the 1960s, it was transformed into a simple hotel, and in 1999, it was upgraded into a well-managed, government-rated three-star hotel. Bedrooms are relatively small but comfortably appointed with nondescript modern furniture. The staff is friendly and hardworking. The hotel has a simple breakfast room, plus a sun deck on the building's roof.

Via del Corso 330, 00186 Roma. ✆ **06-6976361.** Fax 06-6789239. www.hotelregno.com. 62 units. 220€–270€ double; 270€–300€ triple. Rates include buffet breakfast. AE, DC, MC, V. Parking 40€. Metro: Spagna. **Amenities:** Bar; airport transfers (50€); babysitting; room service. *In room:* A/C, TV, hair dryer, minibar, Wi-Fi (free).

La Residenza ★★ In a superb but congested location, this converted villa successfully combines intimacy and elegance. A bit old-fashioned and homelike, this little hotel has an ivy-covered courtyard and a series of upholstered public rooms with Empire divans, oil portraits, and rattan chairs. Terraces are scattered throughout. The guest rooms are generally spacious, containing bentwood chairs and built-in furniture. The dozen or so junior suites boast balconies.

Via Emilia 22–24, 00187 Roma. ✆ **06-4880789.** Fax 06-485721. www.hotel-la-residenza.com. 29 units. 250€–300€ double; 300€–330€ suite. Rates include buffet breakfast. AE, MC, V. Parking (limited) 20€. Metro: Barberini. **Amenities:** Bar; babysitting; room service. *In room:* A/C, TV, hair dryer, minibar.

NEAR ANCIENT ROME

To locate the hotels in this section, see the "Accommodations Near Piazza del Popolo & the Spanish Steps" map on p. 103.

Expensive

Capo d'Africa ★ 🎁 Installed within a beautiful 19th-century building, this hotel lies in the heart of Imperial Rome between the Forum and the Domus Aurea, a few steps from the Colosseum. It attracts visitors with its sophisticated interior design, works of art, high-tech facilities, and impeccable service. Best of all is a splendid rooftop terrace with a panoramic view over some of the dusty ruins of the world's most famous monuments. Rooms are midsize and furnished with good taste; they are spread across three floors. The furnishings are stylized, including tall headboards of beechwood, red leather upholstery, and green marble wash basins.

Via Capo d'Africa 54, 00137 Roma. ✆ **06-772801.** Fax 06-77280801. www.hotelcapodafrica.com. 65 units. 290€–400€ double; 440€–540€ suite. Rates include buffet breakfast. AE, DC, MC, V. Parking 40€. Metro: Colosseo. **Amenities:** Restaurant; bar; babysitting; concierge; exercise room; room service. *In room:* A/C, TV, hair dryer, minibar, Wi-Fi (25€ per day).

Hotel Forum ★ Built around a medieval bell tower off the Fori Imperiali, the Hotel Forum offers old-fashioned elegance and accommodations that range from tasteful to opulent. The rooms look out on the ancient city, and are well appointed with antiques, mirrors, and Oriental rugs. The hotel's lounges are conservative, with paneled walls and furnishings that combine Italian and French Provincial styles. Dining is an event in the rooftop-garden restaurant; reserve well in advance.

Via di Tor de Conti 25–30, 00184 Roma. ✆ **06-6792446.** Fax 06-6786479. www.hotelforumrome.com. 80 units. 260€–400€ double; 400€–600€ suite. Rates include buffet breakfast. AE, DC, MC, V. Parking 30€. Metro: Colosseo. Bus: 40, 75, 85, 87, or 117. **Amenities:** Rooftop restaurant; 2 bars; babysitting; bikes; concierge; room service. *In room:* A/C, TV, hair dryer, Wi-Fi (5€ per hour).

The Inn at the Roman Forum ★ This is one of the secret discoveries of Rome with the Roman Forum itself as a neighbor. A restored 15th-century building dripping with antiquity, the inn even has a small section of Trajan's Marketplace on-site. You enter the front doorway like a resident Roman, greeting your host in the living room. Sleek, classically styled bedrooms are spread across three upper floors, opening onto views of the heart of Rome. Three back bedrooms open onto a walled-in garden complete with fig and palm trees. The most elegant and expensive double has a private patio with a designer bathroom.

Via degli Ibernesi 30, 00184 Roma. ✆ **06-69190970.** Fax 06-45438802. www.theinnattheromanforum.com. 12 units. 352€–800€ double; from 480€ suite. Rates include buffet breakfast. AE, DC, MC, V. Parking 30€. Bus: 64 or 117. **Amenities:** Bar; airport transfers (55€); concierge; room service. *In room:* A/C, TV/DVD, hair dryer, minibar, Wi-Fi (10€ per day).

Moderate

Hotel Nerva Some of the Nerva's walls and foundations date from the 1500s (others from a century later), but the modern amenities date only from 1997. The setting, a few steps from the Roman Forum, will appeal to any student of archaeology or literature, and the warm welcome from the Cirulli brothers will appeal to all. The decor is accented with wood panels and terra-cotta tiles; some rooms retain the original ceiling beams. The furniture is contemporary and comfortable, with tiled bathrooms (mainly with showers) and adequate shelf space. All rooms are soundproof.

Via Tor di Conti 3, 00184 Roma. ✆ **06-6781835.** Fax 06-69922204. www.hotelnerva.com. 19 units. 90€–220€ double; 150€–350€ suite. Rates include buffet breakfast. AE, MC, V. Free on-street parking. Metro: Colosseo. **Amenities:** Bar; airport transfers (50€); babysitting; room service; Wi-Fi (free, in lobby). *In room:* A/C, TV, hair dryer, minibar.

Inexpensive

Hotel Duca d'Alba A bargain near the Roman Forum and the Colosseum, this hotel lies in the Suburra neighborhood, which was once pretty seedy but is being gentrified. Completely renovated, the Duca d'Alba retains an old-fashioned air (it was built in the 19th c.). The guest rooms have elegant Roman styling, with soothing colors, light wood pieces, luxurious beds and bedding, and bathrooms, mainly with showers. The most desirable rooms are the four with private balconies. All rooms are soundproof. ***Warning:*** Some of the rooms are just too cramped, even for Tiny Tim, and not all have safes. Ask to see your room before you check in.

Via Leonina 14, 00184 Roma. ✆ **06-484471.** Fax 06-4884840. www.hotelducadalba.com. 30 units (most with shower only). 139€–260€ double; 100€–550€ suite. Rates include buffet breakfast. AE, DC, MC, V. Parking 26€. Metro: Cavour. **Amenities:** Bar; airport transfers (60€); babysitting; concierge; exercise room; Internet (free, in lobby); room service. *In room:* A/C, TV, hair dryer, minibar, Wi-Fi (free).

Hotel Grifo ☺ In the historical center of Rome, this hotel is a small, cozy, and well-appointed choice that doesn't advertise for its business but depends on word of mouth from satisfied customers. The helpful English-speaking staff will ease you into the Eternal City. An unpretentious family-run hotel, it offers bedrooms that, while comfortably furnished, are in a sober, rather functional style. The hotel's most notable feature is a rooftop garden opening onto a panoramic view. Surprisingly for a hotel of this size, its bar is open 24 hours a day. Some three- and four-bedded rooms are available, making them suitable for small families.

Via del Boschetto 144, 00184 Roma. ✆ **06-4871395.** Fax 06-4742323. www.hotelgrifo.com. 21 units. 114€–178€ double; 164€–390€ triple; 118€–420€ quad. Rates include buffet breakfast. AE, DC, MC, V. Parking in nearby garage 30€. Metro: Cavour. **Amenities:** Bar; bikes; concierge; room service. *In room:* A/C, TV, minibar, Wi-Fi (in some; free).

Nicolas Inn Only 4 blocks from the Colosseum, this small B&B is also convenient for exploring the Roman Forum. In a warm, cozy atmosphere, a few guests are housed on the second floor of an early-20th-century building. Rich fabrics and cherry-colored wood make this hotel a winner, that and its comfortably furnished midsize to spacious bedrooms. A major asset of the inn is the personal attention provided for each of the guests. Guests find a complimentary map of Rome in their bedrooms.

Via Cavour 295, 00184 Roma. ✆ **06-97618483.** www.nicolasinn.com. 4 units. 100€–180€ double. Rates include continental breakfast. No credit cards. Parking 30€. Metro: Cavour. **Amenities:** Airport transfers 50€. *In room:* A/C, TV, fridge, hair dryer, Wi-Fi (free).

NEAR CAMPO DE' FIORI

Expensive

Hotel Ponte Sisto ★ ☺ Occupying prime real estate, this restored Renaissance palazzo lies on an ancient and narrow Roman street leading from the Campo de' Fiori to the Tiber. It is one of Rome's choice small inns. For lovers of landmarks and monuments, the location is idyllic. In neutral colors, the small-to-midsize rooms are handsomely furnished. Ten units have whirlpool tubs. If you've got the cash, go for one of the suites on the fourth floor with private terraces overlooking the rooftop of Old Rome. These have separate living rooms with sofas that can be converted for sleeping, which make them great for families.

Via dei Pettinari 64, 00186 Roma. ✆ **06-6863100.** Fax 06-68301712. www.hotelpontesisto.it. 103 units. 190€–560€ double; 427€–850€ suite. Rates include buffet breakfast. AE, DC, MC, V. Parking 26€. Bus: 116. **Amenities:** Restaurant for guests only; airport transfers (55€); babysitting; concierge; room service. *In room:* A/C, TV, hair dryer, minibar.

Residenza Farnese ★ Among the "boutique hotels" springing up around Campo de' Fiori, the spanking new Farnese in a 15th-century mansion emerges near the top. Opt for one of the front rooms overlooking Palazzo Farnese, with Michelangelo's Renaissance cornice bathed in sunlight. Bedrooms are fresh and modern, ranging in size from small to generous, each with a private bathroom with a shower. The location in the heart of ancient Rome puts you within walking distance of many of the major sights, particularly the Roman Forum. The owner, Signora Zema, is a gracious host who can provide much helpful advice. She has placed contemporary art throughout, and she believes in a generous breakfast to fortify you for the day.

Accommodations near Campo de' Fiori & Piazza Navona

Via del Mascherone 59, 00186 Roma. ✆ **06-68210980.** Fax 06-80321049. www.residenzafarneseroma.it. 31 units. 250€–300€ double; 350€–500€ junior suite. Rates include buffet breakfast. MC, V. Parking 30€. Bus: 64. **Amenities:** Bar; room service. *In room:* A/C, TV, hair dryer, minibar, Wi-Fi (10€ per day).

Moderate

Casa di Santa Brigida ★ Across from the Michelangelo-designed Palazzo Farnese on a quiet square a block from Campo de' Fiori, Rome's best and most comfortable convent hotel is run by the friendly sisters of St. Bridget in the house where that Swedish saint died in 1373. Basically, there isn't much difference between this place and many other little pensioni, except that it's run by sisters (it's not a great place for carousing, let's put it that way). Rooms where Santa Brigida lived and died are on the first floor. The library is quite large. This convent hotel accepts people of every age and creed. The comfy and roomy old-world guest rooms with antiques or reproductions on parquet (lower level) or carpeted (upstairs) floors justify the rates.

Via Monserato 54 (off Piazza Farnese). Postal address: Piazza Farnese 96, 00186 Roma. ✆ **06-68892596.** Fax 06-68891573. www.brigidine.org. 20 units. 190€ double. Rates include continental breakfast. MC, V. Bus: 46, 62, or 64. **Amenities:** Restaurant. *In room:* A/C, hair dryer.

Hotel Teatro di Pompeo ★★ Built atop the ruins of the Theater of Pompey, this small charmer lies near the spot where Julius Caesar met his end on the Ides of March. Intimate and refined, it's on a quiet *piazzetta* near the Palazzo Farnese and Campo de' Fiori. The rooms are decorated in an old-fashioned Italian style with hand-painted tiles, and the beamed ceilings date from the days of Michelangelo. The guest rooms range from small to medium, each with a tidy but cramped shower-only bathroom.

Largo del Pallaro 8, 00186 Roma. ✆ **06-68300170.** Fax 06-68805531. www.hotelteatrodipompeo.it. 13 units (shower only). 180€–210€ double. Rates include buffet breakfast. AE, DC, MC, V. Bus: 46, 62, or 64. **Amenities:** Bar; airport transfers (55€); babysitting; room service; Wi-Fi (3€ per hour, in lobby). *In room:* A/C, TV, hair dryer, minibar.

Inexpensive

Albergo del Sole al Biscione ★ Between Campo de' Fiori and Piazza Navona, the oldest hotel in Rome dates back to the 15th century. In a city of historic hotels, it ranks near the top. In this four-story building, rooms open onto a tranquil courtyard. Over the years the hotel has seen many improvements, including up-to-date plumbing, but it still has few amenities. The midsize bedrooms are furnished with traditional pieces, often in wood, and doubles come with or without private bathroom. The setting of white walls and tiled floors—often beamed ceilings—is suitably old-fashioned.

Via del Biscione 75, 00186 Roma. ✆ **06-68806873.** Fax 06-6893787 www.solealbiscione.it. 62 units (47 with bathroom). 100€–110€ double without bathroom, 125€–165€ double with bathroom. AE, DC, MC, V. Parking 18€–23€. Bus: 46, 62, or 64. *In room:* A/C, TV, Wi-Fi (1.50€ per hour).

Hotel Arenula ★ At last a hotel in Rome's old Jewish ghetto, and not only is it quite affordable, but a winner. It takes its name from Via Arenula, a timeworn street linking Largo Argentina to Ponte Garibaldi and the Trastevere area. The Patta family converted and restored a 19th-century building into a comfortable inn. Close at hand are the Pantheon, the Colosseum, and the Piazza Navona. Rooms are furnished in a tasteful, traditional way, and they are inviting and comfortable, with pale-wood pieces and immaculate bathrooms, each with a shower. There's no elevator, so be prepared to climb some stairs.

Via Santa Maria de' Calderari 47, 00186 Roma. ✆ **06-6879454.** Fax 06-6896188. www.hotelarenula.com. 50 units. 100€–133€ double. Rates include buffet breakfast. AE, DC, MC, V. Parking 40€. Metro: Colosseo. Bus: 40. **Amenities:** Room service; Wi-Fi (free, in lobby). *In room:* A/C, TV, hair dryer.

NEAR PIAZZA NAVONA & THE PANTHEON

Travelers who want to immerse themselves in the atmosphere of ancient Rome, or those looking for romance, will prefer staying in this area. Transportation isn't the greatest and you'll do a lot of walking, but that's the reason many visitors come here in the first place—to wander and discover the glory that was Rome. You're within walking distance of the Vatican and classical ruins, as well as many bars and cafes.

Very Expensive

Hotel Raphael ★★ With a glorious location adjacent to Piazza Navona, the Raphael is often the top choice of Italian politicos in town for the opening of Parliament. The ivy-covered facade invites you to enter the lobby, which is decorated with antiques that rival the cache in local museums (there's even a Picasso ceramics collection). The guest rooms (some quite small) were recently refurbished with a Florentine touch. Some of the suites have private terraces. We love its rooftop restaurant with views of all the major landmarks of Old Rome.

Largo Febo 2, 00186 Roma. ✆ **06-682831.** Fax 06-6878993. www.raphaelhotel.com. 65 units. 238€–380€ double; 450€–1,000€ suite. Rates include American buffet breakfast. AE, DC, MC, V. Parking 50€. Bus: 70, 81, 87, or 115. **Amenities:** Restaurant; bar; babysitting; bikes; concierge; exercise room; room service; sauna. *In room:* A/C, TV, hair dryer, minibar, Wi-Fi (free).

Expensive

Albergo Del Sole al Pantheon ★ You're obviously paying for the million-dollar view, but you might find that it's worth it to be across from the Pantheon. This building was constructed in 1450 as a home, and the first records of it as a hostelry appeared in 1467, making it one of the world's oldest hotels. The layout is amazingly eccentric; prepare to walk up and down a lot of three- or four-step staircases. The guest rooms vary greatly in decor, with compact, tiled full bathrooms. The rooms opening onto the piazza tend to be noisy at all hours. The quieter rooms overlook the quiet courtyard, but we always prefer to put up with the noise to enjoy one of the world's greatest views. For the grandest view of the Pantheon, ask for room no. 106 or 108.

Piazza della Rotonda 63, 00186 Roma. ✆ **06-6780441.** Fax 06-69940689. www.hotelsolealpantheon.com. 30 units. 230€–430€ double; 265€–585€ junior suite. Rates include buffet breakfast. AE, DC, MC, V. Bus: 64. **Amenities:** Bar; airport transfers (55€); babysitting; Jacuzzi; room service; Wi-Fi (free, in lobby). *In room:* A/C, TV, hair dryer, minibar.

Nazionale ★ The Nazionale faces the Piazza Colonna, with its Column of Marcus Aurelius, the Palazzo di Montecitorio, and the Palazzo Chigi. Because it's next to the Parliament buildings, the Albergo is often full of government officials and diplomatic staff. The lobbies are wood-paneled, with many antiques throughout. The guest rooms are high-ceilinged, comfortably proportioned, and individually decorated in a late-19th-century style. They have either carpet or marble floors, and some offer views over the ancient square outside.

Piazza Montecitorio 131, 00186 Roma. ✆ **06-695001.** Fax 06-6786677. www.nazionaleroma.it. 195€–480€ double; 700€–850€ suite. Rates include buffet breakfast. AE, DC, MC, V. Parking 35€–50€, depending on the size of the car. Bus: 116. **Amenities:** Restaurant; bar; airport transfers (65€); babysitting; room service; Wi-Fi (5€ per hour, in lobby). *In room:* A/C, TV, hair dryer, minibar.

Moderate

Albergo Cesàri ★★ If you want to lose yourself on an ancient street in Old Rome, head here. Since 1787, this inn has stood in an offbeat location between the Pantheon and the Trevi Fountain, two of Rome's most enduring landmarks. Its well-preserved exterior harmonizes with the Temple of Neptune and many little antiques shops nearby. The guest rooms have mostly functional modern pieces but contain a few traditional trappings to maintain character.

Via di Pietra 89A, 00186 Roma. ✆ **06-6749701.** Fax 06-67497030. www.albergocesari.it. 47 units (most with shower only). 136€–280€ double; 176€–325€ triple. Rates include buffet breakfast. AE, DC, MC, V. Parking 25€. Bus: 175 or 492 from Stazione Termini. **Amenities:** Bar; babysitting; bikes; room service. *In room:* A/C, TV, hair dryer, minibar, Wi-Fi (5€ per 24 hr.).

Albergo Santa Chiara This is a family-run hotel near the Pantheon in the very inner core of historic Rome. Since 1938, the Corteggiani family has been welcoming sightseers to classic Rome. The hotel's white walls and marble columns speak of former elegance, although the rooms today are simply furnished, yet comfortable. Rooms range from a broom closet to a suite large enough to be classified as a small Roman apartment. We go for those units facing the Piazza della Minerva, although you'll often have to listen to late-night revelers who don't know when to go home.

Via Santa Chiara 21, 00186 Roma. ✆ **06-6872979.** Fax 06-6873144. www.albergosantachiara.com. 98 units (half with shower only). 225€–280€ double; 460€–550€ suite. Rates include buffet breakfast. AE, DC, MC, V. Metro: Spagna. **Amenities:** Bar; airport transfers (55€); babysitting; room service; Wi-Fi (5€ per hour, in lobby). *In room:* A/C, TV, hair dryer, minibar.

Hotel Adriano This hotel is housed within the original walls of a 15th-century palazzo. It's been skillfully converted into a well-run and government-rated three-star hotel that houses guests comfortably. The location is close to some of Rome's major landmarks, including Piazza di Spagna, Piazza Navona, and the Pantheon. You can find a well-upholstered armchair waiting for you under the vaulted ceilings of the public rooms. Bedrooms are simply furnished but tasteful. Bathrooms are small, simple, and clean. You can enjoy breakfast on the hotel's roof terrace.

Via di Pallacorda 2, 00186 Roma. ✆ **06-68802451.** Fax 06-68803926. www.hoteladriano.com. 82 units. 135€–300€ double; 340€–500€ suite. Rates include buffet breakfast. AE, DC, MC, V. Parking 40€. Bus: 116. **Amenities:** Bar; airport transfers (50€); babysitting; bikes; room service; Wi-Fi (5€ per day, in lobby). *In room:* A/C, TV, minibar.

Inexpensive

Mimosa First, the bad news. This friendly little pensione was once an army barracks and hasn't completely erased that former role. That said, it is one of the great bargains of Rome, especially considering its location of prime real estate, a 5-minute walk from the Piazza Navona and only 100m from the Pantheon. The walls are paper-thin but the bedrooms are extremely well maintained and comfortable in a simplistic way, like a well-run frat house. Hallway bathrooms are adequate for those in a room without plumbing, and the breakfast is generous.

Via Santa Chiara 61, 00186 Roma. ✆ **06-68801753.** Fax 06-6833557. www.hotelmimosa.net. 11 units (7 with bathroom). 88€ double without bathroom; 108€ double with bathroom. Rates include continental breakfast. No credit cards. Bus: 116 to Piazza della Rotonda. **Amenities:** Wi-Fi (free, in lobby). *In room:* A/C, no phone.

NEAR PIAZZA DEL POPOLO & THE SPANISH STEPS

This is a great place to stay if you're a serious shopper, but expect to part with a lot of extra dough for the privilege. Think Fifth Avenue all the way.

Accommodations near Piazza del Popolo & the Spanish Steps

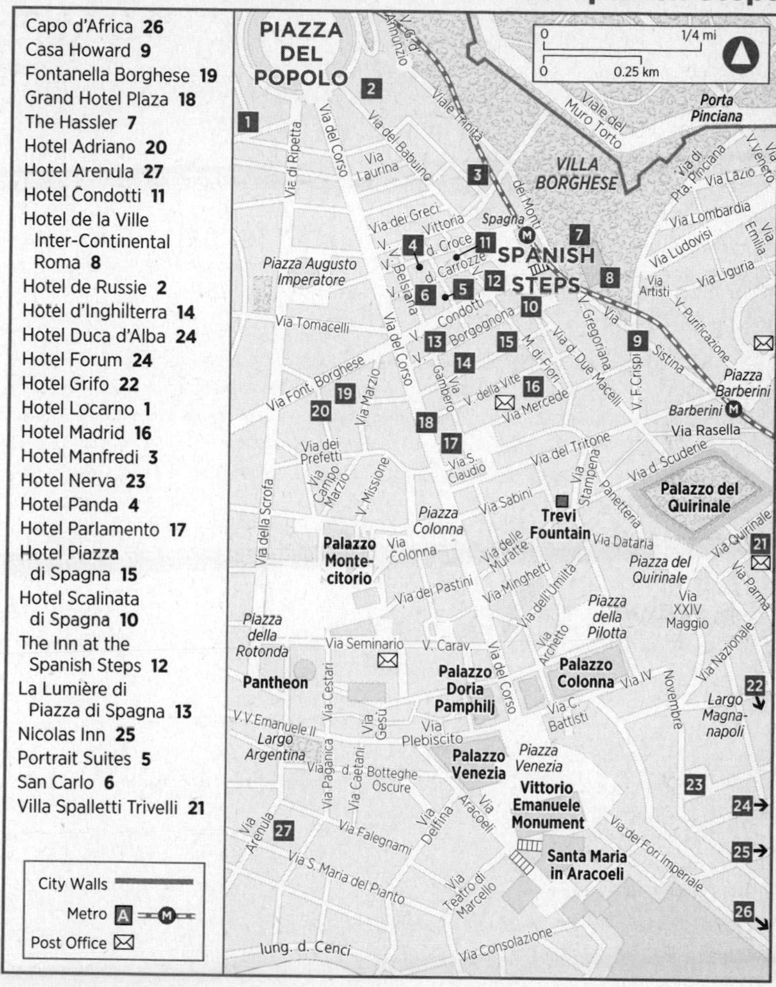

Very Expensive

The Hassler ★★ The Westin Excelsior is a grander palace, and the Eden and the de Russie are more up to date, but the Hassler has something that no other hotel can boast—a coveted location at the top of the Spanish Steps. The Hassler, rebuilt in 1944 to replace the 1885 original, is not quite what it used to be, but because it's such a classic, it gets away with charging astronomical rates. The lounges and the guest rooms still strike a glamorous, if faded, 1930s note. Guest rooms range from small singles to some of the most spacious suites in town. High ceilings make them appear larger than they are, and many of them open onto private balconies or terraces. For panoramas of the Roman rooftops, ask for a room on the top floor. Although some of the accommodations remain a bit dowdy, those on the fourth floor are elegantly renovated.

Piazza Trinità dei Monti 6, 00187 Roma. ✆ **800/223-6800** in the U.S., or 06-699340. Fax 06-69941607. www.hotelhasslerroma.com. 100 units. 350€–850€ double; from 1,100€ suite. AE, DC, MC, V. Parking 45€. Metro: Spagna. **Amenities:** 2 restaurants; bar; airport transfers 100€–250€; babysitting; bikes; exercise room; room service; spa. *In room:* A/C, TV, hair dryer, minibar, Wi-Fi (20€ per day).

Hotel de la Ville Inter-Continental Roma ★★ The hotel looks deluxe (although it's officially rated first class) from the minute you walk through the revolving door, where a smartly uniformed doorman greets you. Once inside this palace, built in the 19th century on the site of the ancient Gardens of Lucullus, you'll find Oriental rugs, marble tables, brocade furniture, and an English-speaking staff. Endless corridors lead to a maze of ornamental lounges. Some of the public rooms have a sort of 1930s elegance, and others are strictly baroque; in the middle of it all is an open courtyard. The guest rooms and public areas are decorated in a beautifully classic and yet up-to-date way. The higher rooms with balconies have panoramic views of Rome. Most units are small but boast chintz-covered fabrics and fine beds.

Via Sistina 67–69, 00187 Roma. ✆ **888/424-6835** in the U.S. and Canada, or 06-67331. Fax 06-6784213. www.ichotelsgroup.com. 192 units. 248€–590€ double; from 639€ suite. Rates include continental breakfast. AE, DC, MC, V. Parking 35€. Metro: Spagna or Barberini. **Amenities:** Restaurant; bar; airport transfers (75€); babysitting; concierge; exercise room; room service. *In room:* A/C, TV/DVD, CD player, hair dryer, minibar, Wi-Fi (23€ per day).

Hotel de Russie ★★★ This government-rated five-star hotel has raised the bar for every other hotel in the city. For service, style, and modern luxuries, it beats out the Eden, the Westin Excelsior, and the St. Regis Grand. Just off the Piazza del Popolo, it opened in the spring of 2000 to rave reviews. In its previous incarnation, it was a favorite of Russian dignitaries (hence its name), and it also has hosted Jean Cocteau, Stravinsky, and Picasso. Public areas are glossy and contemporary. About 30% of the bedrooms are conservative, with traditional furniture, while the remaining 70% are more minimalist, with a stark, striking style. Each is equipped with every conceivable high-tech amenity and offers deeply upholstered comforts. The signature feature is the extensive terraced gardens, which can be seen from many of the bedrooms.

Via del Babuino 9, 00187 Roma. ✆ **800/323-7500** in the U.S., or 06-328881. Fax 06-3288888. www.hotelderussie.it. 125 units. 680€–960€ double; from 1,430€ suite. AE, DC, MC, V. Parking 55€. Metro: Flaminia. **Amenities:** Restaurant; bar; airport transfers (85€); bikes; children's programs; concierge; exercise room; room service; spa. *In room:* A/C, TV, hair dryer, minibar, Wi-Fi (20€ per day).

Hotel d'Inghilterra ★★ Rome's most fashionable small hotel holds on to its traditions and heritage, even though it has been renovated. It's comparable to the Hassler and Inter-Continental. Situated between Via Condotti and Via Borgogna, this hotel in the 17th century was the guesthouse of the Torlonia princes. The rooms have mostly old pieces (gilt and lots of marble, mahogany chests, and glittery mirrors) complemented by modern conveniences. Some, however, are just too cramped. The preferred rooms are higher up, opening onto a tile terrace, with a balustrade and a railing covered with flowering vines and plants.

Via Bocca di Leone 14, 00187 Roma. ✆ **06-699811.** Fax 06-69922243. http://hoteldinghilterra.warwickhotels.com. 98 units. 200€–577€ double; from 630€ suite. AE, DC, MC, V. Parking 40€. Metro: Spagna. **Amenities:** 2 restaurants; bar; airport transfers (70€); babysitting; concierge; room service. *In room:* A/C, TV/DVD, hair dryer, minibar, Wi-Fi (18€ per day).

The Inn at the Spanish Steps ★★★ This intimate, upscale inn is the first new hotel to open in this location in years. The people who run Rome's most famous cafe, Caffé Greco, created it where Hans Christian Andersen once lived. Andersen praised the balcony roses and violets, and so, probably, will you. Every room is furnished in an authentic period decor, featuring antiques, elegant draperies, and parquet floors. The superior units come with a fireplace, a frescoed or beamed ceiling, and a balcony. The hotel is completely modern, with generous wardrobe space. Each marble-paneled bathroom comes with a full tub, and others offer a Jacuzzi as well. Designer boutiques galore lie nearby.

Via dei Condotti 85, 00187 Roma. ✆ **06-69925657.** Fax 06-6786470. www.atspanishsteps.com. 24 units. 170€–820€ double; from 700€ suite. Rates include buffet breakfast. AE, DC, MC, V. Metro: Spagna. **Amenities:** Bar; airport transfers (55€); babysitting; concierge; room service. *In room:* A/C, TV, hair dryer, minibar, Wi-Fi (10€ per day).

Villa Spalletti Trivelli ★★★ On a side street on patrician Quirinal Hill, this gem of a hotel offers a rare opportunity to experience home life as lived by a Roman nobleman and his family a century ago; in this case the Spalletti-Trivelli family. A $4-million renovation has turned the early-20th-century neoclassical villa into a sumptuous address furnished with antiques, tapestries, and Italian art. Just steps from the Piazza del Quirinale and only a 5-minute walk from the Trevi Fountain, the villa opens onto a splendid Italian garden. The spacious bedrooms range from romantically decorated units to grand deluxe suites fit for a visiting president.

Via Piacenza 4, 00184 Roma. ✆ **06-48907934.** Fax 06-4871409. www.villaspalletti.it. 12 units. 363€–900€ double; from 1,067€ suite. AE, DC, MC, V. Metro: Barberini. **Amenities:** Restaurant; honesty bar; concierge; exercise room; room service; spa; Wi-Fi (free, in lobby). *In room:* A/C, TV, minibar.

Expensive

Grand Hotel Plaza ★ This grand old favorite is experiencing a renaissance. Pietro Mascagni composed his *Nerone* in one of the guest rooms here, and Vincent Price stayed here while making what he called, "all those bad movies." When you see the very grand decor, you'll understand why. This hotel's public rooms are vintage 19th century and contain stained-glass skylights, massive crystal chandeliers, potted palms, inlaid marble floors, and a life-size stone lion guarding the ornate stairway. The theatrical grandeur of the lobby carries over into the suites, where the furnishings mimic the gilded-age splendor of the public rooms on a smaller scale. But the standard guest rooms are just that—standard. They're contemporary, midsize, and streamlined, with efficient but comfortable furniture.

Via del Corso 126, 00186 Roma. ✆ **06-69921111.** Fax 06-69941575. www.grandhotelplaza.com. 220 units. 227€–440€ double; 560€–1,800€ suite. AE, MC, V. Parking 52€. Metro: Spagna. **Amenities:** Restaurant; bar; airport transfers (60€); babysitting; concierge; room service. *In room:* A/C, TV, hair dryer, minibar, Wi-Fi (3€ per hour).

Hotel Locarno If you'd like to experience Rome the way visitors such as Mary Pickford and Douglas Fairbanks did in the 1920s, head for this monument to Art Deco. In the heart of Rome, near Piazza del Popolo, this hotel first opened its doors in 1925, and it's been receiving visitors ever since. In fair weather, breakfast is served in the garden or on the rooftop garden. Bedrooms in the older section are a bit chintzy, but the newer wing has brighter, fresher accommodations. All of the original floors, doors, and bathroom fixtures in this newer section were refurbished. Rooms are reached by taking a bird-cage elevator.

Via della Penna 25, 00186 Roma. ✆ **06-3610841.** Fax 06-3215249. www.hotellocarno.com. 66 units. 184€–420€ double; 464€–1,200€ suite. Rates include continental breakfast. AE, DC, MC, V. Parking 25€. Metro: Flaminio. Bus: 116 or 117. **Amenities:** Bar; airport transfers (45€); room service. *In room:* A/C, TV, minibar, Wi-Fi (free).

Hotel Scalinata di Spagna ★★★ This is Rome's most famous little boutique hotel. The deluxe Hassler is across the street but far removed in price and grandeur from this intimate, upscale B&B at the top of the Spanish Steps. This delightful little building—only two floors are visible from the outside—is nestled between much larger structures. The redecorated interior features small public rooms with bright print slipcovers, old clocks, and low ceilings. The decor varies radically from one guest room to the next. Some have low, beamed ceilings and ancient-looking wood furniture; others have loftier ceilings and more run-of-the-mill furniture.

Piazza Trinità dei Monti 17, 00187 Roma. ✆ **06-6793006.** Fax 06-69940598. www.hotelscalinata.com. 16 units (tubs only). 130€–370€ double; 290€–410€ junior suite. Rates include buffet breakfast. AE, MC, V. Parking 40€. Metro: Spagna. **Amenities:** Bar; airport transfers (75€); babysitting; room service. *In room:* A/C, TV, hair dryer, minibar, Wi-Fi (free).

La Lumière di Piazza di Spagna ★ 🎁 We never thought another little inn would open near the Spanish Steps simply because there was no more real estate available. Wrong. Along comes this charmer installed in a five-story 18th-century building with an elevator. Rooms are spacious and exquisitely furnished in a classic style, with a panoramic view of the Spanish Steps. All of them have adjoining bathrooms with Jacuzzi spa showers. While you enjoy your breakfast buffet on the panoramic terrace, the entire city of Rome is at your feet. Outside your door you'll find Rome's best and most exclusive shops.

Via Belsiana 72, 00187 Roma. ✆ **06-69380806.** Fax 06-69294231. www.lalumieredipiazzadispagna.com. 10 units. 120€–350€ double; 150€–410€ junior suite. Rates include breakfast buffet. AE, DC, MC, V. Parking 40€. Metro: Spagna. **Amenities:** Airport transfers (65€); room service. *In room:* A/C, TV, hair dryer, minibar, Wi-Fi (free).

Portrait Suites ★★ For those who don't want to stay at the Hassler, but prefer the luxury of an intimate and deluxe boutique hotel, this all-suite inn is the answer. In a six-story historic building, it is decorated in a very elegant contemporary style, including walls lined with photographs and drawings by Salvatore Ferragamo. It's true *La Dolce Vita* in the heart of Rome. All the accommodations are spacious with such features as large marble bathrooms. On top of the building is a terrace opening onto a panoramic sweep of Rome.

Via Bocca di Leone 23, 00187 Roma. ✆ **06-69380742.** Fax 06-69190625. www.rome-suites-portrait.com. 14 units. 400€–590€ double; 700€–1,590€ suite. Rates include continental breakfast. AE, DC, MC, V. Parking 35€. Metro: Spagna. **Amenities:** Bar; babysitting; room service. *In room:* A/C, TV, hair dryer, minibar, kitchenette, Wi-Fi (free).

Moderate

Casa Howard ★ 🎁 It's rare to make a new discovery in the tourist-trodden Piazza di Spagna area, which is why Casa Howard comes as a pleasant surprise. The little B&B occupies about two-thirds of the second floor of a historic structure. The welcoming owners maintain beautifully furnished guest rooms, each with its own private bathroom with a shower/tub combination (although some bathrooms lie outside the bedrooms in the hallway). The Pink Room is the most spacious, and has an en-suite bathroom. Cristy, at reception, can "arrange anything" in Rome for you and will also invite you to use the house's private Turkish sauna.

Via Capo le Case 18, 00187 Roma. ✆ **06-69924555.** Fax 06-6794644. www.casahoward.com. 5 units. 170€–250€ double. MC, V. Parking 30€. Metro: Spagna. **Amenities:** Babysitting; room service; steam room. *In room:* A/C, TV, hair dryer, Wi-Fi (free).

Fontanella Borghese ★ Close to the Spanish Steps in the exact heart of Rome, this hotel surprisingly remains relatively undiscovered. Much renovated and improved, it has been installed on the third and fourth floor of a palace dating from the end of the 18th century. The building once belonged to the Borghese family, and the little hotel looks out onto the Borghese Palace. It lies within walking distance of the Trevi Fountain, the Pantheon, and the Piazza Navona. The location is also close to Piazza Augusto and the Ara Pacis. In the midsize bedrooms, everything is in a classical tradition, comfortably modernized for today's travelers.

Largo Fontanella Borghese 84, 00186 Roma. ✆ **06-68809504.** Fax 06-6861295. www.fontanellaborghese.com. 29 units. 160€–230€ double. AE, DC, MC, V. Parking nearby 40€. Metro: Spagna. **Amenities:** Babysitting; bikes; room service. *In room:* A/C, TV, hair dryer, minibar.

Hotel Condotti The Condotti is small, choice, and terrific for shoppers intent on staying near the tony boutiques. Book here for an affordable price in a platinum-card neighborhood and a great location. Despite its name, this hotel actually lies 2 blocks to the north of Via Condotti. The staff members, nearly all of whom speak English, are cooperative and hardworking. The mostly modern rooms might not have much historical charm (they're furnished like nice motel units), but they're comfortable and soothing. Each room is decorated with traditional furnishings, including excellent beds (usually twins). Room no. 414 is often requested for its geranium-filled terrace.

Via Mario de' Fiori 37, 00187 Roma. ✆ **06-6794661.** Fax 06-6790457. www.hotelcondotti.com. 21 units (shower only). 99€–355€ double; 119€–385€ triple. Rates include buffet breakfast. AE, DC, MC, V. Metro: Spagna. **Amenities:** Airport transfers (60€); babysitting; room service. *In room:* A/C, TV, hair dryer, minibar, Wi-Fi (free).

Hotel Madrid Despite modern touches in the comfortable, if minimalist, guest rooms, the interior of the Madrid manages to evoke late-19th-century Rome. Guests often take their breakfast amid ivy and blossoming plants on the rooftop terrace with a panoramic view of rooftops and the distant dome of St. Peter's. Some of the doubles are large, with scatter rugs, veneer armoires, and shuttered windows. Others are quite small, so make sure you know what you're getting before you check in.

Via Mario de' Fiori 93–95, 00187 Roma. ✆ **06-6991510.** Fax 06-6791653. www.hotelmadridroma.com. 26 units. 160€–245€ double; 200€–350€ suite. Rates include buffet breakfast. AE, DC, MC, V. Parking nearby 50€. Metro: Spagna. **Amenities:** Babysitting; room service; Wi-Fi (free, in lobby). *In room:* A/C, TV, hair dryer, minibar.

Hotel Manfredi ★ This hotel near the Spanish Steps lies in the art district of Rome. It's a government-rated three-star that enjoys a glamorous address and is housed in a fully renovated 16th-century former private residence. The soundproof rooms are midsize and beautifully decorated in an 18th-century style, with tiled bathrooms with shower/tub combinations. Pastels of pink, green, and blue predominate in this stylish, classic atmosphere.

Via Margutta 61, 00187 Roma. ✆ **06-3207676.** Fax 06-3207736. www.hotelmanfredi.it. 18 units. 224€–380€ double; 315€–480€ junior suite. Rates include buffet breakfast. AE, DC, MC, V. Parking 15€. Metro: Spagna. **Amenities:** Bar; room service. *In room:* A/C, TV, hair dryer, minibar, Wi-Fi (10€ per day).

Hotel Piazza di Spagna About a block from the downhill side of the Spanish Steps, this hotel is small but classic, with an inviting atmosphere made more gracious by the helpful manager, Elisabetta Giocondi. The guest rooms boast a functional streamlined decor; some even have Jacuzzis in the tiled bathrooms. Only eight units come with complete shower/tub combinations. Accommodations are spread across three floors, and the very tidy bedrooms have high ceilings and cool terrazzo floors.

Via Mario de' Fiori 61, 00187 Roma. ✆ **06-6793061.** Fax 06-6790654. www.hotelpiazzadispagna.it. 17 units (some with shower only). 140€–290€ double; 190€–320€ triple. Rates include continental breakfast. AE, MC, V. Parking nearby 25€. Metro: Spagna. Bus: 117. **Amenities:** Bar; airport transfers (50€–65€); room service; Internet (10€ per day, in lobby). *In room:* A/C, TV, hair dryer, minibar.

San Carlo Prices are surprisingly low for a building only 5 minutes on foot from the Spanish Steps and adjacent to the via Condotti with some of the best luxury shops and boutiques in Rome. The structure itself was meticulously renovated from the 17th-century mansion. Accommodations are spread across four floors. Equally desirable rooms lie in an annex with beamed ceilings, terra-cotta floors, and the occasional fresco. Bedrooms throughout are available as a single, double, triple, or quad. Superior rooms open onto private terraces covered with an awning and containing outdoor furniture. Many of the bathrooms are clad in marble.

Via delle Carrozze 92/93, 00187 Roma. ✆ **06-6784548.** Fax 06-69941197. www.hotelsancarloroma.com. 50 units. 125€–210€ double. Rates include buffet breakfast. AE, DC, MC, V. Parking 30€. Metro: Spagna. **Amenities:** Bar; babysitting; concierge; room service. *In room:* A/C, TV, hair dryer, minibar, Wi-Fi (in some; free).

Inexpensive

Hotel Panda This small hotel occupies two floors of a restored 19th-century building only 50m from the Spanish Steps. Bedrooms are simply but adequately furnished, resting (for the most part) under vaulted wood beamed ceilings on stone tiled floors. Some of the accommodations have 19th century frescoes; others have hand-painted tiles in the bathrooms. This is one of the oldest hotels in the historical center of Rome, attracting patrons with its economical prices and its family-like atmosphere. Air-conditioning carries a daily supplement of 6 euros.

Via della Croce 35, 00187 Roma. ✆ **06-6780179.** Fax 06-69942151. www.hotelpanda.it. 20 units (8 with bathroom). 78€ double without bathroom; 108€ double with bathroom; 140€ triple with bathroom. AE, MC, V. Parking 30€. Metro: Spagna. *In room:* A/C, Wi-Fi (free).

Hotel Parlamento This three-story hotel has a four-star government rating at two-star prices. Expect a friendly pensione-style reception. The furnishings are antiques or reproduction, and the firm beds are backed by carved-wood or wrought-iron headboards. Fifteen rooms are air-conditioned, and the bathrooms have heated towel racks, phones, and (in a few) marble sinks. Only three come with a complete shower/tub combination. Rooms differ in style; the nicest are no. 82, with its original

1800s furniture; and nos. 104, 106, and 107, which open onto the rooftop garden. You can enjoy the chandeliered and *trompe l'oeil* breakfast room, or carry your cappuccino up to the small rooftop terrace with its view of San Silvestro's bell tower.

Via delle Convertite 5 (at the intersection with Via del Corso), 00187 Roma. ✆/fax **06-69921000.** www.hotelparlamento.it. 23 units. 90€–195€ double; 110€–205€ triple. Rates include continental breakfast. AE, DC, MC, V. Parking 40€. Metro: Spagna. **Amenities:** Bar; concierge; room service. *In room:* A/C, TV, hair dryer, Wi-Fi (10€ per 6 hr.).

NEAR THE VATICAN

For most visitors, this is a rather dull area in which to be based—it's well removed from the ancient sites, and it's not a great restaurant neighborhood. But if the main purpose of your visit centers on the Vatican, you'll be fine here, and you'll be joined by thousands of other pilgrims, nuns, and priests.

Expensive

Hotel dei Consoli ★ 🎁 In the neighborhood of the Vatican, this refined, rather elegant hotel in the Prati district is newly constructed, lying just a short stroll from the Vatican Museums. The hotel occupies three floors in a building that was painstakingly restored in the imperial style with cornices and columns. Stained glass and fine art create an inviting ambience. All the bedrooms are handsomely furnished and decorated, but units judged deluxe are outfitted with whirlpool baths, as are the junior suites. Draperies and bedding are in elegant silks, the bathrooms adorned with the finest porcelain. There's also a rooftop terrace with panoramic views.

Via Varrone 2 D, 00193 Roma. ✆ **06-68892972.** Fax 06-68212274. www.hoteldeiconsoli.com. 28 units. 250€–320€ double; 360€–380€ suite. Rates include buffet breakfast. AE, DC, MC, V. Parking 20€. Metro: Ottaviano–San Pietro. **Amenities:** Bar; room service; Wi-Fi (8€ per hour, in lobby). *In room:* A/C, TV, minibar.

Hotel dei Mellini ★ This neoclassical hotel is a choice place for Vatican pilgrims. It dates from the early 1900s, when it was a town house. In 1995, after years of neglect, it was turned into a first-class hotel with a certain charm and luxury. It consists of two interconnected buildings, one with four floors and one with six; the top is graced with a terrace overlooking the baroque cupolas of at least three churches. A small staff maintains the lovely guest rooms, whose decor includes Art Deco touches, Italian marble, and mahogany furniture. Accommodations with room numbers ending in "16" come with large sitting areas.

Via Muzio Clementi 81, 00193 Roma. ✆ **06-324771.** Fax 06-32477801. www.hotelmellini.com. 80 units. 260€–400€ double; 450€–550€ suite. Rates include buffet breakfast. AE, DC, MC, V. Parking 30€. Metro: Lepanto. **Amenities:** Restaurant; bar; room service; Wi-Fi (5€ per 30 min.). *In room:* A/C, TV, hair dryer, minibar.

Residenza Paolo VI ★★ 🎁 Established on the premises of a former monastery, this hotel opened in 2000. Its marvelous views of St. Peter's Square rank among the greatest sights in Rome. One reader wrote, "I felt I was at the gates of heaven sitting on the most beautiful square in the Western world." In addition to its incomparable location, the hotel is filled with beautiful, comfortable bedrooms, all with modern bathrooms. In spite of its reasonable prices, this inn is like a small luxury hotel.

Via Paolo VI 29, 00193 Roma. ✆ **06-684870.** Fax 06-6867428. www.residenzapaolovi.com. 29 units. 255€–367€ double; 580€ junior suite. Rates include American buffet breakfast. AE, DC, MC, V. Parking 20€. Metro: Ottaviano–San Pietro. Bus: 62, 64, or 916. **Amenities:** Bar; babysitting; room service. *In room:* A/C, TV, hair dryer, minibar, Wi-Fi (free).

Starhotel Michelangelo ★ How appropriate that this hotel took the name of the great Michelangelo, because it lies only a few minutes' walk from St. Peter's, and many of its well-furnished and midsize bedrooms open onto a view of Michelangelo's dome. The five-story hotel opened back in the glorious heyday of Rome in the '50s. After a slumber, it's back again and better than ever after substantial improvements. The decor of the rooms has been glamorized with rich carpeting, swag draperies, and tasteful furnishings. The best bedrooms here are classified as "executive," and they are more spacious and better accessorized. Naturally, they are booked first. The bar is a good watering hole near the Vatican (yes, priests can be seen here, but drinking only wine). The restaurant has a rich, varied menu of local and international specialties.

Via della Stazione di S. Pietro 14, 00165 Roma. ✆ **06-398739.** Fax 06-632359. www.starhotels.com. 179 units. 160€–350€ double; from 250€ suite. AE, DC, MC, V. Parking 35€. Bus: 64. **Amenities:** Restaurant; bar; babysitting; concierge; exercise room; room service. *In room:* A/C, TV, hair dryer, minibar, Wi-Fi (10€ per hour).

Visconti Palace Hotel ★★ Completely restructured and redesigned, this palatial hotel is graced with one of the most avant-garde contemporary designs in town. Stunningly modern, it uses color perhaps with more sophistication than any other hotel. The location is idyllic, lying in the Prati district between Piazza di Spagna and St. Peter's. The rooms and corridors are decorated with modern art; the bathrooms are in marble; and there are many floor-to-ceiling windows and private terraces. Taste and an understated elegance prevail in this bright, welcoming, yet functional atmosphere.

Via Federico Cesi 37, 00193 Roma. ✆ **06-3684.** Fax 06-3200551. www.viscontipalace.com. 242 units. 350€–380€ double; 450€ junior suite; 650€ suite. AE, DC, MC, V. Metro: Ottaviano. Bus: 40, 62, or 74. Parking 35€. **Amenities:** Bar; exercise room; room service; Wi-Fi (7€ per hour, in lobby). *In room:* A/C, TV, hair dryer, minibar.

Moderate

Bramante Lying just 100m (328 ft.) from St. Peter's Basilica, this hotel is ideal for those who want to spend a lot of time at the Vatican Museums. The location is in what was once the medieval burg of "Borgo Pio" close to the Passetto, the wall that separated the Vatican from Castel San Angelo. In 1574, the present hotel became the home of the famous architect Domenico Fontana, who was Pope Sixtus V's chief architect and whose masterpiece was the Palazzo Lateranense. All the bedrooms have been restored, and many rest under beamed ceilings. The owners call them "cozy"; you might find them cramped. But each is modern and comfortable, with a small shower-only bathroom. Extra services include a private limo to and from the airport.

Vicolo delle Palline 24, 00193 Roma. ✆ **06-68806426.** Fax 06-68133339. www.hotelbramante.com. 16 units. 150€–240€ double. Rates include American buffet breakfast. AE, DC, MC, V. Metro: Ottaviano-San Pietro. Bus: 40. **Amenities:** Airport transfers (55€); babysitting; Wi-Fi (free, in lobby). *In room:* A/C, TV, hair dryer, minibar.

Accommodations & Dining near the Vatican

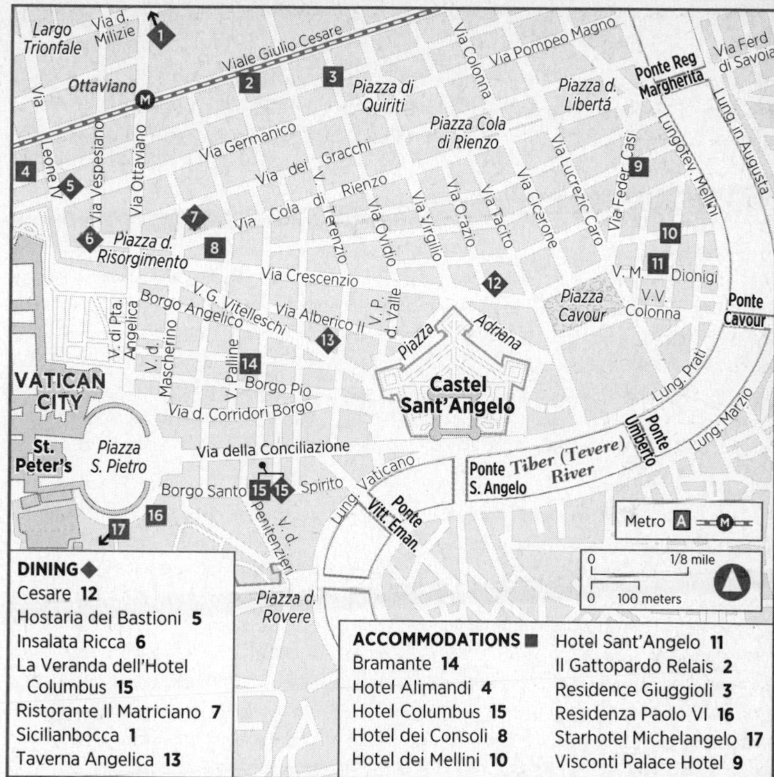

Hotel Alimandi Named after the three brothers who run it (Luigi, Enrico, and Paolo), this friendly guesthouse was built as an apartment house in 1908 in a bland residential neighborhood. The guest rooms are comfortable, albeit a bit small, with unremarkable contemporary furniture and cramped but modern-looking bathrooms. Each of the three upper floors is serviced by two elevators leading down to a simple lobby. The social center and most appealing spot is the rooftop garden, with potted plants and views of St. Peter's dome.

Via Tunisi 8, 00192 Roma. ✆ **06-39745562.** Fax 06-39723943. www.alimandivaticanohotel.com. 35 units. 190€–250€ double; 165€–260€ triple. AE, DC, MC, V. Parking 15€. Metro: Ottaviano-San Pietro. **Amenities:** Bar; airport transfers (50€); concierge; exercise room; room service. *In room:* A/C, TV, hair dryer.

Hotel Columbus ★ This is an impressive 15th-century palace. The Columbus was once the home of the cardinal who became Pope Julius II, the man who tormented Michelangelo into painting the Sistine Chapel. It looks much as it must have centuries ago: a severe time-stained facade, and heavy wooden doors leading from the street to the colonnades and arches of the inner courtyard. The cobbled entranceway leads to a reception hall and a series of baronial public rooms. Note the main salon with its walk-in fireplace, oil portraits, battle scenes, and Oriental rugs. The guest rooms are considerably simpler than the salons and are furnished with comfortable modern pieces. All are spacious, but a few are enormous and still have many original details. The best and quietest rooms front the garden.

Via della Conciliazione 33, 00193 Roma. ✆ **06-6865435.** Fax 06-6864874. www.hotelcolumbus.net. 92 units. 160€–350€ double; 180€–410€ triple. Rates include buffet breakfast. AE, DC, MC, V. Free parking. Bus: 40 or 62. **Amenities:** Restaurant; bar; babysitting; Internet (free, in lobby); room service. *In room:* A/C, TV, hair dryer, minibar.

Hotel Sant'Angelo This hotel, right off Piazza Cavour (northeast of the Castel Sant'Angelo) and a 10-minute walk from St. Peter's, is in a relatively untouristy area. Maintained and operated by the Torre family, it occupies the second and third floors of an imposing 200-year-old building. The rooms are simple, modern, and clean, with wooden furniture and views of either the street or a rather bleak but quiet courtyard. Rooms are small but not cramped.

Via Mariana Dionigi 16, 00193 Roma. ✆ **06-3242000.** Fax 06-3204451. www.hotelsa.it. 31 units (shower only). 86€–300€ double; 140€–350€ triple. Rates include buffet breakfast. AE, DC, MC, V. Parking 35€. Metro: Spagna. **Amenities:** Bar; airport transfers (54€); babysitting; room service. *In room:* A/C, TV, hair dryer, minibar (in some).

Villa Laetitia ★★★ Anna Fendi, of the fashion dynasty, has opened this stylish and super-chic haven of elegance along the Tiber. With its private gardens, this Art Nouveau mansion lies between the Piazza del Popolo and the Prati quarter. The bedrooms are virtual works of art and are decorated with antique tiles gathered by Fendi on her world travels along with other *objets d'art*. For the smart, trendy, and well-heeled traveler, this is a choice address. Many of the rooms contain well-equipped kitchenettes. Accommodations are like small studios with terraces or gardens. Each rental unit has a different design and personality. Artists and designers in particular are attracted to this intimate, personalized hotel.

Lungotevere delle Armi 22-23, 00195 Roma. ✆ **06-3226776.** Fax 06-3232720. www.villalaetitia.com. 15 units. 180€–220€ double; 350€ suite. AE, DC, MC, V. Metro: Lepanto. **Amenities:** Bar; airport transfers (55€); babysitting; room service. *In room:* A/C, TV, hair dryer, minibar, Wi-Fi (free).

Inexpensive

Il Gattopardo Relais Close to St. Peter's and the Vatican Museums, this family-run pensione is located in an elegantly restored building from the 19th century. In the historic Prati district, the Art Nouveau building is decorated in a romantic style with individually designed and soundproof rooms. Locals refer to it as a *hotel de charme*. Antiques, tapestries, and Italian art are scattered throughout.

Viale Giulio Cesare 94, 00192 Roma. ✆ **06-37358480.** Fax 06-37501019. www.ilgattopardorelais.it. 6 units. 110€–220€ double; 150€–250€ triple; 130€–250€ junior suite. AE, DC, MC, V. Metro: Ottaviano. **Amenities:** Bar. *In room:* A/C, TV.

Residence Giuggioli ★ This family-run guesthouse was founded in the 1940s but was recently renovated, adding private bathrooms to each guest room. It occupies most of the second floor of a five-story 1870s apartment house, with high-ceilinged rooms that were originally much grander but whose noble proportions are still obvious. Three of the five rooms have balconies overlooking the street. The Giuggioli is always crowded, partly because the rooms are larger than expected and have a scattering of antiques and reproductions (although the mattresses could use replacing).

If this place is full, walk a few flights up to the similar **Pensione Lady** (✆ **06-3242112;** www.hotelladyroma.it), where up to seven rooms might be available at about the same rates.

Via Germanico 198, 00192 Roma. ✆ **06-36005389.** Fax 06-36790487. www.hotelgiuggioli.it. 19 units. 100€–200€ double; 130€–220€ triple. Rates include buffet breakfast. AE, DC, MC, V. Parking in nearby garage 30€. Metro: Lepanto. **Amenities:** Room service. *In room:* A/C, TV, hair dryer, minibar.

IN TRASTEVERE

Once upon a time, tourists avoided Trastevere, but today, although it's off the beaten track, it's becoming more popular as an up-and-coming neighborhood where you can experience a true slice of Roman life.

Expensive

Ripa Hotel ★ This government-rated four-star hotel provides an unusual opportunity to stay across the Tiber in Trastevere, one of the oldest districts of Rome. The neighborhood may be historic, but the structure itself dates from 1973, although it's been completely restored since that time. The building is in concrete and glass, with a lobby of wooden and marble floors, filled with 1970s style armchairs. The midsize to large bedrooms are furnished in minimalist modern. The Roscioli family, the owners, imbue both the public and private rooms of the hotel with a very contemporary look.

Via degli Orti di Trastevere 3, 00153 Roma. ✆ **06-58611.** Fax 06-5882523. www.ripahotel.com. 170 units. 270€–290€ double; 360€–540€ suite. Rates include buffet breakfast. AE, DC, MC, V. Parking 18€. Bus: H. **Amenities:** Restaurant; bar; babysitting; concierge; exercise room; room service. *In room:* A/C, TV, hair dryer, minibar, Wi-Fi (25€ per day).

Inexpensive

Hotel Trastevere ★ This bargain in Trastevere opened its restored doors in 1998 to meet the demand for accommodations in the neighborhood. This little gem has fresh, bright bedrooms with immaculate tiles. All of the bathrooms have also been renovated and contain showers, although they're small. The price is hard to beat for those who want to stay in one of the most atmospheric sections of Rome. Most of the rooms open onto the lively Piazza San Cosimato, and all of them have comfortable, albeit functional, furnishings. Breakfast is the only meal served, but many good restaurants lie just minutes away.

Via L. Manara 24–25, 00153 Roma. ✆ **06-5814713.** Fax 06-5881016. www.hoteltrastevere.net. 18 units. 103€–105€ double. Rates include buffet breakfast. AE, DC, MC, V. Parking nearby 20€. Bus: H. Tram: 8. **Amenities:** Airport transfers (52€). *In room:* A/C, TV, hair dryer.

IN PARIOLI

Hotel degli Aranci This former villa is on a tree-lined street, surrounded by similar villas that are the homes of consulates and diplomats. Most of the accommodations have tall windows opening onto city views and are filled with provincial furnishings or English-style reproductions and good beds. The tiled, shower-only bathrooms have adequate shelf space. Scattered about the public rooms are medallions of soldiers in profile, old engravings of ruins, and classical vases. From the glass-walled breakfast room, you can see the tops of orange trees.

Via Barnaba Oriani 11, 00197 Roma. ✆ **06-8070202.** Fax 06-8070704. www.hoteldegliaranci.com. 58 units. 153€–200€ double; from 300€ suite. Rates include continental breakfast. AE, DC, MC, V. Free parking. Bus: 910 or 926. **Amenities:** Restaurant; bar; airport transfers (70€); concierge; exercise room; Jacuzzi; room service; sauna. *In room:* A/C, TV, hair dryer, minibar, Wi-Fi (7€ per day).

Hotel delle Muse ★ This little hotel, .5km (⅓ mile) north of the Villa Borghese, is a winning but undiscovered choice run by the efficient, English-speaking Giorgio Lazar. Most rooms have been renovated but remain rather minimalist, with modern furnishings. Nonetheless, you'll be reasonably comfortable and there is a tidy shower-only bathroom in each unit.

Via Tommaso Salvini 18, 00197 Roma. ✆ **06-8088333.** Fax 06-8085749. www.hoteldellemuse.com. 61 units. 80€–220€ double; 110€–245€ triple. Rates include buffet breakfast. AE, DC, MC, V. Parking 20€. Bus: 360. **Amenities:** Garden restaurant; bar; babysitting; Internet (free, in lobby); room service. *In room:* TV, hair dryer, Wi-Fi (free).

Hotel Lord Byron ★★★ Lots of sophisticated travelers are choosing this chic boutique hotel over old landmarks like the St. Regis Grand. In an Art Deco villa set on a residential hilltop in Parioli, an area of embassies and exclusive town houses at the edge of the Villa Borghese, the Lord Byron exemplifies modern Rome. From the curving entrance steps off the staffed parking lot in front, you'll notice striking design touches. Flowers are everywhere, the lighting is discreet, and everything is on an intimate scale. Each guest room is unique, but most have lots of mirrors, upholstered walls, sumptuous beds, spacious bathrooms with gray marble accessories, and big dressing rooms/closets. Ask for room no. 503, 602, or 603 for great views. Bathrooms are medium size. The hotel's restaurant, **Sapori del Lord Byron,** is one of Rome's top restaurants; see the full review on p. 145.

Via G. de Notaris 5, 00197 Roma. ✆ **06-3220404.** Fax 06-3220405. www.lordbyronhotel.com. 32 units. 200€–500€ double; 610€–975€ suite. Rates include buffet breakfast. AE, DC, MC, V. Parking 30€. Metro: Flaminio. Bus: 52. **Amenities:** Restaurant; bar; airport transfers (70€); babysitting; concierge; room service. *In room:* A/C, TV, hair dryer, minibar, Wi-Fi (20€ per day).

IN TORLONIA

Villa del Parco ★ Those who want to escape the hysterical bustle of central Rome, with its tourist hordes, can retreat to this late 1800s restored Liberty-style villa surrounded by greenery in a tranquil residential district right outside the center near the Villa Torlonia park and museum complex. The helpful Bernardini family transformed the private residence into a hotel in the 1950s during Rome's *La Dolce Vita* heyday. The owners personally chose all the furniture in their individually decorated bedrooms, which are fully renovated and attractively and comfortably furnished. Much of the look is Italian country style. The most romantic, but not the largest rooms, are the Mansard quarters in the former attic.

Via Nomentana 110, 00161 Roma. ✆ **06-44237773.** Fax 06-44237572. www.hotelvilladelparco.it. 30 units. 145€–180€ double; 192€ triple. Rates include breakfast. AE, DC, MC, V. Parking 20€. Bus: 90. **Amenities:** Bar; airport transfers (55€); babysitting; Internet (free, in lobby); room service. *In room:* A/C, TV, hair dryer, minibar.

AT THE AIRPORT

Expensive

Hotel Hilton Rome Airport At long last, Rome has a first-class airport hotel for late-night arrivals and early morning departures. Only 200m (656 ft.) from the air terminal, this hotel is approached via a skywalk. The Hilton doesn't pretend to be more than it is—a bedroom factory at the airport. Follow the broad hallways to one of the midsize to spacious "crash pads," each with deep carpeting, generous storage space, and large, full bathrooms. The best units are the executive suites, with luxuries such as separate check-in, and voice mail.

Via Arturo Ferrarin 2, 00050 Fiumicino. ✆ **800/445-8667** in the U.S. and Canada, or 06-65258. Fax 06-65256525. www.hilton.com. 517 units. 220€–380€ double; 345€–465€ suite. AE, DC, MC, V. Parking 25€. Metro: Fiumicino Aeroporto. **Amenities:** 2 restaurants; bar; babysitting; concierge; exercise room; Jacuzzi; indoor pool (heated in winter); room service; sauna; 2 outdoor tennis courts. *In room:* A/C, TV, hair dryer, minibar, Wi-Fi (27€ per day).

Moderate

Hotel Cancelli Rossi If you're nervous about making your flight, you could book into this very simple motel-style place, located 2.5km (1½ miles) from the airport. Two floors are served by an elevator, and the decor is minimal. Rooms range from small to medium and are functionally furnished but reasonably comfortable, with good beds, and clean tiled bathrooms with shower stalls. The atmosphere is a bit antiseptic, but this place is geared more for business travelers than vacationers. A restaurant in an annex nearby serves Italian and international food.

Via Portuense 2467, 00054 Fiumicino. ✆ **06-6507221.** Fax 06-65049168. www.cancellirossi.it. 50 units. 101€–160€ double. Rates include buffet breakfast. AE, DC, MC, V. Free parking. Bus shuttle costing 6€ from/to the Leonardo da Vinci airport Mon–Sat 7–9:45am and 5:15–8:55pm every 20 min. **Amenities:** Restaurant; bar; babysitting; exercise room; room service. *In room:* A/C, TV, hair dryer, minibar, Wi-Fi (12€ per day).

6 WHERE TO DINE IN ROME

Rome remains one of the world's great capitals for dining, with more diversity today than ever. Although most of the trattorie haven't changed their menus in a quarter of a century (except to raise prices), there's an increasing number of chic, upscale spots with chefs willing to experiment, as well as a growing handful of ethnic spots for those days when you just can't face another plate of pasta. The great thing about Rome is that you don't have to spend a fortune to eat really well.

It's difficult to compile a list of the best restaurants in a city such as Rome. Everyone—locals, expatriates, even those who have only visited once—has personal favorites and finds. What follows is not a comprehensive list of all the best restaurants of Rome, but simply a running commentary on a number of our favorites. For the most part, we've chosen not to review every deluxe spot known to all big spenders. We've chosen a handful of splurge restaurants where you'll really get what you pay for, and then we've reviewed a large selection of moderately priced and affordable restaurants where you'll get a wonderful meal, authentic cuisine, and a lovely experience without breaking the bank.

Roman meals customarily include at least three separate courses: pasta, a main course (usually a meat dish with vegetables or salad), and dessert. Meats, though tasty, are definitely secondary to the pasta dishes, which are generous and filling. The wine is so excellent (especially the local white Frascati wine) and affordable that you might want to do as the Romans do and have it with both lunch and dinner.

Roman Cuisine

Some visitors erroneously think of Italian cuisine as one-dimensional. Of course, everybody's heard of minestrone, spaghetti, chicken cacciatore, and spumoni ice cream. But chefs hardly confine themselves to such a limited repertoire.

Rome's cooking isn't subtle, but its kitchens rival anything that the chefs of Florence or Venice can turn out. The city's chefs borrow—and sometimes improve on—the cuisine of other regions. Throughout your Roman holiday you'll encounter such savory treats as *zuppa di pesce* (a soup or stew of various fish, cooked in white wine and herbs), *cannelloni* (tube-shape pasta baked with any number of stuffings), *riso col gamberi* (rice with shrimp, peas, and mushrooms, flavored with white wine and garlic), *scampi alla griglia* (grilled prawns, one of the best-tasting and most expensive dishes in the city), *quaglie con risotto e tartufi* (quail with rice and truffles), *lepre alla cacciatora* (hare flavored with tomato sauce and herbs), *zabaione* (a cream made with sugar, egg yolks, and Marsala), *gnocchi alla romana* (potato-flour dumplings with a sauce made with meat and covered with grated cheese), *stracciatella* (chicken broth with eggs and grated cheese), *abbacchio* (baby spring lamb, often roasted over an open fire), *saltimbocca alla romana* (literally "jump-in-your-mouth"—thin slices of veal with cheese, ham, and sage), *frittata alla romana* (a mixed fry that's likely to include everything from brains to artichokes), *carciofi alla romana* (tender artichokes cooked with mint and garlic, and flavored with white wine), *fettuccine all'uovo* (egg noodles served with butter and cheese), *zuppa di cozze o vongole* (a hearty bowl of mussels or clams cooked in broth), *fritto di scampi e calamaretti* (fast-fried baby squid and prawns), *fragoline* (wild strawberries, in this case from the Alban Hills), and *finocchio* (fennel, a celery-like raw vegetable, often eaten as a dessert and in salads).

Incidentally, except in the south, Italians don't use as much garlic in their food as most visitors seem to believe. Most northern Italian dishes are butter based. Virgin olive oil is preferred in the south. Spaghetti and meatballs is not an Italian dish, although certain restaurants throughout the country have taken to serving it for homesick Americans.

Wines & Other Drinks

Italy is the largest wine-producing country in the world; as far back as 800 B.C., the Etruscans were vintners. It's said that more soil is used in Italy for the cultivation of grapes than for growing food. Many Italian farmers produce wine just for their own consumption or for their relatives. It wasn't until 1965, however, that laws were enacted to guarantee regular consistency in winemaking. Wines regulated by the government are labeled DOC *(Denominazione di Origine Controllata)*. If you see DOCG on a label (the G means *garantita*), it means even better quality control.

Lazio (Rome's region) is a major wine-producing region of Italy. Many of the local wines come from the Castelli Romani, the hill towns around Rome. These wines, experts agree, are best drunk when they are young; and they are most often white, mellow, and dry (or else demi-sec). There are seven different types, including ***Falerno*** (yellowish straw in color) and ***Cecubo*** (often served with roast meat). Try also ***Colli Albani*** (straw-yellow with amber tints and served with both fish and meat). The golden-yellow wines of **Frascati** are famous, produced in both a demi-sec and a sweet variety, the latter served with dessert.

Romans drink other libations as well. Their most famous drink is **Campari,** bright red in color and herb flavored, with a quinine-like bitterness to it. It's customary to serve it with ice cubes and soda.

Beer is also made in Italy and, in general, is lighter than, say, German beer. If you order beer in a Roman bar or restaurant, chances are good that it will be imported unless you specify otherwise, and you'll be charged accordingly. Some famous names in European beer-making now operate plants in Italy, where the brew has been "adjusted" to Italian taste.

High-proof **grappa** is made from the leftovers after the grapes have been pressed. Many Romans drink this before or after dinner (some put it into their coffee). To an untrained foreign palate, it often seems harsh; some say it's an acquired taste.

Other popular drinks include several **liqueurs.** Try herb-flavored Strega, or perhaps an almond-flavored Amaretto. One of the best known is Maraschino, taking its name from a type of cherry used in its preparation. Galliano is also herb flavored, and Sambuca (anisette) is made of aniseed and is often served with a "fly" (coffee bean) in it. On a hot day, the true Roman orders a vermouth, Cinzano, with a twist of lemon, ice cubes, and a squirt of soda water.

NEAR STAZIONE TERMINI

Very Expensive

Agata e Romeo ★★ NEW ROMAN One of the most alluring places near the Vittorio Emanuele Monument is this striking restaurant done up in turn-of-the-20th-century Liberty style. You'll enjoy the creative cuisine of Romeo Caraccio (who manages the dining room) and his wife, Agata Parisella (who prepares her own version of sophisticated Roman food). Look for cream of borlotti beans, chestnuts, and shrimp wrapped in fried pasta noodles, as well as risotto with saffron, *taleggio* cheese, rabbit croquettes, and thyme. For an appetizer consider a flan of aged pecorino cheese from Sogliano with a pear sauce and chestnut honey. Yes, it sounds more like a dessert than a starter. For dessert, consider Agata's *millefoglie,* puff pastry stuffed with almonds and sweetened cream. There's a wine cellar with a wide choice of international and domestic wines.

Via Carlo Alberto 45. ✆ **06-4466115.** www.agataeromeo.it. Reservations recommended. All pastas 30€; meat and fish 40€. AE, DC, MC, V. Mon 8–10:30pm; Tues–Fri 1–2:30pm and 8–10:30pm. Closed Aug 13–Sept 11. Metro: Vittorio Emanuele.

Moderate

Il Quadrifoglio NEAPOLITAN Situated in a grandiose palace, this well-managed restaurant lets you sample the flavors and herbs of Naples and southern Italy. You'll find a tempting selection of antipasti, such as anchovies, peppers, capers, onions, and breaded and fried eggplant, all garnished with fresh herbs and virgin olive oil. Ever had anchovy cake with octopus? The pastas are made daily, usually with tomato- or oil-based sauces and always with herbs and aged cheeses. Try a zesty rice dish (one of the best is *sartù di riso,* studded with vegetables, herbs, and meats), followed by sautéed grouper fish rolls or a simple but savory *granatine* (meatballs, usually of veal, bound together with mozzarella). Dessert anyone? A longtime favorite is *torta caprese,* with hazelnuts and chocolate.

Via del Boschetto 19. ✆ **06-4826096.** Reservations recommended. Main courses 11€–16€. AE, DC, MC, V. Mon–Fri 12:30–3pm and 7pm–midnight; Sat 7pm–midnight. Closed Aug 5–25. Metro: Cavour.

Inexpensive

Monte Arci ROMAN/SARDINIAN On a cobblestone street near Piazza Indipendenza, this restaurant is set behind a sienna facade. It features cheap Roman and Sardinian specialties (you'll spend even less for pizza) such as *nialoreddus* (a regional form of gnocchetti); pasta with clams, lobster, or the musky-earthy notes of porcini

Dining near Stazione Termini, Via Veneto & Piazza Barberini

mushrooms; green and white spaghetti with bacon, spinach, cream, and cheese; and delicious lamb sausage flavored with herbs and pecorino cheese. It's all home cooking: hearty but not particularly creative.

Via Castelfirdardo 33. © **06-4941347.** www.ristorantemontearci.com. Reservations recommended. Main courses 8€-16€. AE, DC, V. Mon-Sat noon-3pm and 6-11:30pm. Closed Aug. Metro: Stazione Termini.

Ristorante Tullio ★ TUSCAN Established in 1945, this longtime favorite was once a dining citadel for Hollywood luminaries such as Henry Fonda and Clark Gable. It was never fancy, really a standard trattoria with cotton tablecloths and wooden chairs. But it quickly became known for its food, including its mozzarella which became famous. The menu is always kept simple and limited, but it reflects whatever is best in any season—perhaps truffles and mushrooms in the fall. Savor some of its specialties such as bread soup with beans and black cabbage, mushroom

TAKE A gelato BREAK

If you're craving luscious gelato, our top choice is **Giolitti ★★**, Via Uffici del Vicario 40 (✆ **06-6991243;** www.giolitti.it), the city's oldest ice-cream shop, open daily from 7am to 1:30am. You'll find the usual *vaniglia* (vanilla), *cioccolato* (chocolate), *fragola* (strawberry), and *caffé* (coffee), but you'll also find great combinations like *gianduia* (chocolate hazelnut), plus such treats as *cassata alla siciliana* (orange-flavored sponge cake with canola cream), zabaione (light custard flavored with Marsala-sweet wine), *mascarpone* (crème fraiche, double cream, and buttermilk), and *maron glace* (chestnuts in a vanilla and butter glaze). The preposterously oversize showpiece sundaes have names such as Coppa Olimpica (made with sponge cake, zabaione, nougat, chocolate, and a touch of liquor flavoring). Other ice-cream flavors include *stracciatella,* champagne, yogurt, coconut, peach, apricot, grape, mandarin, and blackberry.

Another favorite is the **Palazzo del Freddo Giovanni,** Via Principe Eugenio 65–67 (✆ **06-4464740**). More than 100 years old, this ice-cream outlet (part of a gelato factory) turns out yummy concoctions and specializes in rice ice cream. It's open Tuesday through Sunday from noon to 12:30am.

If you're fond of frothy *frullati* frappes, head to **Pascucci,** Via Torre Argentina 20 (✆ **06-6864816**), where blenders work all day grinding fresh fruit into delectable drinks. It's open Monday through Saturday from noon to 1am.

Prices at these shops range from 2€ to 8€.

salad with celery and cheese, or sliced beef grilled and garnished with fresh basil and Parmesan cheese. The location is in the center of Rome just off Piazza Barberini.

Via San Nicola da Tolentino 26. ✆ **06-4745560.** www.tulliioristorante.it. Reservations required. Main courses 7.50€–11€. AE, MC, V. Mon–Sat 12:30–3pm and 7–11pm. Closed Aug. Metro: Barberini.

Trimani Wine Bar ★ CONTINENTAL/WINE BAR Opened as a tasting center for French and Italian wines, spumantis, and liqueurs, this is an elegant wine bar with a stylish but informal decor and comfortable seating. More than 30 wines are available by the glass. To accompany them, you can choose from a bistro-style menu, with dishes such as salad niçoise, vegetarian pastas, herb-laden *fagiole* (bean soup), quiche, and Hungarian goulash. Also available is a wider menu, including meat and fish courses. The specialty is the large choice of little *bruschette* with cheese and prosciutto—the chef orders every kind of prosciutti and cheese, from all over Italy. The dessert specialty is *Verduzzo di Ronco di Viere* (chestnut mousse served with a sauce of white wine), covered by whipped cream and meringue.

Trimani maintains a well-stocked **Italian wine shop** about 37m (120 ft.) from its wine bar, at V. Goito 20 (✆ **06-4469661**), where an astonishing array of wines is for sale. The shop is open Monday to Friday 8:30am to 1:30pm and 3:30 to 8pm.

Via Goito 20. ✆ **06-4469661.** www.trimani.com. Reservations recommended. Main courses 8.50€–18€; glass of wine (depending on vintage) 2€–14€. AE, DC, MC, V. Mon–Sat 11:30am–3pm and 6pm–12:30am (in Dec open also on Sun). Closed 2 weeks in Aug. Metro: Repubblica or Castro Pretorio.

IN SAN LORENZO

To locate the restaurants reviewed below, see the "Dining near Stazione Termini, Via Veneto & Piazza Barberini" map above.

Inexpensive

Arancia Blu ★★ VEGETARIAN/ITALIAN Fabio Bassan and Enrico Bartolucci serve Rome's best vegetarian cuisine. Under soft lighting and wood ceilings, surrounded by wine racks and university intellectuals, the friendly waiters will help you compile a menu to fit any dietary need. The dishes at this trendy spot are inspired by peasant cuisines from across Italy and beyond. The appetizers range from hummus and tabbouleh to asparagus meatballs with a Bergamot tea sauce, soy sauce, and fresh ginger. The main courses might include lasagna with red onions, mushrooms, zucchini, and ginger; couscous *con verdure* (vegetable couscous); or an artichoke, potato, and mint pie with pecorino cheese sauce. The restaurant offers 250 wines and inventive desserts, such as dark-chocolate cake with warm orange sauce.

Via dei Latini 55–65 (at Via Arunci). ✆ **06-4454105.** Reservations highly recommended. Main courses 9€–15€. No credit cards. Daily 8pm–midnight (Sept–July Sun noon–3:30pm). Bus: 71.

NEAR VIA VENETO & PIAZZA BARBERINI

To locate the restaurants in this section, see the "Where to Dine near Stazione Termini, Via Veneto & Piazza Barberini" map above.

Very Expensive

Filippo La Mantia ★★ SICILIAN In the Liberty masterpiece, the Hotel Majestic from the end of the 19th century, a deluxe restaurant with a terrace opens onto the Via Veneto. In the elegant dining rooms, antique elements blend with a contemporary decor. Filippo La Mantia set out to revive the restaurant of a historical hotel, and he has succeeded admirably. The innovative entrance, overlooking the kitchens, lead to a grand lounge in the fin de siècle style, passing through a wine cellar.

The menu is mouthwatering, with dishes brimming over with bright ideas and pronounced flavors. The menu is first class yet rather unsophisticated. Take the starters—octopus salad with diced celery and lemon sauce or anchovy pie with a caper and wild fennel sauce. For the mains, try the couscous with lamb and its broth, or fried cuttlefish with an orange and fennel salad, perhaps baked black suckling Sicilian pig with a honey and citrus glaze. Top it off with roast baby pineapple and an exotic fruit sorbet.

Via Liguria 1. ✆ **06-42144715.** www.filippolamantia.com. Reservations recommended. Main courses 24€–45€. AE, DC, MC, V. Mon–Fri 12:30–2:30pm; Mon–Sat 8:30–11:30pm; Sun 12:30–3:30pm. Metro: Barberini.

La Terrazza ★★★ INTERNATIONAL/ITALIAN La Terrazza and Sapori del Lord Byron (p. 145) serve the city's finest cuisine, but here you get the added bonus of a sweeping view over St. Peter's. The service is formal and flawless, yet not intimidating. The chef, Adriano Cavagnini, is brilliant, creative, and dynamic; and he learned how to cook from his ancestors who founded a restaurant on Lake Garda in 1885. You might start with zucchini blossoms stuffed with ricotta and black olives, or lobster medallions with apple purée and black truffles. Other menu items include oven-baked sole in a crust of green olives, or breast of guinea fowl stuffed with braised endive, robiola cheese, and flavored with a rosemary jus.

M In the Hotel Eden, Via Ludovisi 49. ✆ **06-478121.** www.starwoodhotels.com. Reservations recommended. Jacket required. Main courses 34€–59€; fixed-price menu 110€. AE, DC, MC, V. Daily 12:30–2:30pm and 7:30–10:30pm. Metro: Barberini.

Moderate

Aurora 10 da Pino il Sommelier ITALIAN Skip the tourist traps along Via Veneto and walk another block or two for much better food and a crowd of regulars from the chic neighborhood. The waitstaff is welcoming to foreigners, although the service can be erratic. The place is noted for its array of more than 250 wines, representing every province. The mixed seafood appetizer is one of the best in Rome, a great bowlful of delights from the sea. The exquisite meat dishes include entrecôte with pink pepper sauce or veal escalope with asparagus. Among the more delectable desserts are crème brûlée and Neapolitan *babà,* filled with liqueur.

Via Aurora 10. ✆ **06-4742779.** www.aurora10.it. Reservations recommended. Main courses 14€–24€. AE, DC, MC, V. Tues–Sun noon–3pm and 7–11pm. Metro: Barberini.

Césarina ☺ BOLOGNESE/EMILIANA-ROMAGNOLA/ROMAN Specializing in the cuisines of Rome and the region around Bologna, this place is named for Césarina Masi, who opened it in 1960 (many old-timers fondly remember her strict supervision of the kitchen and how she lectured regulars who didn't finish their tagliatelle). Although Césarina died in the mid-1980s, her traditions are kept going by her family. This has long been a favorite of Roman families. The polite staff rolls a trolley from table to table laden with an excellent *bollito misto* (an array of well-seasoned boiled meats) and often follows with misto Césarina—four kinds of creamy, handmade pasta, each with a different sauce. Equally appealing are the saltimbocca (veal with ham) and the *cotoletta alla bolognese* (tender veal cutlet baked with ham and cheese). A dessert specialty is *semifreddo* Césarina with hot chocolate, so meltingly good that it's worth the 5 pounds you'll gain.

Via Piemonte 109. ✆ **06-4880828.** Reservations recommended. Main courses 9€–25€. AE, DC, MC, V. Mon–Sat 12:30–3pm and 7:30–11pm. Metro: Barberini. Bus: 910.

Colline Emiliane ★★ 🎁 BOLOGNESE/EMILIANA-ROMAGNOLA Serving the *classica cucina bolognese,* Colline Emiliane is a small, family-run place—the owner is the cook, and his wife makes the pasta (about the best you'll find in Rome). The house specialty is an inspired *tortellini alla panna* (with cream sauce and truffles), but the less-expensive pastas, including *maccheroni al funghetto* and *tagliatelle alla bolognese,* are excellent, too. As an opener, we suggest *culatello di Zibello,* a delicacy from a small town near Parma that's known for having the world's finest prosciutto. Main courses include *braciola di maiale* (boneless rolled pork cutlets stuffed with ham and cheese, breaded, and sautéed) and an impressive *giambonetto* (roast veal Emilian-style with roast potatoes).

Via degli Avignonesi 22 (off Piazza Barberini). ✆ **06-4817538.** Reservations highly recommended. Main courses 10€–20€. MC, V. Tues–Sun 12:45–2:45pm; Tues–Sat 7:45–10:45pm. Closed Aug. Metro: Barberini.

QUICK bites

Lunchtime offers you the perfect opportunity to savor Roman fast food: **pizza rustica,** by the slice (often called *pizza à taglio*), half wrapped in waxed paper for easy carrying. Just point to the bubbling, steaming sheet with your preferred toppings behind the counter; 2.50€ buys a healthy portion of "plain" tomato sauce: basil-and-cheese *pizza margherita. Pizza rossa* (just sauce) and *pizza con patate* (with cheese and potatoes) cost even less, as does the exquisitely simple *pizza bianca* (plain dough brushed with olive oil and sprinkled with salt and sometimes rosemary).

A **rosticceria** is a *pizza à taglio* with spits of chickens roasting in the window and a few pasta dishes kept warm in long trays. You can also sit down for a quick pasta or prepared meat dish steaming behind the glass counters at a **tavola calda** (literally "hot table") for about half the price of a trattoria. A Roman **bar,** though it does indeed serve liquor, is what we'd call a cafe, a place to grab a cheap panino (flat roll stuffed with meat, cheese, or vegetables) or *tramezzino* (large triangular sandwiches on white bread with the crusts cut off).

Tuna ★ SEAFOOD This seafood emporium in the center of Rome, overlooking the via Veneto, is dedicated to serving some of the freshest fish in the capital. Not only is the fish fresh, but the chef requires it to be of optimum quality. From crayfish to sea truffles, from oysters to sea urchins, the fish is turned into platters of delight with perfect seasonings and preparation. Started with the midget mussels or the octopus salad or else calamari and artichoke tempura. For a main course, the catch of the day is in general the best choice, or else you may order sliced sea bass with chives and fresh thyme.

Via Veneto11. ✆ **06-4201-6531.** www.tunaroma.it. Reservations required. Main courses 15€–30€. AE, DC, MC, V. Mon–Fri 12:30–3pm; daily 7:30pm–midnight. Closed 2 weeks in Aug. Metro: Barberini.

NEAR CAMPO DE' FIORI & THE JEWISH GHETTO

Very Expensive

Camponeschi ★★ ROMAN/SEAFOOD The fish dishes served here are legendary, and so is the front-row view of the Piazza Farnese. The cuisine is creative, refined, and prepared with only the freshest of ingredients, with a superb wine list guaranteed to appeal to even the most demanding oenophiles. The chefs work hard to make their reputation anew every night, and they succeed admirably with such dishes as lobster with black truffles and raspberry vinegar for an appetizer, or foie gras with port and sultana. We love their generous use of truffles, particularly in a masterpiece of a dish, tagliolini soufflé flavored with white truffles. Among the more succulent pastas is one made with a roe deer sauce. As fine as the meat dishes are, we always enjoy the seafood, too, especially the shrimp with vermouth served with rice pilaf or the filet of turbot with grapes.

Piazza Farnese 50. ✆ **06-6874927.** www.ristorantecamponeschi.it. Reservations required. Main courses 25€–50€. MC, V. Mon–Sat 7:30pm–midnight. Closed 2 weeks in Aug. Metro: Piazza Argentina.

Expensive

Il Drappo ★ SARDINIAN A favorite of the local artsy crowd, Il Drappo lies on a narrow street near the Tiber. You have your choice of two tastefully decorated dining rooms festooned with patterned cotton draped from the ceiling. Fixed-price dinners reflecting diverse choices might begin with wafer-thin *carte di musica* (literally, "sheet-music paper"), a flat, layered bread topped with tomatoes, green peppers, parsley, and olive oil; and then followed with fresh spring lamb in season or fish stew made with tuna caviar. Other temptations on the menu include baked peppers stuffed with artichokes; oven-baked filet of grouper with olives and capers; and a mixed seafood grill of calamari, shrimp, and scampi. The chef's cuisine is a marvelous change of pace from the typical Roman diet, with an inventiveness that keeps us coming back.

Vicolo del Malpasso 9. ✆ **06-6877365.** www.ildrappo.it. Reservations required. Main courses 10€–24€; fixed-price menu 50€. AE, MC, V. Mon–Sat 1–3pm and 7pm–midnight. Closed Aug 12–31. Bus: 46, 62, or 64.

Piperno ★ JEWISH/ROMAN This longtime favorite, opened in 1856 and now run by the Mazzarella and Boni families, celebrates the Jerusalem artichoke (which is not really an artichoke at all, by the way) by incorporating it into a number of recipes. The advice and suggestions put forth by the uniformed crew of hardworking waiters are worth considering. You might begin with aromatic *fritto misto vegetariano* (artichokes, cheese-and-rice croquettes, mozzarella, and stuffed squash blossoms) before moving on to a fish filet, veal, succulent beans, or a pasta creation. Many of the foods are fried or deep-fried but emerge flaky and dry, not at all greasy.

Via Monte de' Cenci 9. ✆ **06-68806629.** www.ristorantepiperno.it. Reservations recommended. Main courses 18€–20€. DC, MC, V. Tues–Sat 12:45–2:20pm and 7:45–10:20pm; Sun 1–2:30pm. Closed Aug. Bus: 23.

Moderate

Ditirambo ★ 🎁 ITALIAN/ROMAN Close to Campo de' Fiori, this is the classic Roman trattoria you dream of finding but rarely do. An antiques dealer, a marketing manager, an actor, and wine merchant bonded to create this simple yet warm-hearted restaurant, a cross between an old-fashioned French bistro and a Roman *hosteria*. All the bread, pasta, and desserts are homemade fresh daily, and the wine list of 200 different vintages comes from 20 different Italian regions. Enticing appetizers range from octopus with chickpeas to Adriatic mackerel stewed in fresh tomato sauce. We prefer the grilled fish of the day, though you may opt for crisp potatoes with cheese fondue and truffle slivers or tagliolini with a julienne of artichokes, pork cheek, and aged ewe's cheese.

Piazza della Cancelleria 74. ✆ **06-6871626.** www.ristoranteditirambo.it. Reservations recommended. Main courses 8.50€–18€. MC, V. Tues–Sun 1–3pm; daily 7:30–11:30pm. Bus: 40, 46, 62, 64, 87, or 492.

Ristorante da Pancrazio ROMAN This place is popular as much for its archaeological interest as for its good food. One of its two dining rooms is decorated in the style of an 18th-century tavern; the other occupies the premises of Pompey's ancient theater and is lined in carved capitals and bas-reliefs. In this historic setting,

Dining near Campo de' Fiori, the Jewish Ghetto & Piazza Navona

you can enjoy time-tested Roman food. Two particular classics are peppered with skill: saltimbocca and tender roast lamb with potatoes. Some superb main courses include beef rolls stuffed with ham, carrots, and celery in a tomato sauce; baby lamb's ribs fried with artichokes; and grouper in a zucchini flower sauce.

Piazza del Biscione 92. ✆ **06-6861246.** www.dapancrazio.it. Reservations recommended. Main courses 13€–25€. AE, DC, MC, V. Thurs–Tues noon–3pm and 7:30–11:15pm. Closed 3 weeks in Aug (dates vary). Bus: 46, 62, or 64.

Ristorante del Pallaro ★★ ROMAN The stern woman in white who emerges in clouds of steam from the bustling kitchen is owner Paola Fazi, who runs two simple dining rooms where value-conscious Romans go for good food at bargain prices. (She also claims—although others dispute it—that Julius Caesar was assassinated on this very site.) The fixed-price menu is the only choice and has made the place famous. Ms. Fazi prepares everything as if she were feeding her extended family. As you sit down, your antipasto, the first of eight courses, appears. Then comes the pasta of the day, followed by roast veal, white meatballs, or (on Fri) dried cod, along with potatoes and eggplant. For your final courses, you're served mozzarella, cake with custard, and fruit in season. The meal also includes bread, mineral water, and half a liter of the house wine. If you're faint-of-heart and not used to Roman rudeness, seek another address for dining.

Largo del Pallaro 15. ✆ **06-68801488.** Reservations recommended. Fixed-price menu 25€. No credit cards. Tues–Sun noon–3:15pm and 7:30pm–12:30am. Closed Aug 10–25. Bus: 40, 46, 60, 62, or 64.

Vecchia Roma ITALIAN/ROMAN Vecchia Roma is a charming, moderately priced trattoria in the heart of the Ghetto. Movie stars have frequented the place, sitting at the crowded tables in one of the four small dining rooms. The owners are known for their frutti di mare (fruit of the sea), a selection of briny fresh seafood. The minestrone is made with fresh vegetables, and an intriguing selection of antipasti, including salmon or vegetables, is always available. The pastas and risottos are savory, spaghetti with squid ragout and shrimp, or linguine with broccoli and clams. The chef's specialties are lamb and *spigola* (a type of whitefish).

Via della Tribuna di Campitelli 18. ✆ **06-6864604.** www.ristorantevecchiaroma.com. Reservations recommended. Main courses 14€–20€. AE, DC, MC, V. Thurs–Tues 1–3:30pm and 8–11pm. Closed 10 days in Aug. Bus: 64, 90, 90B, 97, or 774. Metro: Colosseo.

Inexpensive

Vegetarians looking for monstrous salads (or anyone who just wants a break from heavy meats and starches) can find great food at the neighborhood branch of **Insalata Ricca,** Largo dei Chiavari 85 (✆ **06-68803656;** www.linsalataricca.it).

NEAR PIAZZA NAVONA & THE PANTHEON

To locate these restaurants, see the "Dining near Campo de' Fiori, the Jewish Ghetto & Piazza Navona" map on p. 125.

Very Expensive

La Rosetta ★★ SEAFOOD You won't find any red meat on the menu at this sophisticated choice near Piazza Navona, where the Riccioli family has been directing operations since the mid-1960s. This is one of Rome's best seafood restaurants. An excellent start is insalata di frutti di mare, studded with squid, lobster, octopus, and shrimp. Menu items include just about every fish native to the Mediterranean, as well as a few from the Atlantic coast of France. There's even a sampling of lobster imported from Maine, which can be boiled with drawn butter or served Catalan style with tomatoes, red onions, and wine sauce. Tuck into such main dish delights as risotto with clams and a sweet-onion sauce; spaghetti with red mullet ragout, black olives, and capers; or wild sea bass in lemon sauce with crispy prawns and fresh asparagus.

Via della Rosetta 8–9. ✆ **06-6861002.** www.larosetta.com. Reservations recommended. Main courses 22€–60€. AE, DC, MC, V. Mon–Sat 12:45–2:45pm and 7:30–11pm; Sun 7:30–11pm. Closed Aug 3–25. Bus: 70. Metro: Spagna.

Quinzi & Gabrieli ★★★ SEAFOOD We've never found better or fresher seafood than what's served in this 15th-century building. Don't be put off by the rough-and-ready service; just enjoy the great food. Alberto Quinzi and Anna Gabrieli earned their reputation on their simply cooked and presented fresh fish, such as sea urchin, octopus, sole, and red mullet. They're also known for their raw seafood, including a delicate carpaccio of swordfish, sea bass, and deep-sea shrimp. The house specialty is spaghetti with scampi and white truffles. In summer, French doors lead to a small dining terrace.

Via delle Coppelle 5–6, 00185 Roma. ✆ **06-6879389.** www.quinziegabrieli.it. Reservations recommended. Main courses 25€–40€. AE, DC, MC, V. Tues–Fri 12:30–2:30pm and 7:45–11pm; Sat 7:45–11pm. Closed Aug. Bus: C3, 30, 70, 81,130, or 186.

Expensive

Il Convivio ★★★ INTERNATIONAL/ROMAN This is one of the most acclaimed restaurants in Rome—and one of the very few to have a coveted Michelin star. Its 16th-century building is a classic setting in pristine white with accents of wood. The Troiano brothers turn out an inspired cuisine based on the best and freshest ingredients at the market. Start with caramelized tuna fish with chestnut honey, ginger, green pepper, rosemary, and green apple purée. Other tantalizing menu items include spaghetti with a ragout of sole, artichokes, and tuna roe; breast of guinea fowl in a mustard crust; and salt cod confit with tomatoes, spring onions, olives, Jerusalem artichokes, and eggplant.

Vicolo dei Soldati 31. ✆ **06-6869432.** www.ilconviviotroiani.com. Reservations required. Main courses 28€–44€. AE, DC, MC, V. Mon–Sat 8–11pm. Bus: 40 or 64. Metro: Spagna.

Il Sanlorenzo MEDITERRANEAN/SEAFOOD Right off the Piazza Navonna with its tourist trap restaurants is a bastion of good food and service, all at a moderate price. The decor is both sophisticated and contemporary, with antique wood furniture, plus modern art adorning the walls. Inspired by the bounty of the fields and streams of Latium, the chefs adroitly prepare a cuisine of simplicity and elegance. Try the spaghetti with sea urchins, a real delicacy, or else the risotto with tiger prawns and black truffles. Paccheri is another homemade pasta dish, this one served with swordfish, aubergine (eggplant), and smoked provola cheese. You might start with savory seafood fish soup. Small calamari appear in a delectable fry, or else you can order grilled dentice (a whitefish) with seafood sauce. For dessert, why not the chocolate soup with vanilla ice cream and a raspberry meringue?

Via del Chiavari 4–5. ✆ **06-6865097.** www.ilsanlorenzo.it. Reservations required. Main courses 18€–37€; fixed-price menu 75€. AE, DC, MC, V. Tues–Fri 12:30–3pm and 7:30–11:30pm; Sat–Mon 7:30–11:30pm. Closed 3 weeks in Aug. Bus: 60 or 64.

Moderate

Alfredo alla Scrofa INTERNATIONAL/ROMAN Yes, folks, this is one of two places in Rome claiming to have created fettuccine Alfredo, which almost seems as well known abroad today as it is in Italy. Douglas Fairbanks and Mary Pickford liked this dish so much they presented a golden spoon and fork to the owners when they parted with the recipe. Although the fettuccine is the star of the menu, you can also try a pasta dish that's a little lighter and healthier, like *tagliolini allo scoglio,* served with fresh tomatoes and shellfish. Inventive cookery and sublime ingredients are reflected in such main dishes as pan-fried dumplings with prawns and pumpkin, baked sea bass with wild mushrooms, or filet of turbot in a broccoli and potato crust.

Via della Scrofa 104. ✆ **06-68806163.** www.alfredoallascrofa.com. Reservations recommended. Main courses 11€–22€. AE, DC, MC, V. Daily 12:30–3pm and 7:30–11:30pm. Bus: 87, 492, or 680. Metro: Spagna.

Boccondivino ★ ITALIAN Part of the fun of this restaurant involves wandering through historic Rome to reach it. Inside you'll find delicious food and an engaging mix of Italian Renaissance and imperial and ancient Rome, thanks to recycled columns salvaged from ancient monuments. The hiply dressed staff serve as a tip-off, though, that the menu is completely up to date. You might find fettuccine with shellfish and parsley; carpaccio of beef; various risottos, including a version with black truffles; and grilled steaks and veal. Especially intriguing is whipped codfish resting on spikes of polenta, or grilled ravioli stuffed with scorpion fish and served with pumpkin flower sauce. If you're a seafood lover, look for either the marinated and grilled salmon or a particularly subtle blend of roasted turbot stuffed with foie gras. Desserts feature seasonal fruit, perhaps marinated pineapple or fruit-studded house-made ice creams. The restaurant's name, incidentally, translates as "divine mouthful."

Piazza in Campo Marzio 6. ✆ **06-68308626.** www.boccondivino.it. Reservations required. Main courses 12€–16€; fixed-price lunch 25€. AE, DC, MC, V. Tues–Sat 12:30–3pm and 7:30–11:30pm; Sun 12:30–3pm. Bus: 87 or 175.

Café Mancini Ristorante dal 1905 ITALIAN/SEAFOOD Near the Pantheon and Piazza Navona, this restaurant was originally established in Naples in 1905—hence its name. Five generations of the Mancini family have since turned out a sublime cuisine based on regional fare and fish dishes from their native Campania. The chefs pay special attention to the products of the season. We can make a meal out of the delectable appetizers, especially the *delizie di mare* with a tuna tartare and a skewer of prawns in a taglioni pasta. It comes with a very soft sea bass carpaccio. Or else you might prefer *sfizi di cicci bacco,* with mozzarella, Parma ham, beef tartare, and zucchini flowers. All the pastas are homemade, including fettuccine with prawns and almond pesto sauce. A favorite dish here includes grilled squid with potatoes, zucchini, and a black olive sauce. The setting is elegant and formal, the service top-notch.

Via Metastasio 21. ✆ **06-6872051.** www.cafemancini.com. Reservations recommended. Main courses 7€–25€. AE, DC, MC, V. Mon–Sat noon–3pm and 7–11:30pm. Bus: 44, 46, 55, 60, 61, 62, 64, or 65.

Café Riccioli ★ ITALIAN/JAPANESE Stylish and hip, this restaurant builds its reputation on its sashimi-style raw fish, plus a menu of sophisticated and upscale Italian cuisine. The setting is a trio of artfully minimalist dining rooms painted in bright primary colors; after lunch and dinner, this place becomes a buzzing late-night cafe. Dishes include platters of sashimi, priced at around 50€; salads of raw marinated hake with Italian herbs; and more substantial fare such as roast beef with green apples; sea bass with mango sauce; and richly textured chocolate tortes laced with Marsala wine.

Via delle Coppelle 13. ✆ **06-68210313.** www.ricciolicafe.com. Reservations recommended. Main courses 15€–50€. AE, DC, MC, V. Mon–Sat 10am–3:30pm and 6:30pm–2am. Closed Aug 6–20. Metro: Spagna. Bus: 64 or 492. Tram: 8.

Il Bacaro ★ ITALIAN Unpretentious and very accommodating to foreigners, this restaurant contains only about a half-dozen tables and operates from an ivy-edged hideaway alley near Piazza di Spagna. The restaurant is well known for its fresh and tasty cheese. This was a palazzo in the 1600s, and some vestiges of the building's former grandeur remain. The offerings are time-tested and flavorful: carpaccio of smoked grouper in a tomato sauce with fresh oregano; swordfish roulades stuffed with shrimp, radicchio, and zucchini; or filet of beef in a fresh basil sauce. Pastas come in unusual and tasty combinations, including spaghetti with shrimp, pumpkin flowers, saffron, and coriander.

Via degli Spagnoli 27, near Piazza delle Coppelle. ✆ **06-6872554.** www.ilbacaro.com. Reservations recommended. Main courses 11€–20€. DC, MC, V. Mon–Sat 8pm–midnight. Metro: Spagna.

L'Eau Vive ★ 🎁 FRENCH/INTERNATIONAL Here you'll find an elegant dining experience with unique food and atmosphere. Fine French cuisine and a daily exotic dish are prepared and served by a lay sisterhood of missionary Christians from five continents who dress in traditional costumes. Nonsmokers can skip the plain stuccoed vaulting downstairs and head to the 16th-century Palazzo Lantante della Rovere, where the high ceilings are gorgeously frescoed. You never know until you arrive what will be on the menu. We've enjoyed beef filet flambé with cognac, toasted goat cheese coated with mustard and almond slivers, and duck filet in Grand Marnier sauce with puff-fried potatoes. At 10pm, when most customers are finished with dinner, the recorded classical music is interrupted so that the sisters can sing the "Ave Maria of Lourdes," and some evenings, they interpret a short Bible story in ballet.

Via Monterone 85. ✆ **06-68801095.** www.restaurant-eauvive.it. Reservations recommended. Main courses 7.50€–23€; fixed-price menus 14€–35€. AE, MC, V. Mon–Sat 12:30–2:30pm and 7:30–10:30pm. Closed Aug. Bus: 64, 70, 81, 87, or 115.

Osteria dell'Antiquario ★ 🎁 INTERNATIONAL/ROMAN This virtually undiscovered osteria enjoys a good location a few blocks down the Via dei Coronari as you leave the Piazza Navona and head toward St. Peter's. In a stone-built stable from the 1500s, Osteria dell'Antiquario has three dining rooms used in winter. In nice weather, try to get an outdoor table on the terrace; shaded by umbrellas, they face a view of the Palazzo Lancillotti. We like to begin with the sautéed shellfish (usually mussels and clams), or you could opt for the risotto with porcini mushrooms. For a main course, try grilled lamb chops with a mint sauce, or a risotto with pumpkin flowers, scampi, and saffron.

Piazzetta di S. Simeone 26–27, Via dei Coronari. ✆ **06-6879694.** www.osteriadellantiquario.com. Reservations recommended. Main courses 14€–26€. AE, DC, MC, V. Daily 7:30–11pm. Closed 15 days in mid-Aug, Christmas, and Jan 1–10. Bus: 70, 87, or 90.

Osteria dell'Ingegno ROMAN This is another offbeat trattoria in the vicinity of the much-trodden Piazza Navona. The menu is simple but fairly innovative, and it's adjusted seasonally. The restaurant is decorated in a rather modern style and is warmly welcoming and inviting. The chefs are experts in the use of aromatic herbs and spices, and their dishes are full of flavor. Among our favorite samplings are the walnut-filled ravioli in a sublime cheese sauce, or else codfish fritters with yellow polenta and a Gorgonzola fondue. A true favorite that made us want to return is the roast duck with a sweet-and-sour sauce flavored with wine and raisins.

Piazza di Pietra 45. ✆ **06-6780662.** Reservations required. Main courses 11€–26€. AE, DC, MC, V. Mon–Sat noon–3pm and 7pm–midnight. Closed 2 weeks in Aug (dates vary). Metro: Colosseo.

Inexpensive

Al Bric ITALIAN With four separate and artfully minimalist dining rooms in a 16th-century building close to Campo de' Fiori, this well-managed restaurant combines creative cooks with a polite and efficient waitstaff. Many of the dishes include dollops of goat or herbed cheese, or French brie, flavors that seem to make the wines taste even better. Menu items are based on a combination of traditional and creative modern cuisine. The best examples include spaghetti with anchovies and pecorino cheese, or else another delectable pasta—handmade pappardella with wild boar sauce and Italian sausage. Diners might also enjoy tuna fish stroganoff seasoned with thyme and served in a delicate squid sauce.

Via del Pellegrino 51. ✆ **06-6879533.** www.albric.it. Reservations recommended. Main courses 14€–22€. AE, MC, V. Tues–Sat 7:30–11:30pm; Sun 12:30–2:30pm and 7:30–11:30pm. Closed Aug. Bus: 64.

Filetti di Baccalà FISH/ITALIAN This eatery is dedicated to battered, deep-fried filets of salt cod, long a Roman favorite. The location in the heart of Rome lies off two landmark squares, Piazza Navona and Piazza Campo de Fiori. In a rustic setting, it offers outdoor tables in fair weather. This is a small, snug restaurant that serves a few dishes, other than cod, including golden fried slices of zucchini (courgette). Cold beer is on tap, and there's also bruschette along with plates of beans with onions. In winter, an absolutely delectable salad of puntarelle is served. That's crunchy chicory stems in a savory vinaigrette laced with anchovies, garlic, and lemon.

Largo dei Librari 88. ✆ **06-6864018.** Reservations not accepted. Main courses 6€–9€. No credit cards. Mon–Sat 5–10:30pm. Bus: 64.

Il Miraggio ROMAN/SARDINIAN/SEAFOOD You might want to escape the roar of traffic along Via del Corso by ducking into this informal spot on a crooked side street (about midway between Piazza Venezia and Piazza Colonna). It's a cozy neighborhood setting with rich and savory flavor in every dish. The risotto with scampi, and the fettuccine with porcini mushrooms will have you begging for more. Some dishes are classic, such as roast lamb with potatoes, but others are more inventive, such as sliced stew beef with arugula. We're fond of the house specialty, *spaghetti alla bottarga* with roe sauce, especially if it's followed by *spigola alla vernaccia* (sea bass sautéed in butter and vernaccia wine). For dessert, try the typical Sardinian *seadas,* thin-rolled pastry filled with fresh cheese, fried, and served with honey.

Vicolo Sciarra 59. ✆ **06-6780226.** Reservations recommended. Main courses 10€–19€. AE, MC, V. Daily 11am–11pm. Closed 15 days in Jan. Metro: Barberini. Bus: 62, 95, 117, 119, 160, 175, or 492.

Insalata Ricca 2 ITALIAN/VEGETARIAN This choice fulfills a need for more vegetarian restaurants and lighter, low-fat fare in Rome. Most people call ahead for an outdoor table, although on summer days you might prefer the smoke-free, air-conditioned inside. The more popular of the oversize salads are the *baires* (lettuce, rughetta, celery, walnuts, apples, Gorgonzola) and *siciliana* (lettuce, rughetta, sun-dried tomatoes, green olives, corn, hard salted ricotta). Also on the menu are dishes such as *gnocchi verdi al gorgonzola* (spinach gnocchi with Gorgonzola sauce) and *pasta integrale* (whole-wheat pasta in tomato-and-basil sauce). A few meat dishes are also served. The branches near Campo de' Fiori and near the Vatican (mentioned under their respective neighborhoods) offer the same basic menu, which can be a refreshing relief after too many days of heavy meals and rich sauces.

Piazza Pasquino 72 (southwest of Piazza Navona). ✆ **06-68307881.** www.linsalataricca.it. Reservations recommended. Main courses 8€–20€. AE, DC, MC, V. Daily noon–4pm and 6:30pm–midnight. Bus: 40, 64, or 70.

L'Orso 80 ★ ROMAN/SEAFOOD Fleeing the fancy-schmancy places on Piazza Navona, we recently discovered this nugget on an unpretentious street north and a little west of the Piazza Navona. In-the-know locals have been recommending its fabulous array of tasty Roman dishes for years. The antipasti selection is absolutely delightful, and we quickly plowed into mushrooms with whole peppercorns, succulent little baby artichokes, cauliflower flavored with capers, freshly made mozzarella, fried zucchini fingers, and *fagioli* (beans) in tomato sauce. Terrific main courses include fresh grilled fish; pasta with porcini mushrooms; and our favorite, *abbacchio allo spiedo* (lamb on the spit). End your meal with ricotta cake, a real Roman specialty.

Via dell'Orso 33. ✆ **06-6861710.** www.orso80.it. Reservations recommended. Main courses 8€–18€. AE, DC, MC, V. Tues–Sun 1–3:30pm and 7–11:30pm. Closed in Aug and Dec 24–26. Metro: Lepanto.

Macheroni ROMAN Here in the heart of Rome you can dine in a rustic tavern enjoying traditional Roman food more often found in the Latium countryside. The decor is informal, with wood-paneled walls and pop art, and on a good night the place seats 160 satisfied diners, both visitors and locals. Pasta is the house specialty, and it doesn't get better than the spaghetti with bacon and onion. Also recommended are *maccheroni alla matriciana* (a pasta that comes in a red version with tomatoes, bacon, and pecorino cheese; and a white version that skips the tomatoes). Some very tender and juicy beefsteaks are also served. A well-chosen wine list includes a house chianti.

Piazza della Coppelle 44. ✆ **06-68307895.** www.ristorantemaccheroni.com. Reservations recommended. Main courses 10€–18€. AE, MC, V. Daily 1–3pm and 8pm–midnight. Metro: Spagna. Bus: 64, 70, 75, or 116.

Õbikã ★ CHEESE/MEDITERRANEAN For some a mozzarella bar will be a first-time dining experience. It operates somewhat like a sushi bar—in fact, the decor is Japanese inspired—but the main offering is mozzarella cheese in all its various combinations. The buffalo cheese is delivered fresh daily to the restaurant from the Campania region to the South, with a very creamy burrata variety shipped in from Puglia. Perhaps the most popular item is fried and breaded mozzarella served with crispy wholemeal bread. You are not confined just to mozzarella but can sample such dishes as fresh Sicilian vegetables; a very spicy salami from Calabria; an organic tomato soup made with fresh basil; or else various pastas, including one with a basil pesto and zucchini. Rolled and sliced mozzarella is also served with wild smoked salmon and fresh arugula. The location lies off the landmark Piazza Navona.

Piazza di firenzn 26. ✆ **06-6832630.** www.obika.it. Reservations recommended. Main courses 8.50€-15€. AE, DC, MC, V. Daily 10am-midnight. Bus: 116.

Osteria del Gallo ★ 🎁 ROMAN You can escape the tourist traps of the Piazza Navona by seeking out this place in a narrow little alley off the west/northwest side of the fabled square. It's tiny, with a lovely area for outdoor seating, and definitely off the beaten track. The chef/owner comes out to take your order personally and is justly proud of his homemade pastas. Menu items include a variety of fresh fish dishes roasted in a salt crust to retain their juice and flavor. Other favorites include homemade gnocchi with clams and arugula or spigola fish baked under a potato crust. The homemade desserts include one of the best tiramisus in the area and a traditional favorite, *panna cotta*, an Italian pudding made with cooked fresh cream.

Vicolo di Montevecchio 27. ✆ **06-6873781.** www.osteriadelgalloroma.it. Reservations highly recommended. Main courses 7€-17€. MC, V. Wed-Mon 11:30am-3pm and 6:30-11pm. Closed Aug 8-25 (dates may vary). Metro: Spagna.

NEAR PIAZZA DEL POPOLO & THE SPANISH STEPS

Very Expensive

Imàgo ★★★ INTERNATIONAL/ITALIAN Great food and a sweeping panorama of Ancient Rome lure patrons to the sixth floor of this deluxe hotel on the Spanish Steps. There's so much talk of the view that it is easy to overlook the superb traditional Italian cuisine. The brilliant chef, Francesco Apreda, a Neapolitan, serves Italian food that's influenced by the rest of the world—for example, sea bass with a ginger sauce evocative of Thailand. You are likely to see Italy's leader, Silvio Berlusconi, feasting on pheasant ravioli with truffles. Apreda delights guests with such delectable dishes as breaded sea scallops stuffed with mozzarella and black truffles, or fusilloni pasta with a quail ragout. For dessert, why not the Sicilian cannoli filled with mascarpone cheese and pistachios, served with a raspberry and star anise sorbet?

In the Hotel Hassler, Piazza della Trinità dei Monti 6. ✆ **06-69934726.** www.imagorestaurant.com. Reservations required. Jacket and tie for men at dinner. Main courses 29€-45€. AE, DC, MC, V. Daily 7-10:30pm. Metro: Spagna.

Expensive

Brunello Ristorante ★★ ITALIAN This chicly modern bar, lounge, and restaurant is helping bring back the Via Veneto as an elegant rendezvous place. Your martini will arrive with a few drops of Chanel No. 5 rubbed along its glass stalk. Earthy tones such as brown dominate among the wallcoverings and the upholstered seating in autumnal shades. The menu is impressively innovative, with fresh ingredients that explode in your mouth. Chef Daniele Sera likes to experiment in such dishes as sautéed wild gooseliver in Armagnac sauce and chocolate flakes. Or start with lightly cooked cinnamon-flavored tuna with green apple; going on to such mains as tagliolini with wild fennel, raisins, and fresh anchovies; or perhaps swordfish stuffed with Sicilian salad. The wine cellar boasts 500 labels from every region of Italy.

In the Regina Hotel Baglioni, Via Vittorio Veneto 72. ✆ **06-48902867.** Reservations recommended. Main courses 18€-29€. AE, DC, MC, V. Restaurant Mon-Sat 12:30-3pm and 7:30-11pm. Lounge Mon-Sat noon-1am. Metro: Spagna.

Dining near the Spanish Steps & Ancient Rome

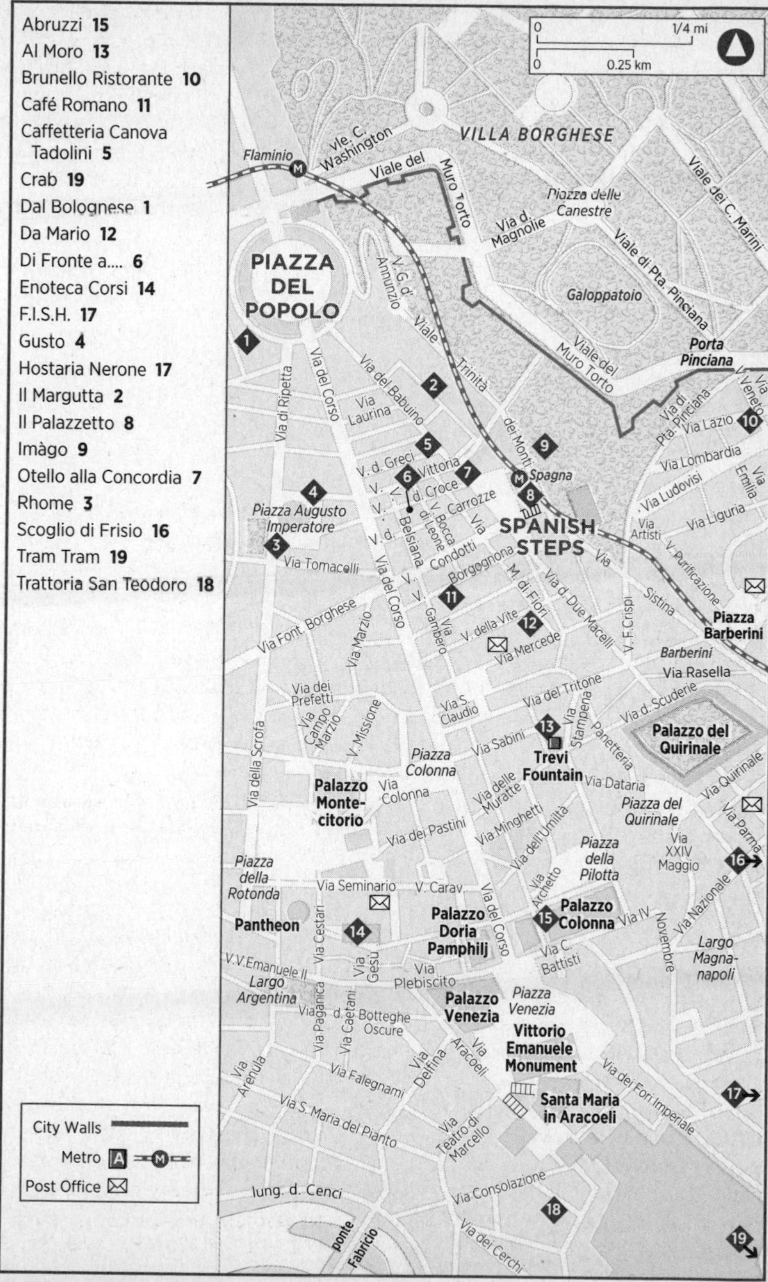

Rhome ★★ ITALIAN The name of the restaurant is a fusion of the words Rome and home. The restaurant and its cuisine are modern and innovative. The chef cleverly selects appropriate herbs, spices, and fresh vegetables, which he transforms into classic dishes such as fettuccine with artichokes and saffron; tonnarelli with goat cheese and sweet red peppers; or simple but tasty, the veal meatballs with creamy mashed potatoes. The bean soup with field chicory is some of the best we've had, and in season you might delight in the deer medallions with chestnut honey. Later in the evening, diners enjoy music selected by a DJ, or, on occasion, live entertainment.

Piazza Augusto Imperatore 42-48. ✆ **06-68301430.** www.ristoranterhome.com. Reservations required. Main courses 18€-35€. AE, DC, MC, V. Sun-Fri noon-3pm and 8-11:30pm; Sat 8-11:30pm. Closed 2 weeks in Aug. Metro: Spagna.

Moderate

Al Moro ★ ITALIAN This 1929 trattoria is a difficult-to-locate place behind the Trevi Fountain. Franco, the son of founding father Moro, is in charge. You're not a true Roman until Franco has thrown you out of his joint at least once. In spite of his scowling, locals recommend that you persevere and get a table. Once you've overcome the initial hostility at the door, you're served some of the most authentic specialties in Rome, including crispy baby goat roasted dark golden and flavored with fresh rosemary. Our favorite vegetables are the crispy fried artichokes. As far as pasta goes, we love the light version of spaghetti carbonara served here. The chef likes to cook with salt, so be sure not to salt anything before you taste it. The wine list is one of the most unusual in the capital.

Vicolo delle Bollette 13. ✆ **06-6783495.** www.ristorantealmororoma.com. Reservations required. Main courses 15€-28€. MC, V. Mon-Sat 1-3:30pm and 7:30-11:30pm. Closed Aug. Metro: Spagna. Bus: 60 or 62.

Café Romano ★ INTERNATIONAL On the most exclusive "fashion street" of Rome, this stylish venue is annexed to the landmark Hotel d'Inghilterra. The cafe can serve you throughout the day, beginning with a late breakfast or concluding with a post theater dinner well after midnight. Two salons are divided by an arch resting on two columns under a barrel-vaulted ceiling with padded settees. The atmosphere is cosmopolitan, with an eclectic, well-chosen menu. You can taste dishes from around the world: from moussaka to fish couscous, from the Lebanese *mezze* (appetizers) to Chicago rib-eye steak, from the Thai-like green chicken curry to the Japanese-inspired salmon teriyaki. Flavors are beautifully blended in such starters as smoked goose breast with candied peaches or beef tartare with thyme-flavored mushrooms. Among the more appealing mains are homemade fusili pasta with wild mushrooms, smoked bacon, and Parmesan, or sautéed roast tuna served with sweet peppers, olives, and capers. Everything is served on fine bone china with silver cutlery and crystal glassware.

In the Hotel d'Inghiterra, Via Borgognona 4. ✆ **06-699811.** www.royaldemeure.com. Main courses 19€-40€. AE, DC, MC, V. Daily noon-10:30pm. Metro: Piazza di Spagna.

Dal Bolognese ★ BOLOGNESE/EMILIANA-ROMAGNOLA This is one of those rare, chic dining spots with food that actually lives up to the scene. Young actors, shapely models, artists from nearby Via Margutta, and even corporate types on expense accounts show up, trying to land one of the few sidewalk tables. To begin, we suggest *misto di pasta:* four pastas, each with a different sauce, arranged on the same plate. For your main course, specialties that win hearts year after year are *lasagne verde* and *tagliatelle alla bolognese.* The chefs also turn out the town's best veal cutlets bolognese topped with cheese. They're not inventive, but they're simply superb.

You might want to cap your evening by dropping into the **Rosati** cafe next door (or its competitor, the **Canova,** across the street) to enjoy a tempting pastry.

Piazza del Popolo 1-2. ✆ **06-3611426.** Reservations required. Main courses 10€–20€. AE, DC, MC, V. Tues–Sun 1–3pm and 8:15pm–midnight. Closed 20 days in Aug. Metro: Flaminio.

Da Mario FLORENTINE/ROMAN Da Mario is noted for its flavorful game specialties and excellent Florentine-style dishes (meats marinated in olive oil with fresh herbs and garlic and lightly grilled). The rich bounty of meats available during hunting season makes this a memorable choice, but even if you aren't feeling game (sorry), you'll find this a convivial and quintessentially Roman trattoria. A good beginning is the wide-noodle pappardelle, best when served with a *caccia* (game sauce) or with chunks of *coniglio* (rabbit), available only in winter. Other main dish specialties include wild boar stew and a delectable and aromatic roast lamb. The wine cellar is well stocked with sturdy reds, the ideal accompaniment for the meat dishes.

Via della Vite 55–56. ✆ **06-6783818.** Reservations recommended. Main courses 12€–25€. AE, DC, MC, V. Mon–Sat noon–11pm. Closed Aug. Metro: Spagna.

Di Fronte a . . . ITALIAN After a hard morning shopping in the Piazza di Spagna area, this is an ideal spot for a lunch break. Its name (which translates as "in front of . . .") comes from the fact that the restaurant lies right in front of a stationery shop (owned by the father of the restaurant's proprietor). The chef prepares tasty cuisine that is simple but good—nothing creative, but a fine boost of energy to hit the stores again. Salads are very large, as are the juicy half-pound burgers. You can also order more substantial food, such as succulent pastas and tender steaks. For dessert, try the pizza blanca, which is a pizza crust topped with chocolate cream or seasonal fruit.

Via della Croce 38. ✆ **06-6780355.** Reservations recommended for dinner. Main courses 12€–18€. AE, DC, MC, V. Daily noon–11pm. Metro: Spagna.

Gusto ★ 🎁 ITALIAN/PACIFIC RIM This restaurant is made up of two separate parts. The simpler and more informal of the two is a street-level pizzeria, where at least a dozen kinds of homemade pastas and pizzas are offered along with freshly made salads and simple platters of such grilled specialties as veal, chicken, steak, and fish. More upscale, and somewhat calmer, is the upstairs restaurant, where big windows, high ceilings, and lots of exposed brick create an appropriately minimalist setting for cutting-edge cuisine. Look for a fusion of Italian and Pacific Rim cuisine in such combinations as spaghetti stir-fried in a Chinese wok with fresh al dente vegetables, prawns and spring baby vegetables tempura style, buffalo mozzarella intriguingly entwined with tuna and arugula, and Middle Eastern staples.

Piazza Augusto Imperatore 9. ✆ **06-3226273.** www.gusto.it. Reservations recommended. Main courses in street-level pizzeria 9€–15€; main courses in upstairs restaurant 16€–28€. AE, MC, V. Daily noon–3:30pm and 7pm–midnight. Metro: Flaminio.

Il Palazzetto ★★★ ROMAN This small restaurant, part of the International Wine Academy of Rome, lies at the top of the Spanish Steps with entrances on both Piazza Trinità dei Monti and Cicolo del Bottino. Created by Roberto E. Wirth, general manager of the swank Hassler, it offers terraces with views of the Spanish Steps. The location is where banquets of Lucullus once took place.

The finest of ingredients go into the carefully crafted dishes, including such starters as an asparagus and pea soup with poached egg or veal and octopus in a green sauce. For your main, sample thin spaghetti with dried tuna roe and red prawns or pork belly roll with soy sauce, spinach, and eggplant. Desserts are luscious, perhaps lemon cheese cake with strawberry and balsamic ice cream.

Il Palazzetto also offers four exquisitely furnished boutique hotel rooms, costing 260€ to 360€.

Vicolo del Bottino 8. ✆ **06-699341000.** www.ilpazzettoroma.com. Reservations recommended. Main courses 13€–26€; fixed-price dinner 65€. AE, MC, V. Tues–Sun noon–2:30pm and 7:30–10:30pm. Metro: Spagna.

Inexpensive

Also consider the **Gusto** pizzeria, reviewed above under "Moderate."

Caffetteria Canova Tadolini ★ 🎁 ROMAN One of Rome's chicest cafes is part of a museum dedicated to Antonio Canova, the neoclassical sculptor, and his student, Adamo Tadolini. Lying only a few steps from the Piazza del Popolo, the museum cafe seats you beneath statues and plaster fragments. It serves a wide selection of drinks, but also full meals, including succulent pastas. Typical Roman specialties include *spaghetti all'amatriciana* or *alla carbonara* (with bacon). *Alla cacio e pepe* is another good selection with lots of creamy cheese and pepper.

Impressions

In Italy, the pleasure of eating is central to the pleasure of living. When you sit down to dinner with Italians, when you share their food, you are sharing their lives.

—Fred Plotkin, *Italy for the Gourmet Traveler*, 1996

Via del Babuino 150 A-B. ✆ **06-32110702.** www.museoateliercanovatadolini.it. Reservations recommended. Main courses 12€–22€. AE, DC, MC, V. Mon–Sat 8am–11pm. Metro: Flaminio or Spagna.

Enoteca Corsi ROMAN Here's a breath of unpretentious fresh air in a pricey neighborhood: an informal wine tavern open for lunch only. Both dining rooms are usually packed and full of festive diners, just as they've been since 1943. The wine list includes affordable choices from around Italy, to go perfectly with the platters of straightforward cuisine. It's nothing fancy, just hearty Italian home cooking like bean soup, gnocchi, Roman tripe, and roasted codfish with garlic and potatoes.

Via del Gesù 87–88. ✆ **06-6790821.** www.enotecacorsi.com. Reservations not necessary. Main courses 11€; pastas 8€; vegetable side dishes 5€. AE, DC, MC, V. Mon–Sat noon–3:30pm. Closed Aug. Metro: Spagna.

Il Margutta ★ VEGETARIAN Although the French would disagree, the Italians seem to know how to make vegetables more tantalizing than almost any other cuisine in the world. In the center of Rome between Piazza di Spagna and Piazza del Popolo, this rare vegetarian restaurant attracts artists who live in the studios lining this street. In such a setting, the owners decorated the walls with modern art. The chefs pay special attention to the quality of their ingredients, including extra-virgin olive oil, stone-ground organic flours such as bulgur, emmer wheat, and wild red rice from the Camargue, plus organically produced ciders, beers, and wines. The sheep and goat cheese served here is aged in vine leaves. Try such dishes as spinach soufflé with deep-fried zucchini flowers and a Parmesan and truffle sauce, or crispy grilled polenta with smoked provola cheese and oyster mushrooms. A dessert might include walnut cake with dried fruit served with hot chocolate and soya ice cream.

Via Margutta 118. ✆ **06-32650577.** www.ilmargutta.it. Reservations recommended for dinner. Main courses 10€–15€. AE, DC, MC, V. Daily 12:30–3:30pm and 7:30–11:30pm. Closed 3 weeks in Aug. Metro: Spagna.

Otello alla Concordia ☺ ROMAN On a side street amid the glamorous boutiques near the northern edge of the Spanish Steps lies one of Rome's most consistently reliable restaurants. A stone corridor from the street leads into the dignified Palazzo Povero. Choose a table in the arbor-covered courtyard or the cramped but convivial dining rooms. Displays of Italian bounty decorate the interior. The *spaghetti alle vongole veraci* (with clams) is excellent, as are Roman-style saltimbocca (veal with ham), *abbacchio arrosto* (roast lamb), eggplant parmigiana, a selection of grilled or sautéed fish dishes (including swordfish), and several preparations of veal.

Via della Croce 81. ✆ **06-6791178.** www.otelloallaconcordia.it. Reservations recommended. Main courses 6.50€–20€; fixed-price menu 25€. AE, DC, MC, V. Mon–Sat 12:30–3pm and 7:30–11pm. Closed 2 weeks in Jan. Metro: Spagna.

NEAR ANCIENT ROME

To locate the restaurants in this section, see the "Dining Near the Spanish Steps & Ancient Rome" map on p. 133.

Expensive

Crab ★ SEAFOOD Eating at this trattoria is ideal after a visit to the nearby Basilica of San Giovanni. Look for fish from around the world, including oysters from France, lobster from the Mediterranean and the Atlantic, and some catches from the Adriatic. The antipasti is practically a meal in itself. Our party devoured a savory sauté of mussels and clams, an octopus salad, and scallops gratin, which was followed by succulent lobster ravioli in *salsa vergine* (a lobster-based sauce). We think the *spaghetti alle vongole* (fresh clams) is the best in all of Rome. For dessert, we recommend an arrangement of sliced tropical fruit that evoked the campy hat worn by Carmen Miranda in all those late-night movies. Most of the main courses, except for some very expensive shellfish platters, are closer to the lower end of the price scale.

Via Capo d'Africa 2. ✆ **06-77203636.** Reservations required. Main courses 12€–85€. AE, DC, MC, V. Mon 7:45–11:30pm; Tues–Sat 1–3:30pm and 8–11:30pm. Closed Aug. Metro: Colosseo. Tram: 3.

Trattoria San Teodoro ★ 🎁 ROMAN At last there's a good place to eat in the former gastronomic wasteland near the Roman Forum and Palatine Hill. The helpful staff welcomes you to a shady terrace or a dimly lit dining room resting under a vaulted brick ceiling and arched alcoves. The chef handles seafood exceedingly well.

His signature dish is seafood carpaccio made with tuna, turbot, or sea bass. Succulent meats, such as medallions of veal in a nutmeg-enhanced cream sauce, round out the menu at this family-friendly place. All the pastas are homemade.

Via dei Fienili 49–51. © **06-6780933.** www.st-teodoro.it. Reservations recommended. Main courses 23€–29€. MC, V. Daily 12:30–3:30pm and 7:30pm–midnight. Closed 2 weeks at Christmas and Sundays Nov–Mar. Metro: Circo Massimo.

Moderate

See also the listing for **Il Quadrifoglio** on p. 118; it's located about midway between Stazione Termini and Ancient Rome.

F.I.S.H. ★ 🎁 SEAFOOD Its initials stand for "Fine International Seafood House," and F.I.S.H. lives up to its acronym. It remains one of Rome's most sought-after restaurants, managing to be both chic and good. It's tiny but choice; count yourself lucky if you can get a table. The decor is sleek and minimalist, but with a touch of elegance. There's an open kitchen, so no culinary secrets here. A sound culinary technique produces such winning platters as a black squid ravioli stuffed with ricotta and tune roe, or else *maltagliate* (homemade egg pasta) with octopus and a sultana ragout. Another worthy specialty is basmati and wild rice with scallops and salmon eggs cooked in banana leaves. Sea perch is cooked into a roll and served with couscous and date pie.

Via dei Serpenti 16. © **06-47824962.** www.f-i-s-h.it. Reservations imperative. Main courses 9€–25€. AE, DC, MC, V. Tues–Fri noon–3pm; Tues–Sun 7:30pm–midnight. Closed Aug 7–26, Dec 24–25, and Dec 31–Jan 4. Metro: Colosseo.

Scoglio di Frisio NEAPOLITAN/PIZZA This trattoria, a longtime favorite, offers a great introduction to the Neapolitan kitchen. Here you can taste a genuine Neapolitan pizza (crunchy, oozy, and excellent) with clams and mussels. Or, you can start with a medley of savory stuffed vegetables and antipasti before moving on to chicken cacciatore or well-flavored tender veal scaloppini. Scoglio di Frisio also makes for an inexpensive night of hokey but still charming entertainment, as cornball "O Sole Mio" renditions and other Neapolitan songs issue forth from a guitar, mandolin, and strolling tenor. The nautical decor (in honor of the top-notch fish dishes) is complete with a high-ceiling grotto of fishing nets, crustaceans, and a miniature three-masted schooner.

Via Merulana 256. © **06-4872765.** www.scogliodifrisio.com. Reservations recommended. Main courses 6€–24€; fixed-price menu 30€. AE, DC, MC, V. Daily 4:30–11:30pm. Metro: Vittorio Emanuele. Bus: 16 or 714.

Tram Tram PUGLIA/ROMAN/SICILIAN Around the Basilica of San Lorenzo, this is a Roman dining oddity, an address rarely frequented by visitors but beloved by locals. The crowded, often hysterically busy dining rooms showcase Signora di Vittorio's robust, hearty, and flavor-filled cuisine. Don't expect professional, or even good, service. But do expect good food and fair prices. We want to rush back soon for some more of the *orecchiette alla Norman,* with Sicilian eggplant, tomato sauce, and *ricotta salata* cheese. Another dish we're definitely reordering is the veal scallops rolled around a filling of prosciutto, bread crumbs, and cheese. We like the *pappardella Tram Tram,* broad noodles in tomato sauce riddled with strips of lamb and roasted sweet peppers, and the stuffed Savoy cabbage filled with an herb-flavored ground meat in a spicy tomato sauce.

Via dei Reti 44–46. ✆ **06-490416.** www.ristorantetramtramroma.com. Reservations recommended. Main courses 11€–18€. AE, DC, MC, V. Tues–Sun 12:30–3:30pm and 7:30–11:30pm. Metro: San Giovanni. Bus: 71 or 492. Tram: 3.

Inexpensive

Abruzzi ABRUZZESE/ROMAN Abruzzi, which takes its name from the region east of Rome, is at one side of Piazza S. S. Apostoli, just a short walk from Piazza Venezia. The good food and reasonable prices make it a big draw for students. The chef offers a satisfying assortment of cold antipasti. With your starter, we suggest a liter of garnet-red wine; we prefer one whose bouquet is suggestive of Abruzzi's wildflowers. The menu is a virtual textbook of classical Italian dishes, everything from a seafood risotto to meltingly tender veal cutlets in the Milanese style (fried with potatoes). No one in Italy does roast lamb better than the Romans, and the selection here is good—tender, grilled to perfection, seasoned with virgin olive oil and fresh herbs, and dished up with roast potatoes.

Via del Vaccaro 1. ✆ **06-6793897.** Reservations recommended. Main courses 7.50€–15€. AE, DC, MC, V. Sun–Fri 12:30–3pm and 7–11pm. Closed 3 weeks in Aug. Bus: 44 or 46.

Hostaria Nerone ★ ITALIAN/ROMAN Built atop the ruins of the Golden House of Nero, this trattoria is run by the energetic de Santis family, who cook, serve, and handle the large crowds of hungry locals and visitors. Opened in 1929 at the edge of the Colle Oppio Park, it contains two compact dining rooms, plus a shrub-lined terrace with views of the Colosseum and the Baths of Trajan. The copious antipasti buffet represents the bounty of Italy's fields and seas. The pastas include savory spaghetti with clams and, our favorite, *pasta fagioli* (with beans). There's also grilled crayfish and swordfish, and Italian sausages with polenta. The broad list of some of the best Italian wines is reasonably priced.

Via Terme di Tito 96. ✆ **06-4817952.** Reservations recommended. Main courses 8.50€–15€. AE, DC, MC, V. Mon–Sat noon–3pm and 7–11pm. Metro: Colosseo. Bus: 75, 85, 87, 117, or 175.

NEAR THE VATICAN

To locate these restaurants, see the "Accommodations & Dining near the Vatican" map on p. 111.

Moderate

Cesare ROMAN/TUSCAN The area around the Vatican is not the place to go for great restaurants, but Cesare is a fine old-world spot known for its deft handling of fresh ingredients. We come here for the fresh and tender seafood salad, brimming with cuttlefish, shrimp, squid, mussels, and octopus, and dressed with olive oil, fresh parsley, and lemon. Our table was blessed with an order of *spaghetti all'amatriciana* in a spicy tomato sauce flavored with hot peppers and tiny bits of salt pork. The *saltimbocca alla romana,* that classic Roman dish, is masterful here. Try the fresh sardines and anchovies if you want to go truly Roman.

Via Crescenzio 13, near Piazza Cavour. ✆ **06-6861227.** www.ristorantecesare.com. Reservations recommended. Main courses 10€–28€; fixed-price Tuscan menu 38€. AE, DC, MC, V. June 15–Aug 7 Mon–Sat 12:30–3pm and 7:30pm–midnight; off season Tues–Sat 12:30–3pm and 7:30pm–midnight, Sun 12:30–3pm. Closed 3 weeks Aug. Metro: Lepanto or Ottaviano-San Pietro. Bus: 23, 34, or 49.

La Veranda dell'Hotel Columbus ★★ ROMAN A few steps from Vatican City, this hotel dining room is one of the most dramatic in Rome, with spectacular frescoes. You also have an option for a courtyard table which is lit by torches at night. The palazzo in which it is housed dates from the 15th century. The menu reflects a supreme artistry in balancing flavors. Starters are savory delights, especially the lobster salad with mango in a ginger sauce or puréed white bean soup with steamed scallops. We urge you to try such mains as thyme-glazed loin of lamb with turnip tops and puréed celeriac, or the piedmontese filet of beef with fried artichokes and crunchy rosemary-infused potatoes. Some of the dishes are based on rare recipes from yesterday, including a 17th-century way of preparing sea beam baked in an almond crust.

In the Hotel Columbus, Borgo Santo Spirito 73. ✆ **06-6872973.** www.laveranda.net. Reservations recommended. Main courses 14€–30€. AE, MC, V. Tues–Sun 12:30–3pm and 7:30–11pm. Metro: Ottaviano.

Ristorante Il Matriciano ★ ☺ ROMAN Il Matriciano is a family restaurant with a devoted following and a convenient location near St. Peter's. The food is good but mostly country fare. For openers, you might enjoy a bracing *zuppa di verdura* (vegetable soup) or creamy ravioli di ricotta. From many dishes, we recommend *scaloppa alla valdostana* (chicken sautéed with ham and mushrooms in a cream sauce) or *abbacchio* (suckling lamb) *al forno,* each evocative of the region's bounty. The specialty, and our personal favorite, is *bucatini matriciana,* a variation on the favorite sauce in the Roman repertoire, *amatriciana,* richly flavored with bacon, tomatoes, and basil. Dining at the convivial tables, you're likely to see an array of Romans, including prelates and cardinals ducking out of the nearby Vatican for a meal.

Via dei Gracchi 55. ✆ **06-3212327.** Reservations required. Main courses 10€–20€. DC, MC, V. Daily 12:30–3pm and 8–11:30pm. Closed Aug 5–31; Wed in winter; Sat in summer. Metro: Ottaviano-San Pietro.

Inexpensive

The sixth branch of **Insalata Ricca,** the popular chain of salad-and-light-meals restaurants, is across from the Vatican walls at Piazza del Risorgimento 5 (✆ **06-39730387;** www.linsalataricca.it).

Hostaria dei Bastioni ROMAN This simple but well-managed restaurant is about a minute's walk from the entrance to the Vatican Museums. Although a warm-weather terrace doubles the size during summer, many diners prefer the inside room as an escape from the roaring traffic. The menu features the staples of Rome's culinary repertoire, including fisherman's risotto (a broth-simmered rice dish studded with fresh fish, usually shellfish), a vegetarian *fettuccine alla bastione* with orange-flavored creamy tomato sauce, an array of grilled fresh fish, and cutlets of tender beef with mushrooms. The food is first-rate—and a real bargain at these prices.

Via Leone IV 29. ✆ **06-39723034.** Reservations recommended Fri–Sat. Main courses 7€–16€. AE, DC, MC, V. Mon–Sat noon–3pm and 7–11:30pm. Closed July 15–Aug 1. Metro: Ottaviano-San Pietro.

Sicilianbocca ★ SICILIAN The best Sicilian restaurant in Rome lies close to the Vatican, ideal for a lunch when visiting either St. Peter's or the papal museums. Natives of Sicily own and operate this place, and their specialties taste virtually the same as those encountered in Sicily itself. The menu features a large variety of delectable smoked fish, including salmon, swordfish, and tuna. The homemade pastas here are the best Sicilian versions in town, especially the classic *Maccheroni alla Norma,* with ricotta, a savory tomato sauce, and sautéed eggplant. You might follow with stuffed grilled calamari or a mixed fish grill. The ricotta and pear cake, topped with steaming hot fudge, is a celestial delight.

Via E. Faà di Bruno 26. © **06-37358400.** www.siciliainboccaweb.com. Reservations not required. Main courses 10€–25€. AE, DC, MC, V. Mon–Sat 1:30–3pm and 8–11:30pm. Closed 3 weeks in Aug. Metro: Ottaviano-San Pietro.

Taverna Angelica SOUTHERN ITALIAN This tavern is not luxurious in any way, but it serves good, affordable food in a position only 200m (656 ft.) from the Vatican. Even priests from St. Peter's come here to dine on such well-prepared dishes as potato ravioli with *guanciale,* an Italian specialty made from dry pig cheeks. The best pasta is the homemade *cavatelli* with chicory and cherry tomatoes. All the dishes are based on fresh regional produce such as broiled lamb chops with eggplant served with polenta.

Piazza A. Capponi 6. © **06-6874514.** www.tavernaangelica.it. Reservations required. Main courses 10€–20€. AE, DC, MC, V. Mon–Sat 7pm–midnight; Sun noon–3:30pm and 7pm–midnight. Closed 10 days in Aug. Metro: Ottaviano-San Pietro.

IN TRASTEVERE

Expensive

Alberto Ciarla ★★ SEAFOOD The Ciarla, in an 1890 building set in an obscure corner of an enormous square, is Trastevere's best restaurant and one of its most expensive. You'll be greeted cordially and with a lavish display of seafood on ice. The specialties include a handful of ancient recipes subtly improved by Signor Ciarla (such as the pasta and bean soup with seafood). Original dishes include gilthead bream in orange sauce, savory spaghetti with clams, and a full array of delicious shellfish. The sea bass filet is prepared in at least three ways, including an award-winning version with almonds.

Piazza San Cosimato 40. © **06-5816068.** www.albertociarla.com. Reservations required. Main courses 17€–33€; fixed-price menus 50€–84€. AE, DC, MC, V. Mon–Sat 8:30pm–midnight. Closed Jan 4–14 and 1 week in Aug. Bus: 44, 75, 170, 280, or 718.

Sabatini ★ ROMAN/SEAFOOD This is a real neighborhood spot in a lively location. (You might have to wait for a table even if you have a reservation.) In summer, tables are placed on the charming piazza, and you can look across at the church's floodlit golden frescoes. The dining room sports beamed ceilings, stenciled walls, lots of paneling, and framed oil paintings. The spaghetti with seafood is excellent, and the fresh fish and shellfish are also very tempting. For a savory treat, try *pollo con peperoni,* chicken with red and green peppers. Wash it all down with the delightful white Frascati wine or the house chianti. (Order carefully; your bill can skyrocket if you choose grilled fish or the Florentine steaks.)

Piazza Santa Maria in Trastevere 13. © **06-5812026.** www.ristorantisabatini.com. Reservations recommended. Main courses 16€–33€. AE, DC, MC, V. Daily 12:30–2:30pm and 7:45–11:30pm. Bus: 45, 65, 170, 181, or 280.

Moderate

Antico Arco ★ ITALIAN Named after one of the gates of early medieval Rome (Arco di San Pancrazio), which rises nearby, Antico Arco is on Janiculum Hill not far from Trastevere and the American Academy. It's a hip restaurant with a young, stylish clientele. Carefully created dishes include homemade fresh cannelloni with rock fish and aged pecorino cheese; or a risotto with red Sicilian shrimp, asparagus, and fresh herbs. The chef has an artisan's devotion to fine ingredients, as evoked by the grilled filet of beef with roasted tomatoes, or the filet of hake from the North Sea.

Piazzale Aurelio 7. ✆ **06-5815274.** www.anticoarco.it. Reservations recommended. Main courses 15€–28€. AE, DC, MC, V. Mon–Sat 6pm–midnight. Bus: 44 or 870.

Asinocotto ITALIAN Within a pair of cramped dining rooms, you'll be served by a cheerful staff that's well practiced in hauling steaming platters of food. The simple white-painted walls accented by dark timbers and panels are a nice background to the flavorful dishes that stream from the busy kitchens of Giuliano Brenna. Look for elaborate antipasti such as quail and watercress in a "Parmesan basket," or smoked sturgeon on a salad of Belgian endive with black olives. You might follow with handmade ravioli filled with sea bass, lettuce, and a sauvignon sauce; or a zesty oxtail soup with artichoke hearts au gratin. Other imaginative dishes include *orecchiette* pasta with eggplant, bacon, and smoked ricotta; or guinea fowl breast with a flavoring of orange and green tea. The restaurant's name, incidentally, translates as "cooked donkey meat," but don't look for that on the menu anytime soon.

Via dei Vascellari 48. ✆ **06-5898985.** www.asinocotto.com. Reservations recommended. Main courses 12€–23€. AE, DC, MC, V. Tues–Sun 7:30–11pm. Tram: 8.

Glass ★ ROMAN/WINE BAR When this chic restaurant and wine bar opened, management claimed it was an "attempt to give Trastevere back to the Romans." Pretend you're a native—not a tourist—and you should have a good time here. Theatrical lighting and lots of glass (including the floors) give the place a modernist aura, rather rare for the district. The cuisine is both innovative and traditional. Some of our favorite bite-downs include gnocchi made with red turnips and served with pecorino, crisp anchovies, and tuna. The tagliolini is homemade and sautéed with cherry tomatoes, duck, and fresh mushrooms. A sublime pigeon comes in a berry sauce encased in a chicory pie. You might also try the celestial fresh fish in an almond and lavender crust with a sweet wine sauce laced with cheese.

Vicolo del Cinque 58. ✆ **06-58335903.** www.glass-hostaria.it. Reservations recommended. Main courses 16€–28€; fixed-price menus 60€–75€. AE, DC, MC, V. Restaurant daily 8–11:30pm. Wine bar daily 8pm–2am. Bus: 23.

La Cisterna ROMAN If you like traditional home cooking based on the best regional ingredients, head here. La Cisterna, named for an ancient well from imperial times discovered in the cellar, lies deep in the heart of Trastevere. For more than 75 years, it has been run by the wonderful Simmi family. In good weather, you can dine at sidewalk tables. From the ovens emerge Roman-style suckling lamb that's amazingly tender and seasoned with fresh herbs and virgin olive oil. The spicy *rigatoni all'amatriciana* is served with red-hot peppers; and the delectable *papalini romana* consists of wide noodles flavored with prosciutto, cheese, and eggs. The

Dining in Trastevere

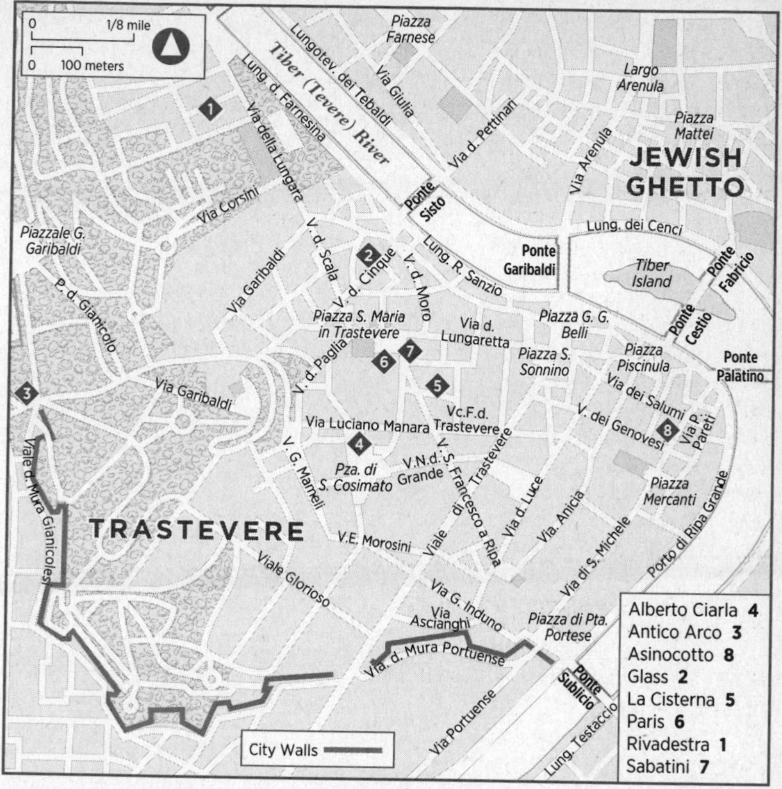

shrimp is perfectly grilled, and an array of fresh fish includes sea bass baked with fresh herbs.

Via della Cisterna 13. ✆ **06-5812543.** www.lacisterna.com. Reservations recommended. Main courses 10€–25€. AE, DC, MC, V. Mon–Sat 7pm–1:30am. Bus: 44, 75, 170, 280, or 710.

Paris ROMAN For about a century, there's been a restaurant here in this weathered stone building erected about 600 years ago in Trastevere. Over the years, this cramped but convivial place has turned out thousands of platters of authentic Roman cuisine, usually with an emphasis on seafood. This is old-fashioned cooking; don't look for the latest foodie trends. Despite that, you're likely to be very happy here, thanks to heaping portions of dishes such as fried filet of sole; turbot with porcini mushrooms, olive oil, and herbs; *coda alla vaccinara* (slow-baked rump steak, Roman style); and succulent grilled baby lamb chops. Vegetarians will appreciate one of the house specialties—a beautifully presented platter of fried, very fresh vegetables that can be a main course for one diner or a shared antipasti for two or three.

Piazza San Calisto 7A. ✆ **06-5815378.** www.ristoranteparis.com. Reservations recommended. Maln courses 12€–20€; fixed-price menu 50€. AE, DC, MC, V. Tues–Sun 12:30–3pm; Tues–Sat 7:45am–11pm. Closed Aug. Bus: H or 44.

Rivadestra ★ MEDITERRANEAN In the heart of Trastevere, this is a Roman eatery of charm and sophistication, with a modern decor of small modular oak tables, handcrafted textiles, and metallic swing lamps inspired by 18th century chandeliers. Young painters and artists who live in Trastevere have made this one a favorite. The carefully crafted cuisine is based on regional products, when available, which are fashioned into deft, delicious, and delightful starters and appetizers.

To open your meal, try the tomato and seabass salad or else fresh tomato soup with prawns and mozzarella. We recommend such mains as tagliolini pasta with shrimp and porcini mushrooms or else risotto with shrimp and fresh asparagus. Guinea fowl is especially intriguing, served with foie gras, artichokes, and a walnut sauce. For dessert, there are such temptations as apple pie with white chocolate or else a chocolate soufflé.

Via della Penitenza 7. ✆ **06-68307053.** www.rivadestra.com. Reservations recommended. Main courses 12€–23€. AE, MC, V. Mon–Fri 1–2:30pm and 8–11:30pm; Sat 8–11:30pm. Closed 2 weeks in Aug. Bus: 125.

IN VILLA BORGHESE

Expensive

Casina Valadier ★ ROMAN After a long hiatus, this chic restaurant has reopened, and once again the glitterati of Rome are flocking here for the to-die-for cocktails, the superb cuisine, and the panoramic views of Rome. Placed on the site of the ancient Collis Hortulorum, the highest point of the Pincio district, the original building dates from 1816 and was the creation of the famous architect, Giuseppe Valadier. In its heyday, this restaurant was the most fashionable place in Rome, attracting people such as King Farouk of Egypt and Pirandello, Gandhi, and Strauss.

The best of the menu is a regionally based repertoire of savory dishes with imaginative, intelligent associations of flavors. Diners take delight in jazzed-up Roman classics such as rigatoni with bacon, onions, peppers, and pecorino; or a cherry- and sesame-encrusted pork filet. Start with a duck breast carpaccio or a warm ricotta cheese round with an olive and pistachio pesto. For dessert, dare you try the fried zucchini flowers stuffed with rice and served with cinnamon ice cream?

Villa Borghese, Piazza Bucarest. ✆ **06-69922090.** www.casinavaladier.it. Reservations required. Main courses 20€–50€. Daily 1–3pm and 8–11pm. Bus: 53.

A Romantic Picnic in the Borghese Gardens

Our favorite place for a picnic in all of Rome is in the Borghese Gardens, followed by a reserved visit to the Galleria Borghese. Gina, 7A Via San Sebastianello (✆ 06-6780251; www.gina roma.com), has come up with a marvelous idea. This deli will provide you with a hamper complete with thermos, glasses, and linen for a picnic to be enjoyed in the fabled gardens. For 40€, two persons can enjoy panini (tomato, eggplant, and mozzarella on focaccia) along with a fresh fruit salad, dessert, and coffee.

IN TESTACCIO

Moderate

Checchino dal 1887 ★ ROMAN During the 1800s, a wine shop flourished here, selling drinks to the butchers working in the nearby slaughterhouses. In 1887, the ancestors of the restaurant's present owners began serving food, too. Many Italian diners come here to relish the *rigatoni con pajata* (pasta with small intestines), *coda alla vaccinara* (oxtail stew), *fagioli e cotiche* (beans with intestinal fat), and other examples of *la cucina povera* (food of the poor). In winter, a succulent wild boar with dried prunes and red wine is served. Safer and possibly more appetizing is the array of salads, soups, pastas, steaks, cutlets, grills, and ice creams. The English-speaking staff is helpful, tactfully proposing alternatives if you're not ready for Roman soul food. The wine cellar stocks more than 600 kinds of wines from all over the world.

Via di Monte Testaccio 30. ✆ **06-5743816.** www.checchino-dal-1887.com. Reservations recommended. Main courses 10€–24€; fixed-price menu 46€–63€. AE, DC, MC, V. Tues–Sat 12:30–3pm and 8pm–midnight. Closed Aug and 1 week at Christmas. Bus: 75 from Termini Station.

Ketumbar ★ 🎁 JAPANESE/ITALIAN How chic can Roma get? Ketumbar (Malay for coriander) has brought sophistication to Testaccio, once known as a *paisano* sector of Roma. Featured in several magazines devoted to the high life in Italy, the decor is sleek and minimalist, or, as one critic dubbed it, "Gothic-cum-Asia-fantasia." The decorator obviously went to Indonesia for much of the furnishings. But the potsherds (pieces of broken Roman amphora) remind us that we're still in an ancient part of Rome. Everything we've sampled here has been a delight: steamed meat-and-vegetable ravioli in soy sauce, fat curried shrimp.

Via Galvani 24. ✆ **06-57305338.** www.ketumbar.it. Reservations required. Main courses 8€–18€. AE, DC, MC, V. Daily 8pm–2am. Closed Aug. Metro: Piramide. Bus: 3, 23, or 75.

IN PARIOLI

Very Expensive

Sapori del Lord Byron ★★★ ITALIAN This luxe restaurant is one of the best places to go for both traditional and creative cuisine. A chichi crowd with demanding palates packs it nightly. There are places in Rome with better views, but the setting here is far more elegant, and the service impeccable. The creative menu features a variety of succulent dishes and one of the best hotel wine *cartes* in Rome. Appetizers are likely to include zucchini carpaccio with pine nuts, fresh mint, and tomato; or a mild smoked salmon with sweet-and-sour red onion. Our favorite Roman specialties include filet of beef with anchovies and fresh marjoram, or sautéed angler fish with lentils and borage flowers. The sea bass steak is a treat, with its flavor of lemon grass. Veal medallions are enlivened with sun-dried tomatoes, fresh olives, and an eggplant confit.

In the Hotel Lord Byron, Via G. de Notaris 5. ✆ **06-3220404.** Reservations required. Main courses 25€–32€. AE, DC, MC, V. Mon–Sat 12:30–2:30pm and 8–10:30pm. Closed Aug. Metro: Flaminio. Bus: 3.

Moderate

Al Ceppo ★ ROMAN Because the place is somewhat hidden (although it's only 2 blocks from the Villa Borghese, near Piazza Ungheria), you're likely to rub elbows with more Romans here than tourists. "The Log" features an open wood-stoked fireplace on which the chef roasts lamb chops, liver, and bacon to perfection. Other intriguing items include fusilli pasta with bacon and artichokes; and a breaded, grilled fish of the day. A true delight is the tender beef filet with black truffles. To warm your soul, order the white chocolate and peach terrine with a fresh mint sauce.

Via Panama 2. ✆ **06-8419696.** www.ristorantealceppo.it. Reservations recommended. Main courses 14€–27€. AE, DC, MC, V. Tues–Sun 12:30–3pm and 7:30–11pm. Closed 1 week in Aug. Bus: 56 or 310.

IN MONTE MARIO

La Pergola ★★★ MEDITERRANEAN Many Roman food critics call this the best restaurant in the city. We too cast our vote for the Cavalieri Hilton's spectacular panoramic restaurant high atop Monte Mario. Arrive early and enjoy the view and Rome's most elegant cocktail bar. In summer, there is alfresco dining on an adjacent terrace. The setting is as elegant as you would expect: *trompe l'oeil* ceilings, wood paneling, beautifully set tables, flickering candles, and sliding glass walls. The staff functions so beautifully they've been compared to a Viennese orchestra.

Since 1994, a talented German chef, Heinz Beck, has been dazzling sophisticated Roman taste buds. Even though he's not a native, he has taken Italian haute cuisine to dizzying new heights, delighting critics and diners with an array of colors and aromas. The surprises go on and on, as you partake of one of the finest meals you are likely to be served in Italy. The cuisine has balance, harmony, and unusual flavor combinations in such dishes as filet of sea bass with olive oil in an avocado crust (served with a green tomato sauce), or spaghetti with cuttlefish in olive oil, cherry tomatoes, and a parsley sauce. The potato gnocchi comes with caviar and chives, or else you might opt for the soy-sauce poached filet of beef with sake sauce.

In the Cavalieri Hilton, Via Cadlolo 101. ✆ **06-35092152.** www.romecavlieri.com. Reservations required. Jacket required. Main courses 39€–59€; fixed-price menu 175€–198€. AE, DC, MC, V. Tues–Sat 7:30–11:30pm. Closed Jan 1–24 and Aug 8–23. Free shuttle bus to and from city center.

IN MONTASACRO

Inexpensive

L'Asino d'Oro ★ 🎁 UMBRIAN/LAZIO Foodies are flocking to northern Rome to taste the enticing menu of Lucio Sforza in an ultramodern Scandinavian interior. Gaining fame in his hometown of Orvieto, he moved to this gentrifying neighborhood. The location is off the Piazza Adriatic. Some of his dishes are based on ancient Etruscan recipes. The handwritten menu changes daily to take advantage of the best ingredients at the market.

Only the most snobbish of gastronomes would call the offerings a peasant cuisine. Try such delightful surprises as the chestnut and bean soup with candied orange or a soup of spelt and shrimps. Tantalizing mains include baked lamb with artichokes; stewed salted codfish with pine nuts, raisins, rosemary, and chickpeas. Fettuccine comes with a tangy wild boar sauce, and one of the best pastas is strangozzi with broccoli and anchovies.

Via Valsavaranche 81. ✆ **06-64491305.** www.trattorialasinodoro.it. Reservations recommended. Main courses 10€–18€; fixed-price lunch menu 12€. AE, DC, MC, V. Mon–Sat 12:30–3:30pm and 7–10:30pm; Sun 12:30–3:30pm. Bus: 38 or 93.

EXPLORING ROME

7

Where else but in Rome could you admire a 17th-century colonnade designed by Bernini while resting against an Egyptian obelisk carried off from Heliopolis while Jesus was still alive? Or stand amid the splendor of Renaissance frescoes in a papal palace built on top of the tomb of a Roman emperor? Where else, for that matter, are Vestal Virgins buried adjacent to the Ministry of Finance?

For the year 2000 Jubilee, decades' worth of grime from car exhaust and other pollution was scrubbed from the city's facades, revealing the original glory of the Eternal City (although Rome could still stand even more work on this front), and ancient treasures such as the Colosseum were shored up. Many of the most popular areas (such as the Trevi Fountain and Piazza Navona) are sparkling and inviting again.

Whether time-blackened or newly gleaming, the city's ancient monuments are a constant reminder that Rome was one of the greatest centers of Western civilization. In the heyday of the empire, all roads led to Rome, and with good reason. It was one of the first cosmopolitan cities, importing slaves, gladiators, great art, and even citizens from the far corners of the world. Despite its carnage and corruption, Rome left a legacy of law; a heritage of great art, architecture, and engineering; and an uncanny lesson in how to conquer enemies by absorbing their cultures.

But ancient Rome is only part of the spectacle. The Vatican has had a tremendous influence on making the city a tourism center. Although Vatican architects looted ancient ruins for their precious marble, they created great Renaissance treasures and even occasionally incorporated the old into the new—as Michelangelo did when turning the Baths of Diocletian into a church. And in the years that followed, Bernini adorned the city with the wonders of the baroque, especially his glorious fountains.

ST. PETER'S & THE VATICAN

If you want to know more about the Vatican, check out its website at **www.vatican.va**.

Rome Attractions

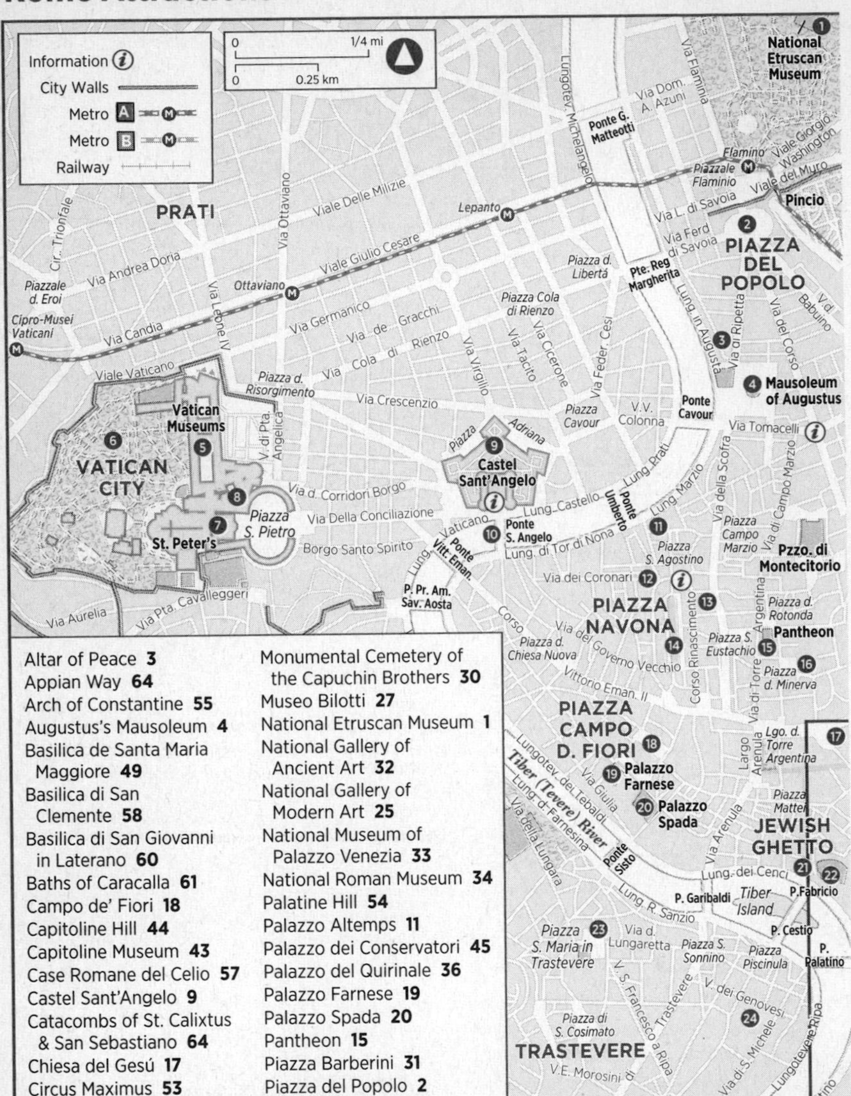

Altar of Peace **3**
Appian Way **64**
Arch of Constantine **55**
Augustus's Mausoleum **4**
Basilica de Santa Maria Maggiore **49**
Basilica di San Clemente **58**
Basilica di San Giovanni in Laterano **60**
Baths of Caracalla **61**
Campo de' Fiori **18**
Capitoline Hill **44**
Capitoline Museum **43**
Case Romane del Celio **57**
Castel Sant'Angelo **9**
Catacombs of St. Calixtus & San Sebastiano **64**
Chiesa del Gesú **17**
Circus Maximus **53**
Colosseum **56**
Forum of Julius Caesar **46**
Forum of Trajan **40**
Galleria Borghese **26**
Galleria Doria Pamphilj **37**
Golden House of Nero **51**
Imperial Forums **47**
Keats-Shelley House **29**
Monumental Cemetery of the Capuchin Brothers **30**
Museo Bilotti **27**
National Etruscan Museum **1**
National Gallery of Ancient Art **32**
National Gallery of Modern Art **25**
National Museum of Palazzo Venezia **33**
National Roman Museum **34**
Palatine Hill **54**
Palazzo Altemps **11**
Palazzo dei Conservatori **45**
Palazzo del Quirinale **36**
Palazzo Farnese **19**
Palazzo Spada **20**
Pantheon **15**
Piazza Barberini **31**
Piazza del Popolo **2**
Piazza Navona **14**
Ponte Sant'Angelo **10**
Protestant Cemetery **62**
Pyramid of Caius Cestius **62**
Roman Forum **48**
St. Peter's Basilica **7**
San Gregorio **22**
San Luigi dei Francesi **13**

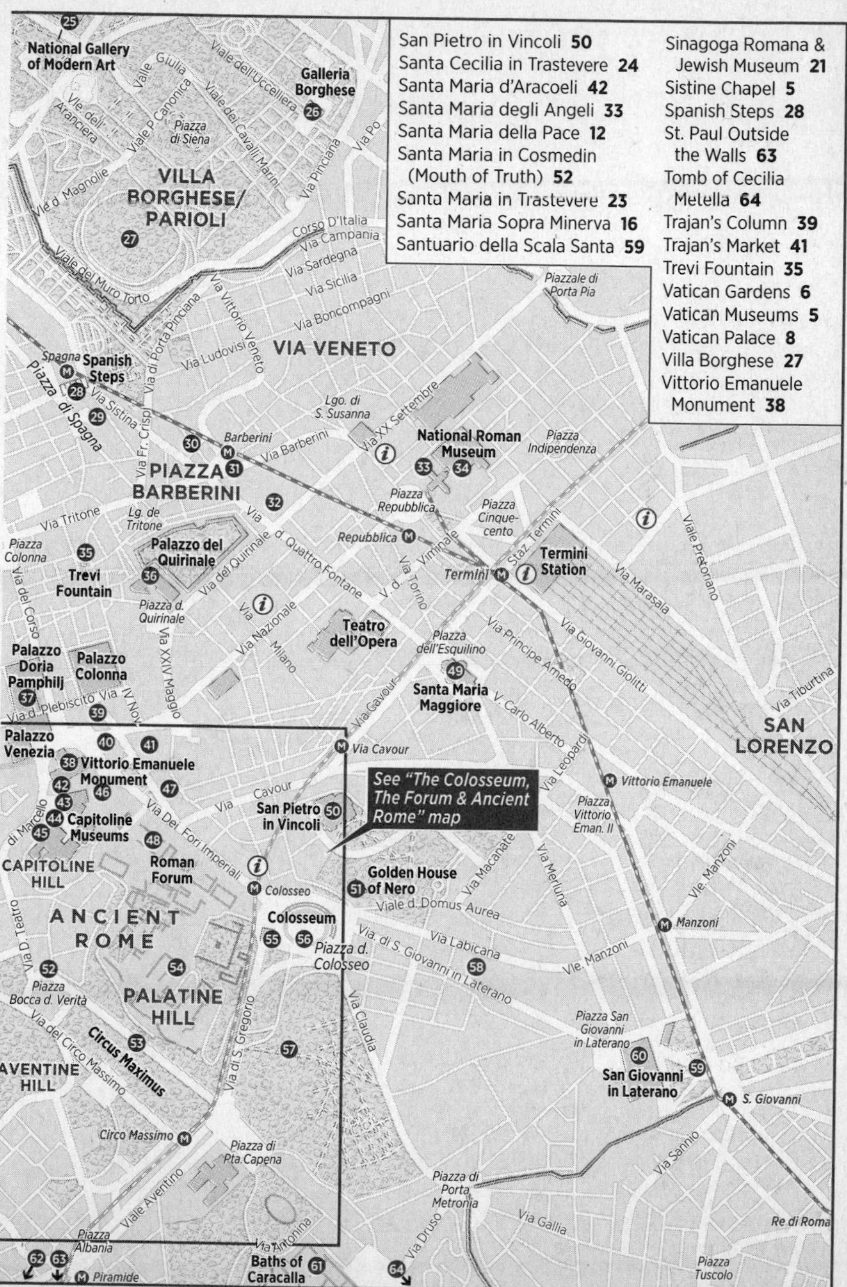
San Pietro in Vincoli 50
Santa Cecilia in Trastevere 24
Santa Maria d'Aracoeli 42
Santa Maria degli Angeli 33
Santa Maria della Pace 12
Santa Maria in Cosmedin (Mouth of Truth) 52
Santa Maria in Trastevere 23
Santa Maria Sopra Minerva 16
Santuario della Scala Santa 59
Sinagoga Romana & Jewish Museum 21
Sistine Chapel 5
Spanish Steps 28
St. Paul Outside the Walls 63
Tomb of Cecilia Metella 64
Trajan's Column 39
Trajan's Market 41
Trevi Fountain 35
Vatican Gardens 6
Vatican Museums 5
Vatican Palace 8
Villa Borghese 27
Vittorio Emanuele Monument 38
National Gallery of Modern Art
Galleria Borghese
VILLA BORGHESE/ PARIOLI
VIA VENETO
Spanish Steps
PIAZZA BARBERINI
National Roman Museum
Palazzo del Quirinale
Trevi Fountain
Termini Station
Teatro dell'Opera
Palazzo Doria Pamphilj
Palazzo Colonna
Santa Maria Maggiore
SAN LORENZO
Palazzo Venezia
Vittorio Emanuele Monument
Capitoline Museums
San Pietro in Vincoli
See "The Colosseum, The Forum & Ancient Rome" map
CAPITOLINE HILL
Roman Forum
Golden House of Nero
ANCIENT ROME
Colosseum
PALATINE HILL
Circus Maximus
AVENTINE HILL
San Giovanni in Laterano
Baths of Caracalla
Spagna
Barberini
Repubblica
Termini
Via Cavour
Vittorio Emanuele
Colosseo
Manzoni
S. Giovanni
Circo Massimo
Piramide
Re di Roma
Piazza di Spagna
Via Veneto
Via Nazionale
Via dei Fori Imperiali
Via Merulana
Via Labicana
Via Claudia
Via di S. Gregorio
Via del Circo Massimo
Viale Aventino
Piazza Bocca d. Verità
Piazza di Pta.Capena
Piazza di Porta Metronia
Piazza San Giovanni in Laterano
Piazza Vittorio Eman. II
Piazza dell'Esquilino
Piazza Indipendenza
Piazza della Repubblica
Piazza Cinquecento
Piazzale di Porta Pia
Piazza Colonna
Piazza d. Quirinale
Piazza d. Colosseo
Piazza Albania
Piazza Tuscolo

In Vatican City

In 1929, the Lateran Treaty between Pope Pius XI and the Italian government created the **Vatican,** the world's second-smallest sovereign independent state. It has only a few hundred citizens and is protected (theoretically) by its own militia, the curiously uniformed (some say by Michelangelo) Swiss guards.

The only entrance to the Vatican for the casual visitor is through one of the glories of the Western world: Bernini's **St. Peter's Square (Piazza San Pietro).** As you stand in the huge piazza, you'll be in the arms of an ellipse partly enclosed by a majestic **Doric-pillared colonnade.** Atop it stands a gesticulating crowd of some 140 saints. Straight ahead is the facade of **St. Peter's Basilica** (Sts. Peter and Paul are represented by statues in front, with Peter carrying the keys to the kingdom), and, to the right, above the colonnade, are the dark-brown buildings of the **papal apartments** and the **Vatican Museums.** In the center of the square is an **Egyptian obelisk,** brought from the ancient city of Heliopolis on the Nile delta. Flanking the obelisk are two 17th-century **fountains.** The one on the right by Carlo Maderno, who designed the facade of St. Peter's, was placed here by Bernini himself; the other is by Carlo Fontana.

On the left side of Piazza San Pietro is the **Vatican Tourist Office** (**© 06-69881662**), open Monday through Saturday from 8:30am to 6:30pm. It sells maps and guides that'll help you make sense of the riches you'll be seeing in the museums. It also schedules tours for the Vatican Gardens and tries to answer questions.

Basilica di San Pietro (St. Peter's Basilica) ★★★ In ancient times, the Circus of Nero, where St. Peter is said to have been crucified, was slightly to the left of where the basilica is now located. Peter was buried here in A.D. 64 near the site of his execution, and in 324 Constantine commissioned a basilica to be built over Peter's tomb. That structure stood for more than 1,000 years until it verged on collapse. The present basilica, mostly completed in the 1500s and 1600s, is predominantly High Renaissance and baroque. Inside, the massive scale showcases some of Italy's greatest artists: Bramante, Raphael, Michelangelo, and Maderno. In a church of such grandeur—overwhelming in its detail of gilt, marble, and mosaic—you can't expect much subtlety. It's meant to be overpowering.

In the nave on the right (the first chapel) stands one of the Vatican's greatest treasures: Michelangelo's exquisite ***Pietà*** **★★★**, created while the master was still in his early 20s but clearly showing his genius for capturing the human form. (The sculpture has been kept behind reinforced glass since a madman's act of vandalism in the 1970s.) Note the incredibly lifelike folds of Mary's robes and her youthful

A St. Peter's Warning

St. Peter's has a strict dress code: no shorts, no skirts above the knee, and no bare shoulders. You will not be let in if you don't come dressed appropriately. In a pinch, men and women alike can buy a big, cheap scarf from a nearby souvenir stand and wrap it around their legs as a long skirt or throw it over their shoulders as a shawl. If you're still showing too much skin, a guard hands out blue paper capes similar to what you wear in a doctor's office. No photographs are allowed.

The Vatican

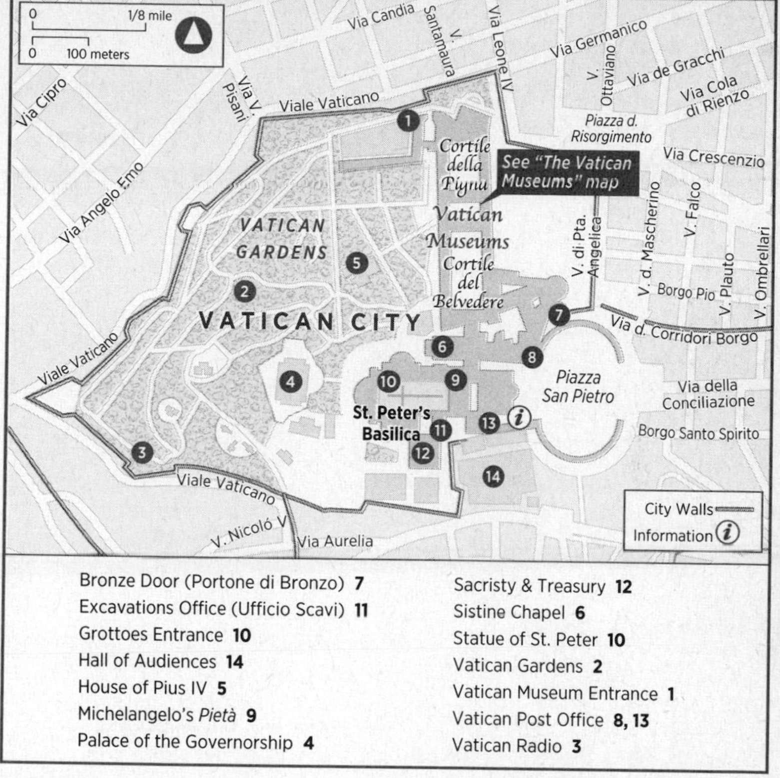

features (although she would've been middle-aged at the time of the Crucifixion, Michelangelo portrayed her as a young woman to convey her purity).

Much farther on, in the right wing of the transept near the Chapel of St. Michael, rests Canova's neoclassical **sculpture of Pope Clement XIII ★★**. The truly devout stop to kiss the feet of the 13th-century **bronze of St. Peter ★**, attributed to Arnolfo di Cambio (at the far reaches of the nave, against a corner pillar on the right). Under Michelangelo's dome is the celebrated twisty-columned **baldacchino ★★** (1524), by Bernini, resting over the papal altar. The 29m-high (96-ft.), ultra-fancy canopy was created in part, so it's said, from bronze stripped from the Pantheon, although that's up for debate.

In addition, you can visit the **Treasury ★**, which is filled with jewel-studded chalices, reliquaries, and copes. One robe worn by Pius XII strikes a simple note in these halls of elegance. The sacristy contains a **Historical Museum (Museo Storico) ★** displaying Vatican treasures, including the large 1400s bronze tomb of Pope Sixtus V by Antonio Pollaiuolo and several antique chalices.

You can also head downstairs to the **Vatican grottoes ★★**, with their tombs of the popes, both ancient and modern (Pope John XXIII gets the most adulation). Behind a wall of glass is the tomb of St. Peter himself.

Impressions

As a whole St. Peter's is fit for nothing but a ballroom, and it is a little too gaudy even for that.

—John Ruskin, letter to the Rev. Thomas Dale, 1840

To go even farther down to the **Vatican necropolis ★★**, the area around St. Peter's tomb, you must apply well in advance at the Ufficio Scavi (© **06-69885318,** scavi@fsp.va), through the arch to the left of the stairs up the basilica. You specify your name, the number in your party, your language, and dates you'd like to visit. They'll notify you by phone or e-mail of your admission date and time. For 10€, you'll take a guided tour of the tombs that were excavated in the 1940s, 7m (23 ft.) beneath the church floor. For details, check **www.vatican.va**.

After you leave the grottoes, you'll find yourself in a courtyard and ticket line for the grandest sight: the climb to **Michelangelo's dome ★★★**, about 113m (375 ft.) high. You can walk up all the steps or take the elevator as far as it goes. The elevator saves you 171 steps, and you'll *still* have 320 to go after getting off. After you've made it to the top, you'll have an astounding view over the rooftops of Rome and even the Vatican Gardens and papal apartments—a photo op, if ever there was one.

Piazza San Pietro. © **06-69881662** (for information on celebrations). Basilica (including grottoes) free admission. Guided tour of excavations around St. Peter's tomb 10€; children 14 and under are not admitted. Stairs to the dome 4€; elevator to the dome 5€; sacristy (w/Historical Museum) free. Basilica (including the sacristy and treasury) daily 9am–6pm. Grottoes daily 8am–5pm. Dome Oct–Mar daily 8am–5pm; Apr–Sept 8am–6pm. Metro: Ottaviano-San Pietro, and then a long stroll. Bus: 23, 34, 40, or 271.

Vatican Museums (Musei Vaticani) & the Sistine Chapel (Cappella Sistina) ★★★ The Vatican Museums boast one of the world's greatest art collections. They're a gigantic repository of treasures from antiquity and the Renaissance, all housed in a labyrinthine series of lavishly adorned palaces, apartments, and galleries leading you to the real gem: the Sistine Chapel. The Vatican Museums occupy a part of the papal palaces built from the 1200s onward. From the former papal private apartments, the museums were created over a period of time to display the vast treasure-trove of art acquired by the Vatican.

To reach the ticket windows, you take an escalator, although you exit down a magnificent spiral ramp. Signs will direct you on your way to the highlights. Obviously, 1, 2, or even 20 trips will not be enough to see the wealth of the Vatican, much less to digest it. With that in mind, we've previewed only a representative sampling of the masterpieces on display (in alphabetical order).

Borgia Apartments ★: Frescoed with biblical scenes by Pinturicchio of Umbria and his assistants, these rooms were designed for Pope Alexander VI (the infamous Borgia pope). They might be badly lit, but they boast great splendor and style. At the end of the Raphael Rooms (see below) is the Chapel of Nicholas V, an intimate room frescoed by the Dominican monk Fra Angelico, the most saintly of all Italian painters.

Chiaramonti Museum: Founded by Pope Pius VII, also known as Chiaramonti, the museum includes the *Corridoio* (Corridor), the Galleria Lapidaria, and the *Braccio Nuovo* (New Side). The Corridor holds more than 800 Greek and Roman works,

The Vatican Museums

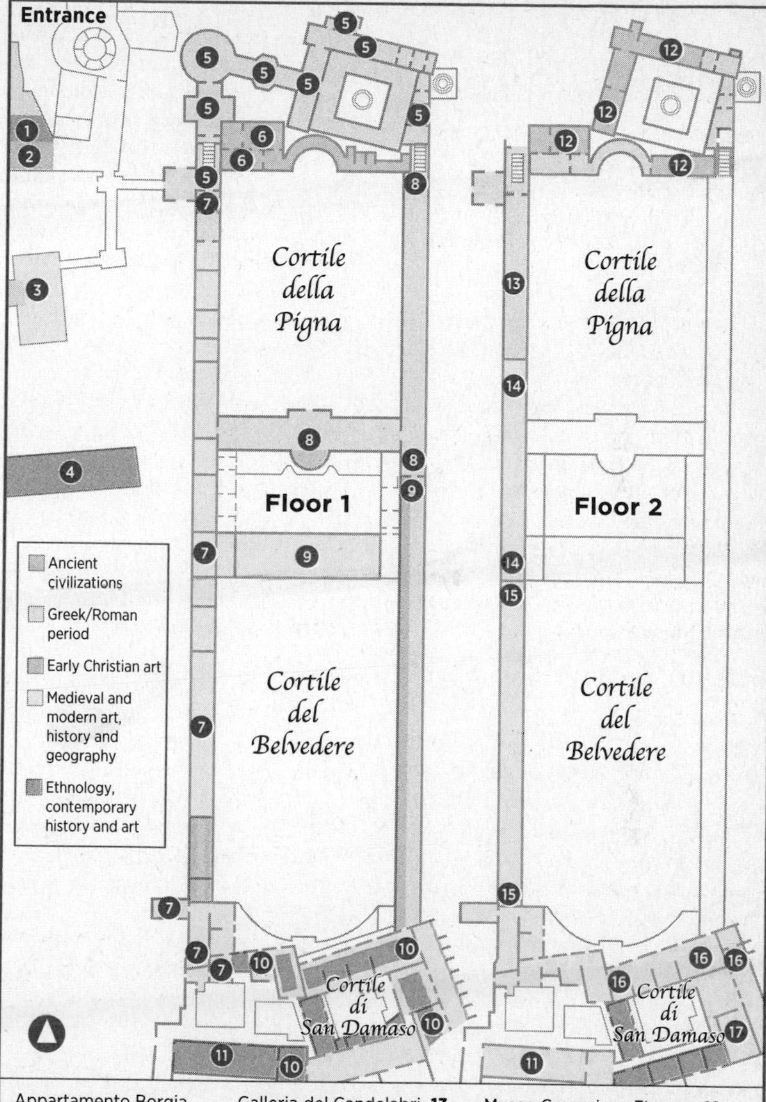

Appartamento Borgia & Collezione d'Arte Religiosa Moderna **10**
Cappella di Nicholas V **17**
Cappella Sistina (Sistine Chapel) **11**
Galleria degli Arazzi **14**
Galleria del Candelabri **13**
Galleria delle Carte Geografiche **15**
Galleria Lapidaria **9**
Library **7**
Museo Chiaramonti **8**
Museo Gregoriano Egizio **6**
Museo Gregoriano Etrusco **12**
Museo Gregoriano Profano **1**
Museo Missionario Ethnologico **2**
Museo Pio-Clementino **5**
Museo Storico **4**
Pinacoteca **3**
Stanze di Raffaello **16**

including statues, reliefs, and sarcophagi. In the Galleria Lapidaria are about 5,000 Christian and pagan inscriptions. In the Braccio Nuovo, built as an extension of the Chiaramonti, you can admire ***The Nile*** ★, a magnificent reproduction of a long-lost Hellenistic original and one of the most remarkable pieces of sculpture from antiquity. The imposing statue of Augustus of Prima Porta presents him as a regal commander.

Collection of Modern Religious Art: This museum, opened in 1973, represents American artists' first invasion of the Vatican. Of the 55 rooms, at least 12 are devoted to American artists. All the works chosen were judged on their "spiritual and religious values." Among the American works is Leonard Baskin's 1.5m (5-ft.) bronze sculpture of *Isaac*. Modern Italian artists such as De Chirico and Manzù are also displayed, and there's a room of paintings by the Frenchman Georges Rouault. You'll also see works by Picasso, Gauguin, Gottuso, Chagall, Henry Moore, Kandinsky, and others.

Egyptian Gregorian Museum: Experience the grandeur of the pharaohs by studying sarcophagi, mummies, and statues of goddesses, vases, jewelry, sculptured pink-granite statues, and hieroglyphics.

Ethnological Museum: This is an assemblage of works of art and objects of cultural significance from all over the world. The principal route is a .5km (⅓-mile) walk through 25 geographical sections, displaying thousands of objects covering 3,000 years of world history. The section devoted to China is especially interesting.

Etruscan Gregorian Museum ★: This was founded by Gregory XIV in 1837 and then enriched year after year, becoming one of the most important and complete collections of Etruscan art. With sarcophagi, a chariot, bronzes, urns, jewelry, and terra-cotta vases, this gallery affords remarkable insights into an ancient civilization. One of the most acclaimed exhibits is the Regolini–Galassi tomb, unearthed in the 19th century at Cerveteri. It shares top honors with the *Mars of Todi,* a bronze sculpture probably dating from the 5th century B.C.

Historical Museum: This museum tells the history of the Vatican. It exhibits arms, uniforms, and armor, some dating from the early Renaissance. The carriages displayed are those used by the popes and cardinals in religious processions.

Pinacoteca (Picture Gallery) ★★★: The Pinacoteca houses paintings and tapestries from the 11th to the 19th centuries. In room no. 1, note the oldest picture at the Vatican, a keyhole-shape wood panel of the *Last Judgment* from the 11th century. In room no. 2 is one of the finest pieces—the *Stefaneschi Triptych* (six panels), by Giotto and his assistants. Bernardo Daddi's masterpiece of early Italian Renaissance art, *Madonna del Magnificat,* is also here. You'll see works by Fra Angelico, the 15th-century Dominican monk who distinguished himself as a miniaturist (his *Virgin with Child* is justly praised—check out the Madonna's microscopic eyes).

Pio Clementino Museum ★★★: Here you'll find Greek and Roman sculptures, many of which are immediately recognizable. The rippling muscles of the ***Belvedere Torso*** ★★★, a partially preserved Greek statue (1st c. B.C.) much admired by the artists of the Renaissance, especially Michelangelo, reveal an intricate knowledge of the human body. In the rotunda is a large gilded bronze of *Hercules* from the late 2nd century B.C. Other major sculptures are under porticoes opening onto the Belvedere courtyard. From the 1st century B.C., one sculpture shows ***Laocoön*** ★★★ and his two sons locked in eternal struggle with the serpents. The incomparable ***Apollo Belvedere*** ★★★ (a late Roman reproduction of an authentic Greek work from the 4th c. B.C.) has become the symbol of classic male beauty, rivaling Michelangelo's *David.* Some members of the Vatican staff once discovered Michelangelo in front of the Belvedere Apollo "publicly aroused in defilement." He was caned and shamed accordingly and had to promise to "create something grand" to compensate for his "shocking" behavior.

Raphael Rooms ★★: While still a young man, Raphael was given one of the greatest assignments of his short life: to decorate a series of rooms in the apartments of Pope Julius II. Raphael and his workshop carried out the commission from 1508 to 1524. In these works, Raphael achieves the Renaissance aim of blending classic beauty with realism. In the Stanza dell'Incendio, you'll see much of the work of Raphael's pupils but little of the master—except in the fresco across from the window. The partially draped Aeneas rescuing his father (to the left of the fresco) is attributed to Raphael, as is the surprised woman with a jug balanced on her head to the right.

Raphael reigns supreme in the next and most important salon, the Stanza della Segnatura, the first room decorated by the artist, where you'll find the majestic ***School of Athens*** **★★★**, one of his best-known works, depicting such philosophers from the ages as Aristotle, Plato, and Socrates. Many of the figures are actually portraits of some of the greatest artists of the Renaissance, including Bramante (on the right as Euclid, bent over to draw on a chalkboard), Leonardo da Vinci (as Plato, the bearded man in the center pointing heavenward), and even Raphael himself (looking out at you from the lower-right corner). While he was painting this masterpiece, Raphael stopped work to walk down the hall for the unveiling of Michelangelo's newly finished Sistine Chapel ceiling. He was so impressed that he returned to his *School of Athens* and added to his design a sulking Michelangelo sitting on the steps.

The *Stanza d'Eliodoro,* also by the master, manages to flatter Raphael's papal patrons (Julius II and Leo X) without compromising his art (although one rather fanciful fresco depicts the pope driving Attila from Rome). Finally, there's the *Sala di Constantino,* which was completed by his students after Raphael's death. Raphael designed the loggia, which is frescoed with more than 50 scenes from the Bible, but his students did the actual work.

Raphael Salon ★★★: In room no. 8, you can view three paintings by the Renaissance giant himself: the *Coronation of the Virgin,* the *Virgin of Foligno,* and the massive *Transfiguration* (completed shortly before his death). There are also eight tapestries made by Flemish weavers from cartoons by Raphael. In room no. 9, seek out Leonardo da Vinci's masterful but uncompleted ***St. Jerome with the Lion*** **★★**, as well as Giovanni Bellini's *Pietà* and one of Titian's greatest works, the *Virgin of Frari.* Finally, in room no. 10, feast your eyes on one of the masterpieces of the baroque, **Caravaggio's *Deposition from the Cross* ★★**.

Sistine Chapel ★★★: Michelangelo considered himself a sculptor, not a painter. While in his 30s, he was commanded by Julius II to stop work on the pope's own tomb and to devote his considerable talents to painting ceiling frescoes (an art form of which the Florentine master was contemptuous). Michelangelo labored for 4 years (1508–12) over this epic project, which was so physically taxing that it permanently damaged his eyesight. All during the task, he had to contend with the pope's incessant urgings to hurry up; at one point, Julius threatened to topple Michelangelo from the scaffolding—or so Vasari relates in his *Lives of the Artists.*

It's ironic that a project undertaken against the artist's wishes would form his most enduring legend. Glorifying the human body as only a sculptor could, Michelangelo painted nine panels, taken from the pages of Genesis, and surrounded them with prophets and sibyls. The most notable panels detail the expulsion of Adam and Eve from the Garden of Eden and the creation of man. ***Tip:*** Bring along binoculars so you can see the details better.

The Florentine master was in his 60s when he began the masterly ***Last Judgment*** ★★★ on the altar wall. Here, Michelangelo presents a more jaundiced view of people and their fate; God sits in judgment and sinners are plunged into the mouth of hell. A master of ceremonies under Paul III, Monsignor Biagio da Cesena, protested to the pope about the "shameless nudes" painted by Michelangelo. Michelangelo showed that he wasn't above petty revenge by painting the prude with the ears of a jackass in hell. When Biagio complained to the pope, Paul III maintained that he had no jurisdiction in hell.

On the side walls are frescoes by other Renaissance masters, such as Botticelli, Perugino, Signorelli, Pinturicchio, Roselli, and Ghirlandaio. Unfortunately, because they compete with Michelangelo's artistry, they're virtually ignored by visitors.

The twisting *ignudi* or male nudes that decorate the corners of the ceiling were terribly controversial when executed.

The restoration of the Sistine Chapel in the 1990s touched off a worldwide debate among art historians. The restoration took years as restorers used advanced computer analyses in their painstaking and controversial work. They reattached the fresco and repaired the ceiling, ridding the frescoes of their dark and shadowy look. Critics claim that in addition to removing centuries of dirt and grime—and several of the added "modesty" drapes—the restorers removed a vital second layer of paint

PAPAL audiences

When the pope is in Rome, he gives a public audience every Wednesday beginning at 10:30am (sometimes at 10am in summer). It takes place in the Paul VI Hall of Audiences, although sometimes St. Peter's Basilica and St. Peter's Square are used to accommodate a large attendance. Anyone is welcome, but you must first obtain a **free ticket** from the office of the Prefecture of the Papal Household, accessible from St. Peter's Square by the Bronze Door, where the colonnade on the right (as you face the basilica) begins. The office is open from Monday through Saturday from 9am to 1pm. Tickets are readily available on Monday and Tuesday; sometimes you won't be able to get into the office on Wednesday morning. Occasionally, if there's enough room, you can attend without a ticket.

You can also write ahead to the **Prefecture of the Papal Household,** 00120 Città del Vaticano (✆ **06-69883273**), indicating your language, the dates of your visit, the number of people in your party, and (if possible) the hotel in Rome to which the cards should be sent the afternoon before the audience. American Catholics, armed with a letter of introduction from their parish priest, should apply to the **North American College,** Via dell'Umiltà 30, 00187 Roma (✆ **06-684931;** www.pnac.org).

At noon on Sunday, the pope speaks briefly from his study window and gives his blessing to the visitors and pilgrims gathered in St. Peter's Square. From about mid-July to mid-September, the Angelus and blessing take place at the summer residence at Castelgandolfo, some 26km (16 miles) out of Rome and accessible by Metro and bus.

as well. Purists argue that many of the restored figures seem flat compared with the originals, which had more shadow and detail. Others have hailed the project for saving Michelangelo's masterpiece for future generations to appreciate and for revealing the vibrancy of his color palette.

Vatican Library ★: The library is richly decorated, with frescoes created by a team of Mannerist painters commissioned by Sixtus V. The library is open only to qualified researchers.

Vatican City, Viale Vaticano (a long walk around the Vatican walls from St. Peter's Square). © **06-69883333.** www.vaticanlibrary.va. Admission 14€ adults, 8€ children 13 and under, free for children 5 and under. Nov–Feb Mon–Sat 10am–12:20pm; Mar–Oct Mon–Fri 10am–3:20pm, Sat 8:45am–12:20pm. Closed Jan 1 and 6, Easter, May 1 and 20, Nov 1, and Dec 8, 25, and 26. Metro: Cipro-Musei Vaticani.

Vatican Gardens ★ Separating the Vatican from the secular world on the north and west are 23 hectares (58 acres) of lush gardens filled with winding paths, brilliantly colored flowers, groves of massive oaks, and ancient fountains and pools. In the midst of this pastoral setting is a small summerhouse, Villa Pia, built for Pope Pius IV in 1560 by Pirro Ligorio. The gardens contain medieval fortifications from the 9th century to the present. Water spouts profusely from a variety of fountains.

To make a reservation to visit the gardens, **it is necessary to book online at www.vatican.va**. Once the reservation is accepted, you must go to the Vatican information office (at Piazza San Pietro, on the left side looking at the facade of St. Peter's) and pick up the tickets 2 or 3 days before your visit. Tours of the gardens last for 2 hours, and the first half-hour is by bus. The cost of the tour is 18€. Visits are March to October on Tuesday, Thursday, and Saturday at 11am, November to February only on Saturday at 11am. For further information, contact the **Vatican Tourism Office** (**© 06-69881662**).

North and west of the Vatican. See previous paragraph for tour information.

Near Vatican City

The trio of arches in the Tiber River's center has been basically unchanged since the **Ponte Sant'Angelo** was built around A.D. 135; the arches abutting the river's embankments were added late in the 19th century as part of a flood-control program. On December 19, 1450, so many pilgrims gathered on this bridge (which at the time was lined with wooden buildings) that about 200 of them were crushed to death.

Since the 1960s, the bridge has been reserved for pedestrians, who can stroll across and admire the statues designed by Bernini. On the southern end is **Piazza Sant'Angelo,** the site of one of the most famous executions of the Renaissance. In 1599, Beatrice Cenci and several members of her family were beheaded on orders of Pope Clement VIII. Their crime? Plotting the murder of their rich and brutal father. Their tale inspired a tragedy by Shelley and a novel by 19th-century Italian politician Francesco Guerrazzi.

Castel Sant'Angelo ★ This overpowering castle on the Tiber was Rome's chief citadel and dungeon and has seen more blood, treachery, and turmoil than any other left in Rome. Even those on a rushed visit to Rome might want to spend some time here. It was built in the 2nd century as a tomb for Emperor Hadrian; it continued as an imperial mausoleum until the time of Caracalla. If it looks like a fortress, it should—that was its function in the Middle Ages. It was built over the Roman walls and linked to the Vatican by an underground passage that was much used by the fleeing papacy, who escaped from unwanted visitors such as Charles V during his 1527 sack of the city. In the 14th century it became a papal residence, enjoying various connections with Boniface IX, Nicholas V, and Julius II, patron of Michelangelo and Raphael. However, its legend rests largely on its link with Pope Alexander VI, whose mistress bore him two children (those darlings of debauchery, Cesare and Lucrezia Borgia).

The highlight is a trip through the Renaissance apartments, with their coffered ceilings and lush decoration. Their walls have witnessed some of the most diabolical plots and intrigues of the High Renaissance. You can go through the dank cells that once echoed with the screams of Cesare's torture victims. The most famous figure imprisoned here was Benvenuto Cellini, the eminent sculptor/goldsmith, remembered for his candid *Autobiography.* Now a museum, the castle halls display the history of the Roman mausoleum, along with a wide-ranging selection of ancient arms and armor. You can climb to the top terrace for another one of those dazzling views of the Eternal City. An audio guide is available to help you understand what you're seeing.

Lungotevere Castello 50. ✆ **06-6819111.** www.castelsantangelo.com. Admission 5€. Tues–Sun 9am–7pm. Metro: Ottaviano-San Pietro, and then a long stroll. Bus: 23, 34, 40, or 271.

THE COLOSSEUM, THE ROMAN FORUM & HIGHLIGHTS OF ANCIENT ROME

The Top Sights in Ancient Rome

If you'd like more guidance as you explore this area, see "Walking Tour 1: Rome of the Caesars," on p. 193.

The Colosseum (Colosseo) ★★★ Now a mere shell, the Colosseum still remains ancient Rome's greatest architectural legacy. Vespasian ordered the construction of the elliptical bowl, called the Amphitheatrum Flavium, in A.D. 72; it was inaugurated by Titus in A.D. 80 with a bloody combat between gladiators and wild beasts that lasted many long weeks. At its peak, under the cruel Domitian, the Colosseum could seat 50,000. The Vestal Virgins from the temple screamed for blood, as more exotic animals were shipped in from the far corners of the empire to satisfy jaded tastes (lion versus bear, two humans vs. hippopotamus). Not-so-mock naval battles were staged (the canopied Colosseum could be flooded), and the defeated combatants might have their lives spared if they put up a good fight. Many historians now believe that one of the most enduring legends about the Colosseum (that Christians were fed to the lions) is unfounded.

Long after the Colosseum ceased to be an arena to amuse sadistic Romans, it was struck by an earthquake. Centuries later it was used as a quarry, its rich marble facing stripped away to build palaces and churches. On one side, part of the original four tiers remains; the first three levels were constructed

> **Impressions**
>
> ***Rome reminds me of a man who lives by exhibiting to travelers his grandmother's corpse.***
>
> **—James Joyce, letter to Stanislaus Joyce, September 1906**

The Colosseum, the Forum & Ancient Rome Attractions

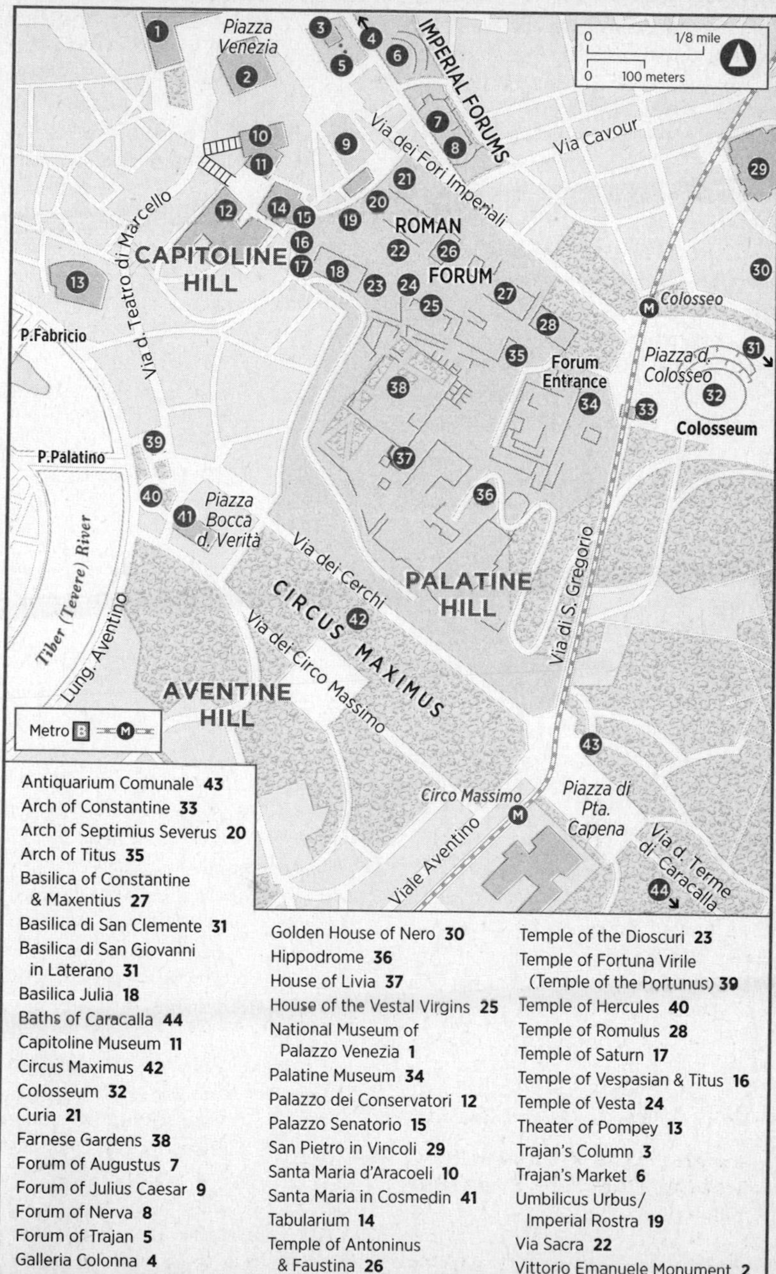

in Doric, Ionic, and Corinthian styles, respectively, to lend variety. Inside, the seats are gone, as is the wooden floor.

On a user-friendly note, two elevators have been installed to allow visitors to reach the second tier without having to climb steps 10 inches high. The Colosseum has become the turnstile for Rome's largest traffic circle, around which thousands of cars whip daily, spewing exhaust over this venerable monument. You can explore on your own or rent an audio guide for 12€.

The **Arch of Constantine ★★**, the highly photogenic memorial next to the Colosseum, was erected by the Senate in A.D. 315 to honor Constantine's defeat of the pagan Maxentius (in 306). Many of the reliefs have nothing whatsoever to do with Constantine or his works, but they tell of the victories of earlier Antonine rulers (they were apparently lifted from other, long-forgotten memorials).

Historically, the arch marks a period of great change in the history of Rome and thus the history of the world. Converted to Christianity by a vision on the battlefield, Constantine ended the centuries-long persecution of the Christians (during which many followers of the new religion had been put to death gruesomely). While Constantine didn't ban paganism (which survived officially until the closing of the temples more than half a century later), he espoused Christianity himself and began the inevitable development that culminated in the conquest of Rome by the Christian religion.

Piazzale del Colosseo, Via dei Fori Imperiali. ✆ **06-39967700.** Admission 12€ all levels. Nov–Feb 15 daily 8:30am–4:30pm; Feb 16–Mar 15 daily 8:30am–5pm; Mar 16–27 daily 8:30am–5:30pm; Mar 28–Aug daily 8:30am–7:15pm; Sept daily 8:30am–7pm; Oct daily 8:30am–6pm. Guided tours in English with an archaeologist 7 times per day Mar 28–Oct 30 (9:30am, 10:15am, 11:15am, 12:30pm, 3pm, 4:15pm, and 5:15pm) 4€. ***Note:*** Admission to the Colosseum also includes a visit to the Roman Forum and the Palatine Hill. Metro: Colosseo.

Roman Forum (Foro Romano), Palatine Hill (Palatino), and Palatine Museum (Museo Palatino) ★★★ When it came to cremating Caesar, purchasing a harlot for the night, or sacrificing a naked victim, the Roman Forum was the place to be. Traversed by the **Via Sacra (Sacred Way) ★**, the Broadway of ancient Rome, the Forum was built in the marshy land between the Palatine and Capitoline hills, and it flourished as the center of Roman life in the days of the Republic before it gradually lost prestige to the Imperial Forums.

You'll see only ruins and fragments, an arch or two, and lots of overturned boulders, but with some imagination you can feel the rush of history here. That any semblance of the Forum remains today is miraculous because it was used for years

No More Lines

The endless lines outside Italian museums and attractions are a fact of life. But reservation services can help you avoid the wait, at least for some of the major museums. Select Italy allows you to reserve tickets for the Colosseum, the Palatine and Forum and Museum, Palazzo Altemps, the Galleria Borghese, and more, plus many other museums in Florence and Venice. The cost varies from 17€ to 35€, depending on the museum, and several combination passes are available. Contact Select Italy at (✆ 800/877-1755), or buy your tickets online at www.selectitaly.com.

(like the Colosseum) as a quarry. Eventually it reverted to what the Italians call a *campo vaccino* (cow pasture). But excavations in the 19th century began to bring to light one of the world's most historic spots.

By day, the columns of now-vanished temples and the stones from which long-forgotten orators spoke are mere shells. Bits of grass and weeds grow where a triumphant Caesar was once lionized. But at night, when the Forum is silent in the moonlight, it isn't difficult to imagine Vestal Virgins still guarding the sacred temple fire. The best view of the Roman Forum at night is from Campidoglio, or Capitoline Hill, Michelangelo's Renaissance piazza that overlooks the Forum.

You can spend at least a morning wandering through the ruins of the Forum. Or, to imbue the stones with some meaning, buy a detailed plan at the gate (the temples are hard to locate otherwise).

Turn right at the bottom of the entrance slope to walk west along the old Via Sacra toward the arch. Just before it on your right is the large brick **Curia ★★** built by Julius Caesar, the main seat of the Roman Senate (if the doors are open, you can lean in to see the 3rd-c. marble inlay floor).

The triumphal **Arch of Septimius Severus ★★** (A.D. 203) displays time-bitten reliefs of the emperor's victories in what are today Iran and Iraq. During the Middle Ages, Rome became a provincial backwater, and frequent flooding of the nearby river helped to rapidly bury most of the Forum. This former center of the empire became a cow pasture. Some bits did still stick out aboveground, including the top half of this arch, which was used to shelter a barbershop! It wasn't until the 19th century that people really became interested in excavating these ancient ruins to see what Rome in its glory must have been like.

Just to the left of the arch, you can make out the remains of a cylindrical lump of rock with some marble steps curving off it. That round stone was the **Umbilicus Urbus,** considered the center of Rome and of the entire Roman Empire; the curving steps are those of the **Imperial Rostra ★**, where great orators and legislators stood to speak, and the people gathered to listen. Nearby, the much-photographed trio of fluted columns with Corinthian capitals supporting a bit of architrave form the corner of the **Temple of Vespasian and Titus ★★**.

Start heading to your left toward the eight Ionic columns marking the front of the **Temple of Saturn ★★** (rebuilt 42 B.C.), which housed the first treasury of Republican Rome. It was also the site of one of the Roman year's biggest annual blowout festivals, the December 17 feast of *Saturnalia,* which, after a bit of tweaking, is now celebrated as Christmas. Now turn left to start heading back east, past the worn steps and stumps of brick pillars outlining the enormous **Basilica Julia ★★**, built by Julius Caesar. Past it are the three Corinthian columns of the **Temple of the Dioscuri ★★★**, dedicated to the Gemini twins, Castor and Pollux. Forming one of the most celebrated sights of the Roman Forum, a trio of columns supports an architrave fragment. The founding of this temple dates from the 5th century B.C.

Beyond the bit of curving wall that marks the site of the little round **Temple of Vesta** (rebuilt several times after fires started by the sacred flame housed within), you'll find the partially reconstructed **House of the Vestal Virgins ★★** (3rd–4th c. A.D.) against the south side of the grounds. This was the home of the consecrated young women who tended the sacred flame in the Temple of Vesta. Vestals were young girls chosen from patrician families to serve a 30-year-long priesthood.

During their tenure, they were among Rome's most venerated citizens, with unique powers such as the ability to pardon condemned criminals. The cult was quite serious about the "virgin" part of the job description—if any of Vesta's earthly servants were found to have "misplaced" her virginity, the miscreant Vestal was summarily buried alive. (Her amorous accomplice was merely flogged to death.) The overgrown rectangle of their gardens is lined with broken, heavily worn statues of senior Vestals on pedestals.

The path dovetails back to join Via Sacra at the entrance. Turn right and then left to enter the massive brick remains and coffered ceilings of the 4th-century **Basilica of Constantine and Maxentius ★★**. These were Rome's public law courts, and their architectural style was adopted by early Christians for their houses of worship (the reason so many ancient churches are called "basilicas").

Return to the path and continue toward the Colosseum, veering right to the second great surviving triumphal arch, the **Arch of Titus ★★** (A.D. 81), on which one relief depicts the carrying off of treasures from Jerusalem's temple—look closely and you'll see a menorah among the booty. The war that this arch glorifies ended with the expulsion of Jews from the colonized Judea, signaling the beginning of the Jewish Diaspora throughout Europe. From here you can climb the **Palatine Hill ★** (admission is included with your combined ticket to the Forum and Colosseum). Before you make the climb, look for a sign pointing to **Santa Maria Antigua,** the oldest Christian church in the Roman Forum, dating from the 16th century.

The Palatine, tradition tells us, is the spot on which the first settlers built their huts, under the direction of Romulus. In later years, the hill became a patrician residential district that attracted such citizens as Cicero. In time, however, the area was gobbled up by imperial palaces and drew a famous and infamous roster of tenants, such as Livia (some of the frescoes in the House of Livia are in miraculous condition), Tiberius, Caligula (murdered here by members of his Praetorian Guard), Nero, and Domitian.

Only the ruins of its former grandeur remain today, and you really need to be an archaeologist to make sense of them because they're more difficult to understand than those in the Forum. But even if you're not interested in the past, it's worth the climb for the panoramic view of the ruins of Rome.

The **Palatine Museum (Museo Palatino) ★** displays a good collection of Roman sculpture from the ongoing digs in the Palatine villas. In summer you can take guided tours in English daily at 11:30am for 4€; call in winter to see whether they're still available. If you ask the museum's custodian, he might take you to one of the nearby locked villas and let you in for a peek at surviving frescoes and stuccoes. **Orti Farnesiani ★**, or the Farnese Gardens, were ordered laid out by Cardinal Alessandro Fernese, Pope Paul III's nephew, in the 16th century. The designer was Gincomo de Vignola, the great Renaissance architect. Resplendent with wildflowers, spring-scented orange groves, and delightful walkways, the site is one of the world's first botanical gardens. It has pavilions, rose gardens, terraces, and **panoramic views ★★** of the Forum over Ancient Rome. Certain sections are sometimes closed due to reconstruction work and ongoing excavations.

Largo Romolo e Remo. ✆ **06-39967700.** Admission 12€; ticket good for same-day admission to the Colosseum and Palatine Hill. Guided tours of Roman Forum daily 1pm, 4€. Oct 30–Feb 15 daily 8:30am–4:30pm; Feb 16–Mar 15 daily 8:30am–5pm; Mar 16–26 daily 8:30am–5:30pm; Mar 27–Aug 31 daily 8:30am–7:15pm; Sept daily 8:30am–7pm; Oct 1–29 daily 8:30am–6:30pm. Last admission 1 hr. before closing. Closed holidays. Metro: Colosseo. Bus: 40, 46, 62, 63, 64, 70, 87, 119, 271, or 280.

Imperial Forums (Fori Imperiali) ★★ It was Mussolini who issued the controversial orders to cut through centuries-old neighborhoods to carve out Via dei Fori Imperiali, thereby linking the Colosseum to the grand 19th-century monuments of Piazza Venezia. Excavations under his fascist regime revealed many archaeological treasures, but destroyed countless others.

Begun by Julius Caesar as an answer to the overcrowding of Rome's older forums, the Imperial Forums were, at the time of their construction, flashier, bolder, and more impressive than the buildings in the Roman Forum. This site conveyed the unquestioned authority of the emperors at the height of their absolute power. On the street's north side, you'll come to a large outdoor restaurant, where Via Cavour joins the boulevard. Just beyond the small park across Via Cavour are the remains of the **Forum of Nerva,** built by the emperor whose 2-year reign (A.D. 96–98) followed that of the paranoid Domitian. You'll be struck by just how much the ground level has risen in 19 centuries. The only really recognizable remnant is a wall of the Temple of Minerva with two fine Corinthian columns. This forum was once flanked by that of Vespasian, which is now gone. It's possible to enter the Forum of Nerva from the other side, but you can see it just as well from the railing.

The next forum you approach is the **Forum of Augustus ★★**, built before the birth of Christ to commemorate the emperor's victory over the assassins Cassius and Brutus in the Battle of Philippi (42 B.C.). Like the Forum of Nerva, you can enter this forum from the other side (cut across the tiny footbridge).

Continuing along the railing, you'll see the vast semicircle of **Trajan's Market ★★**, Via Quattro Novembre 144 (© **06-6790048,** p. 163), whose teeming arcades stocked with merchandise from the far corners of the Roman world collapsed long ago, leaving only a few cats to watch after things. The shops once covered a multitude of levels, and you can still wander around many of them. Trajan's Market is worth the descent below street level. To get there, follow the service road you're on until you reach Trajan's Column on your left; turn right and go up the steep flight of stairs leading to Via Nazionale. At the top, about half a block farther on the right, you'll see the entrance. It's open Tuesday to Sunday from 9am to 7pm. Admission is 8€.

You can enter the **Forum of Trajan ★★** on Via Quattro Novembre near the steps of Via Magnanapoli. Once through the tunnel, you'll emerge into the newest and most beautiful of the Imperial Forums, built between A.D. 107 and 113, and designed by Greek architect Apollodorus of Damascus (who laid out the adjoining market). There are many statue fragments and pedestals bearing still-legible inscriptions, but more interesting is the great Basilica Ulpia, whose gray marble columns rise roofless into the sky. This forum was once regarded as one of the architectural wonders of the world.

Beyond the Basilica Ulpia is **Trajan's Column ★★★**, in magnificent condition, with intricate bas-relief sculpture depicting Trajan's victorious campaign (though, from your vantage point, you'll be able to see only the earliest stages). The next stop is the **Forum of Julius Caesar ★★**, the first of the Imperial Forums. It lies on the opposite side of Via dei Fori Imperiali. This was the site of the Roman stock exchange as well as the Temple of Venus.

After you've seen the wonders of ancient Rome, you might continue up Via dei Fori Imperiali to **Piazza Venezia ★★**, where the white Brescian marble **Vittorio Emanuele Monument** dominates the scene. (You can't miss it.) Italy's most flamboyant landmark, it was built in the late 1800s to honor the first king of Italy. An

Before & After

To appreciate the Colosseum, the Roman Forum, and other ruins more fully, buy a copy of the small red book *Frommer's Rome Past & Present* (Wiley Publishing), sold in bookstores or by vendors near the Forum. Its plastic overleafs show you the way things looked 2,000 years ago.

eternal flame burns at the Tomb of the Unknown Soldier. You'll come to use the monument as a landmark as you figure your way around the city.

Via dei Fori Imperiali. Free admission. Metro: Colosseo. Keep to the right side of the street.

Circus Maximus (Circo Massimo) The Circus Maximus, with its elongated oval proportions and ruined tiers of benches, still evokes the setting of *Ben-Hur.* Today a formless ruin, the once-grand circus was pilfered repeatedly by medieval and Renaissance builders in search of marble and stone. At one time, 250,000 Romans could assemble on the marble seats while the emperor observed the games from his box high on the Palatine Hill. What the Romans called a "circus" was a large arena enclosed by tiers of seats on three or four sides, used especially for sports or spectacles.

The circus lies in a valley formed by the Palatine on the left and the Aventine on the right. Next to the Colosseum, it was the most impressive structure in ancient Rome, located in one of the most exclusive neighborhoods. For centuries, the pomp and ceremony of imperial chariot races filled this valley with the cheers of thousands.

When the dark days of the 5th and 6th centuries fell, the Circus Maximus seemed symbolic of Rome's complete ruin. The last games were held in A.D. 549 on the orders of Totilla the Goth, who had seized Rome in 547 and established himself as emperor. It must've been a pretty miserable show because the decimated population numbered something like 500 when Totilla captured the city. After the travesty of 549, the Circus Maximus was never used again, and the demand for building materials reduced it, like so much of Rome, to a great dusty field.

Between Via dei Cerchi and Via del Circo Massimo. Metro: Circo Massimo. Bus: 81, 60, 160, 715, or 628.

Capitoline Museum (Museo Capitolino) and Palazzo dei Conservatori ★★ Of Rome's seven hills, the Capitoline (Campidoglio) is the most sacred—its origins stretch way back into antiquity (an Etruscan temple to Jupiter once stood on this spot). Climbing Michelangelo's long, sloping steps makes for a dramatic approach. At the top is a perfectly proportioned square, **Piazza del Campidoglio ★★**, also laid out by the Florentine artist. Michelangelo positioned the bronze equestrian statue of Marcus Aurelius in the center, but it has now been moved inside for protection from pollution (a copy was placed on the pedestal in 1997). The other steps adjoining Michelangelo's approach will take you to Santa Maria d'Aracoeli (see "Other Attractions near Ancient Rome," below).

One side of the piazza is open; the others are bounded by the **Senatorium (Town Council),** the statuary-filled **Palace of the Conservatori (Curators),** and the **Capitoline Museum.** These museums house some of the greatest pieces of classical sculpture in the world.

The **Capitoline Museum,** built in the 17th century, was based on an architectural sketch by Michelangelo. In the first room is ***The Dying Gaul* ★★**, a work of majestic skill that's a copy of a Greek original dating from the 3rd century B.C. In a special gallery all her own is the ***Capitoline Venus*** ★★, who demurely covers herself. This statue was the symbol of feminine beauty and charm down through the centuries (also a Roman copy of a 3rd-c.-B.C. Greek original). *Amore* (Cupid) and *Psyche* are up to their old tricks near the window.

The famous **equestrian statue of Marcus Aurelius** ★★, whose years in the piazza made it a victim of pollution, has recently been restored and is now kept in the museum for protection. This is the only bronze equestrian statue to have survived from ancient Rome, mainly because it was thought for centuries that the statue was that of Constantine the Great, and papal Rome respected the memory of the first Christian emperor. The statue is housed in an impressive, newly opened exhibition area, along with several other Capitoline treasures.

The **Palace of the Conservatori** ★★, across the way, was also based on a Michelangelo architectural plan and is rich in classical sculpture and paintings. One of the most notable bronzes, a Greek work of incomparable beauty dating from the 1st century B.C., is ***Lo Spinario*** ★★★ (a little boy picking a thorn from his foot). In addition, you'll find ***Lupa Capitolina (Capitoline Wolf)*** ★★★, a rare Etruscan bronze that could date from the 5th century B.C. (Romulus and Remus, the legendary twins who were suckled by the wolf, were added at a later date.) The palace also contains a *Pinacoteca* (Picture Gallery)—mostly works from the 16th and 17th centuries. Notable canvases are Caravaggio's *Fortune Teller* and his curious *John the Baptist; The Holy Family,* by Dosso Dossi; *Romulus and Remus,* by Rubens; and Titian's *Baptism of Christ.* The entrance courtyard is lined with the remains (head, hands, a foot, and a kneecap) of an ancient colossal statue of Constantine the Great.

A View to Remember

Standing on Piazza del Campidoglio, walk around the right side of the Palazzo Senatorio to a terrace overlooking the city's best panorama of the Roman Forum, with the Palatine Hill and the Colosseum as a backdrop. At night, the Forum is dramatically floodlit, and the ruins look even more impressive.

Piazza del Campidoglio. ✆ **06-67102071.** www.museicapitolini.org. Admission (to both) 11€. Tues–Sun 9am–8pm. Bus: 44, 84, 190, or 780.

Baths of Caracalla (Terme di Caracalla) ★ Named for Emperor Caracalla, the baths were completed in the early 3rd century. The richness of decoration has faded, and the lushness can be judged only from the shell of brick ruins that remain. In their heyday, they sprawled across 11 hectares (27 acres) and could handle 1,600 bathers at one time. As such, these baths are the largest to survive from Rome's imperial era. Most tours start with a visit to the *palestra* or gym, followed by a look at the *laconicum* or Turkish bath. You can also view the *caldarium* which was the "boiling pot" section of the baths. Sweaty bodies cooled down afterward with a soak in the lukewarm waters of the *tepidarium.* The session for the Romans ended at the *frigidarium* with a dip in cold waters. These hot immersions and cold dips were followed by massages and rubdowns by slave boys, many of whom were also recruited for their sexual services to their Roman masters. There remain the ruins of an open-air *natatio* or swimming pool.

Via delle Terme di Caracalla 52. © **06-39967700.** Admission 6€. Oct daily 9am–6pm; Nov and Dec daily 9am–4:30pm; Jan–Feb 15 daily 9am–4:30pm; Feb 16–Mar 15 daily 9am–5pm; Mar 16–27 daily 9am–5:30pm; Mar 28–Aug daily 9am–7:15pm; Sept daily 9am–7pm. Last admission 1 hr. before closing. Closed holidays. Bus: C3, 81, 118, or 160.

Other Attractions near Ancient Rome

Basilica di San Clemente ★ From the Colosseum, head up Via San Giovanni in Laterano to this basilica. It isn't just another Roman church—far from it. In this church-upon-a-church, centuries of history peel away. In the 4th century A.D., a church was built over a secular house from the 1st century, beside which stood a pagan temple dedicated to Mithras (god of the sun). Down in the eerie grottoes, you'll discover well-preserved frescoes from the 9th to the 11th centuries. The Normans destroyed the lower church, and a new one was built in the 12th century. Its chief attraction is the bronze-orange mosaic (from that period) adorning the apse, as well as a chapel honoring St. Catherine of Alexandria with frescoes by Masolino.

Via San Giovanni in Laterano at Piazza San Clemente, Via Labicana 95. © **06-7740021.** Basilica free admission; excavations 5€. Mon–Sat 9am–noon and 3–6pm; Sun 10am–noon and 3–6:30pm. Metro: Colosseo. Bus: C3, 85, 87, 117, 186, or 571.

Basilica di San Giovanni in Laterano ★ This church is the cathedral of the diocese of Rome, where the pope comes to celebrate Mass on certain holidays. Built in A.D. 314 by Constantine, it has suffered the vicissitudes of Rome, forcing it to be rebuilt many times. Only fragmented parts of the original baptistry remain.

The present building is characterized by its 18th-century facade by Alessandro Galilei (statues of Christ and the Apostles ring the top). A 1993 terrorist bomb caused severe damage, especially to the facade. Borromini gets the credit (some say blame) for the interior, built for Innocent X. It's said that, in the misguided attempt to redecorate, frescoes by Giotto were destroyed (remains believed to have been painted by Giotto were discovered in 1952 and are now on display against a column near the entrance on the right inner pier). In addition, look for the unusual ceiling and the sumptuous transept, and explore the 13th-century cloisters with twisted double columns. Next door, **Palazzo Laterano** (not open to the public) was the original home of the popes before they became voluntary "Babylonian captives" in Avignon, France, in 1309.

Across the street is the **Santuario della Scala Santa (Palace of the Holy Steps),** in the Piazza San Giovanni in Laterano (© **06-7726641**). It's alleged that

Rome from a Tiber Perspective

Battelli di Roma (© 06-97745498; www.battellidiroma.it) runs tours aboard a "water bus" that passes under the bridges of Rome. You'll see such landmarks as St. Peter's Basilica (in the distance); Castel Sant'Angelo; and the little island in the Tiber, Isola Tiberina. The cost of a one-way ticket is just 1€. For a 75-minute guided tour, you'll pay 15€. Children ages 6 to 12 pay 6€; ages 5 and under ride for free. Tours start at Ponte Sant'Angelo near the Vatican and are conducted daily at 10am, 11:30am, 3:30pm, and 5pm. An evening tour that includes a four-course dinner departs nightly from Ponte Sant'Angelo at 8pm and lasts 2½ hours. The cost is 54€ for adults and 35€ for kids.

the 28 marble steps (now covered with wood for preservation) were originally at Pontius Pilate's villa in Jerusalem and that Christ climbed them the day he was brought before Pilate. According to tradition, Constantine's mother, Helen, brought the steps from Jerusalem to Rome in 326, and they've been in this location since 1589. Today pilgrims from the world over come to climb the steps on their knees. This is one of the holiest sites in Christendom, although some historians say the stairs may date only to the 4th century. **Santuario della Scala Santa** is open daily 6:15am to noon and 3:30 to 6:30pm.

Piazza San Giovanni in Laterano 4. ✆ **06-69886452.** Basilica free admission; cloisters 2€. Summer daily 7am–6:45pm (off season to 6pm). Metro: San Giovanni.

Galleria Colonna ★ For those who saw the classic Audrey Hepburn film, *Roman Holiday,* this spectacular private palazzo, with its 17th-century *Sala Grande,* is already familiar to you. In it, Hepburn, playing a princess, held a press conference where she bid an elegant adieu to the handsome reporter she'd fallen in love with, Gregory Peck. Today the palace houses a celebrated art collection in its *Galleria Colonna,* which has extremely limited visiting times. The art collection is one of the most prestigious in Rome, all of it acquired after the Renaissance. The greatest art is from the 17th century, and the collection embraces many grand masters of Europe, including small paintings on copper by Jan Bruegel the Elder. There are also several magnificent paintings by Gasper van Wittel, among others. The beautiful, even lavishly decorated rooms of the palace compete with the art itself. Frescoes, for example, by the famous Bernardino di Betto (better known as "Pinturicchio"), decorate the ceiling of "the Room of the Fountain."

Piazza SS, Apostoli 66. ✆ **06-6784350.** www.galleriacolonna.it. Admission 10€, 8€ for those 10 and under and 65 and over. Sat only 9am–1pm. Metro: Colosseo.

National Museum of Palazzo Venezia (Museo Nazionale di Palazzo Venezia) ★ The Palazzo Venezia, in the geographic heart of Rome near Piazza Venezia, served as the seat of the Austrian Embassy until the end of World War I. During the fascist regime (1928–43), it was the seat of the Italian government. The balcony from which Mussolini used to speak to the people was built in the 15th century. You can now visit the rooms and halls containing oil paintings, porcelain, tapestries, ivories, and ceramics. No one particular exhibit stands out—it's the sum total that adds up to a major attraction. The State Rooms occasionally open to host temporary exhibits.

Via del Plebiscito 118. ✆ **06-69994318.** www.galleriaborghese.it. Admission 4€. Tues–Sun 8:30am–7pm. Bus: 30, 40, 46, 60, 62, 64, 70, 87, 119, 130, or 916.

Santa Maria d'Aracoeli ★ On the Capitoline Hill, this landmark church was built for the Franciscans in the 13th century. According to legend, Augustus once ordered a temple erected on this spot, where a sibyl forecast the coming of Christ. In the interior are a coffered Renaissance ceiling and a mosaic of the Virgin over the altar in the Byzantine style. If you poke around, you'll find a tombstone carved by the great Renaissance sculptor Donatello. The church is known for its **Bufalini Chapel,** a masterpiece by Pinturicchio, who frescoed it with scenes illustrating the life and death of St. Bernardino of Siena. He also depicted St. Francis receiving the stigmata. These frescoes are a high point in early Renaissance Roman painting. You have to climb a long flight of steep steps to reach the church, unless you're already

DID YOU know?

- Along with miles of headless statues and acres of paintings, Rome has 913 churches.
- Some Mongol khans and Turkish chieftains pushed westward to conquer the Roman Empire after it had ceased to exist.
- At the time of Julius Caesar and Augustus, Rome's population reached one million—it was the largest city in the Western world. Some historians claim that by the year A.D. 500, only 10,000 inhabitants were left.
- Pope Leo III snuck up on Charlemagne and set an imperial crown on his head, a surprise coronation that launched a precedent of Holy Roman Emperors being crowned by popes in Rome.
- More than 90% of Romans live in apartment buildings, some of which rise 10 floors and have no elevators.
- The Theater of Marcellus incorporated a gory realism in some of its plays: Condemned prisoners were often butchered before audiences.
- Christians might not have been fed to the lions at the Colosseum, but in a single day 5,000 animals were slaughtered (about 1 every 10 seconds). North Africa's native lions and elephants were rendered extinct.

on neighboring Piazza del Campidoglio, in which case you can cross the piazza and climb the steps on the far side of the Museo Capitolino (see above).

Piazza d'Aracoeli. ✆ **06-69763839.** Free admission. Daily 9am-12:30pm and 3:30-6:30pm. Bus: 30, 40, 46, 62, 63, 64, 70, 87, 119, 130,186, 190, or 271.

Santa Maria in Cosmedin This little church was begun in the 6th century but was subsequently rebuilt, and a Romanesque campanile was added at the end of the 11th century, although its origins go back to the 3rd century. The church was destroyed several times by earthquakes or by foreign invasions, but it has always been rebuilt.

People come not for great art treasures, but to see the **"Mouth of Truth,"** a large disk under the portico. As Gregory Peck demonstrated to Audrey Hepburn in the film *Roman Holiday,* the mouth is supposed to chomp down on the hands of liars who insert their paws. (According to local legend, a former priest used to keep a scorpion in back to bite the fingers of anyone he felt was lying.) The purpose of this disk (which is not of particular artistic interest) is unclear. One hypothesis says that it was used to collect the faithful's donations to God, which were introduced through the open mouth.

Piazza della Bocca della Verità 18. ✆ **06-6781419.** Free admission. Summer daily 9am–8pm; off season daily 9am–5pm. Metro: Circo Massimo.

St. Peter in Chains (San Pietro in Vincoli) ★ This church was founded in the 5th century to house the chains that bound St. Peter in Palestine (they're preserved under glass). But its drawing card is the tomb of Pope Julius II, with one of the world's most famous sculptures: **Michelangelo's *Moses* ★★★**. Michelangelo was to have carved 44 magnificent figures for the tomb. That didn't happen, but the pope was given a great consolation prize—a figure intended to be "minor" that's now counted among Michelangelo's masterpieces. In the *Lives of the Artists,* Vasari wrote about the stern father symbol of Michelangelo's *Moses:* "No modern work will ever equal it in beauty, no, nor ancient either."

Piazza San Pietro in Vincoli 4A (off Via degli Annibaldi). © **06-4882865.** Free admission. Spring/summer daily 7:30am-12:30pm and 3:30-7pm; fall/winter to 6pm. Metro: Colosseo or Cavour, and then cross the boulevard and walk up the flight of stairs. Turn right, and you'll head into the piazza; the church will be on your left.

THE PANTHEON & ATTRACTIONS NEAR PIAZZA NAVONA & CAMPO DE' FIORI

The Pantheon & Nearby Attractions

The Pantheon stands on **Piazza della Rotonda,** a lively square with cafes, vendors, and great people-watching.

The Pantheon ★★★ Of all ancient Rome's great buildings, only the Pantheon (All the Gods) remains intact. It was built in 27 B.C. by Marcus Agrippa and was reconstructed by Hadrian in the early 2nd century A.D. This remarkable building, 43m (142 ft.) wide and 43m (142 ft.) high (a perfect sphere resting in a cylinder) and once ringed with white marble statues of Roman gods in its niches, is among the architectural wonders of the world because of its dome and its concept of space. Hadrian himself is credited with the basic plan, an architectural design that was unique for the time. The dome, a perfect hemisphere of cast concrete, rests on a solid ring wall, supporting this massive structure. Before the 20th century, this was the biggest pile of concrete ever constructed. The ribbed dome outside is a series of almost weightless cantilevered brick. Animals were sacrificed and burned in the center, and the smoke escaped through the only means of light, the oculus, an opening at the top 5.4m (18 ft.) in diameter. Michelangelo came here to study the dome before designing the cupola of St. Peter's (whose dome is .6m/2 ft. smaller than the Pantheon's). The walls are 7.5m (25 ft.) thick, and the bronze doors weigh 20 tons each. About 125 years ago, Raphael's tomb was discovered here (fans still bring him flowers). Vittorio Emanuele II, king of Italy, and his successor, Umberto I, are interred here as well.

Impressions

Rome, Italy, is an example of what happens when the buildings in a city last too long.

—Andy Warhol, *The Philosophy of Andy Warhol (From A To B And Back Again),* 1975

Piazza della Rotonda. © **06-68300230.** Free admission. Mon-Sat 8:30am-7:30pm; Sun 9am-6pm. Bus: C3, 30, 46, 62, 63, 64, 116, 170, or 492 to Largo di Torre.

Galleria Doria Pamphilj ★ This museum offers a look at what it was like to live in an 18th-century palace. It has been restored to its former splendor and expanded to include four rooms long closed to the public. It's partly leased to tenants (on the upper levels), and there are shops on the street level—but you'll overlook all this

Where Emperors Ruled & Cats Now Reign

At the site where it is believed that Julius Caesar was stabbed to death, right in the heart of historic Rome, you can visit the city's vast feline population. The **Torre Argentina Cat Sanctuary,** at Largo di Torre Argentina (✆ 06-6872133; www.romancats.de), is at the intersection of via Arenula and via Florida, right off Corso Vittorio Emanuele, a short walk from the Pantheon and Piazza Navona. Where four Republican-era temples dating from 200 to 300 B.C. once stood, today some 300 abandoned house cats are cared for by a group of volunteers. Cats in all shapes and sizes are everywhere, craving human attention. Some of them find homes with visitors from around the world. The attraction can be visited daily from noon to 6pm (until 8pm in summer). The cats will be waiting.

after entering the grand apartments of the Doria Pamphilj family, which traces its lineage to before the great 15th-century Genoese admiral Andrea Doria. The apartments surround the central court and gallery. The **ballroom, drawing rooms, dining rooms,** and **family chapel** are full of gilded furniture, crystal chandeliers, Renaissance tapestries, and family portraits.

Skirting the central court is a **picture gallery** with a memorable collection of frescoes, paintings, and sculpture. Most important are the portrait of Innocent X, by Velázquez; *Salome,* by Titian; works by Rubens and Caravaggio; the *Bay of Naples,* by Pieter Bruegel the Elder; and a copy of Raphael's portrait of Principessa Giovanna d'Aragona de Colonna (who looks remarkably like Leonardo's *Mona Lisa*).

Piazza del Collegio Romano 2 (off Via del Corso). ✆ **06-6797323.** www.doriapamphilj.it. Admission 9.50€ adults, 7€ students/seniors. Daily 10am–5pm. Closed on holidays. Private visits can be arranged. Metro: Barberini or Colosseo.

Santa Maria Sopra Minerva Beginning in 1280, early Christian leaders ordained that the foundation of an ancient temple dedicated to Minerva (goddess of wisdom) be reused as the base for Rome's only Gothic church. Architectural changes and redecorations in the 1500s and 1900s stripped it of some of its magnificence, but it still includes an awe-inspiring collection of medieval and Renaissance tombs. You'll find a beautiful chapel frescoed by Fillipino Lippi and, to the left of the apse, a muscular *Risen Christ* carrying a rather small marble cross carved by Michelangelo (the bronze drapery covering Christ's nudity was added later). Under the altar lie the remains of St. Catherine of Siena. After St. Catherine died, her head was separated from her body, and now the head is in Siena, where she was born. In the passage to the left of the choir is the floor tomb of the great monastic painter Fra Angelico. The amusing baby elephant carrying a small obelisk in the piazza outside was designed by Bernini.

Piazza della Minerva 42. ✆ **06-6793926.** www.basilicaminerva.it. Free admission. Daily 8am–7pm. Bus: C3, 30, 70, 64, 70, 87, 116, or 492.

Piazza Navona & Nearby Attractions

Piazza Navona ★★★, one of the most beautifully baroque sites in all Rome, is an ocher-colored gem, unspoiled by new buildings or traffic. Its shape results from the ruins of the Stadium of Domitian, lying underneath. Great chariot races were once

The Pantheon & Nearby Attractions

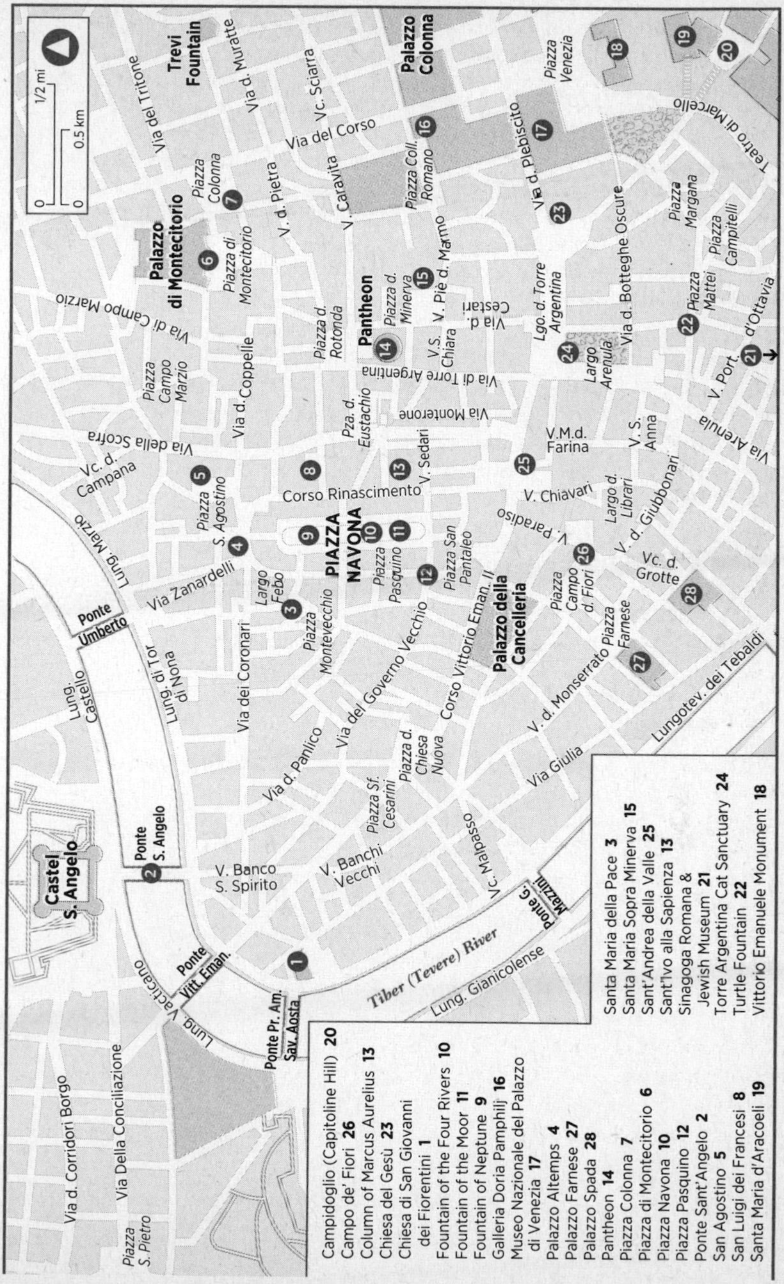
Campidoglio (Capitoline Hill) 20
Campo de' Fiori 26
Column of Marcus Aurelius 13
Chiesa del Gesù 23
Chiesa di San Giovanni dei Fiorentini 1
Fountain of the Four Rivers 10
Fountain of the Moor 11
Fountain of Neptune 9
Galleria Doria Pamphilj 16
Museo Nazionale del Palazzo di Venezia 17
Palazzo Altemps 4
Palazzo Farnese 27
Palazzo Spada 28
Pantheon 14
Piazza Colonna 7
Piazza di Montecitorio 6
Piazza Navona 10
Piazza Pasquino 12
Ponte Sant'Angelo 2
San Agostino 5
San Luigi dei Francesi 8
Santa Maria d'Aracoeli 19
Santa Maria della Pace 3
Santa Maria Sopra Minerva 15
Sant'Andrea della Valle 25
Sant'Ivo alla Sapienza 13
Sinagoga Romana & Jewish Museum 21
Torre Argentina Cat Sanctuary 24
Turtle Fountain 22
Vittorio Emanuele Monument 18
0 1/2 mi
0 0.5 km
Trevi Fountain
Palazzo Colonna
Palazzo di Montecitorio
Pantheon
PIAZZA NAVONA
Palazzo della Cancelleria
Castel S. Angelo
Piazza Venezia
Via del Corso
Via del Tritone
Corso Rinascimento
Corso Vittorio Eman. II
Tiber (Tevere) River
Ponte S. Angelo
Ponte Umberto
Ponte Vitt. Eman.
Ponte Pr. Am. Sav. Aosta
Ponte G. Mazzini
Lungotev. dei Tebaldi
Teatro di Marcello
Via Giulia
Via della Conciliazione

913 CHURCHES, 1 SYNAGOGUE: JEWS IN THE capital OF CHRISTENDOM

Nestled midway between the Isola Tiberina and the monument to Vittorio Emanuele II, Rome's Jewish ghetto was designated during the administration of Pope Paul IV between 1555 and 1559. At the time, it enclosed several thousand people in a cramped 1-hectare (2½-acre) tract of walled-in, overcrowded real estate that did much to contribute to the oppression of the Jews during the Italian Renaissance.

Jews had played an important part in the life of Rome prior to that time. They migrated to the political center of the known world during the 1st century B.C., and within 200 years, their community had grown to a very noticeable minority. Most of it was based in Trastevere, which for many years was referred to as the *Contrada Iudaeorum* (Jewish Quarter). By 1309, ordinances were passed that forced Jews to indicate their religious and cultural backgrounds with special garments, and their ability to worship as they wished depended on the indulgence of the pope.

In 1363, additional ordinances were passed that limited Jewish cemeteries to an area adjacent to the Tiber, near the present-day Church of San Francesco a Ripa. During the 1400s, the Jewish population regrouped onto the opposite side of the Tiber, in an area around the square that's known today as Piazza Mattei.

In 1492, Queen Isabella and King Ferdinand of Spain killed, tortured, forcibly converted, or forced the emigration of thousands of Jews from Spain. Many came to Rome, swelling the ranks of the city. Pope Alexander VI (1492–1503), whose political sympathies lay firmly with the Spanish monarchs, grudgingly admitted the refugees into his city, on condition that each pay a hefty fee in gold. His papal bull defined the borders of the Jewish ghetto within the boundaries of the Sant'Angelo district and later enlarged them to include the muddy, frequently flooded banks of the Tiber. Water levels often reached the

held here (some rather unusual, such as the one in which the head of the winning horse was lopped off as it crossed the finish line and was then carried by runners to be offered as a sacrifice by the Vestal Virgins atop the Capitoline). In medieval times, the popes used to flood the piazza to stage mock naval encounters. Today the piazza is packed with vendors and street performers, and lined with pricey cafes where you can enjoy a cappuccino or gelato and indulge in unparalleled people-watching.

In addition to the twin-towered facade of 17th-century Santa Agnes, the piazza boasts several baroque masterpieces. The best known, in the center, is Bernini's **Fountain of the Four Rivers (Fontana dei Quattro Fiumi) ★★★**, whose four stone personifications symbolize the world's greatest rivers: the Ganges, Danube, della Plata, and Nile. It's fun to try to figure out which is which. (***Hint:*** The figure with the shroud on its head is the Nile, so represented because the river's source was unknown at the time.) At the south end is the **Fountain of the Moor (Fontana del Moro),** also by Bernini. The **Fountain of Neptune (Fontana di Nettuno),** which balances that of the Moor, is a 19th-century addition; it was restored after a demented 1997 attack by two men broke the tail of one of its sea creatures. To get there, take bus no. C3, 30, 70, 81, 87, 130, or 186.

third floors of the houses of the poorest families, who were forced, by law and economics, to settle here. Piling humiliation on humiliation, the residents of the nearly uninhabitable riverbanks were forced to pay for the construction of the embankments that prevented the neighborhood from flooding. For centuries, no one could enter or leave the ghetto between sundown and sunrise.

In 1848, the walls that had defined and confined the ghetto were demolished under the auspices of the relatively lenient Pope Leo XII. In 1883, during the surge of nationalism that preceded the unification of Italy, the ghetto was abolished altogether.

Tragically, on October 16, 1943, the segregation of Rome's Jews was reestablished when German Nazi soldiers rounded up most of the Jews from throughout Rome into a re-creation of the medieval ghetto and imposed a ridiculously high ransom on them. Amazingly, this fee—more than 100 pounds of gold per resident—was eventually collected. Having made the payment, the Jews were rounded up and deported to the death camps anyway, one of the most horrible episodes of Italy's participation in the war years.

Today the neighborhood, centered on Piazza Mattei and its elegant Renaissance fountain, lacks any coherent architectural unity; it's a colorful hodgepodge of narrow, twisting streets and occasionally derelict buildings. One of the most unusual streets is Via del Portico d'Ottavia, where medieval houses and pavements adjoin kosher food stores and simple trattorie that almost invariably feature *carciofi alla Giudea* (deep-fried Jerusalem artichokes).

Although it bears the scars and honors of centuries of occupation by Jews, today this is a Jewish neighborhood mostly in name only. Its centerpiece is the synagogue on Via Catalana.

Palazzo Altemps ★ This branch of the National Roman Museum is housed in a 15th-century palace that was restored and opened to the public in 1997. It is home to the fabled Ludovisi Collection of Greek and Roman sculpture. Among the masterpieces of the Roman Renaissance, you'll find the *Ares Ludovisi,* a Roman copy of the original dated 330 B.C. and restored by Bernini during the 17th century. In the *Sala delle Storie di Mosè* is *Ludovisi's Throne,* representing the birth of Venus. The *Sala delle Feste* (the Celebrations' Hall) is dominated by a sarcophagus depicting the Romans fighting against the Ostrogoth Barbarians; this masterpiece, carved from a single block, dates back to the 2nd century A.D. and today is called *Grande Ludovisi* (Great Ludovisi). Other outstanding art from the collection includes a copy of Phidias's celebrated *Athena,* which once stood in the Parthenon in Athens. (The Roman copy here is from the 1st c. B.C. because the original *Athena* is lost to history.) The huge *Dionysus with Satyr* is from the 2nd century A.D.

Piazza di Sant Apollinare 48, near the Piazza Navona. ✆ **06-39967700.** Admission 7€. Tues–Sun 9am–7:45pm. Last admission 1 hr. before closing. Bus: C3, 30, 70, 81, 87, or 130.

San Luigi dei Francesi This has been the national church of France in Rome since 1589, and a stone salamander (the symbol of the Renaissance French monarch François I) is subtly carved into its facade. Inside, in the last chapel on the left, is a noteworthy series of oil paintings on canvas by Caravaggio: the celebrated *Calling of St. Matthew* on the left, *St. Matthew and the Angel* in the center, and the *Martyrdom of St. Matthew* on the right. Of these, Caravaggio's masterpiece is the "divine" *Calling of St. Matthew,* with his familiar motif—a beautiful young man with a slightly scornful leer.

Via Santa Giovanna d'Arco 5. ✆ **06-688271.** Free admission. Fri–Wed 10am–12:30pm and 4–7pm; Thurs 10am–12:30pm. Bus: C3, 30, 70, 81, or 87.

Santa Maria della Pace According to legend, blood flowed from a statue of the Virgin above the altar here after someone threw a pebble at it. This legend motivated Pope Sixtus to rebuild the church in the 1500s on the foundations of an even older sanctuary. For generations after that, its curved porticos, cupola atop an octagonal base, cloisters by Bramante, and frescoes by Raphael helped make it one of the most fashionable churches for aristocrats residing in the surrounding palazzos.

Vicolo del Arco della Pace 5 (off Piazza Navona). ✆ **06-6861156.** Free admission. Mon–Sat 10am–noon and 4–6pm; Sun 10am–noon. Bus: C3, 30, 70, 81, or 87.

Campo De' Fiori & the Jewish Ghetto

During the 1500s, **Campo de' Fiori ★** was the geographic and cultural center of secular Rome, site of dozens of inns. From its center rises a statue of the severe-looking monk Giordano Bruno, whose presence is a reminder that religious heretics were occasionally burned at the stake here. Today, circled by venerable houses, the campo is the site of an **open-air food market** held Monday through Saturday from early in the morning until around noon (or whenever the food runs out). Take bus no. 30, 40, 62, 64, 70, 87, 116, 492, 571, or 628 to Corso Vittorio Emanuele.

Built from 1514 to 1589, the **Palazzo Farnese ★**, on Piazza Farnese, was designed by Sangallo and Michelangelo, among others, and was an astronomically expensive project for the time. Its residents have included members of the Farnese family, plus Pope Paul III, Cardinal Richelieu, and the former Queen Christina of Sweden, who moved to Rome after abdicating. During the 1630s, when the heirs couldn't afford to maintain the palazzo, it became the site of the French Embassy, as it still is (it's closed to the public). For the best view of it, cut west from Via Giulia along any of the narrow streets (we recommend Via Mascherone or Via dei Farnesi).

Palazzo Spada ★, Capo di Ferro 3 (✆ **06-6861158;** www.galleriaborghese.it), built around 1550 for Cardinal Gerolamo Capo di Ferro and later inhabited by the descendants of several other cardinals, was sold to the Italian government in the 1920s. Its richly ornate facade, covered in high-relief stucco decorations in the Mannerist style, is the finest of any building from 16th-century Rome. The State Rooms are closed, but the richly decorated courtyard and a handful of galleries of paintings are open. Admission is 6€; it's open Tuesday through Saturday from 8:30am to 7:30pm. To get there, take bus no. 46, 56, 62, 64, 70, 87, or 492.

Also in this neighborhood stands the **Sinagoga Romana** (✆ **06-6840061**), open only for services. Trying to avoid all resemblance to a Christian church, the building (1874–1904) evokes Babylonian and Persian details. The synagogue was attacked by terrorists in 1982 and since then has been heavily guarded by *carabinieri* (a division of the Italian army) armed with machine guns.

On the premises of the synagogue is the **Museo Ebraico di Roma** (Jewish Museum of Rome), first opened in 1959, displaying the works of 17th and 18th century silversmiths, precious textiles from all over Europe, parchments, and marble carvings saved when the ghetto synagogues were demolished. The exhibits trace 2,000 years of the history of the Jews of Rome. Open Sunday to Thursday 10am to 5pm (June 11–Sept 4, 10am–7pm), Friday 9am to 2pm (June 11–Sept 4, 10am–4pm). Admission (includes guided tour) is 7.50€ for adults, 4€ for students, and free for children 10 and under. For more information about the museum, check www.museoebraico.roma.it.

THE SPANISH STEPS, THE TREVI FOUNTAIN & NEARBY ATTRACTIONS

On or Around Piazza Di Spagna

The Spanish Steps ★★ (Scalinata di Spagna; Metro: Spagna) are filled in spring with azaleas and other flowers, flower vendors, jewelry dealers, and photographers snapping pictures of visitors. The steps and the square (Piazza di Spagna) take their names from the Spanish Embassy, which used to be headquartered here. Designed by Italian architect Francesco de Sanctis and built from 1723 to 1725, they were funded almost entirely by the French as a preface to Trinità dei Monti at the top. The steps and the piazza below are always packed with a crowd: strolling, reading in the sun, browsing the vendors' carts, and people-watching.

Keats-Shelley House At the foot of the Spanish Steps is this 18th-century house where John Keats died of consumption on February 23, 1821, at age 25. Since 1909, when it was bought by well-intentioned English and American literary types, it has been a working library established in honor of Keats and Percy Bysshe Shelley, who drowned off the coast of Viareggio with a copy of Keats's poems in his pocket. Mementos range from the kitsch to the immortal. The apartment where Keats spent his last months, carefully tended by his close friend Joseph Severn, shelters a strange death mask of Keats, as well as the "deadly sweat" drawing by Severn.

Piazza di Spagna 26. © **06-6784235.** www.keats-shelley-house.org. Admission 4€. Mon–Fri 10am–1pm and 2–6pm; Sat 11am–2pm and 3–6pm. Guided tours by appointment. Metro: Spagna.

Palazzo del Quirinale ★★ Until the end of World War II, this palace was the home of the king of Italy; before that, it was the residence of the pope. Despite its Renaissance origins (nearly every important architect in Italy worked on some aspect of its sprawling premises), it's rich in associations with ancient emperors and deities. The colossal statues of the twin heroes, or dioscuri Castor and Pollux, which now form part of the fountain in the piazza, were found in the nearby great Baths of Constantine; in 1793 Pius VI had the ancient Egyptian obelisk moved here from the Mausoleum of Augustus. The sweeping view of Rome from the piazza, which crowns the highest of the seven ancient hills of Rome, is itself worth the trip.

Piazza del Quirinale. www.quirinale.it. Admission 5€. Sun 8:30am–noon. Metro: Barberini. ***Note:*** Palazzo del Quirinale remains closed June 22–Sept 7.

Great Art in the Stables

Across from the Palazzo del Quirinale, the 18th-century Quirinal stables called the **Scuderie del Quirinale or Scuderie Papali,** Via XXIV Maggio 16 (✆ 06-39967500; www.scuderiequirinale.it), originally built for the pope's horses, have been transformed into an art gallery that hosts changing exhibitions. Recent exhibits have ranged from 100 masterpieces on loan from the Hermitage to Botticelli's drawings illustrating Dante's *Divine Comedy.* The stables were built on the site of the 3rd-century Temple of Serapis (some of the ruins can still be seen from the glass-enclosed stairs overlooking a private garden). The galleries are open Sunday to Thursday 10am to 8pm, Friday and Saturday 10am to 10:30pm. Admission is 10€.

Trevi Fountain (Fontana dei Trevi) ★★ As you elbow your way through the summertime crowds around the Trevi Fountain, you'll find it hard to believe that this little piazza was nearly always deserted before the film *Three Coins in the Fountain* brought the stampede of tour buses. Today this newly restored gem is a must on everybody's itinerary.

Supplied by water from the Acqua Vergine aqueduct and a triumph of the baroque style, it was based on the design of Nicolo Salvi and was completed in 1762. The design centers on the triumphant figure of Neptunus Rex, standing on a shell chariot drawn by winged steeds and led by a pair of tritons. Two allegorical figures in the side niches represent good health and fertility.

On the southwestern corner of the piazza is a somber **SS. Vincenzo e Anastasio,** with a strange claim to fame. Within it survive the hearts and intestines of several centuries of popes. According to legend, the church was built on the site of a spring that burst from the earth after the beheading of St. Paul; the spring is one of the *three* sites where his head is said to have bounced off the ground.

Piazza di Trevi. Metro: Barberini. Bus: 62, 81, 85,175, 492, or 590.

Around Via Veneto & Piazza Barberini

To find these attractions, see the map titled "Attractions near Stazione Termini, Via Veneto & Piazza Barberini," on p. 183. Metro: Barberini.

Piazza Barberini lies at the foot of several Roman streets, among them Via Barberini, Via Sistina, and Via Vittorio Veneto. It would be a far more pleasant spot were it not for the heavy traffic swarming around its principal feature, Bernini's **Fountain of the Triton (Fontana del Tritone) ★**. For more than 3 centuries, the strange figure sitting in a vast open clam has been blowing water from his triton.

As you go up Via Vittorio Veneto, look for the small fountain on the right corner of Piazza Barberini—it's another Bernini, the small **Fountain of the Bees (Fontana delle Api).** At first they look more like flies, but they're the bees of the Barberini, the crest of that powerful family complete with the crossed keys of St. Peter above them (the keys were always added to a family crest when a son was elected pope).

Monumental Cemetery of the Capuchin Brothers (Cimitero Monumentale dei Padri Cappuccini) One of the most horrifying sights in all Christendom, this is a series of chapels with hundreds of skulls and crossbones woven into

Attractions near the Spanish Steps & Piazza del Popolo

mosaic "works of art." To make this allegorical dance of death, the bones of more than 4,000 Capuchin brothers were used. Some of the skeletons are intact, draped with Franciscan habits. The creator of this chamber of horrors? The tradition of the friars is that it was the work of a French Capuchin. Their literature suggests that you should visit the cemetery while keeping in mind the historical moment of its origins, when Christians had a rich and creative cult for their dead, and great spiritual masters meditated and preached with a skull in hand. Those who've lived through the days of crematoria and other such massacres might view the graveyard differently, but to many who pause to think, this sight has a message. It's not for the squeamish, however. The entrance is halfway up the first staircase on the right of the church.

Impressions

Rome's just a city like anywhere else. A vastly overrated city, I'd say. It trades on belief just as Stratford trades on Shakespeare.

—Anthony Burgess, *Inside Mr. Enderby*, 1963

Beside the Church of the Immaculate Conception, Via Vittorio Veneto 27. ✆ **06-4871185.** www.cappucciniviaveneto.it. Donation required. Fri–Wed 9am–1pm and 3–6pm. Metro: Barberini.

National Gallery of Ancient Art (Galleria Nazionale d'Arte Antica) ★★ **Palazzo Barberini,** right off Piazza Barberini, is one of the most magnificent baroque palaces in Rome. It was begun by Carlo Maderno in 1627 and completed in 1633 by Bernini, whose lavishly decorated rococo apartments, the **Gallery of Decorative Art (Galleria d'Arte Decorativa),** are on view. This gallery is part of the National Gallery of Ancient Art.

The bedroom of Princess Cornelia Costanza Barberini and Prince Giulio Cesare Colonna di Sciarra stands just as it was on their wedding night, and many household objects are displayed in the decorative art gallery. In the chambers, which boast frescoes and hand-painted silk linings, you can see porcelain from Japan and Bavaria, canopied beds, and a wooden baby carriage.

On the first floor is a splendid array of paintings from the 13th to the 16th centuries, most notably *Mother and Child,* by Simone Martini, and works by Fillipino Lippi, Andrea Solario, and Francesco Francia. Il Sodoma has some brilliant pictures here, including *The Rape of the Sabines* and *The Marriage of St. Catherine.* One of the best-known paintings is Raphael's beloved *La Fornarina,* the baker's daughter who was his mistress and who posed for his Madonna portraits. Titian is represented by his *Venus and Adonis.* Also here are Tintorettos and El Grecos. Many visitors come just to see the magnificent Caravaggios, including *Narcissus.*

Via Barberini 18. ✆ **06-32810.** www.galleriaborghese.it. Admission 6€. Tues–Sun 8:30am–7:30pm. Metro: Barberini.

Near Piazza Del Popolo

The restored **Piazza del Popolo ★★** is haunted with memories. According to legend, the ashes of Nero were enshrined here until 11th-century residents began complaining to the pope about his imperial ghost. The **Egyptian obelisk** dates from the 13th century B.C., removed from Heliopolis to Rome during Augustus's reign (it stood at the Circus Maximus). The piazza was designed in the early 19th century by Valadier, Napoleon's architect. The lovely **Santa Maria del Popolo ★★**, with two Caravaggios, is at its northern curve, and opposite are almost-twin baroque churches, overseeing the never-ending traffic. Take the Flaminio Metro.

Altar of Peace (Ara Pacis) ★ In an airy glass-and-concrete building beside the Tiber rests a reconstructed treasure from the reign of Augustus. It was built by the Senate as a tribute to that emperor and the peace he brought to the Roman world. On the marble wall, you can see portraits of the imperial family—Augustus, Livia (his second wife), Tiberius (Livia's son from her first marriage and Augustus's successor), and even Julia (Augustus's unfortunate daughter, who divorced her first husband to marry Tiberius and then was exiled by her father for her sexual excesses). The altar was reconstructed from literally hundreds of fragments scattered in museums for centuries. A major portion came from the foundations of a Renaissance palace on the Corso. The reconstruction took place during the 1930s.

Lungotevere Augusta. ✆ **06-82059127.** www.arapacis.it. Admission 6.50€. Tues–Sun 9am–9pm. Bus: 70, 81, 186, or 628.

Augustus's Mausoleum (Mausoleo Augusteo) ★ This seemingly indestructible pile of bricks has been here for 2,000 years and will probably remain for another 2,000. Like the larger tomb of Hadrian across the river, this was once a circular marble-covered affair with tall cypresses, symmetrical groupings of Egyptian obelisks, and some of Europe's most spectacular ornamentation. Many of the 1st-century emperors had their ashes deposited in golden urns inside, and it was probably because of this crowding that Hadrian decided to construct an entirely new tomb (the Castel Sant'Angelo) for himself in another part of Rome. The imperial remains stayed intact here until the 5th century, when invading barbarians smashed the bronze gates and stole the golden urns, emptying the ashes on the ground outside. You can't enter, but you can walk along the four streets encircling it.

Piazza Augusto Imperatore. No phone. Metro: Spagna. Bus: C3, 81, 224, or 913.

IN THE VILLA BORGHESE

Villa Borghese ★★, in the heart of Rome, is 5.5km (3½ miles) in circumference. One of Europe's most elegant parks, it was created by Cardinal Scipione Borghese in the 1600s. Umberto I, king of Italy, acquired it in 1902 and presented it to the city of Rome. With lovely landscaped vistas, the greenbelt is crisscrossed by roads, but you can escape the traffic and seek a shaded area to enjoy a picnic or simply relax. On a sunny weekend afternoon, it's a pleasure to stroll here and see Romans at play, relaxing or in-line skating. There are a few casual cafes and some food vendors throughout; you can also rent bikes here. In the northeast of the park is a small zoo; the park is also home to a few outstanding museums.

Galleria Borghese ★★★ This fabulous treasure-trove includes such masterpieces as Bernini's *Apollo and Daphne,* Titian's *Sacred and Profane Love,* Raphael's *Deposition,* and Caravaggio's *Jerome.* The collection began with the gallery's founder, Scipione Borghese, who by the time of his death in 1633 had accumulated some of the greatest art of all time, even managing to acquire Bernini's early sculptures. Some paintings were spirited out of Vatican museums or even confiscated when their rightful owners were hauled off, too. The great collection suffered at the hands of Napoleon's notorious sister, Pauline, who married Prince Camillo Borghese in 1807 and sold most of the ancient collection (many works are now in the Louvre in Paris). One of the most popular pieces of sculpture in today's gallery, ironically, is Canova's life-size sculpture of Pauline in the pose of *Venus Victorious*. (When Pauline was asked whether she felt uncomfortable posing in the nude, she replied, "Why should I? The studio was heated.")

Important information: No more than 360 visitors at a time are allowed on the ground floor, and no more than 90 are allowed on the upper floor. Reservations are essential, so call ✆ **06-32810** (Mon–Fri 9am–6pm). However, the number always seems to be busy. If you'll be in Rome for a few days, try stopping by in person on your first day to reserve tickets for a later day. Better yet, before you leave home, contact **Select Italy** (✆ **800/877-1755;** www.selectitaly.com).

Piazza Scipione Borghese 5 (off Via Pinciano). ✆ **06-32810** for information. www.galleriaborghese.it. Admission 11€. Tues–Sun 8:30am–7:30pm. Bus: 116 or 910.

National Etruscan Museum (Museo Nazionale di Villa Giulia) ★★★ This 16th-century papal palace shelters a priceless collection of art and artifacts from the mysterious Etruscans, who predated the Romans. Known for their sophisticated art and design, they left a legacy of sarcophagi, bronze sculptures, terra-cotta vases, and jewelry, among other items. If you have time for only the masterpieces, head for room no. 7, with a remarkable 6th-century-B.C. *Apollo from Veio* (clothed, for a change). The other two widely acclaimed statues here are *Dea con Bambino (Goddess with a Baby)* and a greatly mutilated but still powerful *Hercules* with a stag. In room no. 8, you'll see the lions' sarcophagus from the mid–6th century B.C., which was excavated at Cerveteri, north of Rome.

Finally, one of the world's most important Etruscan art treasures is the bride and bridegroom coffin from the 6th century B.C., also dug out of the tombs of Cerveteri (in room no. 9). Near the end of your tour, another masterpiece of Etruscan art awaits you in room no. 33: the Cista Ficoroni, a bronze urn with paw feet, mounted by three figures, dating from the 4th century B.C.

Piazzale di Villa Giulia 9. ✆ **06-3201951.** Admission 4€. Tues–Sun 8:30am–7:30pm. Metro: Flaminio. Tram: 2, 3, or 19.

National Gallery of Modern Art (Galleria Nazionale d'Arte Moderna) ★ This gallery of modern art is a short walk from the Etruscan Museum (see above). With its neoclassical and romantic paintings and sculpture, it makes a dramatic change from the glories of the Renaissance and ancient Rome. Its 75 rooms also house the largest collection in Italy of 19th- and 20th-century works by Balla, Boccioni, De Chirico, Morandi, Manzù, Burri, Capogrossi, and Fontana. There are also many works of Italian optical and pop art and a good representation of foreign artists, including Degas, Cézanne, Monet, and van Gogh. Surrealism and expressionism are well represented by Klee, Ernst, Braque, Mirò, Kandinsky, Mondrian, and Pollock. You'll also find sculpture by Rodin. You can see the collection of graphics, the storage rooms, and the Department of Restoration by appointment Tuesday through Friday.

Viale delle Belle Arti 131. ✆ **06-32298221.** www.gnam.arti.beniculturali.it. Admission 10€. Tues–Sun 8:30am–7:30pm. Bus: 19, 95, or 910.

THE APPIAN WAY & THE CATACOMBS

Of all the roads that led to Rome, **Via Appia Antica** (built in 312 B.C.) was the most famous. It eventually stretched all the way from Rome to the seaport of Brindisi, through which trade with the colonies in Greece and the East was funneled. (According to Christian tradition, it was along the Appian Way that an escaping Peter encountered the vision of Christ, causing him to go back to the city to face subsequent martyrdom.) The road's initial stretch in Rome is lined with the great monuments and ancient tombs of patrician Roman families—burials were forbidden within the city walls as early as the 5th century B.C.—and, beneath the surface, miles of tunnels hewn from tufa stone.

These tunnels, or catacombs, were where early Christians buried their dead and, during the worst times of persecution, held church services discreetly out of the public eye. A few of them are open to the public, so you can wander through mile after mile of musty-smelling tunnels whose soft walls are gouged out with tens of thousands of burial niches (long shelves made for 2–3 bodies each). In some dank, dark grottoes, you can still discover the remains of early Christian art. The requisite guided tours feature a smidgen of extremely biased history and a large helping of sermonizing.

The Appia Antica has long been a popular Sunday lunch picnic site for Roman families (following the half-forgotten pagan tradition of dining in the presence of one's ancestors on holy days). A 1990s initiative that closed the Via Appia Antica to cars on Sundays brings out the picnickers and bicyclists—along with in-line skaters and a new Sunday-only bus route to get out here.

You can take **bus no. 218** from the San Giovanni Metro stop, which follows the Appia Antica for a bit and then veers right on Via Ardeatina at Domine Quo Vadis Church. After another long block, the bus stops at the square Largo M.F. Via d. Sette Chiese. From here, you can follow the signs to the San Domitilla catacombs; or, walk left down Via d. Sette Chiese to the San Sebastiano catacombs.

An alternative is to ride the **Metro** to the Colli Albani stop and catch **bus no. 660,** which wraps up the Appia Antica from the south, veering off it at the San Sebastiano catacombs (if you're visiting all three, you can take bus no. 218 to the first two, walk to San Sebastiano, and then catch bus no. 660 back to the Metro). On Sundays, the road is closed to traffic, but **bus no. 118** trundles from the Circo Massimo Metro stop down the Via Appia Antica, turning around after it passes the Tomb of Cecilia Metella.

Of the monuments on the Appian Way, the most impressive is the **Tomb of Cecilia Metella ★**, within walking distance of the catacombs. The tomb honors the wife of one of Julius Caesar's military commanders from the Republican era. Why such an elaborate tomb for such a minor person in history? Cecilia Metella was singled out for enduring fame because her tomb has remained while others have decayed.

Catacombs of St. Callixtus (Catacombe di San Callisto) ★★ "The most venerable and most renowned of Rome," said Pope John XXIII of these funerary tunnels. The founder of Christian archaeology, Giovanni Battista de Rossi (1822–94), called them "catacombs par excellence." These catacombs are often packed with tour-bus groups, and their tour is perhaps the cheesiest, but the tunnels are simply phenomenal. They're the first cemetery of Rome's Christian community and burial place of 16 popes in the 3rd century. They bear the name of St. Callixtus, the deacon hired to run the catacombs by Pope St. Zephyrinus, who was later elected pope (A.D. 217–22) in his own right. The complex is a network of galleries stretching for nearly 19km (12 miles), structured in five levels and reaching a depth of about 20m (65 ft.). There are many sepulchral chambers and almost half a million tombs of early Christians. Paintings, sculptures, and epigraphs (with such symbols as the fish, anchor, and dove) provide invaluable material for the study of the life and customs of the ancient Christians and the story of their persecutions.

Entering the catacombs, you see at once the most important crypt, that of nine popes. Some of the original marble tablets of their tombs are still preserved. The next crypt is that of St. Cecilia, the patron of sacred music. This early Christian martyr received three ax strokes on her neck, the maximum allowed by Roman law, which failed to kill her outright. Farther on, you'll find the famous Cubicula of the Sacraments with its 3rd-century frescoes.

Via Appia Antica 110-126. ✆ **06-5130151.** www.catacombe.roma.it. Admission 8€ adults, 5€ children 6-15, free for children 5 and under. Apr-Oct Thurs-Tues 9am-noon and 2:30-5pm (to 4pm Nov-Mar). Closed Feb. Bus: 118.

Catacombs of St. Domitilla (Catacombe di San Domitilla) ★★★ This oldest of the catacombs is also the hands-down winner for most enjoyable catacomb experience. Groups are small, most guides are genuinely entertaining and personable, and, depending on the mood of the group and your guide, the visit can last anywhere from 20 minutes to over an hour. You enter through a sunken 4th-century church. There are fewer "sights" than in the other catacombs—although the 2nd-century fresco of the Last Supper is impressive. This is the only catacomb where you'll still see bones; the rest have emptied their tombs to rebury the remains in ossuaries on the inaccessible lower levels.

Via d. Sette Chiese 283. ✆ **06-5110342.** www.domitilla.soverdi.eu. Admission 8€ adults, 5€ children 6-14. Wed-Mon 8:30am-noon and 2:30-5pm. Closed Jan. Bus: 118.

Catacombs of St. Sebastian (Catacombe di San Sebastiano) ★ Today the tomb of St. Sebastian is in the basilica, but his original resting place was in the catacombs underneath it. From the reign of Valerian to the reign of Constantine, the bodies of Sts. Peter and Paul were hidden in the catacombs. The big church was built in the 4th century. The tunnels here, if stretched out, would reach a length of 11km (6⅔ miles). In the tunnels and mausoleums are mosaics and graffiti, along with many other pagan and Christian objects from centuries even before the time of Constantine. Though the catacombs themselves are fascinating, the tour here is one of the shortest and least satisfying of all the catacomb visits.

Via Appia Antica 136. ✆ **06-7850350.** www.catacombe.org. Admission 8€ adults, 5€ children 6-15, free for children 5 and under. Mon-Sat 9am-noon and 2-5pm. Closed mid-Nov to mid-Dec. Bus: 118.

MORE ATTRACTIONS

Around Stazione Termini

Basilica di Santa Maria Maggiore ★ This great church, one of Rome's four major basilicas, was built by Pope Liberius in A.D. 358 and was rebuilt by Pope Sixtus

Attractions near Stazione Termini, Via Veneto & Piazza Barberini

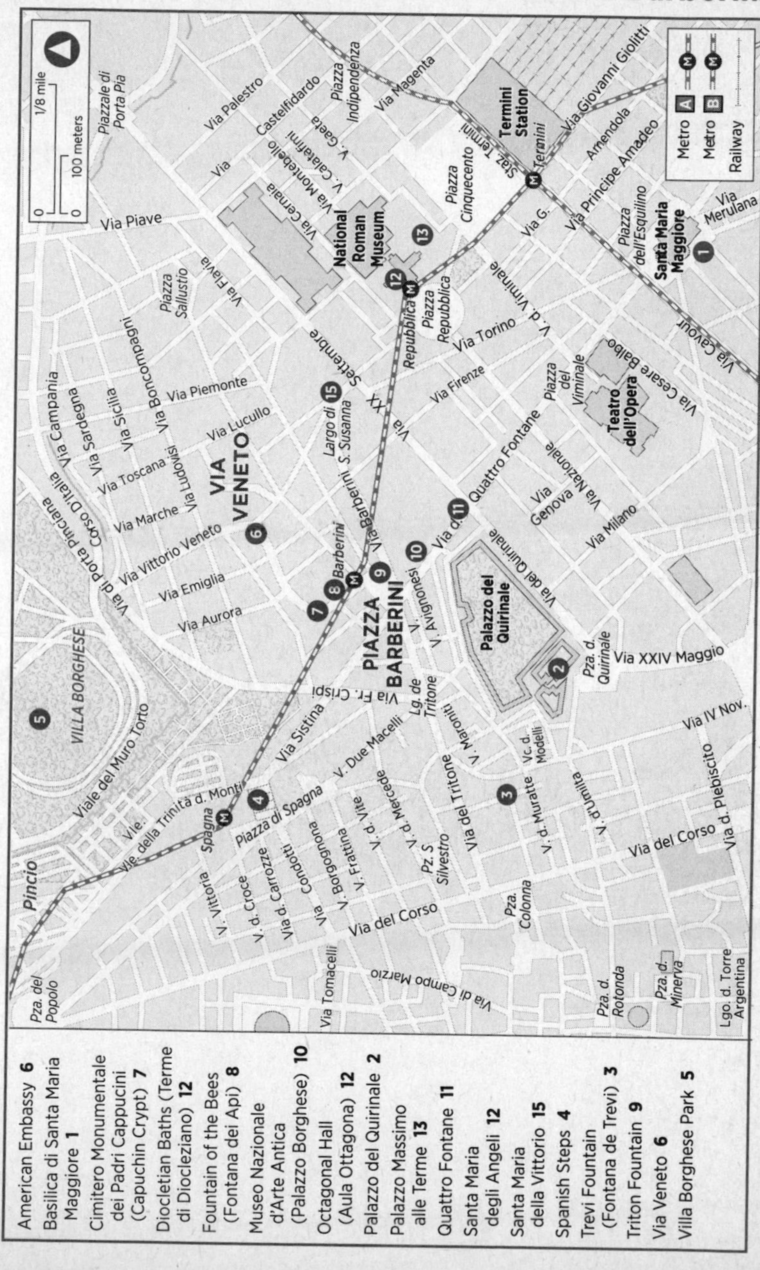

III from 432 to 440. Its 14th-century **campanile** is the city's loftiest. Much doctored in the 18th century, the church's facade isn't an accurate reflection of the treasures inside. The basilica is especially noted for the 5th-century Roman mosaics in its nave, as well as for its coffered ceiling, which is said to have been gilded with gold brought from the New World. In the 16th century, Domenico Fontana built a now-restored "Sistine Chapel." In the following century, Flaminio Ponzo designed the **Pauline (Borghese) Chapel** in the baroque style. The church also contains the **tomb of Bernini,** Italy's most important baroque sculptor/architect. Ironically, the man who changed the face of Rome with his elaborate fountains is buried in a tomb so simple that it takes a sleuth to track it down (to the right near the altar).

Piazza di Santa Maria Maggiore. ✆ **06-69886800.** Free admission. Daily 7am–7pm. Metro: Termini.

MUSEO NAZIONALE ROMANO

Originally, this museum occupied only the Diocletian Baths. Today it is divided into four different sections: Palazzo Massimo alle Terme; the Terme di Diocleziano (Diocletian Baths), with the annex Octagonal Hall; and Palazzo Altemps (which is near Piazza Navona; see p. 173 for a complete listing).

Diocletian Bath (Terme di Diocleziano) and the Octagonal Hall (Aula Ottagona) ★ Near Piazza dei Cinquecento, which fronts the rail station, this museum occupies part of the 3rd-century-A.D. Baths of Diocletian and part of a convent that might have been designed by Michelangelo. The Diocletian Baths were the biggest thermal baths in the world. Nowadays they host a marvelous collection of funereal artworks, such as sarcophagi, and decorations dating back to the Aurelian period. The Baths also have a section reserved for temporary exhibitions.

The **Octagonal Hall** occupies the southwest corner of the central building of the Diocletian Baths. Here you can see the *Lyceum Apollo,* a copy of the 2nd-century-A.D. work inspired by the Prassitele. Also worthy of note is the *Aphrodite of Cyrene,* a copy dating back to the second half of the 2nd century A.D. and discovered in Cyrene, Libya.

Viale E. di Nicola 79. ✆ **06-39967700.** Admission to the Baths 8€; Octagonal Hall free admission. The same ticket will admit you to Palazzo Massimo alle Terme. Tues–Sun 9am–7:45pm. Last admission 1 hr. before closing. Metro: Termini.

Palazzo Massimo alle Terme ★ If you ever wanted to know what all those emperors from your history books looked like, this museum makes them live again, togas and all. In the central hall are works representing the political and social life of Rome at the time of Augustus Caesar. Note the statue of the emperor with a toga covering his head, symbolizing his role as the head priest of state. Other works include an altar from Ostia Antica, the ancient port of Rome, plus a statue of a wounded Niobid from 440 B.C. that is a masterwork of expression and character. Upstairs, stand in awe at all the traditional art from the 1st century B.C. to the Imperial Age. The most celebrated mosaic is of the *Four Charioteers.* In the basement is a rare numismatic collection and an extensive collection of Roman jewelry.

Largo di Villa Peretti 67. ✆ **06-39967700.** Admission 8€; the same ticket will admit you to the Diocletian Baths. Tues-Sun 9am–7:45pm. Last admission 1 hr. before closing. Metro: Termini.

In the Testaccio Area, the Aventine & South

Montemartini Museum (Museo Centrale Di Montemartini) ★ 🎁 Hike out to this old power plant if you want to see some of the finest sculptures in ancient

Rome, including many items from the Capitoline Museum stockpile that haven't been exhibited in Rome since Mussolini was in power. They're displayed against a backdrop of Industrial Age machinery that once supplied electricity to the area. The prize here is the *Togato Barberini,* a berobed aristocrat from Rome of 90 B.C. He carries two heads, the symbol of an old custom in Republican Rome when patricians maintained hollow wax portrait busts of their former ancestors.

You'll find everything from a Greek Aphrodite from the 5th century B.C. to an endless array of marble busts and statues, many of which might have come from the area of the Imperial Forum. Many of the statues are superb Roman copies of Greek originals. The most stunning of these is a towering goddess statue from 100 B.C. that once graced the Temple of Fortuna in Largo di Teatro Argentina.

Via Ostiense 106. ✆ **06-5748030.** www.centralemontemartini.org. Admission 4.50€ adults, free for ages 18 and under. Tues–Sun 9am–7pm. Metro: Piramide or Garbatella. Bus: 23 or 271.

Museum of Roman Civilization (Museo della Civilità Romana) Some 5.5km (3½ miles) south of the historic center of Rome is a more modern city conceived by the fascist-era dictator Mussolini. At the height of his power, he launched a complex of impersonal modern buildings to dazzle Europe with a scheduled world's fair in 1942 that never happened. Il Duce got strung up, and EUR—the neighborhood in question—got hamstrung. The new Italian government that followed inherited the unfinished project and turned it into a center of government and administration.

The most intriguing sight here is this Museum of Roman Civilization, which houses two fascinating scale models that reproduce Rome in two different epochs: the early Republican Rome and the city in its imperial heyday in the 4th century A.D. You'll see the intact Circus Maximus, Colosseum, Baths of Diocletian—and lots more. You can also see examples of late imperial and paleochristian art, including more than a hundred casts of the reliefs that climb Trajan's Column in the Imperial Forum.

Piazza Giovanni Agnelli 10 (in EUR, south of the city center). ✆ **06-5926041.** www.museocivilta romana.it. Admission 6.50€, free for ages 18 and under. Metro: EUR-Fermi.

Protestant Cemetery (Cimitero Protestante) Near Porta San Paola, in the midst of cypress trees, lies the old cemetery where John Keats is buried. In a grave nearby, Joseph Severn, his "deathbed" companion, was interred beside him 6 decades later. Dejected and feeling that his reputation as a poet was being diminished by the rising vehemence of his critics, Keats asked that the following epitaph be written on his tombstone: "Here lies one whose name was writ in water." A great romantic poet Keats certainly was, but a prophet, thankfully not. Percy Bysshe Shelley, author of *Prometheus Unbound,* drowned off the Italian Riviera in 1822, before his 30th birthday, and his ashes rest beside those of Edward John Trelawny, a fellow romantic.

Via Caio Cestio 6. ✆ **06-5741900.** www.protestantcemetery.it. Free admission (but a 2€ offering is customary). Year-round Mon–Sat 9am–5pm, Sun 9am–1pm. Bus: 3, 23, 30, or 60. Metro: Piramide.

Pyramid of Caius Cestius ★ From the 1st century B.C., the Pyramid of Caius Cestius, about 36m (120 ft.) high, looks as if it belongs to the Egyptian landscape. It was constructed during the "Cleopatra craze" in architecture that swept across Rome. You can't enter the pyramid, but it's a great photo op. And who was Caius

Cestius? He was a rich magistrate in imperial Rome whose tomb is more impressive than his achievements. You can visit at any time.

Piazzale Ostiense. Metro: Piramide.

St. Paul Outside the Walls (Basilica di San Paolo Fuori le Mura) ★ The Basilica of St. Paul, whose origins go back to the time of Constantine, is Rome's fourth great patriarchal church; it was erected over the tomb of St. Paul. The basilica fell victim to fire in 1823 and was subsequently rebuilt. It is the second-largest church in Rome after St. Peter's. From the inside, its windows might appear to be stained glass, but they're actually translucent alabaster. With its forest of single-file columns and mosaic medallions (portraits of the various popes), this is one of the most streamlined and elegantly decorated churches in Rome. Its most important treasure is a 12th-century candelabrum by Vassalletto, who was also responsible for the remarkable cloisters. Of particular interest is the *baldacchino* (richly embroidered fabric of silk and gold, usually fixed or carried over an important person or sacred object) of Arnolf di Cambio, dated 1285, that miraculously wasn't damaged in the fire. The Benedictine monks and students sell a fine collection of souvenirs, rosaries, and bottles of Benedictine every day except Sunday and religious holidays.

Via Ostiense 184. ✆ **06-45434185.** www.abbaziasanpaolo.net. Free admission. Basilica daily 7am–6:30pm; cloisters daily 9am–1pm and 3–6pm. Metro: San Paolo Basilica.

Santa Sabina ★ A rarity, Santa Sabina is Rome's best remaining example of a paleochristian church. It dates from A.D. 422, and its original wooden doors from that time are still intact. The doors alone are worth the trek here. They are handsomely carved with Bible scenes, including one that depicts the Crucifixion, one of the earliest examples of this in the art of the Western world. You'll find it carved on a door at the end of a "porch" from the 1400s. The porch itself contains ancient sarcophagi.

Santa Sabina was the site of the temple of Juno Regina, the patroness of Rome's Etruscan archrival, Veii, who was seduced into switching sides in 392 B.C. Sabina was martyred to the Christian cause. In 1936 much of the church was restored to its original appearance, and today it is one of Rome's most beautiful churches. The surviving two dozen Corinthian columns might have come from the Temple of Juno. The delicate windows were pieced together from 9th-century fragments. In the floor of the nave is Rome's only surviving mosaic tomb, dating to around 1300.

Piazza Pietro d'Illiria. ✆ **06-5743573.** Free admission. Daily 6am–12:45pm and 3–7pm. Bus: 23, 30, 44, 60, 75, 95, or 170.

In Trastevere

Rome boasts many wonderful views, but one of the best spots for a memorable vista is the **Gianicolo (Janiculum Hill) ★★**, across the Tiber. It's not considered one of the "Seven Hills" of Rome, but it's certainly one of the most visited. Not even included within the original city walls (the area was built by Urban VII for defensive purposes), today most of Gianicolo is parkland. We like to come here at dawn and watch the sun rise over Rome. Here you can also look at the **Tempietto of Bramante,** the most evocative work of the High Renaissance in Rome.

Legend has it that Gianicolo was the site of the city founded by the god Janus. One of his kids, Tiber, lent his name to the river of Rome. For the best view, position yourself at the open space in front of the church, San Pietro in Montorio, which was

Attractions in Trastevere

constructed at the end of the 1400s during the reign of Sixtus IV. There is no grander panorama of Rome than the one you'll see here. Later you can follow the Passeggiata del Gianicolo or Janiculum Walk, which winds along the crest of the hill.

If you don't want to walk up the hill, you can catch bus no. 41 from the Ponte Sant'Angelo. But we prefer to walk along the medieval Via Garibaldi reached from Via della Scale in Trastevere. You'll reach the summit of the hill in about 15 minutes of steady climbing.

Galleria Nazionale di Palazzo Corsini After you've seen Italy's National Gallery of Art at the Palazzo Barberini, head to Trastevere to view the other half of the collection. This collection is installed in what was the 18th-century mansion of Pope Clemente XII (whose real name was Lorenzo Corsini, of the famous banking family). Before it was damaged by French attacks in 1849, the palace was the grandest in Rome. Queen Christina died here in her bedroom (room no. 5) in 1689, and Napoleon's mother, Letizia, once lived here as well. The palace is still rich in neoclassical works of the Napoleonic era.

The gallery hosts a wide array of paintings from the 16th and 17th centuries, although they are bunched together and badly displayed. Nonetheless, this is an outstanding treasure-trove of such European masters, although Italian artists dominate. Seek out in particular Caravaggio's *St. John the Baptist* and a rendition of the same subject by Guido Reni, who painted *Salome with the Head of St. John the Baptist.* Murillo's *Madonna and Bambino* is one of his less saccharine efforts, and some Rubens paintings are a bit overripe, notably a *St. Sebastian* and a *Madonna.* For sheer gore, Salvator Rosa's version of *Prometheus* tops them all.

Via della Lungara 10. © **06-68802323.** www.galleriaborghese.it. Admission 4€ adults, free for children 14 and under. Tues–Sun 8:30am–7:30pm. Bus: 23, or 125.

Santa Cecilia in Trastevere ★ A cloistered and still-functioning convent with a fine garden, Santa Cecilia contains *The Last Judgment,* by Pietro Cavallini (ca. 1293), a masterpiece of Roman medieval painting. Another treasure is a late-13th-century baldacchino by Arnolfo di Cambio over the altar. The church is built on the reputed site of Cecilia's long-ago palace, and for a small fee you can descend under the church to inspect the ruins of some Roman houses as well as peer through a gate at the stuccoed grotto beneath the altar.

Piazza Santa Cecilia 2. © **06-5899289.** Church free admission; Cavallini frescoes 2.50€; excavations 2.50€. Main church and excavations Mon–Sat 9:30am–noon and 4–6:30pm; frescoes Mon–Sat 10am–noon. Bus: 23, 271, 280, or 780.

Santa Maria in Trastevere ★ This Romanesque church at the colorful center of Trastevere was built around A.D. 350 and is one of the oldest in Rome. The body was added around 1100, and the portico was added in the early 1700s. The restored mosaics on the apse date from around 1140, and below them are the 1293 mosaic scenes depicting the life of Mary done by Pietro Cavallini. The faded mosaics on the facade are from the 12th or 13th centuries, and the fountain in the piazza is an ancient Roman original that was restored and added to in the 17th century by Carlo Fontana.

Piazza Santa Maria in Trastevere. © **06-5814802.** Free admission. Daily 8:30am–9pm. Bus: 23, 280, or 780.

Villa Farnesina ★★ Agostino "il Magnifico" Chigi (1465–1520), the richest man in Europe, once lived in this sumptuous villa built for him by the architect Baldassare Peruzzi between 1508 and 1511. Some of Rome's grandest feasts and parties, the likes of which were unknown since the days of imperial Rome, were staged here, often for popes, diplomats, artists, philosophers, and even high-priced courtesans. The Siennese banker would order his guests to toss their gold and silver plates into the Tiber after every course. Unknown to the guests, the savvy banker had placed nets under the water so that he could retrieve his treasures.

Even before this outrageous banker came to live here, the site was famous. Once it was the country villa of Julius Caesar, and Cleopatra stayed here in 44 B.C. with their illegitimate child, Caesarion.

Chigi was Raphael's patron and friend, and he called upon this great artist to help decorate part of his villa, along with such towering figures as Francesco Penni, Giulo Romano, Sebastian del Piombo, and "Il Sodoma" (so called because of his sexual practices). Together these artists created a series of paintings that stand as one of the treasures of the Renaissance, especially the ***Loggia of Cupid and Psyche*** **★**.

Also stunning is the ***Galatea*** ★★ from 1511—Raphael painted Nereus's sea-maiden riding in a shell drawn by pug-nosed dolphins in a frolicking romp. Paintings depicting scenes from Ovid's *Metamorphoses* are by Sebastiano del Piombo; frescoes of the constellations on the ceiling are by Baldassare Peruzzi.

Upstairs you can see Peruzzi's masterful *Salone delle Prospettive,* an early example of *trompe l'oeil* views of Rome and Il Sodoma's masterpiece *Scenes from the Life of Alexander the Great.*

Via d. Lungara 230. ✆ **06-68027268.** Admission 5€ adults, 4€ ages 17 and under. Mon–Sat 9am–1pm. Bus: 23 or 125.

Near Circus Maximus

Case Romane del Celio ★ The 5th-century Basilica of SS Giovanni e Paolo stands over a residential complex consisting of several Roman houses of different periods. According to tradition, this was the dwelling of two Roman officers, John and Paul (not the apostles), who were beheaded during the reign of Julian the Apostate (361–62), when they refused to serve in a military campaign. They were later made saints, and their bones were said to have been buried at this site. A visit here will provide you with a unique picture of how several generations of Romans lived. Preserved at the site is a residence from the 2nd century A.D., a single home of a wealthy family, and a 3rd-century-A.D. apartment building for artisans. A religious sect, the Passionists, excavated the site in 1887, discovering naked genii figures painted on the walls. Scandalized at such a realistic depiction of male genitalia, they blurred some of the most obvious anatomical details. The two-story construction, with some 20 rooms, also contains a labyrinth of well-preserved pagan and Christian paintings.

Piazza Santi Giovanni e Paolo 13 (entrance on Clivo di Scauro). ✆ **06-70454544.** www.caseromane.it. Admission 6€ adults, 4€ ages 12–18, free for ages 11 and under. Thurs–Mon 10am–1pm and 3–6pm. Metro: Colosseo or Circo Massimo.

In Salario

MACRO (Museo d'Arte Contemporanea Roma) Opened in a former brewery, this daringly avant-garde museum took over a striking industrial space near Piazza Fiume. Even Romans travel to see Rome's first contemporary art museum. "We're not all ancient," said the curator. "We can be on the cutting edge of *moderno* as well." There are galleries for temporary art shows, an art studio, a bookstore, and a cafe—all a dynamic center for cultural activity. There is also a permanent collection of modern art.

MACRO overflows into a cutting-edge annex, MACRO al Mattatoio housed in the city's former slaughterhouse in Testaccio, south of the center. The Testaccio annex, Piazza Orazio Giustiniani, is surrounded by an enclave of underground music clubs and late-night restaurants, so this MACRO here keeps hours in tune with the neighborhood—4pm to midnight Tuesday to Sunday.

Piazza Orazio Giustiniani 4. ✆ **06-671070400.** www.macro.roma.museum. Admission 4.50€. Tues–Sun 9am–7pm. Metro: Fiume.

In Flaminio

MAXXI (National Museum of Art of the XXI Century) ★ The city of Michelangelo has gone modern with the opening of this stunning building constructed on the site of former army barracks. The complex, costing 60€ million, was the creation of an Iraqi-born architect, Zaha Hadid, who is known for her daring architecture. MAXXI (the first two letters stand for the Museum of Art), with the Roman numerals denoting the 21st century, houses Italy's growing national collection of contemporary art. In addition to its permanent collection, MAXXI will also host the most avant-garde exhibitions of modern art in Italy. The museum is divided into two sections—MAXXI art and MAXXI architecture.

Via Guido Reni 10, Flaminio. ✆ **06-32101829**. www.maxxi.beniculturali.it. Free admission. Tues–Sun 11am–7pm. Metro to Flaminio stop, then tram 2.

Museo Carlo Bilotti ★ The aristocratic collector of modern art, Carlo Bilotti, who made a fortune in international cosmetics, donated his celebrated collection to the city of Rome upon his death in 2006. He not only purchased great pieces of modern art but also became friends with many of the artists, including Andy Warhol, Lichtenstein, Dalí, Rivers, Rotella, and de Chirico. The works are displayed in a restored orangery that had been allowed to decay for many years. Works donated by Bilotti are displayed in rooms arranged specifically for a certain artist; other salons are devoted to changing exhibits of some of the major modern artists in the world.

Viale Fiorello La Guardia. ✆ **06-85357446.** www.museocarlobilotti.it. Admission 4.50€ adults, 2.50€ children 17 and under. Tues–Sun 9am–7pm. Metro: Flaminio.

Via Nomentana

This legendary boulevard of elegant villas, embassies, and parkland begins at Porta Pia, built to the designs of Michelangelo. It's being visited by more foreigners with the opening of Mussolini's villa (see below).

Villa Torlonia ★ Il Duce lived here for 18 years, but now the public can visit. Designed in 1802 by Giuseppe Valadier, the villa was taken over by Benito Mussolini in 1925. The dictator paid a nominal rent of one lira a year to the descendants of Prince Giovanni Torlonia who owned the villa. Allied soldiers occupied it for 3 years, beginning in 1944. After that, it fell into disrepair.

The villa today contains an art museum dedicated to the Roman school of 20th-century art. The Allied soldiers left two large murals—one of a banjo player, the other of a dancing girl, both of which have been preserved as part of the villa's heritage. Among the curiosities preserved are Mussolini's bed and a "Thinking Room" upstairs. In addition, there's an impressive collection of 18th-century neoclassical sculpture by Antonio Canova and Bartolomeo Cavaceppi.

The villa houses a museum of the Holocaust, dedicated to the 2,000 Jews who were deported from Rome during the German occupation (1943–44). Fearing an allied attack, Mussolini had a bomb shelter constructed beneath the building with two-inch-thick steel doors and filtered air intakes. This, too, is open to visitors.

Via Nomentana 70. ✆ **06-44231185.** www.museivillatorlonia.it. 9€ adults, 5.50€ ages 17 and under. Last Sat of Mar until last Sat of Oct daily 9am–7pm; other times, daily 9am–4:30pm. Bus: 36 from Termini but a walk of 1km (.6 miles).

THE GARDENS OF ROME

The greatest garden of Rome is the **Villa Borghese,** which has already been previewed, as have the gardens of the Vatican. But there are other "secret gardens" of Rome where you can slip away from the hordes and the traffic.

Villa dei Medici Gardens were called "the most enchanting place" in Rome by Henry James, who went on to write that the gardens were possessed with an "incredible, impossible charm." Covering 17 sprawling acres on Pincio Hill above the Piazza di Spagna, they offer our favorite panoramic view of Rome. In the 1st century B.C., the site was covered by the Gardens of Lucullus. With their tree-lined avenues, statues, and fountains, these gardens were built around the severe, fortresslike facade of the Villa dei Medici in 1540. When Galileo was under house arrest by the Inquisition (1630–33), the dukes offered him shelter here.

In 1801, Napoleon purchased the villa to make it the seat of the French Academy. *Prix de Rome* scholars stay here, studying art, architecture, and archaeology. In front of the villa is a round fountain with a wide basin. Its spout was made from a cannonball shot from Castel Sant'Angelo.

Viale Trinità dei Monti 2. ✆ **06-67611.** www.villamedici.it. Admission 6.50€. Tours daily at 11:45am. Metro: Spagna. Bus: 117 or 119.

Orto Botanico ★ Originally belonging to the aristocratic Corsini family, this 30-acre botanical garden today is run by the University of Rome. In her exile, Queen Christina of Sweden once strolled past its magnificent grottoes and gushing fountains. Regrettably, many of the ancient trees were sold by the city fathers for firewood in 1878, much to the objections of the Italian queen, Margherita. But there is much that remains to delight us, including 7,000 plant species from all over the world. The exotic plants are grouped together into botanical families. Stone steps and tiered fountains invite you to linger and relax among the orchids, bamboo grove, and Japanese tea garden. There are two greenhouses—one for orchids, another for cacti. As a special, thoughtful touch, gardeners have planted a scented garden for the blind.

Largo Cristina di Svezia 24. ✆ **06-6864193.** www.horti.unimore.it. Admission 4€ adults, 2€ ages 6–11; free for ages 5 and under. June–Sept Tues–Sat 9am–6:30pm; off season Tues–Sat 9am–5:30pm. Closed Aug. Bus: 125.

ORGANIZED TOURS

Because of the sheer number of sights to see, some first-time visitors like to start out with an organized tour. While few things can really be covered in any depth on these overview tours, they're sometimes useful for getting your bearings.

One of the leading tour operators is **American Express,** Piazza di Spagna 38 (✆ **06-67641;** www.americanexpress.com; Metro: Spagna). A popular tour is their 4-hour orientation of Rome and the Vatican, which departs most mornings at 8:30am and costs 68€ per person. Another 4-hour tour, which focuses on the Rome of antiquity (including visits to the Colosseum, the Roman Forum, the ruins of the Imperial Palace, and San Pietro in Vincoli), costs 68€. From April to October, a good excursion outside Rome is a 5-hour bus tour to Tivoli, where tours are conducted of the Villa d'Este and its spectacular gardens and the ruins of the Villa Adriana, all for 58€ per person.

Through Eternity Tours, Via Sinuessa 8 (✆ **06-7009336;** www.througheternity.com), is staffed by a team of art historians, archaeologists, and experts on ancient Rome. Its guided tour of Vatican City is the best in Rome, a comprehensive 5-hour tour that brings life to the artifacts in this vast treasure-trove. The cost is 32€ per person. Other tours include Rome at Twilight, a 2½-hour evening tour of the city's beautiful piazzas and fountains, costing 29€ per person. Lasting 4 hours, a tour of Underground Rome costs 49€.

Another option is **Context Travel,** Via Baccina 40 (© **06-4820911;** www.contexttravel.com), which has a network of architects, historians, and art historians who organize walking seminars for intellectually curious travelers. These walks last anywhere from 3 hours to all day and provide an in-depth alternative to traditional tours. Groups are small, never more than 6 participants. For example, 1 tour lasting 2 hours and costing 35€ per person takes you into the subterranean chambers of the Circus Maximus (not open to the general public). Yet another 3-hour tour, costing 55€ per person, takes you on a tour of the development of Rome during the Imperial period, including the Colosseum and the Roman Forum.

STROLLING THROUGH ROME

8

Rome is a great city for walking—be sure to allow yourself enough time to just wander and let yourself get lost. Those of you who want more guidance in your exploration might enjoy the walking tours we've designed in this chapter. Visitors with very limited time might want to concentrate on Walking Tour 1, "Rome of the Caesars," and Walking Tour 2, "The Heart of Rome." Those with more time can try out "Renaissance Rome" and "Trastevere." Many of the major sights along these routes, especially on walking tours 2 to 4, are covered fully in chapter 7. These tours serve both to string the sights together and to reveal some lesser-known hidden gems along the way.

WALKING TOUR 1: ROME OF THE CAESARS

START:	**Via Sacra, in the Roman Forum**
FINISH:	**Circus Maximus**
TIME:	**5½ hours**
BEST TIMES:	**Any sunny day**
WORST TIMES:	**After dark or midday, when the place is overrun with tour groups**

This tour takes in the most central of the monuments and ruins that attest to the military and architectural grandeur of ancient Rome. As a whole, they make up the most famous and evocative ruins in the world, despite such drawbacks as roaring traffic that's the bane of the city's civic planners and a general dustiness and heat that can test even the hardiest amateur archaeologists.

After the collapse of Rome and during the Dark Ages, the forums and many of the other sites on this tour were lost to history, buried beneath layers of debris, their marble mined by medieval builders, until Benito Mussolini set out to restore the grandeur of Rome by reminding his compatriots of their glorious past.

The Roman Forum

The western entrance to the Roman Forum (there are two entrances) is at the corner of Via dei Fori Imperiali and Via Cavour, adjacent to Piazza Santa Maria Nova. The nearest Metro is the Colosseo stop. As you walk down into the Forum along a masonry ramp, you'll be heading for Via Sacra, the ancient Roman road that ran through the Forum connecting the Capitoline Hill, to your right, with the Arch of Titus (1st c. A.D.), off to your left. The Roman Forum is the more dignified and austere of the two forums you'll visit on this walking tour. Although it consists mostly of artfully evocative ruins scattered confusingly around a sun-baked terrain, it represents almost 1,000 years of Roman power during the severely disciplined period that preceded the legendary decadence of the later Roman emperors.

Arriving at Via Sacra, turn right. The random columns on the right as you head toward the Arch of Septimius Severus belong to the:

1 Basilica Aemilia

This was once the site of great meeting halls and shops, all maintained for centuries by the noble Roman family who gave it its name. At the corner nearest the Forum entrance are some traces of melted bronze decoration that was fused to the marble floor during a great fire set by invading Goths in A.D. 410.

The next important building is the:

2 Curia, or Senate House

It's the large brick building on the right that still has its roof. Romans had been meeting on this site for centuries before the first structure was erected, and that was still centuries before Jesus was born. The present building is the fifth (if you count all the reconstructions and substantial rehabilitations) to stand on the site. Legend has it that the original building was constructed by an ancient king with the curious name of Tullus Hostilius. The tradition he began was noble indeed, and our present legislative system owes much to the Romans who met in this hall. Unfortunately, the high ideals and inviolate morals that characterized the early Republican senators gave way to the bootlicking of imperial times, when the Senate became little more than a rubber stamp. Caligula, who was only the third emperor, had his horse appointed to the Senate, which pretty much sums up the state of the Senate by the middle of the 1st century A.D.

The building was a church until 1937, when the fascist government tore out the baroque interior and revealed what we see today. The original floor of Egyptian marble and the tiers that held the seats of the senators have miraculously survived. In addition, at the far end of the great chamber we can see the stone on which rested the fabled golden statue of Victory. Originally installed by Augustus, it was disposed of in the 4th century by a fiercely divided Senate whose Christian members convinced the emperor that it was improper to have a pagan statue in such a revered place.

Walking Tour: Rome of the Caesars

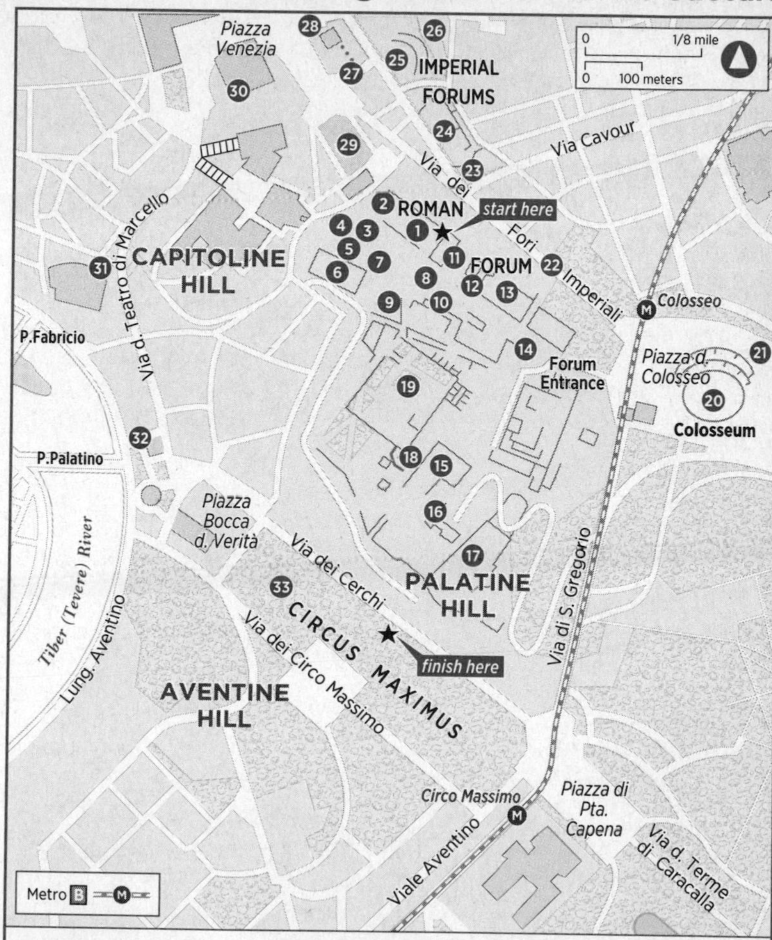

1 Basilica Aemilia
2 Curia
3 Lapis Niger
4 Arch of Septimius Severus
5 Rostra
6 Basilica Julia
7 Column of Phocas
8 Temple of Julius Caesar
9 Temple of the Castors
10 Temple of Vesta
11 Temple of Antoninus and Faustina
12 Temple of Romulus
13 Basilica of Constantine
14 Arch of Titus
15 Flavian Palace
16 Domus Augustana
17 Hippodrome
18 House of Livia
19 Orti Farnesiani (Farnese Gardens)
20 The Colosseum
21 Bar Martini
22 Via dei Fori Imperiali
23 Forum of Nerva
24 Forum of Augustus
25 Trajan's Market
26 Tower of the Milizie
27 Forum of Trajan
28 Trajan's Column
29 Forum of Julius Caesar
30 Vittorio Emanuele Monument
31 Teatro di Marcello
32 Temple of Fortuna Virile
33 Circus Maximus

Outside, head down the Curia stairs to the:

3 Lapis Niger

These are the remains of black marble blocks that reputedly mark the tomb of Romulus. Today they bask under a corrugated metal roof. Go downstairs for a look at the excavated tomb. There's a stone here with the oldest Latin inscription in existence, which, unfortunately, is nearly illegible. All that can be safely assumed is that it genuinely dates from the Rome of the kings, an era that ended in a revolution in 510 B.C.

Across from the Curia, you'll see the:

4 Arch of Septimius Severus

The arch was dedicated at the dawn of the troubled 3rd century to the last decent emperor to govern Rome for some time. The friezes on the arch depict victories over Arabs and Parthians by the cold but upright Severus and his two dissolute sons, Geta and Caracalla. Severus died on a campaign to subdue the unruly natives of Scotland. At the end of the first decade of the 3rd century, Rome unhappily fell into the hands of the young Caracalla, chiefly remembered today for the baths he ordered built.

Walk around to the back of the Severus arch, face it, and look to your right. There amid the rubble can be discerned a semicircular stair that led to the famous:

5 Rostra

This was the podium from which dictators and Caesars addressed the throngs on the Forum below. You can just imagine the emperor, shining in his white toga, surrounded by imperial guards and distinguished senators, gesticulating grandly like one of the statues on a Roman roofline. The motley crowd falls silent, the senators pause and listen, the merchants put down their measures, and even the harlots and unruly soldiers lower their voices in such an august presence. Later emperors didn't have much cause to use the Rostra; they made their policies known through edicts and assassinations instead.

Now, facing the colonnade of the Temple of Saturn, once the public treasury, and going to the left, you'll come to the ruins of the:

6 Basilica Julia

Again, little more than a foundation remains. The basilica is named for Julius Caesar, who dedicated the first structure in 46 B.C. Like many buildings in the Forum, the basilica was burned and rebuilt several times, and the last structure dated from the shaky days after the Gothic invasion in A.D. 410. Throughout its history, it was used for the hearing of civil court cases, which were conducted in the pandemonium of the crowded Forum, open to anyone who happened to pass by. The building was also reputed to be particularly hot in the summer, and it was under these sweaty and unpromising circumstances that Roman justice, the standard of the world for a millennium, was meted out.

Walking back down the ruined stairs of the Basilica Julia and into the broad area whose far side is bounded by the Curia, you'll see the:

7 Column of Phocas

Probably lifted from an early structure in the vicinity, this was the last monument to be erected in the Roman Forum, and it commemorates the Byzantine Emperor Phocas's generous donation of the Pantheon to the pope of Rome, who almost immediately transformed it into a church.

Now make your way down the middle of the Forum, nearly back to the ramp from which you entered. The pile of bricks with the semicircular indentation that stands in the middle of things was the:

8 Temple of Julius Caesar

It was erected some time after the dictator was deified, and judging from the reconstruction, it was quite an elegant building.

As you stand facing the ruins, with the entrance to the Forum on your left, you'll see on your right three columns originally belonging to the:

9 Temple of the Castors

This temple perpetuated the legend of Castor and Pollux, who appeared out of thin air in the Roman Forum and were observed watering their horses at the fountain of Juturna (still visible today), just as a major battle against the Etruscans turned in favor of Rome. Castor and Pollux, the heavenly twins (and the symbol of the astrological sign Gemini), are a favorite of Rome.

The next major monument is the circular:

10 Temple of Vesta

Here dwelt the sacred flame of Rome and the Atrium of the Vestal Virgins. A Vestal Virgin was usually a girl of good family who signed a contract for 30 years. During that time she lived in the ruin you're standing in right now. Of course, back then it was an unimaginably rich marble building with two floors. There were only six Vestal Virgins at a time during the imperial period, and even though they had the option of going back out into the world at the end of their 30 years, few did. The cult of Vesta came to an end in A.D. 394, when a Christian Rome secularized all its pagan temples. A man standing on this site before then would have been put to death immediately.

Stand in the atrium with your back to the Palatine and look beyond those fragmented statues of the former vestals to the:

11 Temple of Antoninus and Faustina

It's the building with the free-standing colonnade just to the right of the ramp where you first entered the Forum. Only the colonnade dates from imperial times; the building behind it is a much later church dedicated to San Lorenzo.

After you inspect the beautifully proportioned Antoninus and Faustina temple, head up Via Sacra away from the entrance ramp toward the Arch of Titus. Pretty soon, on your left, you'll see the twin bronze doors of the:

12 Temple of Romulus

It's the doors themselves that are really of note—they're the original Roman doors, swinging on the same massive hinges they were mounted on in A.D. 306. In this case, the temple is not dedicated to the legendary cofounder of Rome, but to the son of its builder, Emperor Maxentius, who named his son Romulus in a fit of antiquarian patriotism. Unfortunately for both father and son, they competed with a general who deprived them of their empire and their lives. That man was Constantine, who, while camped outside Rome during preparations for one of his battles against Maxentius, saw the sign of the cross in the heavens with the insignia *In hoc signo vinces* (In this sign shall you conquer). Raising the standard of Christianity above his legions, he defeated Maxentius and became the first Christian emperor.

Those three gaping arches up ahead on your left were part of the:

13 Basilica of Constantine

At the time of Constantine's victory (A.D. 306), the great Basilica was only half finished, having been started by the unfortunate Maxentius. Constantine finished the job and affixed his name to this, the largest and most impressive building in the Forum. To our taste, the delicate Greek-influenced temples are more attractive, but you have to admire the scale and engineering skill that erected this monument. The fact that portions of the original coffered ceiling are still intact is amazing. The basilica once held a statue of Constantine so large that his little toe was as wide as an average man's waist. You can see a few fragments from this colossus—the remnants were found in 1490—in the courtyard of the Conservatory Museum on the Capitoline Hill. As far as Roman emperors went, Christian or otherwise, ego knew no bounds.

From Constantine's basilica, follow the Roman paving stones of Via Sacra to a low hill just ahead, where you'll find the:

14 Arch of Titus

Titus was the emperor who sacked the great Jewish temple in Jerusalem, and the bas-relief sculpture inside the arch shows the booty of the Jews being carried in triumph through the streets of Rome while Titus is crowned by Victory, who comes down from heaven for the occasion. You'll notice, in particular, the candelabrum, for centuries one of the most famous pieces of the treasure of Rome. In all probability, it lies at the bottom of the Busento River in the secret tomb of Alaric the Goth.

The Palatine Hill

When you've gathered your strength in the shimmering sun, head up the Clivus Palatinus—the road to the palaces of the Palatine Hill, or *Palatino*. With your back to the Arch of Titus, it's the road going up the hill to the left.

It was on the Palatine Hill that Rome first became a city. Legend tells us that the date was 753 B.C. The new city originally consisted of nothing more than the Palatine, which was soon enclosed by a surprisingly sophisticated wall, remains of which can still be seen on the Circus Maximus side of the hill. As time went on and Rome grew in power and wealth, the boundaries were extended and later enclosed by the Servian Wall. When the last of the ancient kings was overthrown (510 B.C.), Rome had already extended over several of the adjoining hills and valleys. As Republican times progressed, the Palatine became a fashionable residential district. So it remained until Tiberius—who, like his predecessor, Augustus, was a bit too modest to call himself "emperor" out loud—began the first of the monumental palaces that eventually covered the entire hill.

It's difficult today to make sense out of the Palatine. First-time viewers might be forgiven for suspecting it to be an entirely artificial structure built on brick arches. Those arches, visible on practically every flank of the hill, are actually supports that once held imperial structures. Having run out of building sites, the emperors, in their fervor, simply enlarged the hill by building new sides on it.

The road goes on only a short way, through a small sort of valley filled with lush, untrimmed greenery. After about 5 minutes (for slow walkers), you'll see the ruins of a monumental stairway just to the right of the road. The Clivus Palatinus turns sharply to the left here, skirting the monastery of San Bonaventura, but we'll detour to the right and take a look at the remains of the:

15 Flavian Palace

As you walk off the road and into the ruins, you'll be able to discern that there were once three rooms here. But it's impossible for anyone but the most imaginative to comprehend quite how splendid they were.

The entire Flavian Palace was decorated in the most lavish of colored marbles and gold. Much of the decoration survived as late as the 18th century, when the greedy duke of Parma removed most of what was left. The room closest to the Clivus Palatinus was called the lararium and held statues of the divinities that protected the imperial family. The middle room was the grandest of the three. It was the imperial throne room, where sat the ruler of the world, the emperor of Rome. The far room was a basilica and was used for miscellaneous court functions, among them audiences with the emperor. This part of the palace was used entirely for ceremonial functions.

Adjoining these three rooms are the remains of a spectacularly luxurious peristyle. You'll recognize it by the hexagonal remains of a fountain in the middle. Try to imagine this fountain surrounded by marble arcades planted with mazes and equipped with mica-covered walls. On the opposite side of the peristyle from the throne room are several other great reception and entertainment rooms. The banquet hall was here; beyond it, looking over the Circus Maximus, are a few ruins of former libraries. Although practically nothing remains except the foundations, every now and then you'll catch sight of a fragment of colored marble floor in a subtle, sophisticated pattern.

Toward the Circus Maximus, slightly to the left of the Flavian Palace, is the:

16 Domus Augustana

This is where the imperial family lived. The remains lie toward the Circus Maximus, slightly to the left of the Flavian Palace. The new building that stands here—it looks old to us, but in Rome it qualifies as a new building—is a museum. It stands in the absolute center of the Domus Augustana. In the field adjacent to the stadium, well into the last century stood the Villa Mills, a gingerbread Gothic villa of the 19th century. The Villa Mills was the scene of fashionable entertainment in Victorian times, and it's interesting to note, as H. V. Morton pointed out, that the last dinner parties that took place on the Palatine Hill were given by an Englishman. At any of several points along this south-facing gazebo of the Palatine Hill, you'll be able to see the faraway oval walls of the Circus Maximus.

Continue with your exploration of the Palatine Hill by heading across the field parallel to the Clivus Palatinus until you come to the north end of the:

17 Hippodrome, or Stadium of Domitian

The field was apparently occupied by parts of the Domus Augustana, which, in turn, adjoined the enormous stadium. The stadium alone is worth examination, although sometimes it's difficult to get down inside it. The perfectly proportioned area was usually used for private games staged for the amusement of the imperial family. As you look down the stadium from the north end, you can see, on the left side, the semicircular remains of a structure identified as Domitian's private box. Some archaeologists claim that this stadium was actually an elaborate sunken garden.

The aqueduct that comes up the wooded hill used to supply water to the Baths of Septimius Severus, whose difficult-to-understand ruins lie in monumental poles of arched brick at the far end of the stadium.

Returning to the Flavian Palace, leave the peristyle on the opposite side from the Domus Augustana and follow the signs for the:

18 House of Livia

They take you down a dusty path to your left. Although legend says that this was the house of Augustus's consorts, it actually was Augustus's all along. The place is notable for some rather well-preserved murals showing mythological scenes. But more interesting is the aspect of the house itself—it's smallish, and there never were any great baths or impressive marble arcades. Even though Augustus was the first emperor, he lived simply compared to his successors. His wife, Livia, was a fiercely ambitious aristocrat who divorced her first husband to marry the emperor (the ex-husband was made to attend the wedding, incidentally) and, according to some historians, was the true power behind Roman policy between the death of Julius Caesar and the ascension of Tiberius. She even controlled Tiberius, her son, since she had engineered his rise to power through a long string of intrigues and poisonings.

After you've examined the frescoes in Livia's parlor, head up the steps that lead to the top of the embankment to the north. Once on top, you'll be in the:

19 Orti Farnesiani (Farnese Gardens)

This was the 16th-century horticultural fantasy of a Farnese cardinal. They're constructed on top of the Palace of Tiberius, which, you'll remember, was the first of the great imperial palaces to be built on this hill. It's impossible to see any of it, but the gardens are cool and laid out nicely. You might stroll up to the promontory above the Forum and admire the view of the ancient temples and the Capitoline heights off to the left.

You've now seen the best of the Forum and the Palatine. To leave the archaeological area, continue walking eastward along the winding road that meanders steeply down from the Palatine Hill to Via di San Gregorio. When you reach the roaring traffic of that busy thoroughfare, walk north toward the ruins so famous that they symbolize the city itself:

20 The Colosseum

Its crumbling, oval bulk is the greatest monument of ancient Rome, and visitors are impressed with its size, its majesty, and its ability to conjure up the cruel games that were played out for the pleasure of the Roman masses. Visit it now or return later.

21 Bar Martini

On a hill in back of the landmark Colosseum is the Bar Martini, Piazza del Colosseo 3B (✆ 06-7004431), surrounded by flowery shrubs. Have your coffee, cool drink, plate of pasta, or simple sandwich outside at one of the tables and absorb one of the world's greatest architectural views: that of the Colosseum itself.

The Imperial Forums

Begun by Julius Caesar as an answer to the overcrowding of Rome's older forums during the days of the empire, the Imperial Forums were, at the time of their construction, flashier, bolder, and more impressive than the old Roman Forum, and as such represented the unquestioned authority of the Roman emperors at the height of their absolute power. After the collapse of Rome and during the Dark Ages, they, like many other ancient monuments, were lost to history, buried beneath layers of debris. Mussolini, in an egomaniacal attempt to draw comparisons between his fascist regime and the glory of ancient Rome, later helped restore the grandeur of Rome.

With your back to the Colosseum, walk westward along the:

22 Via dei Fori Imperiali

Keep to the right side of the street. It was Mussolini who issued the controversial orders to cut through centuries of debris and junky buildings to reveal many archaeological treasures and carve out this boulevard linking the Colosseum to the grand 19th-century monuments of Piazza Venezia. The vistas over the ruins of Rome's Imperial Forums from the northern side of the boulevard make for one of the most fascinating walks in Rome.

Some of the rather confusing ruins you'll see from the boulevard include the shattered remnants of the colonnade that once surrounded the Temple of Venus and Roma. Next to it, you'll see the back wall of the Basilica of Constantine.

Shortly, on the street's north side, you'll come to a large outdoor restaurant, where Via Cavour joins the boulevard. Just beyond the small park across Via Cavour are the remains of the:

23 Forum of Nerva

Your best view is from the railing that skirts it on Via dei Fori Imperiali. It was built by the emperor whose 2-year reign (A.D. 96–98) followed that of the paranoid Domitian. You'll be struck by just how much the ground level has risen in 19 centuries. The only really recognizable remnant is a wall of the Temple of Minerva with two fine Corinthian columns. This forum was once flanked by that of Vespasian, which is now completely gone. It's possible to enter the Forum of Nerva from the other side, but you can see it just as well from the railing.

The next forum you approach is the:

24 Forum of Augustus

This was built to commemorate the emperor's victory over the assassins Cassius and Brutus in the Battle of Philippi (42 B.C.). Fittingly, the temple that once dominated this forum—its remains can still be seen—was that of Mars Ultor, or Mars the Avenger, in which stood a mammoth statue of Augustus that, unfortunately, has vanished completely. You can enter the Forum of Augustus from the other side (cut across the tiny footbridge).

Continuing along the railing, you'll see next the vast semicircle of:

25 Trajan's Market

Its teeming arcades, stocked with merchandise from the far corners of the Roman Empire, long ago collapsed, leaving only the ubiquitous cats to watch over things. The shops once covered a multitude of levels. In front of the perfectly proportioned semicircular facade, designed by Apollodorus of Damascus at the beginning of the 2nd century, are the remains of a great library. Fragments of delicately colored marble floors still shine in the sunlight between stretches of rubble and tall grass. Admission is 8€. Entrance is at the Column of Trajan, a prominent landmark clearly visible.

26 Tower of the Milizie

This 12th-century structure was part of the medieval headquarters of the Knights of Rhodes. The view from the top (if it's open) is well worth the climb. From the tower, you can wander down to the ruins of the market, admiring the sophistication of the layout and the sad beauty of the bits of decoration that remain.

When you've examined the brick and travertine corridors, head out in front of the semicircle to the site of the former library; from here, scan the retaining wall that supports the modern road and look for the entrance to the tunnel that leads to the:

27 Forum of Trajan

It's entered on Via IV Novembre near the steps of Via Magnanapoli. Once through the tunnel, you'll emerge in the newest and most beautiful of the Imperial Forums, designed by the same man who laid out the adjoining market. There are many statue fragments and pedestals that bear still-legible inscriptions, but more interesting is the great Basilica Ulpia, with gray marble columns rising roofless into the sky. You wouldn't know it to judge from what's left, but the Forum of Trajan was once regarded as one of the architectural wonders of the world. Constructed between A.D. 107 and 113, it was designed by the Greek architect Apollodorus of Damascus.

Beyond the Basilica Ulpia is:

28 Trajan's Column

This column is in magnificent condition, with intricate bas-relief sculptures depicting Trajan's victorious campaign (although from your vantage point you'll be able to see only the earliest stages). The emperor's ashes were kept in a golden urn at the base of the column. If you're fortunate, someone on duty at the stairs next to the column will let you out there. Otherwise, you'll have to walk back the way you came.

The next stop is the:

29 Forum of Julius Caesar

This is the first of the Imperial Forums. It lies on the opposite side of Via dei Fori Imperiali, the last set of sunken ruins before the Vittorio Emanuele Monument. Although it's possible to go right down into the ruins, you can see everything just as well from the railing. This was the site of the Roman stock exchange, as well as of the Temple of Venus, a few of whose restored columns stand cinematically in the middle of the excavations.

On to the Circus Maximus

From here, retrace your last steps until you're in front of the white Brescian marble monument around the corner on Piazza Venezia, the:

30 Vittorio Emanuele Monument

This flamboyant landmark, which has been compared to a frosted wedding cake or a Victorian typewriter, was constructed in the late 1800s to honor Italy's first king. An eternal flame burns at the Tomb of the Unknown Soldier. The interior of the monument has been closed to the public for many years.

Keep close to the monument and walk to your left, in the opposite direction from Via dei Fori Imperiali. You might like to pause at the fountain that flanks one of the monument's great white walls and splash some icy water on your face. Stay on the same side of the street and just keep walking around the monument. You'll be on Via del Teatro Marcello, which takes you past the twin lions that guard the sloping stairs and on along the base of the Capitoline Hill.

Keep walking along this street until you come to the:

31 Teatro di Marcello

It'll be on your right, and you'll recognize the two rows of gaping arches, which are said to be the models for the Colosseum. Julius Caesar is credited with starting the construction of this theater, but it was finished many years after his death (in 11 B.C.) by Augustus, who dedicated it to his favorite nephew, Marcellus. A small corner of the 2,000-year-old arcade has been restored to what presumably was the original condition. Here, as everywhere, numerous cats stalk around the broken marble.

The bowl of the theater and the stage were adapted many centuries ago as the foundation for the Renaissance palace of the Orsini family. The other ruins belong to old temples. To the right is the Porticus of Octavia, dating from the 2nd century B.C. Note how later cultures used part of the Roman structure without destroying its original character. There's another good example of this on the other side of the theater. Here you'll see a church with a wall that completely incorporates part of an ancient colonnade.

Keep walking along Via del Teatro Marcello away from Piazza Venezia for 2 more long blocks, until you come to Piazza della Bocca della Verità. The first item to notice in the attractive piazza is the rectangular:

32 Temple of Fortuna Virile

You'll see it on the right, a little off the road. Built a century before the birth of Jesus, it's still in magnificent condition. Behind it is another temple, dedicated to Vesta. Like the one in the Roman Forum, it is round, symbolic of the prehistoric huts where continuity of the hearth fire was a matter of survival.

About a block to the south you'll pass the facade of the Church of Santa Maria in Cosmedin, set on Piazza della Bocca della Verità. Even more noteworthy, a short walk east is the:

33 Circus Maximus

Its elongated oval proportions and ruined tiers of benches will make you think of *Ben-Hur*. Today a formless ruin, the victim of countless raids on its stonework by medieval and Renaissance builders, the remains of the once-great arena lie directly behind the church. At one time, 250,000 Romans could assemble on the marble seats, while the emperor observed the games from his box high on the Palatine Hill.

The circus lies in a valley formed by the Palatine Hill on the left and the Aventine Hill on the right. Next to the Colosseum, it was the most impressive structure in ancient Rome, located certainly in one of the most exclusive neighborhoods. Emperors lived on the Palatine, and the great palaces of patricians sprawled across the Aventine, which is still a nice neighborhood. For centuries, the pomp and ceremony of imperial chariot races filled this valley with the cheers of thousands.

When the dark days of the 5th and 6th centuries fell on the city, the Circus Maximus seemed a symbol of the complete ruination of Rome. The last games were held in 549 on the orders of Totilla the Goth, who had seized Rome in 547 and established himself as emperor.

To return to other parts of town, head for the bus stop adjacent to the Church of Santa Maria in Cosmedin, or walk the length of the Circus Maximus to its far end and pick up the Metro to the Termini of anywhere else in the city that appeals to you.

WALKING TOUR 2: THE HEART OF ROME

START:	**Palazzo del Quirinale**
FINISH:	**Piazza Santi Apostoli**
TIME:	**3½ hours**
BEST TIMES:	**Sunday mornings**
WORST TIMES:	**Morning and afternoon rush hours on weekdays**

This walking tour will lead you down narrow, sometimes traffic-clogged streets that have witnessed more commerce and religious fervor than any other neighborhood in Rome. Be prepared for glittering and very unusual shops that lie cheek by jowl with churches dating back to A.D. 500.

Walking Tour: The Heart of Rome

1 Piazza del Quirinale
2 Trevi Fountain
3 Piazza della Trinità dei Monti
4 Spanish Steps (Scalinata della Trinita dei Monti)
5 Keats-Shelley House (Casina Rossa)
6 Babington's Tea Rooms
7 Collegio di Propoganda Fide
8 Via Condotti
9 Augustus's Mausoleum (Mausoleo Augusteo)
10 Altar of Peace (Ara Pacis)
11 Borghese Palace (Palazzo Borghese)
12 Via del Corso
13 Palazzo Ruspoli
14 Chiesa dl San Lorenzo in Lucina
15 Piazza Colonna
16 Piazza di Montecitorio
17 Chiesa San Marcello al Corso
18 Chiesa S.S. Apostoli

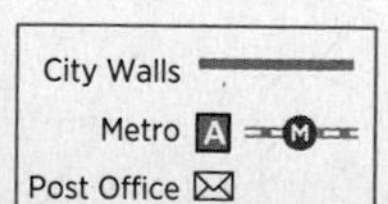

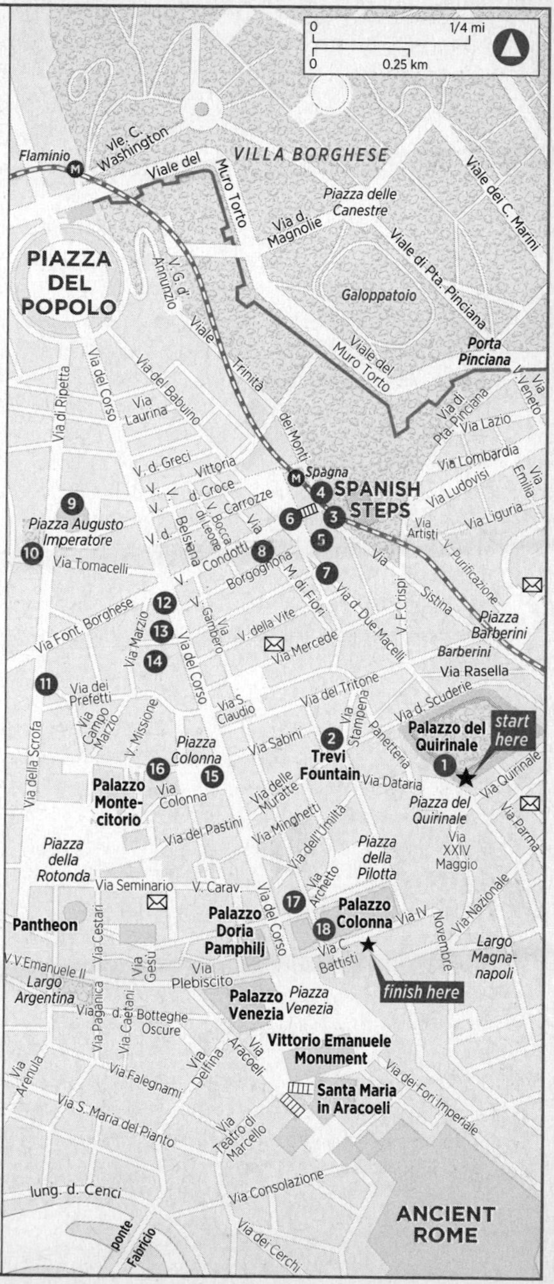

Begin in the monumental, pink-toned:

1 Piazza del Quirinale

Crowning the highest of the seven ancient hills of Rome, this is where Augustus's Temple of the Sun once stood (the steep marble steps that now lead to Santa Maria d'Aracoeli on the Capitoline Hill once serviced this spot), and part of the fountains in the piazza were built from the great Baths of Constantine, which also stood nearby. The palace, today home to the president of Italy, is open to the public only on Sunday mornings.

You can admire a nice view of Rome from the piazza's terrace, and then meander along the curiously lifeless streets that surround it before beginning your westward descent along Via della Dataria and your northerly descent along Via San Vincenzo to one of the most famous waterworks in the world, the:

2 Trevi Fountain

Supplied by water from the Acqua Vergine aqueduct, and a triumph of the baroque style, it was based on the design of Nicolo Salvi (who is said to have died of illness contracted during his supervision of the project) and completed in 1762. On the southwestern corner of the fountain's piazza you'll see a somber, not particularly spectacular church (Chiesa SS. Vincenzo e Anastasio) with a strange claim to fame: In it are contained the hearts and intestines of several centuries' worth of popes. This was the parish church of the popes when they resided at the Quirinal Palace on the hill above, and for many years each pontiff willed those parts of his body to the church. According to legend, the church was built on the site of a spring that burst from the earth after the beheading of St. Paul at one of three sites where his head is said to have bounced off the ground.

Throw a coin or two into the fountain to ensure your return to Rome, and then walk around to the right of the fountain along streets whose names will include Via di Stamperia, Via del Tritone, and Via F. Crispi. These lead to a charming street, Via Gregoriana, whose relatively calm borders and quiet apartments flank a narrow street that inclines upward to one of the most spectacular public squares in Italy:

3 Piazza della Trinità dei Monti

Partly because of its position at the top of the Spanish Steps (which you'll descend in a moment), partly because of its soaring Egyptian obelisk, and partly because of its lavish and perfect baroque symmetry, this is one of the most theatrical piazzas in Italy. Flanking the piazza are buildings that have played a pivotal role in French (yes, French) politics for centuries, including the Church of Trinità dei Monti, begun by the French monarch Louis XII in 1502 and restored during Napoleon's occupation of Rome in the early 1800s. The eastern edge of the square, adjacent to Via Gregoriana, is the site of the 16th-century Palazzetto Zuccaro, built for the mannerist painter Federico Zuccaro, with doorways and window openings fashioned into deliberately grotesque shapes inspired by the mouths of sea monsters. (It lies between Via Gregoriana, Via Sistina, and Piazza Trinità dei Monti.) In this building, at the dawn of the French Revolution, Jacques-Louis David painted the most politicized canvas in the history of France,

The Oath of the Horatii (1784), which became a symbol of the Enlightenment then sweeping through the salons of Paris. Today the palazzetto is owned by the German Institute for Art History.

Begin descending the most famous staircase in the world, the:

4 Spanish Steps

This azalea-flanked triumph of landscape design takes its name from the Spanish Embassy, which was in a nearby palace during the 19th century. The Spanish, however, had nothing to do with the construction of the steps. Designed by Italian architect Francesco de Sanctis between 1723 and 1725, they were funded almost entirely by the French as a preface to the above-mentioned French church, Trinità dei Monti.

The Spanish Steps are at their best in spring, when they're filled with flowers that seem to cascade down into Piazza di Spagna, a piazza designed like two interconnected triangles. Curiously, in the early 19th century, the steps were famous for the sleek young men and women who lined the travertine steps, flexing muscles and exposing ankles in hopes of attracting an artist and being hired as a model.

The boat-shape Barcaccia fountain, in the piazza at the foot of the steps, was designed by Bernini's father at the end of the 16th century.

There are two nearly identical houses at the foot of the steps on either side. One is the home of Babington's Tea Rooms (see "Take a Break," below); the other is the house where the English romantic poet John Keats lived—and died. That building, at 26 Piazza di Spagna, contains the:

5 Keats-Shelley House

Keats died here on February 23, 1821, at the age of 25, during a trip he made to Rome to improve his failing health. Since 1909, when well-intentioned English and American aficionados of English literature bought the building, it has been a working library established in honor of Keats as well as Shelley, who drowned off the coast of Viareggio with a copy of Keats's work in his pocket. Mementos inside range from the kitschy to the immortal and are almost relentlessly laden with literary nostalgia.

6 Babington's Tea Rooms

Babington's Tea Rooms, Piazza di Spagna 23 (✆ 06-6786027; www.babingtons.com), has been serving homemade scones and muffins, along with a good cuppa, ever since it opened in 1893 by Miss Anna Maria Babington, using her original recipes. Celebrities and thousands of visitors have stopped off here to rest in premises inspired by England's Victorian age. Prices are high, however.

In the past, the Piazza di Spagna area was a favorite of English lords, who rented palaces hereabout and parked their coaches on the street. Americans now dominate the scene, especially since the main office of American Express is right on Piazza di Spagna and dispenses all those letters (and money) from home. Much to the dismay of many Romans, the piazza is also home to a **McDonald's;** however, it's not your average Golden Arches—we've never seen one so lavish, and it's a good place to duck in if you need a restroom.

To the extreme southern edge of the square—flanked by Via Due Macelli, Via Propaganda, and Piazza di Spagna—is an odd vestige of the Catholic church's sense of missionary zeal, the:

7 Collegio di Propoganda Fide

Established in 1627 as the headquarters of a religious organization devoted to the training of young missionaries, this later became one of the most important centers for missionary work in the world. Owned and administered by the Vatican, it is therefore exempt from most of the laws and legalities of Italy. It contains design elements by two of the 17th century's most bitter artistic rivals, Bernini and Borromini.

The street that runs east-west as the logical continuation of the descent of the Spanish Steps is one of the most celebrated for style and fashion in Italy:

8 Via Condotti

It's lined with windows displaying the latest offerings from the Italian fashion industry. Even the least materialistic will enjoy window-shopping along this impressive lineup of the most famous names in international design. (Via Condotti is only the most visible of several upscale shopping streets in the neighborhood. For more of the same temptations, detour onto a smaller but equally glamorous parallel street, Via della Croce, 2 blocks to the north, and wander at will with your platinum card in hand. You'll need to return to Via Condotti eventually for the continuation of this walking tour.)

Via Condotti ends at a shop-lined plaza, Largo Goldoni, where your path will fork slightly to the right onto Via Tomacelli. Staying on the right (northern) edge of the street, turn right at the second intersection into Piazza Augusto, site of the:

9 Augustus Mausoleum

Once covered with marble and cypress trees, this tomb housed the ashes of many of the emperors of the 1st century all the way up to Hadrian (who built what is now Castel Sant'Angelo across the river for his own tomb). The imperial remains stayed intact within this building until the 5th century, when invading barbarians smashed the bronze gates and stole the golden urns, probably emptying the ashes onto the ground outside. The tomb was restored by Mussolini, and although you cannot enter the mausoleum itself, you can walk around it.

At the mausoleum's southwestern corner (Largo San Rocco), veer northwest until you reach the edge of the Tiber, stopping for a view of a bizarre, almost surreal compendium of ancient archaeological remnants restored and, in some cases, enhanced by Mussolini. It sits in an airy glass-and-concrete building beside the eastern banks of the Tiber at Ponte Cavour. Inside is one of the treasures of antiquity, the:

10 Altar of Peace (Ara Pacis)

The altar was built by the Senate as a tribute to Augustus and the peace he had brought to the Roman world. Look closely at the marble walls for portraits of Augustus's imperial family. Mussolini collected the few fragments of this monument that were scattered in museums throughout the world and gave his archaeological engineers a deadline for digging out the bulk of the altar, which remained underground—below the water table and forming part of the foundation of a Renaissance palace on the Corso. Fearful of failing Il Duce, the engineers hit on the idea of chemically freezing the water surrounding the altar and simply chipping the relic out in huge chunks of ice, building new supports for the palace overhead as they went.

Proceed southward along Via Ripetta, cross over Piazza di Porto di Ripetta, and then fork left, walking southeast along Via Borghese for a block until you reach the austere entrance to the:

11 Borghese Palace (Palazzo Borghese)

Although many of the art treasures that once graced its interior now form part of the Galleria Borghese collections (for details, see the listing on p. 179—you can't just duck in quickly on a whim), this huge and somewhat disjointed palazzo retains its status as the modern-day Borghese family's seat of power and prestige. Bought from another family in 1605 by the cardinal who later became Pope Paul V, it was later occupied by Pauline Borghese, Napoleon's scandalous sister, a noted enemy of opera composer Rossini. Regrettably, the palace, carefully preserving its status as one of the most prestigious private homes in the world, is not open to the public.

From your vantage point, walk in a westerly direction along Via Fontanella Borghese back to a square you've already visited, Largo Goldoni, the western terminus of Via Condotti. The busy avenue on your right is one of the most richly stocked treasure-troves of Italian merchandise in Rome:

12 Via del Corso

When compared with the many meandering streets with which it merges, the rigidly straight lines of Via del Corso are unusual. In the 18th century, residents of Rome commandeered the street to race everything from horses to street urchins, festooning the windows of buildings on either side of the narrow street with banners and flags. Although today its merchandise is not as chic (or as expensive) as what you'll find along Via Condotti, it's well worth a browse to see what's up in the world of Italian fashion.

Walk south along Via del Corso's western edge, turning right (west) after 1 block into Piazza San Lorenzo in Lucina. The severely massive building on the piazza's northern edge is the:

13 Palazzo Ruspoli

This is a 16th-century testament to the wealth of the Florentine Rucellai family. Family members commissioned the same architect (Bartolommeo Ammannati) who designed parts of the Pitti Palace in Florence to build their Roman headquarters. Today the building belongs to a private foundation, although it's occasionally open for temporary, infrequently scheduled exhibitions. The entrance is at Via del Corso 418A, although your best vantage point will be from Piazza San Lorenzo in Lucina.

On the piazza's southern edge rises the:

14 Chiesa di San Lorenzo in Lucina

Most of what you'll see today was rebuilt around 1650, although if you look carefully, the portico and most of the bell tower have survived almost unchanged since the 1100s. According to tradition, this church was built on the site of the mansion of Lucina, a prosperous Roman matron who salvaged the corpses of Christian martyrs from prisons and amphitheaters for proper burials. The church was founded by Sixtus III, who reigned for 8 years beginning in A.D. 432. Inside, look for the tomb of the French painter Poussin (1594–1665), which was carved and consecrated on orders of the French statesman Chateaubriand in 1830.

After your visit, retrace your steps back to Via del Corso and walk southward until you reach the venerable perimeter of:

15 Piazza Colonna

Its centerpiece is one of the most dramatic obelisks in town, the Column of Marcus Aurelius, a hollow bronze column rising 25m (83 ft.) above the piazza. Built between A.D. 180 and 196, and restored (some say "defaced") in 1589 by a pope who replaced the statue of the Roman warrior on top with a statue of St. Paul, it's one of the ancient world's best examples of heroic bas-relief and one of the most memorable sights of Rome. Beside the piazza's northern edge rises the Palazzo Chigi, official residence of the Italian prime minister.

Continue walking west from Piazza Colonna into another square a few steps to the east, and you'll find yourself in a dramatic piazza designed by Bernini:

16 Piazza di Montecitorio

This was the site during ancient times of the cremations of the Roman emperors. In 1792, the massive obelisk of Psammetichus II, originally erected in Egypt in the 6th century B.C., was placed here as the piazza's centerpiece. Brought to Rome by barge from Heliopolis in 10 B.C., it was unearthed from a pile of rubble in 1748 at a site close to the Church of San Lorenzo in Lucina. The Palazzo di Montecitorio, which rises from the piazza's northern edge, is the modern-day site of the Italian legislature (the Chamber of Deputies) and is closed to the public.

Retrace your steps back to Via del Corso, and then walk south, this time along its eastern edge. Within 6 blocks, just after crossing over Via dell'Umilità, you'll see the solid stone walls of the namesake church of this famous shopping boulevard:

17 Chiesa San Marcello al Corso

Originally founded in the 4th century and rebuilt in 1519 after a disastrous fire, it was ornamented in the late 1600s with a baroque facade by Carlo Fontana. A handful of ecclesiastical potentates from the 16th and 17th centuries, many resting in intricately carved sarcophagi, are contained inside.

After your visit, return to the piazza in front of the church, and then continue walking for half a block south along Via del Corso. Turn left (eastward) onto Via SS. Apostoli, then turn right onto Piazza SS. Apostoli, and conclude this tour with a visit to a site that has witnessed the tears of the penitent since the collapse of the Roman empire, the:

18 Chiesa SS. Apostoli

Because of alterations to the site, especially a not-very-harmonious rebuilding that began in the early 1700s, there's very little to suggest the ancient origins of this church of the Holy Apostles. Pope Pelagius founded it in the dim, early days of the Roman papacy, sometime between A.D. 556 and 561, as a thanksgiving offering for the short-term defeat of the Goths at a battle near Rome. The most interesting parts of this ancient site are the fluted stone columns at the end of the south aisle, in the Cappella del Crocifisso; the building's front portico, added in the 1300s, which managed to incorporate a frieze from ancient Rome; and one of the first works executed by Canova, a painting near the high altar completed in 1787 shortly after his arrival in Rome. The church is open daily from 6:30am to noon and 4 to 7pm.

WALKING TOUR 3: RENAISSANCE ROME

START:	**Via della Conciliazione (Piazza Pia)**
FINISH:	**Galleria Doria Pamphilj**
TIME:	**4 hours, not counting a tour of the Castel Sant'Angelo and visits to the Palazzo Spada and the Galleria Doria Pamphilj**
BEST TIMES:	**Early and midmornings**
WORST TIMES:	**After dark**

The threads that unify this tour are the grandiose tastes of Rome's Renaissance popes and the meandering Tiber River that has transported building supplies, armies, pilfered treasures from other parts of Europe, and such famous personages as Cleopatra and Mussolini into Rome. Slower and less powerful than many of Italy's other rivers (such as the mighty Po, which irrigates the fertile plains of Lombardy and the north), the Tiber varies from a sluggish ribbon of sediment-filled water only 1.2m deep (4 ft.) to a 6m-deep (20-ft.) torrent capable of flooding the banks that contain it.

The last severe flood to destroy Roman buildings occurred in 1870. Since then, civic planners have built mounded barricades high above its winding banks, a development that has diminished the river's visual appeal. The high embankments, as well as the roaring traffic arteries that parallel them, obscure views of the water along most of the river's trajectory through Rome. In any event, the waters of the Tiber are so polluted that many modern Romans consider their concealment something of a plus.

Begin your tour at Piazza Pia. (Don't confuse Piazza Pia with nearby Piazza Pio XII.) Piazza Pia is the easternmost end of Rome's most sterile and impersonal boulevard. Start at:

1 Via della Conciliazione

Construction of this boulevard, conceived by Mussolini as a monumental preface to the faraway dome of St. Peter's Basilica, required the demolition of a series of medieval neighborhoods between 1936 and 1950, rendering it without challenge the most disliked avenue in Rome.

Walk east toward the massive and ancient walls of the:

2 Castel Sant'Angelo

Originally built by Emperor Hadrian in A.D. 135 as one of the most impressive mausoleums in the ancient world, it was adapted for use as a fortress, a treasure vault, and a pleasure palace for the Renaissance popes. Visit its interior, noting the presence near the entrance of architectural models showing the castle at various periods of its history. Note the building's plan (a circular tower set atop a square foundation) and the dry moats (used today for impromptu soccer games by neighborhood kids), which long ago were the despair of many an invading army.

After your visit, walk south across one of the most ancient bridges in Rome:

3 Ponte Sant'Angelo

The trio of arches in the river's center is basically unchanged since the bridge was built around A.D. 135; the arches that abut the river's embankments were added late in the 19th century as part of a flood-control program. On December 19, 1450, so many pilgrims gathered on this bridge (which at the time was lined with wooden buildings) that about 200 of them were crushed to death. Today the bridge is reserved exclusively for pedestrians; vehicular traffic was banned in the 1960s.

On the southern end of the bridge is the site of one of the most famous executions of the Renaissance:

4 Piazza Sant'Angelo

Here, in 1599, Beatrice Cenci and several members of her family were beheaded on the orders of Pope Clement VIII for plotting the murder of their very rich and very brutal father. Their tale later inspired a tragedy by Shelley and a novel by 19th-century Italian politician Francesco Guerrazzi.

From the square, cut southwest for 2 blocks along Via Paola (crossing the busy traffic of Corso Vittorio Emanuele in the process) onto:

5 Via Giulia

Laid out during the reign of Pope Julius II (1503–13), Via Giulia and its straight edges were one of Renaissance Rome's earliest examples of urban planning. Designed to facilitate access to the Vatican, it was the widest, straightest, and longest city street in Rome at the time of its construction and was bordered by the 16th-century homes of such artists as Raphael, Cellini, and Borromini, and the architect Sangallo. Today the street is lined with some of the most spectacular antiques stores in Rome.

At the terminus of Via Paola, the first building on Via Giulia you're likely to see is the soaring dome of the:

6 Florentine Church (Chiesa di San Giovanni dei Fiorentini)

This is the premier symbol of the city of Florence in papal Rome. Its design is the result of endless squabbling among such artistic rivals as Sansovino, Sangallo, and Maderno, each of whom added embellishments of his own. Michelangelo also submitted a design for the church, although his drawing did not

Walking Tour: Renaissance Rome

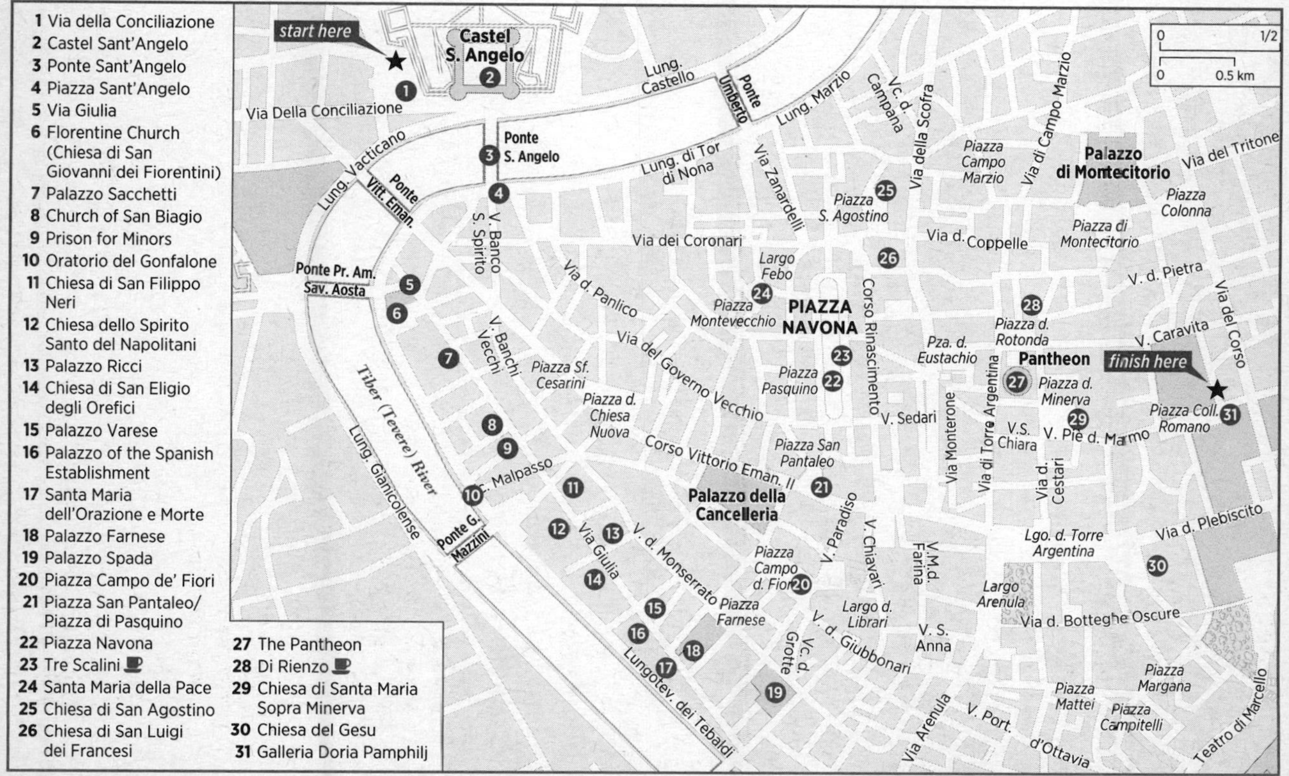

prevail during the initial competition. Most of the building was completed during the 1620s, and Lorenzo Corsini added the facade during the 1700s.

Now walk in a southeasterly direction along Via Giulia, making special note of houses at **no. 82** (built in the 1400s, it was offered by Pope Julius II to the Florentine community), **no. 85** (the land it sits on was once owned by Raphael), and **no. 79** (built in 1536 by the architect Sangallo as his private home, it was later snapped up by a relative of Cosimo de' Medici).

In less than 3 short blocks, on the northwest corner of Vicolo del Cefalo, rises the symmetrical bulk of the:

7 Palazzo Sacchetti

Completed by Vasari in the mid-1500s, it was built for the Sacchetti family, a Florence-based clan of bankers and merchants who moved to Rome after they lost an epic power struggle with the Medicis.

Continue walking south along Via Giulia. On your right rises the baroque facade of the unpretentious:

8 Chiesa di San Biagio

Although its front was added in the early 1700s, it's actually one of the oldest churches in Rome, rebuilt from an even earlier model dating to around 1070. The property of an Armenian Christian sect based in Venice, the church is named after an early Christian martyr (St. Biagio), a portion of whose throat is included among the sacred objects inside.

Walk another short block south along Via Giulia. Between Via del Gonfalone and Vicolo della Scimia are the barred windows of what was originally built early in the 19th century as a:

9 Prison for Minors

This, along with another nearby building (at Via Giulia 52, a few blocks to the south, which was built during the mid-1600s), incarcerated juvenile delinquents, political prisoners, debtors, common rogues, and innocent victims of circumstance for almost a hundred years. During its Industrial Revolution heyday, armed guards supervised all comings and goings along this section of Via Giulia.

Turn right onto Vicolo della Scimia and descend toward the Tiber. On your left, at no. 18, is a building used since the early 1500s as a guildhall for the flag-bearers of Rome, the:

10 Oratorio del Gonfalone

The guild of flag-bearers had, by the time this building was constructed, evolved into a charitable organization of concerned citizens and a rather posh social and religious fraternity. The frescoes inside were painted in 1573 by Zuccari. Restored during the early 1980s, they now form a backdrop for concerts held inside. The building is usually open Monday through Friday from 10am to 4pm—guided visits only. Make a reservation in advance by calling **✆ 06-85301758.**

Walk to the very end of Vicolo della Scimmia and make a hard left onto Vicolo Prigioni, which will eventually lead back to Via Giulia. At this point, as you continue to walk south along Via Giulia, you'll notice a swath of trees and a curious absence of buildings flanking the corner of Via Moretta. In 1940, Mussolini ordered the demolition of most of the buildings along Via Moretta for the construction of a triumphal boulevard running from east to west. His intention—which was never fulfilled—was to link together the nearby Ponte Mazzini with Corso Vittorio Emanuele. One building that suffered was the building near the corner with a baroque facade, the:

11 Chiesa di San Filippo Neri

Originally funded during the early 1600s by a wealthy but ailing benefactor in hopes of curing his gout, the church retains only its facade—the rest of the building was demolished. Where choirs once sang and candles burned during Mass, there is now a market for fruit and vegetables.

About another block to the south, on your right, rises the bulk of the:

12 Chiesa dello Spirito Santo del Napolitani

Once one of the headquarters of the Neapolitan community in Rome, the version you see today is a product of a rebuilding during the 1700s, although parts of the foundation were originally constructed during the 1300s.

Slightly farther south, at Via Giulia 146, rises the:

13 Palazzo Ricci

This is one of the many aristocratic villas that once flanked this historic street. For a better view of its exterior frescoes, turn left from Via Giulia into Piazza Ricci to admire this building from the rear.

Returning to Via Giulia, walk south for a block, and then turn right onto Via Barchetta. At the corner of Via di San Eligio, notice the:

14 Chiesa di San Eligio degli Orefici

According to popular belief, this church was designed by Raphael in 1516. Completed about 60 years later, it was dedicated to (and funded by) the city's gold- and silversmiths.

Return to Via Giulia and notice, near its terminus at Via Giukua 16, the:

15 Palazzo Varese

This structure was built as an aristocratic residence in the Tuscan style.

Nearby, at Via Giulia 151, is the:

16 Palazzo of the Spanish Establishment

Constructed in anticipation of the 1862 visit of Queen Elizabeth II of Spain, for the occasion of her charitable visit to Rome, it was designed by Antonio Sarti.

Continue walking south along Via Giulia, past the faded grandeur of at least another half-dozen palazzi. These will include the **Palazzo Cisterno** (from about 1560), at no. 163; **Palazzo Baldoca/Muccioli/Rodd** (about 1700), at no. 167; and **Palazzo Falconieri** (about 1510), at no. 1.

Opposite the corner of Via dei Farnesi rise the walls of one of the most macabre buildings in Rome, the church of:

17 Santa Maria dell'Orazione e Morte

Built around 1575 and reconstructed about 160 years later, it was the property of an order of monks whose job it was to collect and bury the unclaimed bodies of the indigent. Notice the depictions of skulls decorating the church's facade. During the Renaissance, underground chambers lined with bodies led from the church to the Tiber, where barges carried the corpses away. Although these vaults are not open to the public, the church's interior decoration carries multiple reminders of the omnipresence of death.

After exiting the church, notice the covered passageway arching over Via Giulia. Built in 1603 and designed by Michelangelo, it connected the church with the:

18 Palazzo Farnese

The rear side of the palazzo rises to your left, with the Tiber and a series of then-opulent gardens and villas that no longer exist. The Palazzo Farnese was designed by Sangallo and Michelangelo, among others, and has housed dignitaries ranging from Pope Paul III to Queen Christina of Sweden. Today the French Embassy, it's closed to the public. For the best view of the building, cut west from Via Giulia along any of the narrow streets (Via Mascherone or Via dei Farnesi will do nicely) to reach Piazza Farnese.

To the southwest is a satellite square, Piazza Quercia, at the southern corner of which rises the even more spectacular exterior of the:

19 Palazzo Spada

Built around 1550 for Cardinal Gerolamo Capo di Ferro, its ornate facade is stuccoed in high relief in the mannerist style. Although the staterooms are closed to the public, the courtyard and several galleries are open.

From here, walk 2 blocks north along either Vicolo del Grotte or Via Balestrari until you reach one of the most famous squares of Renaissance Rome:

20 Piazza Campo de' Fiori

During the 1500s, this square was the geographic and cultural center of secular Rome, with inns and the occasional burning at the stake of religious heretics. Today the campo hosts a morning open-air food market every day except Sunday.

After your visit, continue to walk north for 3 meandering blocks along the narrow confines of Via Baullari to:

21 Piazza San Pantaleo/Piazza di Pasquino

Its edges are the site of both the Palazzo Massimo (to the east) and the Palazzo Braschi (Museo di Roma) to the north. The Palazzo Massimo (currently home to, among other things, the Rome campus of Cornell University) was begun as a private home in 1532 and designed with an unusual curved facade that corresponded to the narrow confines of the street. Regrettably, because it's open to the public only 1 day a year (Mar 17), it's viewed as a rather odd curiosity from the Renaissance by most passersby. More accessible is the **Palazzo**

Braschi, built during the late 1700s by Pope Pius VI, né Giovanni Angelo Braschi, for his nephews. Severe and somewhat drab, it was the last palace ever constructed in Rome by a pope. Since 1952, it has contained the exhibits of the Museo di Roma, a poorly funded entity whose visiting hours and future are uncertain.

Continue walking north for 2 blocks until you reach the southernmost entrance of the most thrilling square in Italy:

22 Piazza Navona

Originally laid out in A.D. 86 as a stadium by Emperor Domitian, stripped of its marble in the 4th century by Constantine, and then embellished during the Renaissance into the lavish baroque form you see today, Piazza Navona has witnessed as much pageantry and heraldic splendor as any site in Rome. The fact that it's reserved exclusively for pedestrians adds enormously to its charm but makes parking in the surrounding neighborhood almost impossible.

23 Tre Scalini

Established in 1882, Tre Scalini, Piazza Navona 30 (© 06-6879148; www.ristorante-3scalini.com), is the most famous cafe on the square, although it is too tourist ridden for most tastes. Literally hundreds of people go here every day to sample the *tartufo* (ice cream disguised with a coating of bittersweet chocolate, cherries, and whipped cream). There are simpler versions of gelato as well.

After you've perked yourself up with sugar or caffeine or both, head for the piazza's northwestern corner, adjacent to the startling group of heroic fountains at the square's northern edge, and exit onto Via di Lorenesi. Walk westward for 2 crooked blocks, forking to the left onto Via Parione until you reach the edge of one of the district's most charming churches:

24 Santa Maria della Pace

According to legend, blood flowed from a statue of the Virgin above the altar after someone threw a pebble at it. This legend motivated Pope Sixtus IV to rebuild the church in the 1500s on the foundations of an even older sanctuary. For generations after that, its curved porticos, cupola atop an octagonal base, and frescoes by Raphael helped make it one of the most fashionable churches for aristocrats residing in the surrounding palazzos.

After admiring the subtle, counterbalancing curves of the church, retrace your steps to the welcoming confines of Piazza Navona, and then exit from it at its northernmost (narrow) end. Walk across the broad expanse of Via Zanardelli to its northern edge, and then head east for 2 blocks to Piazza San Agostino, on whose northern flank rises the:

25 Chiesa di San Agostino

Built between 1479 and 1483 and originally commissioned by the archbishop of Rouen, France, it was one of the first churches erected in Rome during the Renaissance. Its interior was altered and redecorated in the 1700s and 1800s. A painting by Caravaggio, *Madonna of the Pilgrims* (1605), hangs over the first altar on the left as you enter.

After your visit, continue walking east along Via Zanardelli, turning south in about a block onto Via della Scrofe. Be alert to the fact that this street changes its name in rapid order to Largo Toniolo and Via Dogana. Regardless of how it's marked, walk for about 2 blocks south. On the right, you'll see a particularly charming church, the:

26 Chiesa di San Luigi dei Francesi

This has functioned as the national church of France in Rome since 1589. Subtly carved into its facade is a stone salamander, the symbol of the Renaissance French monarch François I. Inside is a noteworthy series of frescoes by Caravaggio, *The Martyrdom of St. Matthew.*

Continue walking south for less than a block along Via Dogana, and then turn left for a 2-block stroll along the Salita dei Crescenzi. Suddenly, at Piazza della Rotonda, there will emerge a sweeping view of one of our favorite buildings in all of Europe:

27 The Pantheon

Rebuilt by Hadrian around A.D. 125, it's the best-preserved ancient monument in Rome, a remarkable testimony to the skill of ancient masons, whose (partial) use of granite helped ensure the building's longevity. Originally dedicated to all the gods, it was transformed into a church (Santa Maria ad Martyres) by Pope Boniface IV in A.D. 609. Many archaeologists find the building's massive, slightly battered dignity thrilling. Its flattened dome is the widest in the world, exceeding the width of the dome atop St. Peter's by about .6m (2 ft.).

28 Di Rienzo

Di Rienzo, Piazza della Rotonda 9 (✆ 06-6869097), is a great cafe. Here you can sit at a table enjoying a pick-me-up while you view not only one of the world's premier ancient monuments, but also the lively crowd of people who come and go on this square, one of the most interesting in Rome. Open daily from 7am to 3am.

After your coffee, walk southward along the eastern flank (Via Minerva) of the ancient building. That will eventually lead you to Piazza di Minerva. On the square's eastern edge rises the massive and severe bulk of a site that's been holy for more than 3,000 years:

29 Chiesa di Santa Maria Sopra Minerva

Beginning in 1280, early Christian leaders ordained that the foundation of an already ancient temple dedicated to Minerva (goddess of wisdom) be reused as the base for Rome's only Gothic church. Unfortunately, architectural changes and redecorations during the 1500s and the 1900s weren't exactly improvements. Despite that, the awe-inspiring collection of medieval and Renaissance tombs inside creates an atmosphere that's something akin to a religious museum.

After your visit, exit Piazza di Minerva from the square's easternmost edge, following Via del Gesù in a path that proceeds eastward, and then meanders to the south. Continue walking southward until you eventually cross over the roaring traffic of Corso Vittorio Emanuele II/Via del Plebiscito. On the southern side of that busy avenue, you'll see a church that for about a century after the Protestant Reformation was one of the most influential in Europe, the:

30 Chiesa del Gesù

Built between 1568 and 1584 with donations from a Farnese cardinal, this was the most powerful church in the Jesuit order for several centuries. Conceived as a bulwark against the perceived menace of the Protestant Reformation, it's sober, monumental, and historically very important to the history of the Catholic Counter-Reformation. The sheathing of yellow marble that covers part of the interior was added during the 1800s.

After your visit, cross back over Via del Plebiscito, walk eastward for 2 blocks, and turn left (north) onto Via de Gatta. Pass through the first piazza (Piazza Grazioli), and then continue northward to Piazza del Collegi Romano, site of the entrance to one of Rome's best-stocked museums, the:

31 Galleria Doria Pamphilj

This wonderful museum has a full listing on p. 169.

WALKING TOUR 4: TRASTEVERE

START: **Isola Tiberina**

FINISH: **Palazzo Corsini**

TIME: **3 hours, not counting museum visits**

BEST TIMES: **Daylight hours during weekday mornings, when the outdoor food markets are open, or early on a Sunday, when there's very little traffic**

WORST TIMES: **After dark**

Not until the advent of the Fellini films did Trastevere make a name for itself. Set on the western bank of the Tiber, away from the main tourist path, Trastevere (whose name translates as "across the Tiber") seems a world apart from the rest of Rome. Its residents have traditionally been considered more insular than the Romans across the river.

Because only a fraction of Trastevere has been excavated, it remains one of Rome's most consistently unchanged medieval neighborhoods, despite a trend toward gentrification. Dotted with ancient and dimly lit churches, crumbling buildings angled above streets barely wide enough for a Fiat, and very articulate inhabitants who have stressed their independence from Rome for many centuries, the district is the most consistently colorful of the Italian capital.

Be warned that street crime, pickpockets, and purse snatchers are more plentiful here than in Rome's more frequently visited neighborhoods, so leave your valuables behind and be alert to what's going on around you.

Your tour begins on the tiny but historic:

1 Tiber Island (Isola Tiburtina)

Despite its location in the heart of Rome, this calm and sun-flooded island has always been a refuge for the sick. The oldest bridge in Rome, the Ponte Fabricio, constructed in 62 B.C., connects the island to the Tiber's eastern bank. The church at the island's eastern end, **San Bartolomeo,** was built during the 900s by Holy Roman Emperor Otto III, although dozens of subsequent renovations have removed virtually everything of the original structure. The complex of structures at the island's western end contains the hospital of Fatebenefratelli, whose foundations and traditions date back to the ancient world (the island was associated with the healing powers of the god Aesculapius, son of Apollo).

Walk south along the bridge (Ponte Cestio) that connects the island to the western bank of the Tiber. After crossing the raging traffic, which runs parallel to the riverbanks, continue south for a few steps. Soon you'll reach:

2 Piazza Piscinula

Named after the Roman baths *(piscina)* that once stood here, the square contains the tiny but ancient Church of San Benedetto, whose facade was rebuilt in a simplified baroque style during the 1600s. It's classified as the smallest Romanesque church in Rome and supposedly is constructed on the site where St. Benedict, founder of the Benedictine order, lived as a boy. Directly opposite the church rises the intricate stonework of the Casa dei Mattei. Occupied during the Renaissance by one of the city's most powerful and arrogant families (the Mattei), it was abandoned as unlucky after several family members were murdered during a brawl at a wedding held inside. In reaction, the family moved to more elegant quarters across the Tiber.

Exit the piazza at the northwest corner, walking west along either the narrow Via Gensola or the somewhat wider Via della Lungaretta. In about 2 jagged blocks you'll reach the first of a pair of connected squares:

3 Piazza Sidney Sonnino

This first square was named after the Italian minister of foreign affairs during World War I. A few hundred feet to the north, facing the Tiber, is **Piazza G. G. Belli,** with a statue commemorating Giuseppe Gioacchino Belli (1791–1863), whose more than 2,000 satirical sonnets (written in Roman dialect) on Roman life have made him a particular favorite of the Trasteverans. From one edge of the piazza rise the 13th-century walls of the Torre degli Anguillara and the not-very-famous church of St. Agatha; on the southern edge, across the street, stand the walls of the Church of San Crisogono. Founded in the 500s and rebuilt in the 1100s (when the bell tower was added), it contains stonework and mosaics that merit a visit.

Now, from a point near the southernmost expanses of these connected squares, cross the traffic-clogged Viale di Trastevere and head southeast into a maze of narrow alleyways. We suggest that you ask a passerby for Via dei Genovesi because street signs in this maze of piazzas might be hard to find. Walking along Via dei Genovesi, traverse Via della Luce, and then turn right onto Via Anicia (which was named after the family that produced the medieval leader Pope Gregory the Great). Then, at Via Anicia 12, on the west side of the street, you'll see the simple but dignified walls of the:

4 Chiesa di San Giovanni dei Genovesi

Built during the 1400s for the community of Genoan sailors who labored at the nearby port, it has a tranquil garden on the opposite side of the street, which you might or might not be able to visit, according to the whim of the gatekeeper.

Walking Tour: Trastevere

After your visit, look across Via Anicia to the forbidding rear walls and ancient masonry of:

5 Santa Cecilia in Trastevere

To reach its entrance, continue walking another block southeast along Via dei Genovesi; then turn right onto Via Santa Cecilia, which soon funnels into Piazza dei Mercanti. A cloistered and still-functioning convent with a fine garden, Santa Cecilia contains in its inner sanctum hard-to-visit frescoes by Cavallini. (If you want to see the frescoes, call © **06-5899289** to make an appointment. Viewing hours are daily 10:15am–12:15pm.) The church is more easily visited and contains a white marble statue of the saint herself. The church is built on the reputed site of Saint Cecilia's long-ago palace and contains sections dating from the 12th to the 19th centuries. Admission to see the frescoes and subterranean areas is 3€. The church is open daily 9:30am to 12:30pm and 4 to 6:30pm.

St. Cecilia, who proved of enormous importance in the history of European art as a symbol of the struggle of the early church, was a wealthy Roman aristocrat condemned for her faith by a Roman prefect around A.D. 300. According to legend, her earthly body proved extraordinarily difficult for Roman soldiers to slay, affording the saint ample opportunity to convert bystanders to the Christian cause as she slowly bled to death over a period of 3 days.

About half a dozen cafes are near this famous church. Any of them serves frothy cups of cappuccino, tasty sandwiches, ice cream, and drinks.

After your snack, take the opportunity to wander randomly down three or four of the narrow streets outward from Piazza dei Mercanti. Of particular interest might be Via del Porto, which stretches south to the Tiber. The largest port in Rome once flourished at this street's terminus (Porto di Ripa Grande). During the 1870s redesign of the riverfront, when the embankments were added, the port was demolished.

Retrace your steps northward along Via del Porto, turning left onto Via di San Michele. At no. 22, inside a stucco-covered, peach-colored building that never manages to lose its bureaucratic anonymity despite its age, you'll see:

6 San Michele a Ripa Grande

For many years, this was the temporary home of the paintings of the Borghese Gallery until that gallery was restored and reopened.

After your visit, turn north onto Via Madonna dell'Orto, a narrow street that intersects Via di San Michele. One block later, at the corner of Via Anicia, you'll see the baroque:

7 Santa Maria dell'Orto

This church was originally founded by the vegetable gardeners of Trastevere during the early 1400s, when the district provided most of the green vegetables for the tables of Rome. Famous for the obelisks that decorate its cornices (added in the 1760s) and for the baroque gilding inside, it's one of the district's most traditional churches.

Now walk southwest along Via Anicia. In 2 blocks, the street funnels into Piazza di San Francesco d'Assisi. On your left, notice the ornate walls of the:

8 Chiesa di San Francesco a Ripa

Built in the baroque style and attached to a medieval Franciscan monastery, the church contains a mannerist statue by Bernini depicting Ludovica Albertoni. It's Bernini's last known sculpture and supposedly one of his most mystically transcendental.

Exit from Piazza di San Francesco d'Assisi and walk north along Via San Francesco a Ripa. After traversing the feverish traffic of Viale di Trastevere, take the first left onto a tiny street with a long name, Via Natale del Grande Cardinale Merry di Val. (Its name is sometimes shortened to simply "Via Natale," if it's marked at all on your map.) This funnels into:

9 Piazza di San Cosimato

A busy food market operates here every weekday from early morning until around noon. On the north side of the square lies the awkwardly charming church of San Cosimato, sections of which were built around A.D. 900; it's closed to the public.

Exit from the piazza's north side, heading up Via San Cosimato (its name might not be marked). This will lead into:

10 Piazza di San Callisto

Much of the real estate surrounding this square, including the 17th-century Palazzo San Callisto, belongs to the Vatican.

The edges of this piazza will almost imperceptibly flow into one of the most famous squares of Rome:

11 Piazza di Santa Maria in Trastevere

The Romanesque church that lends the piazza its name (**Santa Maria in Trastevere**) is the most famous building in the entire district. Originally built around A.D. 350 and thought to be one of the oldest churches in Rome, it sports a central core that was rebuilt around 1100 and an entrance and portico that were added in the 1840s. The much-restored mosaics both on the facade and in the interior, however, date from around 1200. Its sense of timelessness is enhanced by the much-photographed octagonal fountain in front (and the hundreds of pigeons).

12 Café Bar di Marzio

Try one of the many cafes that line this famous square. We especially like the Café Bar di Marzio, Piazza di Santa Maria in Trastevere 14B (© 06-5816095), where rows of tables, both inside and out, offer an engaging view of the ongoing carnival of Trastevere. Open Tuesday through Sunday from 7am to 3am.

After your stop, walk to the church's north side, toward its rear. Stretching from a point beginning at its northwestern edge is an ancient square, Piazza di San Egidio, with its own drab and rather nondescript 16th-century church (Chiesa di San Egidio) set on its western edge. Use it as a point of reference for the left street that funnels from its base in a northeasterly direction, Via della Scala.

The next church you'll see on your left, just after Via della Scala, is:

13 Santa Maria della Scala

This 17th-century baroque monument belongs to the Discalced Carmelite order of nuns. The interior contains works by Caravaggio and his pupils. There's also a pharmacological oddity in the annexes associated with the building: They include a modern pharmacy as well as a room devoted to arcane jars and herbal remedies that haven't changed very much since the 18th century.

In about 5 blocks, you'll reach a triumphal archway that marks the site of one of the ancient Roman portals to the city, the:

14 Porta Settimiana

During the 3rd century it was a vital link in the Roman defenses of the city, but its partially ruined masonry provides little more than poetic inspiration today. Much of its appearance dates from the age of the Renaissance popes, who retained it as a site marking the edge of the ancient Aurelian wall.

The narrow medieval-looking street leading off to the right is:

15 Via Santa Dorotea

Site of a rather drab church (**Chiesa San Dorotea,** a few steps from the intersection with Via della Scala), the street also marks a neighborhood that was, according to legend, the home of "La Fornarina," the baker's daughter. She was the mistress of Raphael, and he painted her as the Madonna, causing a scandal in his day.

Return to Via della Scala (which at this point has changed its name to Via della Lungara) and continue walking north. After Via Corsini, the massive palace on your left is the:

16 Palazzo Corsini

Built in the 1400s for a nephew of the pope, it was acquired by Queen Christina of Sweden, the fanatically religious monarch who abdicated the Protestant throne of Sweden for a life of devotion to Catholic causes. Today it houses some of the collection of the **National Gallery of Ancient Art,** plus European paintings of the 17th and 18th centuries. It is open Tuesday to Sunday 8:30am to 7:30pm.

After your visit, cross Via della Lungara, heading east toward the Tiber, for a look at what was once the most fashionable villa in Italy, the:

17 Villa Farnesina

It was built between 1508 and 1511 by a Sienese banker, Agostino Chigi (Il Magnifico), who was believed to be the richest man in Europe at the time. After his death in 1520, the villa's frescoes and carvings were partially sacked by German armies in 1527. After years of neglect, the building was bought by the Farnese family, after whom it is named today, and then by the Bourbons of Naples in the 18th century. Graced with sculpture and frescoes (some by Raphael and his studio), it now belongs to the Italian government and is the home of the National Print Cabinet (Gabinetto Nazionale delle Stampe), whose collections are open for view only by appointment. The public rooms, however, are open Monday to Saturday 9am to 1pm.

SHOPPING

Rome offers temptations of every kind. You might find hidden oases of charm and value in lesser-known neighborhoods, but in our limited space here, we've summarized certain streets known throughout Italy for their shops. Keep in mind that the monthly rent on these places is very high, and those costs will be passed on to you. Nonetheless, a stroll down some of these streets presents a cross section of the most desirable wares found in Italy.

Although Rome has many wonderful boutiques, you'll find better shopping in Florence and Venice. If you're continuing on to either of these cities, hold off a bit.

Shopping hours are generally Monday from 3:30 to 7:30pm, and Tuesday through Saturday from 9:30 or 10am to 1pm and 3:30 to 7 or 7:30pm. Some shops are open on Monday mornings, however, and some shops don't close for the afternoon break.

THE SHOPPING SCENE

SHIPPING Shipping can be a problem, but—for a price—any object can be packed, shipped, and insured. For major purchases, you should buy an all-risks insurance policy to cover damage or loss in transit. Because these policies can be expensive, check into whether using a credit card to make your purchase will provide automatic free insurance.

TAX REBATES ON PURCHASES IN ITALY Visitors are sometimes appalled at the high taxes and add-ons that seem to make so many things expensive in Italy. Those taxes, totaling as much as 19% to 35% for certain goods, apply to big-ticket purchases of more than 155€ but can be refunded if you plan ahead and perform a bit of sometimes tiresome paperwork. When you make your purchase, get a receipt from the vendor. When you leave Italy, find an Italian Customs agent at the point of your exit from the country. The agent will want to see the item you've bought, confirm that it's physically leaving Italy, and stamp the vendor's receipt.

You should then mail the stamped receipt (keeping a photocopy for your records) back to the original vendor. The vendor will, sooner or later, send you a check representing a refund of the tax you paid. Reputable stores view this as a matter of ordinary paperwork and are very businesslike about it. Less honorable stores might lose your receipts. It pays to deal with established vendors on purchases of this size.

Major Shopping Streets

VIA BORGOGNONA This street begins near Piazza di Spagna, and both the rents and the merchandise are chic and ultra-expensive. Like its neighbor, Via Condotti, Via Borgognona is a mecca for wealthy, well-dressed men and women from around the world. Its storefronts have retained their baroque or neoclassical facades.

VIA COLA DI RIENZO Bordering the Vatican, this long, straight street runs from the Tiber to Piazza Risorgimento. Since the street is wide and clogged with traffic, it's best to walk down one side and then up the other. Via Cola di Rienzi is known for stores selling a wide variety of merchandise at reasonable prices—from jewelry to fashionable clothes and shoes.

VIA CONDOTTI Easy to find because it begins at the base of the Spanish Steps, this is Rome's poshest and most prominent shopping street—the Madison Avenue of Rome. Even the recent incursion of some less elegant stores hasn't diminished the allure of Via Condotti as a consumer's playground for the rich and super-rich. For us mere mortals, it's a great place for window-shopping and people-watching.

VIA DEL CORSO Not attempting the stratospheric image or prices of Via Condotti or Via Borgognona, Via del Corso boasts styles aimed at younger consumers. There are some gems scattered amid the shops selling jeans and sporting equipment. The most interesting stores are nearest the fashionable cafes of Piazza del Popolo.

VIA FRANCESCO CRISPI Most shoppers reach this street by following Via Sistina (see below) 1 long block from the top of the Spanish Steps. Near the intersection of these streets are several shops for unusual and less expensive gifts.

VIA FRATTINA Running parallel to Via Condotti, it begins, like its more famous sibling, at Piazza di Spagna. Part of its length is closed to traffic. Here the concentration of shops is denser, although some aficionados claim that its image is slightly less chic and prices are slightly lower than at its counterparts on Via Condotti. It's usually thronged with shoppers who appreciate the lack of motor traffic.

VIA NAZIONALE The layout recalls 19th-century grandeur, but the traffic is horrendous; crossing Via Nazionale requires a good sense of timing and a strong understanding of Italian driving patterns. It begins at Piazza della Repubblica and runs down almost to the 19th-century monuments of Piazza Venezia. You'll find an abundance of leather stores (more reasonable in price than those in many other parts of Rome) and a handful of stylish boutiques.

VIA SISTINA Beginning at the top of the Spanish Steps, Via Sistina runs to Piazza Barberini. The shops are small and stylish, and pedestrian traffic is less dense than on other major streets.

VIA VITTORIO VENETO Via Veneto is filled with expensive hotels and cafes and relatively expensive stores selling shoes, gloves, and leather goods.

SHOPPING A TO Z

Antiques

Some visitors to Italy consider the many antiques for sale the country's greatest treasure. But prices have risen to alarming levels as increasingly wealthy Europeans outbid one another in a frenzy. Any antiques dealer who risks the high rents of

Rome Shopping

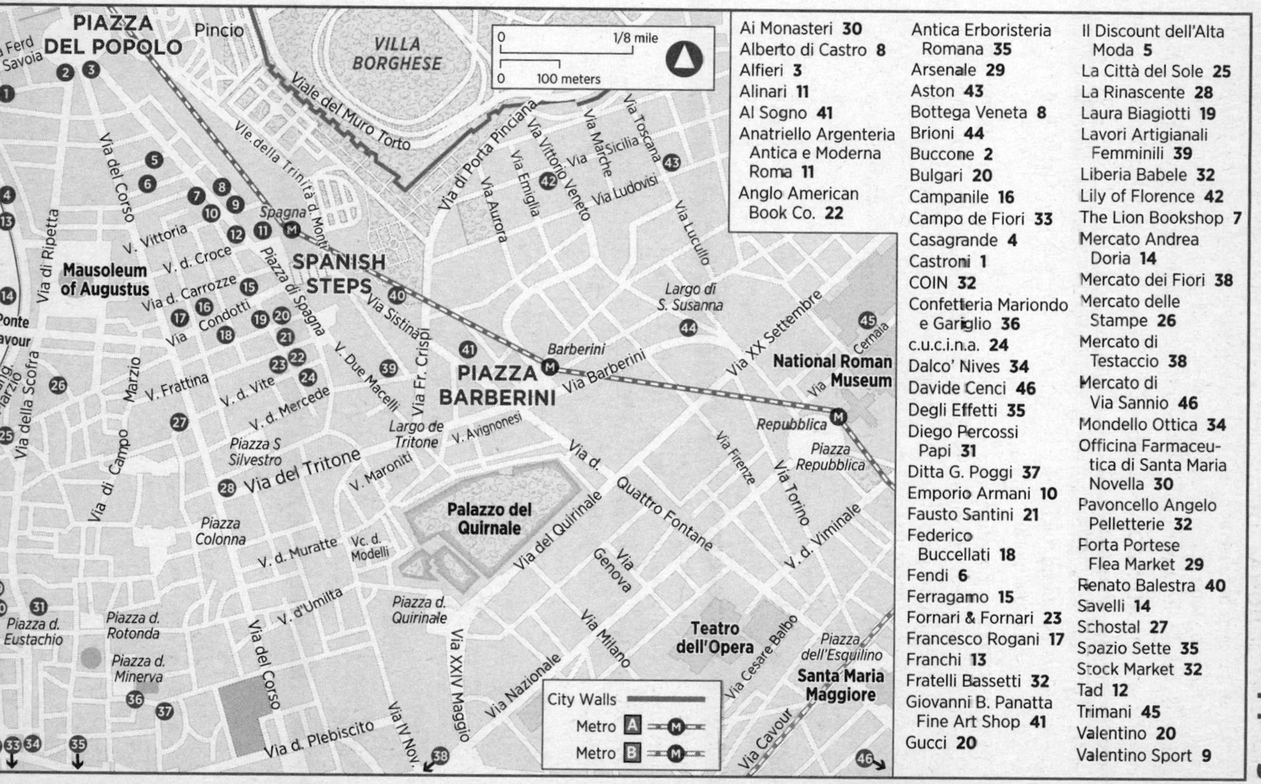

Ai Monasteri 30
Alberto di Castro 8
Alfieri 3
Alinari 11
Al Sogno 41
Anatriello Argenteria Antica e Moderna Roma 11
Anglo American Book Co. 22
Antica Erboristeria Romana 35
Arsenale 29
Aston 43
Bottega Veneta 8
Brioni 44
Buccone 2
Bulgari 20
Campanile 16
Campo de Fiori 33
Casagrande 4
Castroni 1
COIN 32
Confetteria Mariondo e Gariglio 36
c.u.c.i.n.a. 24
Dalco' Nives 34
Davide Cenci 46
Degli Effetti 35
Diego Percossi Papi 31
Ditta G. Poggi 37
Emporio Armani 10
Fausto Santini 21
Federico Buccellati 18
Fendi 6
Ferragamo 15
Fornari & Fornari 23
Francesco Rogani 17
Franchi 13
Fratelli Bassetti 32
Giovanni B. Panatta Fine Art Shop 41
Gucci 20
Il Discount dell'Alta Moda 5
La Città del Sole 25
La Rinascente 28
Laura Biagiotti 19
Lavori Artigianali Femminili 39
Liberia Babele 32
Lily of Florence 42
The Lion Bookshop 7
Mercato Andrea Doria 14
Mercato dei Fiori 38
Mercato delle Stampe 26
Mercato di Testaccio 38
Mercato di Via Sannio 46
Mondello Ottica 34
Officina Farmaceutica di Santa Maria Novella 30
Pavoncello Angelo Pelletterie 32
Porta Portese Flea Market 29
Renato Balestra 40
Savelli 14
Schostal 27
Spazio Sette 35
Stock Market 32
Tad 12
Trimani 45
Valentino 20
Valentino Sport 9

central Rome is acutely aware of valuations. So while you might find gorgeous pieces, you're not likely to find any bargains.

Beware of fakes, remember to insure anything you have shipped home, and for larger purchases—anything more than 155€ at any one store—keep your paperwork in order to obtain your tax refund (p. 225).

Via dei Coronari is buried in a colorful section of the Campo Marzio. To find the street, turn left out of the north end of Piazza Navona and pass the excavated ruins of Domitian's Stadium—it will be just ahead. There are more than 40 antiques stores in the next 4 blocks, offering inlaid secretaries, gilded consoles, vases, urns, chandeliers, marble pedestals, chaises, refectory tables—you name it. Bring your pocket calculator and keep in mind that stores are frequently closed between 1 and 4pm.

Via del Babuino is another major street for antiques in Rome, with some of the most prestigious stores found here, including Alberto di Castro (our favorite store for prints—see "Art," below), but many others as well.

A few minutes south of Piazza del Popolo, via Laurina lies midway between via del Corso and via del Babuino. It is filled with beautiful stores where you can find anything from an antique print to a 17th-century chandelier.

Ad Antiqua Domus This shop practically feels like a museum of Italian furniture design through the ages. You'll find furniture from the days of Caesar through the 19th century for sale here. Via dei Coronari 41. ✆ **06-6861186.** Bus: 46B, 98, 870, or 881.

Art

Alberto di Castro ★★ Alberto di Castro is one of the largest dealers in antique prints and engravings in Rome. You'll find depictions of everything from the Colosseum to the Pantheon, each evocative of the Mediterranean world, priced between 21€ to 7,967€ depending on the age and rarity of the engraving. Piazza di Spagna 5. ✆ **06-6792269.** www.dicastro.com. Metro: Spagna.

Alinari This shop takes its name from the famed Florentine photographer of the 19th century. Original Alinari prints are almost as prized as antique paintings, and they record Rome as it was more than a century ago. Via Alibert 16A. ✆ **06-6792923.** www.alinari.it. Metro: Spagna.

Giovanni B. Panatta Fine Art Shop In business since 1890, this store is up the hill toward the Villa Borghese. Here you'll find excellent prints in color and black and white, covering a variety of subjects from 18th-century Roman street scenes to astrological charts. There's a good selection of attractive and reasonably priced reproductions of medieval and Renaissance art as well. Via Francesco Crispi 117. ✆ **06-6795948.** Metro: Spagna or Barberini.

Bookstores

Anglo American Book Co. Near the Spanish Steps, this is one of the best outlets for English language books, especially if you're interested in Italian art and architecture. Via della Vite 102 at Via Mario de'Fiori. ✆ **06-6795222.** www.aab.it. Metro: Spagna.

Libreria Babele This is Rome's major gay and lesbian bookstore. Besides the usual stock, it sells a gay map of the city. Via dei Banchi Vecchi 116. ✆ **06-687628.** www.libreriababeleroma.it. Bus: 40, 46, 62, or 64.

The Lion Bookshop The Lion Bookshop is the oldest English-language bookshop in town, specializing in both American and English titles. It also sells children's books and photographic volumes on both Rome and Italy. English-language videos are for sale or rent. Closed in August. Via del Greci 33. ✆ **06-32654007.** www.thelionbookshop.com. Metro: Spagna.

Chocolates

Confetteria Moriondo e Gariglio There is no finer chocolatier in Rome than this family-run outlet that's mobbed at Easter and before Valentine's Day. The dark, liqueur-filled confections and other treats are molded and made right on-site. The staff also sells confections made out of almonds, chestnuts, and other nuts. Closed in August. Via di Pie' di Marmo 21–22. ✆ **06-6990856.** Bus: C3, 30, 40, 46, 64, or 119.

Cosmetics & Perfumes

Ai Monasteri ★★ This shop, evoking a medieval apothecary, was founded here in 1892 and has since been managed by four generations of the Nardi family. It sells products from monastic orders around Italy, many of them based on centuries-old and closely guarded recipes. Merchandise ranges from liqueurs to "products from the beehive," rare oils and vinegar to some of the best tasting jams we've ever had. Expect to be dazzled by items that include some of the world's best chocolates to rare cosmetic products. Corso del Rinascimento 72. ✆ **06-68802783.** www.aimonasteri.it. Bus: 30, 81, or 87.

Antica Erboristeria Romana 🎁 Charles Dickens might call it the curiosity shop. Since the 18th century it has been dispensing "wonders" from its tiny wooden drawers, some of which are labeled with skulls and crossbones. Scented aper, licorice, hellbane, and herbal remedies . . . it's all here and more. Via di Torre Argentina 15. ✆ **06-6879493.** www.anticaerboristeriaromana.it. Metro: Spagna or Barberini.

Officina Farmaceutica di Santa Maria Novella ★ This highly scented perfumery and apothecary's shop is a branch of its more famous parent in Florence. The staff sells creams, exotic soaps and essences, and lotions based on formulas created in the 16th century by Dominican monks in Tuscany. The potpourri is a wonderful gift to take home. Closed 1 week in mid-August. Corso del Rinascimento 47. ✆ **06-6872446.** Bus: C3, 30, 70, 81, 87, or 130.

Department Stores

COIN Close to the Vatican, this is hardly the Harrods of Rome, but might come in handy for any number of purchases. The store sells clothing of medium but affordable quality along with accessories, shoes, underwear, jewelry—you name it. If you shop carefully here, you can find some great buys. There is a good section of cosmetics, even a department for kids clothing and a good selection of Italian household wares. Via Cola di Rienzo 173 (at Via Poolo Emilio). ✆ **06-36004298.** www.coin.it. Metro: Ottaviano.

La Rinascente This upscale department store offers clothing, hosiery, perfume, cosmetics, and other goods. It also has its own line of clothing (Ellerre) for men, women, and children. This is the largest of the Italian department-store chains. Piazza Colonna, Via del Corso 189. ✆ **06-6797691.** www.rinascente.it. Bus: 117.

Discount Shopping

Certain stores that can't move their merchandise at any price often consign their unwanted goods to discounters. In Italy, the original labels are usually still inside the garment, and you'll find some very chic labels strewn in with mounds of more generic garments. Know in advance that these pieces couldn't be sold at higher prices in more glamorous shops; and some garments are the wrong size, are the wrong look, or have a stylistic mistake. If you're willing to sift through a lot, you might find a gem.

Il Discount dell'Alta Moda The honest and genuinely helpful staff here will help you pick through the constantly changing racks of women's and men's clothing, with discounts of up to 50% on such labels as Versace, Donna Karan, Armani, Krizia, and Ferré. The shop also sells irregulars and overstock at cut-rates. Near the Spanish Steps at Via di Gesù e Maria 16A. ✆ **06-3613796.** Metro: Flaminio. Another branch is near Termini at Via Viminale 35. ✆ **06-47825672**. Metro: Repubblica.

McArthur Glen Designer Outlet Bargain hunters seeking major labels at prices 35% to 75% below normal head for the Roman hill town of Castel Romano 10km (6 miles) east of Rome. In a faux Roman setting, this shopping complex takes in nearly 110 stores. Here you'll have all your needs met in clothing, footwear, and accessories. Designer names include Versace, Dolce & Gabbana, Hilfiger, and Ferragamo. There is also a large playground here, along with restaurants and bars. Take the B line of the Metro to the Laurentina stop. From this point, catch a Cotral bus toward Pomezia-Latina to the Castel Romano stop. From this point, it's a 5-minute walk to Castel Romano Outlet. Via Ponte di Piscina Cupa 64, Castel Romano. ✆ **06-5050050.** www.mcarthurglen.it.

Eyewear

Mondello Ottica At Campo de' Fiori, this is one of the best places to shop for eyewear in all of Rome, with a wide selection ranging from sunglasses to prescription frames. A few steps from Corso Vittorio Emanuele II, it offers a very wide selection of both Italian and foreign brands of eyewear. Naturally, it's also well equipped to supply contact lenses. Via del Pellegrino 98. ✆ **06-6861955.** www.mondelloottica.it. Bus: 46, 64, 190, 571, or 916.

Fabrics

Aston Right on the tourist-trodden Via Veneto, this elegant outlet sells some of the finest Italian and continental fabrics, including silks. It also stocks fashionable ready-to-wear clothing for both men and woman. Sometimes remnants (*scampolia*) are sold, and these are true deals. Via Boncompagni 27. ✆ **06-42871227.** www.astontessuti.com. Metro: Barberini. Bus: 52, 53, or 63.

Fratelli Bassetti About 300m (984 ft.) from Piazzo Campo de' Fiori, this antique palazzo is the showcase for a fabulous collection of exquisite Italian silks and other couture fashion fabrics. The Bassetti company also makes and sells sheets, bed coverings, rugs, tablecloths, curtains, and upholstery fabrics. Closed 2 weeks in August. Corso Vittorio Emanuele II 73. ✆ **06-6892326.** www.fratellibassetti.com. Bus: 40, 46, 62, or 64.

Fashion

See also "Department Stores," "Discount Shopping," "Leather," "Lingerie," and "Shoes."

FOR MEN

Brioni ★★ This is the finest men's clothing store in Rome, opening in 1945 and dressing ambassadors, actors, and presidents over the years. It numbers among its clientele a virtual who's who that includes Donald Trump, Clark Gable, John Wayne, Gary Cooper, and Luciano Pavarotti. Brioni even outfitted 007 in some of the James Bond films. The custom tailoring is impeccable, but you can also purchase ready-to-wear garments. Via Barberini 79. ✆ **06-484517.** www.brioni.com. Metro: Repubblica. Bus: 150 or 175.

Emporio Armani This store stocks relatively inexpensive menswear crafted by the couturier who has dressed perhaps more stage and screen stars than any other designer in Italy. The designer's more expensive line—sold at sometimes staggering prices that are nonetheless up to 30% less than what you'd pay in the United States—is a short walk away at **Giorgio Armani,** Via Condotti 77 (✆ **06-6991460;** www.giorgioarmani.com). Via del Babuino 140. ✆ **06-36002197.** www.emporioarmani.com. Metro: Spagna.

Schostal Dating to 1870, this is the clothing store for men who like their fashion conservative and well crafted. It features everything from underwear to cashmere overcoats. The prices are more reasonable than you might think. Via del Corso 158. ✆ **06-6791240.** www.schostalroma.com. Bus: C3, 62, 63, 81, or 117.

Valentino ★★★ If you can afford the high prices in this swank emporium, you'll be the most fashionable man in town. Valentino's women's haute couture is sold around the corner in an even bigger showroom at Via Bocca di Leone 15 (✆ **06-6787585**). Via dei Condotti 13. ✆ **06-6790479.** www.valentino.com. Metro: Spagna.

FOR WOMEN

Arsenale ★ Most of the inventory displayed here is the creative statement of owner Patrizia Pieroni. Her design preferences include lots of ultra-rich fabrics, nothing too frilly or girlish, and a dignified kind of severity that many foreign visitors find captivating. Favorite colors include a spectrum of pinks, pale grays, and lilacs, with accents of bright orange, celadon green, bordeaux, and off-whites. Via del Governo Vecchio 64. ✆ **06-6861380.** www.patriziapieroni.it. Bus: 40, 46, 62, or 64.

Laura Biagiotti ★★ One of Rome's born-and-bred designers remains our favorite. Stylish *signoras* still come here to buy cashmere knits from a woman known as the "Queen of Cashmere." A Biagiotti dress fits casually, loosely, but flatteringly on a woman's frame and often contains topstitching and *ajourée,* or fretwork. She calls her own fashions "behavioral modern art." The designer also creates stylish fashions for men. Via Mario de' Fiori 26. ✆ **06-6791205.** www.laurabiagiotti.it. Metro: Spagna.

Renato Balestra Rapidly approaching the stratospheric upper levels of Italian fashion is Renato Balestra, whose women's clothing exudes a lighthearted elegance. Via Abruzzi 3. ✆ **06-4882586.** www.renatobalestra.it. Metro: Barberini.

Tad For one-stop shopping—perfume, accessories, shoes, fashion—this is the address. A textile line and a collection of home furnishings are only two features of what is called a "concept shop." Another section is devoted to music with a large CD collection. The Roman press has hailed Tad as the city's "coolest lifestyle store." The Tad Café serves breakfast, light lunches, and luscious desserts in an Asian-style inner courtyard. Via del Babuino 155. ✆ **06-96842086.** www.wetad.it. Metro: Spagna.

FOR CHILDREN

Lavori Artigianali Femminili Near Piazza di Spagna is an unusual clothing store for children and infants. The shop features what many a little Roman aristocrat might be wearing, including handmade velvet and chiffon lace-trimmed party dresses. They also sell embroidered crib and carriage linens. It's expensive and occasionally impractical, but what a delight. Closed in August. Via di Capo Le Case 6. ✆ **06-6781100.** Metro: Spagna.

CLASSICAL CLOTHING FOR MEN & WOMEN

Davide Cenci This upscale specialty store opened in 1926 and has long been popular with well-heeled locals. There's a wide choice of men's jackets (some in cashmere) and well-tailored shirts. Women gravitate to the beautifully tailored skirts and trousers, as well as the knitwear made of natural fibers. Even shoes and children's clothing are sold. Via Campo Marzio 1–7. ✆ **06-6990681.** www.davidecenci.com. Bus: 116.

Degli Effetti Near the Pantheon, this funky but classic trio of designer boutiques stocks name labels. These are mostly from designers that can't afford their own showcase outlets. The store sells sophisticated menswear at number 75, chic women's apparel at 79, and unisex offerings at 93. The latter has the most high-quality apparel but at expensive prices. Piazza Capranica 75, 79, 93. ✆ **06-6790202.** Bus: 62, 63, or 116.

SPORTSWEAR FOR MEN & WOMEN

Valentino Sport Specializing exclusively in sportswear, this is Valentino's least expensive line of clothing. His easy-to-wear, stylish clothing has warm climates in mind. In summer, there's more emphasis on women's clothes than men's, but the rest of the year the inventories are about equal. Via del Babuino 61. ✆ **06-36001906.** Metro: Spagna.

Food & Wine

See also "Markets," below.

Castroni ★★ At this old-fashioned store, you'll find an array of unusual foodstuffs from around the Mediterranean. If you want herbs from Apulia, cheese from the Valle d'Aosta, or an obscure brand of balsamic vinegar, Castroni will have it. Filled to the rafters with the abundance of agrarian Italy, it also carries foods that are exotic in Italy but commonplace in North America, such as taco shells, corn curls, and peanut butter. Via Cola di Rienzo 196. ✆ **06-6874383.** www.castronicoladirienzo.com. Bus: 81 or 590.

Franchi ★★ Near the Vatican, this gourmet deli is claimed as the market leader. It's great for either a picnic or place to order hot food to go. Deeper into the store are prepared some of the best stuffed tomatoes in Rome, or else shelled prawns and a selection of the favorite "fried nibbles." There is a varied and carefully chosen selection of wines as well. Franchi has arguably the finest *salumeria* counter in Rome, piled high with every form of culinary temptation, including cheese from Italy, France, and Great Britain. Via Cola di Rienzo 204. ✆ **06-6874651.** www.franchi.it. Metro: Ottaviano.

Volpetti ★★ This emporium of food and wine, among the finest gourmet delis in Italy, is the major competition to Franchi (see above). Located in the typical Roman neighborhood of Testaccio, it originated in 1973 and still is a family business run by the Volpetti brothers. There is an infinite variety of exceptional cheese, hams, and salami, plus a varied and tempting offering of first-rate breads and sumptuous desserts made by hand. You can even order pizza, plates to go, honey, fresh truffles, and also varied pastas also made by hand. The deli is dedicated to rediscovering the ancient flavors of Rome. Via Marmorata 47. ✆ **06-5742352.** www.volpetti.com. Metro: Piramide.

Housewares

c.u.c.i.n.a. This is a stainless-steel shrine to everything you need for a proper Italian kitchen, sporting designs that are as beautiful in their simplicity as they are utilitarian. Via Mario de' Fiori 65. ✆ **06-6791275.** www.cucinastore.com. Metro: Spagna.

Spazio Sette This is far and away Rome's best housewares emporium, a design boutique of department-store proportions. It goes way beyond the Alessi teakettles to fill three huge floors with the greatest names in Italian and international design. Via D. Barbieri 7, off Largo di Torre Argentina. ✆ **06-6869747.** Metro: Colosseo.

Stock Market Here you'll find great prices on last year's models, overstock, irregulars, and artistic misadventures in design that the pricier boutiques couldn't move. Most is moderately funky household stuff, but you never know when you'll find a gem. Via D. Banchi Vecchi 51–52. ✆ **06-6864238.** Bus: 40, 46, 62, or 64. Another location is at Via Alessandria 133. ✆ **06-6864238.** Metro: Castro Pretorio.

Jewelry

Since the days when the ancient Romans imported amethysts and pearls from the distant borders of their empire, and the great trading ships of Venice and Genoa carried rubies and sapphires from Asia, Italians have collected jewelry.

Bulgari ★★★ Bulgari is the capital's most prestigious jeweler and has been since the 1890s. The shop window, on a conspicuously affluent stretch of Via Condotti, is a visual attraction in its own right. Bulgari designs combine classical Greek aesthetics with Italian taste. Over the years, Bulgari has managed to follow changes in style while still maintaining its tradition. Prices range from affordable to insane. Via Condotti 10. ✆ **06-6793876.** www.bulgari.com. Metro: Spagna.

Diego Percossi Papi ★ Look here for the ornate jewelry Lucrezia Borgia might wear if she were alive and kicking. Most of the designs are inspired by Renaissance themes, many crafted from gemstones and accented with iridescent patches of enameling. Jade, opal, and semiprecious gemstones are heavily featured. Via Sant'Eustachio 16. ✆ **06-68801466.** www.percossipapi.com. Metro: Barberini or Colosseo. Bus: C3, 30, 70, or 116.

Federico Buccellati ★★★ At this, one of the best gold- and silversmiths in Italy, neo-Renaissance creations will change your thinking about gold and silver designs. You'll discover the Italian tradition and beauty of handmade jewelry and holloware whose principles sometimes hark back to the designs of Renaissance gold master Benvenuto Cellini. Via Condotti 31. ✆ **06-6790329.** www.federicobuccellati.it. Metro: Spagna.

Leather

Italian leather is among the very best in the world and, at its best, can attain butter-soft textures more pliable than cloth. You'll find hundreds of leather stores in Rome, many of them excellent.

Alfieri Virtually every leather garment imaginable is sold in this richly stocked store. Established in the 1960s, with a somewhat more funky and counterculture slant than Casagrande or Campanile, Alfieri sells a wide range of jackets, boots, bags, belts, shirts, hats, and pants for men and women; shorts reminiscent of German lederhosen; and skirts in at least 10 different colors. Everything sold is made in Italy, but this place prides itself on reasonable prices rather than ultra-high quality. Check the stitching and zippers carefully before you invest. Via del Corso 1-2. ✆ **06-3611976.** Bus: 117.

Bottega Veneta ★★ Overlooking one of Rome's most upscale squares, this is the largest Bottega store in Europe, an offshoot of a family business launched in Venice. Housed in a 17th-century palazzo, its elegant interior is the setting from some of the finest leather purses among other items sold in Rome. Piazza San Lorenzo in Lucina 8. ✆ **06-68210024.** www.bottegaveneta.com. Metro: Spagna.

Campanile Belying the postmodern sleekness of its premises, this outfit has a pedigree going back to the 1870s and an impressive inventory of well-crafted leather jackets, belts, shoes, bags, and suitcases for both men and women. Quality is relentlessly high (as are prices). Via Condotti 58. ✆ **06-6783041.** Metro: Spagna.

Casagrande If famous names in leather wear appeal to you, you'll find most of the biggies here—Fendi and its youth-conscious offspring, Fendissime, plus Cerruti, Mosquino, and Valentino. This well-managed store has developed an impressive reputation for quality and authenticity since the 1930s. Prices are more reasonable than in some other parts of town. Via Cola di Rienzo 206. ✆ **06-6874610.** Bus: 81 or 590.

Fendi ★★★ The House of Fendi is mainly known for its leather goods, but it also has furs, stylish purses, ready-to-wear clothing, and a new men's line of clothing and accessories. Gift items, home furnishings, and sports accessories are also sold here, all emblazoned with an F. It's closed Saturday afternoons from July to September. Via Borgognona 36–40. ✆ **06-334501.** Metro: Spagna.

Francesco Rogani ★ Francesco Rogani has become one of Rome's most famous leather stores, offering a wide selection of bags for every occasion. At Rogani, you'll find a good price-quality relation also for wallets, belts, and handmade ties. Via Condotti 47. ✆ **06-6784036.** Metro: Spagna.

Gucci ★★★ Gucci has been a legend since 1900, selling high-class leather suitcases, handbags, wallets, shoes, and accessories. It also has elegant men's and women's wear, including shirts, blouses, and dresses, as well as ties and scarves. *La bella figura* is alive and well at Gucci; prices have never been higher. Among the many temptations is Gucci's own perfume. Via Condotti 8. ✆ **06-6790405.** Metro: Spagna. There is another location at Via Borgognona 7D. ✆ 06-69190661. www.gucci.com. Metro: Spagna.

Markets

Piles of fresh vegetables arranged above ancient pavements in the streaming Italian sunshine—well, what visitor can resist? Here's a rundown on the Roman markets known for fresh produce, uninhibited merchants, and long-running traditions.

Campo de' Fiori During the Renaissance, this neighborhood contained most of the inns that pilgrims and merchants from other parts of Europe used for lodgings. Today its battered and slightly shabby perimeter surrounds about a hundred merchants who arrange their produce artfully every day. The market is open Monday to Saturday 7am to 1:30pm. Campo de' Fiori. Bus: 46, 62, 64, or 116.

Mercato Andrea Doria After a visit to this open-air festival, you'll never look at frozen vegetables in the supermarket the same way again. Near the Vatican between Via Tunisi and Via Santamaura, the merchandise includes meats, poultry, eggs, dairy products, wines, an endless assortment of fruit and vegetables, and even some scruffy-looking racks of secondhand clothing. The market is open only on Monday and Saturday 7am to 1pm. Via Andrea Doria. Metro: Ottaviano.

Mercato dei Fiori Most of the week this vast covered market sells flowers only to retail florists, who resell them to consumers. Every Tuesday, however, the industrial-looking premises are open to the public, who crowd in for access to exotic Mediterranean flowers at bargain-basement prices. Open to the public Tuesday from 10:30am to 1pm. Via Trionfale. © **06-39741403.** Metro: Ottaviano.

Mercato delle Stampe Virtually everything that's displayed in the dozens of battered kiosks here is dog-eared and evocatively ragtag. You'll find copies of engravings, books, magazines from the 1960s (or before); and prints and engravings that are either worthless or priceless, depending on your taste. If your passion is the printed word, this is your place, and bargaining is part of the experience. Monday to Saturday 7am to 7pm. Largo della Fontanella di Borghese. Bus: 70, 81, 87, or 117.

Mercato di Testaccio Because their stalls are covered from the wind, rain, and dust, the vendors here are able to retain an air of permanence about their setups that most outdoor markets simply can't provide. Inside you'll find fishmongers, butchers, cheese sellers, a wide array of dairy products, and the inevitable fruit and vegetables. Piazza Testaccio. Bus: 95, 170, or 781.

Mercato di Via Sannio If you like street fairs loaded with junky items but occasional nuggets of value or eccentric charm, this is the market for you. Regrettably, rare or unusual items are harder to find here because every antiques dealer in Italy seems to have combed through the inventories long ago. Despite that, you'll find some ragtag values. Via Sannio. Metro: S. Giovanni.

Porta Portese Flea Market On Sundays from 6:30am to 2pm, every peddler from Trastevere and the surrounding Castelli Romani sets up shop at the sprawling Porta Portese open-air flea market. Vendors are likely to sell merchandise ranging from secondhand paintings of Madonnas and termite-eaten Il Duce wooden medallions, to pseudo-Etruscan hairpins, rosaries, 1947 TVs, and books printed in 1835. Serious shoppers can often ferret out a good buy. If you've ever been impressed with the bargaining power of the Spaniard, you haven't seen anything until you've bartered with an Italian. As at any street market, beware of pickpockets. Near the end of Viale Trastevere. Bus: 780 to Porta Portese, and then a short walk to Via Portuense.

Mosaics

Savelli ★ This company specializes in the manufacture and sale of mosaics, an art form as old as the Roman Empire itself. Many objects in the company's gallery were inspired by ancient originals discovered in thousands of excavations throughout the Italian peninsula, including those at Pompeii and Ostia. Others, especially the floral designs, rely on the whim and creativity of the artists. Objects include tabletops, boxes, and vases. The cheapest mosaic objects begin at around 80€ and are unsigned products crafted by art students at a school that is partially funded by the Vatican. Objects made in the Savelli workshops that are signed by the individual artists tend to be larger and more elaborate. The outlet also sells small souvenirs, such as key chains and carved statues. Via Paolo VI 27–29. ✆ **06-68307017.** www.savellireligious.com. Metro: San Paola.

Shoes

Dalco' Nives If you've ever suspected that a shoe fetish might be lurking deep inside you, a visit to this store will probably unleash it. Everything is handmade and usually can be matched to a handbag that provides a reasonably close approximation. Most of the shoes are low-key and conservative, but a few are wild, whimsical, and outrageous enough to appeal to RuPaul. But sorry, only women's shoes are stocked. Via Vittoria 65. ✆ **06-6786536.** www.dalco-roma.com. Metro: Spagna.

Fausto Santini ★★ This is the outlet for Rome's most celebrated designer of shoes for both men and women. Each pair of shoes is almost a work of art, and signs invite you to "please touch," since the feel of the shoes is a reward unto itself. Fausto Santini honors its commitment "to organic shapes and fundamental simplicity." Via Frattina 120. ✆ **06-6784114.** www.faustosantini.it. Metro: Spagna. Bus: 52, 53, 61, or 71.

Ferragamo ★★★ Ferragamo sells elegant and fabled footwear, plus women's clothing and accessories. The name became famous in America when such silent-screen vamps as Pola Negri and Greta Garbo began appearing in Ferragamo shoes. There are always many customers waiting to enter the shop; management allows them to enter in small groups. (Wear comfortable shoes for what could well be a 30-min. wait.) Via Condotti 66–73. ✆ **06-6781130.** www.ferragamo.com. Metro: Spagna.

Lily of Florence This famous Florentine shoemaker now has a shop in Rome, with the same merchandise that made the outlet so well known in the Tuscan capital. Colors come in a wide range, the designs are stylish, and leather texture is of good quality. Shoes for both men and women are sold, and American sizes are a feature. Via Lombardia 38A (off Via Vittorio Veneto). ✆ **06-4740262.** www.lilyofflorence.com. Bus: C3, 95, 116, or 150.

Pavoncello Angelo Pelletterie Near the Vatican, this store offers footwear in chic styles but at affordable prices. It also sells an assortment of handbags and other Italian leather goods and accessories. It's worth a detour out of your way to see the ever-changing repertoire. Piazza del Risorgimento 38. ✆ **06-39737247.** Metro: Ottaviano–San Pietro.

Silver

Anatriello Argenteria Antica e Moderna Roma ★ This store is known for stocking new and antique silver, some of it the most unusual in Italy. New items are made by Italian silversmiths, in designs ranging from the whimsical to the formal and dignified. Also on display are antique pieces from England, Germany, and Switzerland. Via Frattina 27. ✆ **06-6789601.** Metro: Spagna.

Fornari & Fornari This two-story showroom is filled with silver, lamps, porcelain, crystal, furniture, and upscale gift items from many manufacturers throughout Italy and Europe. Virtually anything can be shipped around the world. Closed in August. Via Frattina 133. ✆ **06-6780105.** www.fornariandfornari.com. Metro: Spagna.

Toys

Al Sogno The name of this store, launched in 1945, means "Into the Dream," and for children it opens onto a fabulous world of dolls, trolls, huge bears, and tiny tin soldiers, among dozens of other items. All of these creatures eye you, awaiting purchase the way animals do in a pet store. The Manfredini family, including a daughter, Annamaria, continues to carry on in the tradition of the founding mother, Dolores. Piazza Navona 53. ✆ **06-6864198.** www.alsogno.com. Bus: 30, 70, 81, 87, or 130.

La Città del Sole Other than the branch in Milan, this is the best stocked of any of the stores in its 40-member chain. It specializes in amusements for children and adults, with a wide range of toys and games that don't make beeping noises. Many games are configured in English; others in Italian. You'll find role-playing games, family games, and games that will challenge a young person and probably drive his parents crazy. Also for sale are such rainy-day distractions as miniature billiards tables and tabletop golf sets. Via della Scrofa 65. ✆ **06-68803805.** www.cittadelsole.com. Metro: Spagna. Bus: 70, 87, or 116.

Wines & Liquors

Ai Monasteri Italy produces a staggering volume of wines, liqueurs, and after-dinner drinks, and here you'll find a treasure-trove of selections: liquors, honey, and herbal teas made in monasteries and convents all over Italy. You can buy excellent chocolates and other candies here as well. The shop will ship some items home for you. In a quiet atmosphere reminiscent of a monastery, you can choose your spirits as they move you. Corso del Rinascimento 72. ✆ **06-68802783.** www.aimonasteri.it. Bus: C3, 70, 81, or 87.

Buccone This is a historic wine shop, right near Piazza del Popolo. Its selection of wines and gastronomic specialties is among the finest in Rome. Via Ripetta 19. ✆ **06-3612154.** www.enotecabuccone.com. Bus: 70, 87, or 116.

Trimani Established in 1821, Trimani sells wines and spirits from Italy, with a selection of thousands of bottles. It collaborates with the Italian wine magazine *Gambero Rosso,* organizing wine lectures in which enthusiasts can improve their knowledge and educate their taste buds. Via Goito 20. ✆ **06-4469661.** www.trimani.com. Metro: Castel Pretorio. Bus: 86, 92, 140, 217, or 360.

ROME AFTER DARK

When the sun goes down, lights across the city bathe palaces, ruins, fountains, and monuments in a theatrical glow. There are few evening pursuits as pleasurable as a stroll past the solemn pillars of old temples or the cascading torrents of Renaissance fountains glimmering under the blue-black sky.

10

Of these fountains, the **Naiads (Piazza della Repubblica),** the **Tortoises (Piazza Mattei),** and, of course, the **Trevi** are particularly beautiful at night. The **Capitoline Hill,** with its measured Renaissance facades, is magnificently lit after dark. The view of the **Roman Forum** from the rear of the trapezoidal Piazza del Campidoglio is the grandest in Rome, more so than even the Colosseum. If you're across the Tiber, **Piazza San Pietro** (in front of St. Peter's Basilica) is particularly impressive at night. Illuminated architecture, Renaissance fountains, sidewalk shows, and art expos all enliven **Piazza Navona.**

Even if you don't speak Italian, you can generally follow the listings of special events and entertainment in ***La Repubblica,*** one of the leading Italian newspapers. The minimag ***Wanted in Rome*** (www.wantedinrome.com) has listings of jazz, rock, and such. The daily ***Il Messaggero*** lists current cultural news. ***Un Ospite a Roma*** (www.unospitearoma.it), available free from the concierge desks of top hotels, is full of details on what's happening.

THE PERFORMING ARTS

Rome's premier cultural venue is the **Teatro dell'Opera** (see below), which may not be Milan's legendary La Scala, but offers stellar performances nevertheless. The outstanding local troupe is the **Rome Opera Ballet** (see below).

Rome doesn't have a major center for classical music concerts, although performances of the most important orchestra, the **RAI Symphony Orchestra,** most often take place at the RAI Auditorium or the Academy of St. Cecilia.

Rome is a major stopover for international stars. Rock headliners often perform at **Stadio Flaminio, Foro Italico,** and in the EUR, at **Palazzo della Civilità del Lavoro** or **Palazzo dello Sport.** Most concerts are at the Palazzo dello Sport.

Classical Music

Parco della Musica ★ This is the largest concert facility in Europe, an ultramodern building constructed in 2002 by Renzo Piano, a world-famous architect. It has 40,000 sq. m (430,556 sq. ft.) of gardens and three separate concert halls, plus one massive open-air theater. In the summer, concerts are often outside, and you can listen to the strains of Brahms or Schumann under a star-studded sky. Viale de Coubertin 30. ✆ **06-802411.** www.auditorium.com. Tickets and prices depend on the event. Bus: 53, 217, 231, or 910.

Teatro Olimpico Large and well publicized, this echoing stage hosts a widely divergent collection of singers, both classical and pop. Occasionally, the space is devoted to chamber orchestras or visits by foreign orchestras. Piazza Gentile Da Fabriano 17. ✆ **06-3265991.** www.teatroolimpico.it. Tickets 19€–50€, depending on the event. Metro: Flaminio.

Opera

Teatro dell'Opera If you're in the capital for the opera season—usually October to June—you might want to attend a performance at the historic Rome Opera House, located off Via Nazionale. From July 9 to August 5, performances are held at the Teatro delle Terme di Caracalla (Metro: Circo Massimo). You can buy tickets at the box office (closed Mon), at any Banca di Roma bank, or by phone at ✆ **800-907080.** Piazza Beniamino Gigli 1 off Via Nazionale. ✆ **06-48160252.** www.operaroma.it. Tickets 11€–130€. Metro: Termini.

THE CLUB & MUSIC SCENE

Nightclubs/Dance Clubs

Alpheus ★ One of Rome's largest and most energetic nightclubs, Alpheus contains three sprawling rooms, each with a different musical sound and an ample number of bars. You'll find areas devoted to Latin music, to rock, and to jazz. Live bands come and go, and there's enough variety in the crowd to keep virtually anyone amused throughout the evening. Locals and visitors frequent this club, and the clients span a wide age range. It's open Tuesday through Sunday from 10pm to 4am. Via del Commercio 36. ✆ **06-5747826.** www.alpheus.it. Cover 7€–15€. Bus: 713.

Caruso Café de Oriente As the hippest district in Rome today, Testaccio attracts late-night revelers, many of whom turn up at Caruso. If you'd like to join Rome's beautiful people, head here, the later the better. Latin music, especially

Nocturnal Outdoor Entertainment

In summer, the streets of Rome become a kind of outdoor festival. Many Romans live in hot apartments without air-conditioning, and they spill into the cooler streets at night to enjoy evening concerts and other events.

The best of these occur along Via di Monte Testaccio in the Testaccio sector, which becomes a venue for jam sessions, jazz concerts, and other entertainment. Bars and restaurants overflow onto the streets, and there are food stalls, markets, and shops operating until late at night. From June until August, the street is blocked off from 8:30pm to 2am, and entry is free.

salsa, is played for the wildly gyrating dancers, stepping to the sounds of the Caribbean or Brazil. The average age of the patrons ranges from 25 to 40. Open Tuesday to Sunday 10pm to 4am. Via Monte Testaccio 36. ✆ **06-5745019.** www.carusocafe.com. Cover (including 1 drink) 8€–15€. Metro: Piramide.

Jonathan's Angels This extraordinary space is decorated with colorful kitsch, pop art, and plastic furniture evoking Andy Warhol's famous old "Factory" in New York. Hip Romans come here for live piano music played by eccentric local musicians. This is one of the best nightspots if you're in and around the Piazza Navona. Check out the outlandish "loos" here, entered through a veritable pleasure garden. Take Via Pasquino from Piazza Navona and turn right onto Via Parione, and then left on Via della Fossa. Open Monday to Friday 8pm to 2:30am, Saturday and Sunday 8pm to 3:30am. Via della Fossa 14–16. ✆ **06-6893426.** Beer 5€; cocktails 9€. No cover.

Jazz & Other Live Sounds

The places we've recommended appeal to a wide age group, especially the jazz joints.

Alexanderplatz At this leading jazz club, you can listen to the music or enjoy the cooking, everything from *pesto alla genovese* to Japanese cuisine. It's open Monday through Saturday from 9pm to 2am, with live music from 10:30pm. Via Ostia 9. ✆ **06-39742171.** www.alexanderplatz.it. Club membership (valid for 1 month) 10€. Bus: 23, 490, 492, or 495.

Arciliuto This place reputedly once housed Raphael's studio, and is now home to one of the most romantic candlelit spots in Rome. Musical offerings include Neapolitan love songs, Italian madrigals, and hits from Broadway. Highly recommended, it's within walking distance of Piazza Navona. It's open Monday through Saturday from 10pm to 1:30am and is closed July 20 to September 3. Piazza Monte Vecchio 5. ✆ **06-6879419.** www.arciliuto.it. Cover (including 1 drink) 20€. Bus: 42, 62, or 64. From the west side of Piazza Navona, take Via di S. Agnese in Agone, which leads to Via di Tor Milliana; then follow this street to Piazza Monte Vecchio.

Big Mama Big Mama is a hangout for jazz and blues musicians, where you're likely to meet the up-and-coming jazz stars of tomorrow and sometimes even the big names. It's open Monday to Saturday 9pm to 1:30am, and is closed July through September. Vicolo San Francesco a Ripa 18. ✆ **06-5812551.** www.bigmama.it. Cover 15€–30€ for big acts (free for minor shows), plus 13€ seasonal membership fee. Bus: 75, 170, or 780.

Fonclea Fonclea offers live music every night—jazz, Dixieland, rock, rhythm and blues, and funk. This is basically a cellar jazz bar that attracts folks from all walks of Roman life. There's also a restaurant that features moderately priced grilled meats, salads, and crepes. Music usually starts at 9:15pm and lasts until about 12:30am. It's open daily from 7pm to 2am. The club is closed in July and August. Via Crescenzio 82A. ✆ **06-6896302.** www.fonclea.it. Cover Fri–Sat 6€. Bus: 23, 34, 49, or 492.

Gay & Lesbian Clubs

Edoardo This is the most popular gay restaurant and bar in Rome. With its top-rate food and drink, you can come here and make an evening of it. This restaurant and bar attracts a young professional class of Romans. A trendy choice for a night out, the bar is named for the gay monarch himself. It's open Wednesday to Monday 7pm to midnight. Vicolo Margana 14. ✆ **06-69942419.** www.edoardosecondo.com. Bus: C3, 30, 40, 46, 84, 87, 119, 130, 170, or 175.

The Hangar Having survived since 1984, the Hangar is a landmark on the gay nightlife scene. It's on one of Rome's oldest streets, adjacent to the Forum. Women are welcome any night except Monday, when the club features videos and entertainment for men. The busiest nights are Saturday, Sunday, and Monday, when as many as 500 people cram inside. It's open Wednesday to Monday 10:30pm to 2:30am. The Hangar is closed 3 weeks in August. Via in Selci 69. ✆ **06-4881397.** www.hangaronline.it. Annual club membership 10€. Metro: Cavour.

Muccassassina This is one of the most popular gay bars in Rome, spread across three floors. Each floor is different, the most popular being the ground level with its popular music. Upstairs the mood and the music is darker, including the back room. The third floor is devoted to house music. Some of the most attractive young Romans show up here to cruise. The bar is open every Friday from 11:30pm to 5:30 am. At the Qube Club. Via di Portonaccio 212. ✆ **06-5413985.** www.muccassassina.com. Cover 16€. Metro: Tiburtina.

THE CAFE & BAR SCENE

It seems there's nothing Romans like better than sitting and talking over a beverage—usually wine or coffee. Unless you're dead set on making the Roman nightclub circuit, try what can be a far livelier and less expensive scene—sitting late at night on **Via Veneto, Piazza della Rotonda, Piazza del Popolo,** or one of Rome's other piazzas, all for the cost of an espresso, a cappuccino, or a Campari.

If you're looking for some scrumptious **ice cream,** refer to the listings below for Caffé Rosati and Giolitti, as well as the box titled "Take a Gelato Break," on p. 120.

Cafes & Bars

ON VIA VENETO

Back in the 1950s (a decade *Time* magazine gave to Rome, in the way it conceded the 1960s and later the 1990s to London), **Via Vittorio Veneto** rose in fame as the hippest street in Rome, crowded with aspiring and actual movie stars, their directors, and a fast-rising group of card-carrying members of the jet set. Today the beautiful people wouldn't be caught dead on touristy Via Veneto—but regardless, visitors flock here by the thousands. As one Roman cafe owner told us, "You can see Romans all over the city. But on Via Veneto, sit at one of our tables and catch people from all over the world go by. It's worth the price we charge for an espresso."

Cafè de Paris This spot has been around for decades. It's popular in summer, when the tables spill right out onto the sidewalk and the passing crowd walks through the maze. This is the most famous cafe in all of Rome for people-watching along Via Veneto, although locals shun it. It's open daily from 8am to 2am (Tues till midnight). Via Vittorio Veneto 91. ✆ **06-4815631.** www.cafedeparisroma.eu. Metro: Barberini.

Harry's Bar Sophisticated Harry's Bar is a perennial favorite of post-40 foreign visitors. If you want to dine outdoors but avoid the scorching sun, there's an air-conditioned sidewalk cafe open from May to November. Meals inside cost about double what you'd pay outside. In back is a small dining room serving some of the finest (and priciest) food in central Rome. The restaurant inside is open Monday to Saturday 12:30 to 3pm and 7:30pm to 1am. Outside you can eat from noon to midnight. The bar is open daily from 11am to 2am (closed 1 week in mid-Aug), and the piano bar is open nightly from 9:30pm, with music starting at 11pm. Via Vittorio Veneto 150. ✆ **06-484643.** www.harrysbar.it. Metro: Barberini.

NEAR THE TERMINI

Bar Marani This century-old coffee bar by the marketplace attracts all kinds—students, visitors, Japanese tourists, shopkeepers, artists, pickpockets, and rock stars. Espresso is one of the lures, as is the delicious ice cream. Grab a table on the vine-covered terrace. Via dei Volsci 57. ✆ **06-490016.** Metro: Termini.

Fiddler's Elbow Fiddler's Elbow, near Piazza di Santa Maria Maggiore and the railway station, is reputedly the oldest pub in the capital. Sometimes, however, the place is so packed you can't find room to drink. It's open Monday to Friday from 5pm to 2am, Saturday and Sunday from 3pm to 2am. Via dell'Olmata 43. ✆ **06-4872110.** www.thefiddlerselbow.com. Metro: Termini.

NEAR CAMPO DE' FIORI

Roof Top Lounge Bar This is a summertime rendezvous, attracting a fashionable young crowd, with its panoramic sweep over the rooftops and domes of Rome at night. Waiters at the wine bar serve at least 120 vintages by the glass, along with snacks. The location is a block from the Tiber, off Campo de'Fiori. Open June to September daily 6:30am to 10:30pm. In the St. George Hotel, via Giulia 62. ✆ **06-686611.** www.stgeorgehotel.it. Bus: 46, 62, or 65.

NEAR PIAZZA NAVONA

Caffè della Pace Caffè della Pace has elegant neighbors, such as Santa Maria della Pace, a church with sibyls by Raphael and a cloister designed by Bramante. The bar dates from the beginning of the 20th century and is decorated with wood, marble, and mirrors. It's open Monday 3pm to 3am, and Tuesday to Sunday 9am to 3am. Via della Pace 3–5. ✆ **06-6861216.** Bus: 64.

Fluid Only a short walk from the Piazza Navona, this super modern bar has a liquid theme. Some of the seating is on plastic cubes evoking ice. Walls and ceilings are sculpted to give the impression of a waterworld grotto. Mostly it attracts patrons in the age range of 25 to 40 who enjoy a small buffet and a respectable wine carte. Open daily 6pm to 2am. Via del Governo Becchio Vecchio 46–47. ✆ **06-6832361.** Bus: 64.

NEAR THE PANTHEON

Caffè Sant'Eustachio Strong coffee is liquid fuel to Italians, and many Romans will walk blocks for what they consider to be a superior brew. Caffè Sant'Eustachio is one of Rome's most celebrated espresso shops, where the water supply is funneled into the city by an aqueduct built in 19 B.C. Rome's most experienced espresso judges claim the water plays an important part in the coffee's flavor. Buy a ticket from the cashier for as many cups as you want, and then leave a small tip (about 1€) for the counter-person when you present your receipt. It's open Sunday to Thursday 8:30am to 1am, Friday 8:30am to 1:30am, and Saturday 8:30am to 2am. Piazza Sant'Eustachio 82. ✆ **06-68802048.** www.santeustachioilcaffe.it. Bus: C3, 81, 87, or 116.

Di Rienzo This is the top cafe at the Pantheon. In fair weather, try to snag one of the sidewalk tables. In cooler weather, you can retreat inside, where the walls are inlaid with the type of marble found on the Pantheon's floor. It's open daily from 7am to 1 or 2am. Piazza della Rotonda 8–9. ✆ **06-6869097.** www.ristorantedirienzo.com. Bus: 116.

Le Bain In the heart of Rome, a few steps from the Pantheon and near Campidoglio, this is a minimalist and chic restaurant and cocktail bar, with a wide variety of wines. It's something of a launchpad for new artists in Rome, who often exhibit their latest works here. There's never a cover for patrons seen reclining on banquettes or in armchairs, listening to the recorded music. Open Monday to Saturday 12:30 to 3:30pm and 7pm to 2am. Via delle Botteghe Oscure 32A. © **06-6865673.** Bus: 30, 40, 46, or 62.

Riccioli Café Formally known as Hemingway's Pub, this sleek nightspot is a chic oyster and champagne bar. In elegant yet informal surroundings, you can order drinks as well as oysters on the half shell. It's a scene, but the food in the upscale loftlike wine cellar is quite good. It's open daily 9am to 3:30pm and 6:30pm to 2am. Piazza delle Coppelle 10A. © **06-68210313.** www.ricciolicafe.com. Bus: 64.

Tazza d'Oro This cafe is known for serving its own brand of espresso. Another specialty, ideal on a hot summer night, is *granità di caffè* (coffee that has been frozen, crushed into a velvety slushlike ice, and placed in a glass between layers of whipped cream). It's open daily from 7:30am to 1am. Piazza della Rotonda, Via degli Orfani 84. © **06-6789792.** www.tazzadorocoffeeshop.com. Bus: 116 or 117.

ON THE CORSO & PIAZZA COLONNA

Giolitti Near Piazza Colonna, this is one of the city's most popular nighttime gathering spots and the oldest ice-cream shop. Some of the sundaes look like Vesuvius about to erupt. Many people take gelato out to eat on the streets; others enjoy it in the post-empire splendor of the salon inside. You can have your "coppa" daily 7am to 2am (closed at 1am in winter). Via Uffici del Vicario 40. © **06-6991243.** www.giolitti.it. Bus: 116.

ON OR NEAR PIAZZA DEL POPOLO

According to legend, the ashes of Nero were enshrined here until 11th-century residents began complaining to the pope about his imperial ghost. The Egyptian obelisk seen here today dates from the 13th century B.C.; it was removed from Heliopolis to Rome during the reign of Augustus (it originally stood at the Circus Maximus). The present piazza was designed in the early 19th century by Valadier, Napoleon's architect. Two almost-twin baroque churches stand on the square, overseeing the never-ending traffic.

Caffé Rosati Caffé Rosati, which has been around since 1923, attracts guys and dolls of all persuasions, both foreign and domestic, who drive up in Maseratis and Porsches. It's really a combination of sidewalk cafe, ice-cream parlor, candy store, confectionery, and ristorante that has been swept up in the fickle world of fashion. The later you go, the more interesting the action. It's open daily from 7:30am to 11:30pm. Piazza del Popolo 5A. © **06-3225859.** www.rosatibar.it. Bus: 117 or 119.

Canova Café Although the management has filled it with boutiques selling expensive gift items, such as luggage and cigarette lighters, many Romans still consider Canova Café *the* place to be on the piazza. The Canova has a sidewalk terrace for people-watching, plus a snack bar, a restaurant, and a wine shop. In summer, you'll have access to a courtyard whose walls are covered with ivy and where flowers grow in terra-cotta planters. The restaurant is open daily from noon to 3:30pm and 7 to 11pm; the bar is open daily from 8am till midnight or 1am. Piazza del Popolo 16. © **06-3612231.** www.canovapiazzadelpopolo.it. Bus: 117 or 119.

NEAR THE SPANISH STEPS

Antico Caffè Greco ★★ Since 1760, this has been Rome's poshest coffee bar. Stendhal, Goethe, Keats, and D'Annunzio have sipped coffee here. Today you're more likely to see ladies who lunch and Japanese tourists, but there's plenty of atmosphere. In front is a wooden bar, and beyond is a series of small salons. You sit at marble-topped tables of Napoleonic design, against a backdrop of gold or red damask, romantic paintings, and antique mirrors. It was Giorgio de Chirico who suggested that this is the cafe where you sit and await the end. The house specialty is *paradisi,* made with lemon and orange. The coffee bar is open daily from 9am to 7pm; it is closed 10 days in August (dates vary). Via Condotti 84. ✆ **06-6791700.** www.anticocaffegreco.eu. Metro: Spagna.

IN TRASTEVERE

Several cafes in Trastevere, across the Tiber, are attracting crowds. Fans who saw Fellini's *Roma* know what **Piazza di Santa Maria in Trastevere** looks like at night. The square, filled with milling throngs in summer, is graced with an octagonal fountain and a 12th-century church. Children play in the piazza, and occasional spontaneous guitar fests break out when the weather's good.

Café-Bar di Marzio This warmly inviting place, which is strictly a cafe (not a restaurant), has narrow wood-paneled furnishings and outdoor tables at the edge of the square, with the best view of its famous fountain. Everybody from blue-collar workers to artists and writers goes here to see and be seen. The cafe is open daily from 7am to 2am and is closed on Tuesdays, from October to March. Piazza di Santa Maria in Trastevere 15. ✆ **06-5816095.** Bus: 115 or 125.

Friends Art Café Named for the long-running American TV sitcom, this is one of our favorite hangouts in the historic district of Trastevere across the Tiber. It's an ideal place to hit on your pre-dinner rounds. Big glass windows overlook Piazza Trilussa, and the decor is modern with metal furnishings. The staff serves a cold vegetarian buffet and various cocktails. Piazza Trilussa 34, Trastevere. ✆ **06-5816111.** www.cafefriends.it. Bus: 23 or 125.

NEAR TESTACCIO

Il Barone Rosso This is the biggest and best German beer garden in Rome, and on a summer night the "Red Baron" can be a lot of fun. Opened in 1996, this 380-seat club has a summer garden that always overflows in fair weather. The staff serves lots of beer and other drinks, along with Italian pizzas and German snacks, salads, and sandwiches. Beer costs 4.50€ a mug, and hours are daily 7pm to 3am. Via Libetta 13. ✆ **06-57288961.** www.baronerosso.com. Metro: Garbatella.

Wine Bars

Casa Bleve ★★ Rome's most luxurious wine bar occupies the former courtyard of the 16th-century Palazzo Medici. Long roofed over with an Art Deco style glass canopy, it's the latest offering of the Bleve family, who are local fixtures on the wine-and-dine scene in Rome. Their selection of wines by the glass is one of the best in Rome, costing from 4.50€ to 10€. Their lunchtime buffet is seriously gourmet, ranging from fresh Pugliese Burrata (near liquid mozzarella) to Calabrian peppers to cookies and desserts from Sicily. Ask to visit their wine cellar. Open Tuesday to Saturday 10am to 3pm, and also on Wednesday and Thursday 6 to 10pm. Via del Teatro Valle 48-49. ✆ **06-6865970.** www.casableve.it. Bus: 40, 46, 62, 64, or 116.

Enoteca Antica A drink in this dark, atmospheric spot is the perfect ending to a visit to the nearby Spanish Steps. Set behind a discreet facade in a chic shopping district, this is the city's best repository for Italian wines, brandies, and grappa. You can opt for a postage-stamp-size table in the back or stand at the bar with its impressive display of wines stacked in every available corner. It's open daily 11am to 1am. Via della Croce 76B. ✆ **06-6797544.** www.anticaenoteca.com. Metro: Spagna.

Il Goccetto Set near Campo de' Fiori, Il Goccetto specializes in French and Italian wines by the glass at prices that range from 4€ for a simple chianti to as much as 17€ for a glass of French champagne. Cold platters of food, including an extensive list of Italian cheeses and processed meats, especially salami and pâtés, as well as an occasional salad, are available. Overall, this place provides an excellent site for the *degustazione* of a wide assortment of unusual Italian wines, many of them from less well-known small producers. It's open Monday to Saturday 5pm to midnight. Via dei Banchi Vecchi 14. ✆ **06-6864268.** Bus: 46, 62, 64, or 116.

Tazio Wine Bar This trendy bar at night attracts a lively crowd to its location near the rail terminal, fronting the Baths of Diocletian and Michelangelo's Basilica degli Angeli. It serves reasonably priced Italian wines along with champagnes and tasty meat or fish platters. In summer the Tazio Bar moves to the terrace overlooking the square. Open daily 10am to 1am. In the Tazio Hotel Exedra, Piazza della Repubblica 47. ✆ **06-489381.** www.boscolohotels.com. Metro: Repubblica.

11 SIDE TRIPS FROM ROME

Most European capitals are surrounded by a number of worthwhile attractions, but Rome tops them all for sheer variety. Just a few miles from Rome, you can go back to the dawn of Italian history and explore the dank tombs the Etruscans left as their legacy, or drink the golden wine of the towns in the Alban Hills (Castelli Romani). You can wander the ruins of Hadrian's Villa, the "queen of villas of the ancient world," or be lulled by the baroque fountains in the Villa d'Este. You can loll on the beaches of Ostia di Lido or explore the ruins of Ostia Antica, Rome's ancient seaport.

If you have time, the attractions in the environs can fill at least 3 days. We've highlighted the best of the lot here.

TIVOLI & THE VILLAS ★★

32km (20 miles) east of Rome

Tivoli, known as Tibur to the ancient Romans, is 32km (20 miles) east of Rome on Via Tiburtina, about an hour's drive with traffic. If you don't have a car, take Metro Line B to the end of the line, the Rebibbia station. After exiting the station, board a CoTral bus (✆ **800-174471;** www.cotralspa.it) for the trip the rest of the way to Tivoli. Generally, buses depart about every 20 minutes during the day. For information about the town, check with **Azienda Autonoma di Turismo,** Piazzale Nazioni Unite (no phone), Tivoli. Hours are Tuesday to Sunday 10am to 1pm and 4 to 6pm.

Exploring the Villas

Hadrian's Villa (Villa Adriana) ★★★ In the 2nd century A.D., the globe-trotting Hadrian spent the last 3 years of his life in grand style. Less than 7km (4 miles) from Tivoli, he built one of the greatest estates ever erected, and he filled acre after acre with some of the architectural wonders he'd seen on his many travels. Perhaps as a preview of what he envisioned for himself, the emperor even created a representation of hell. Hadrian was a patron of the arts, a lover of beauty, and even something

Side Trips from Rome

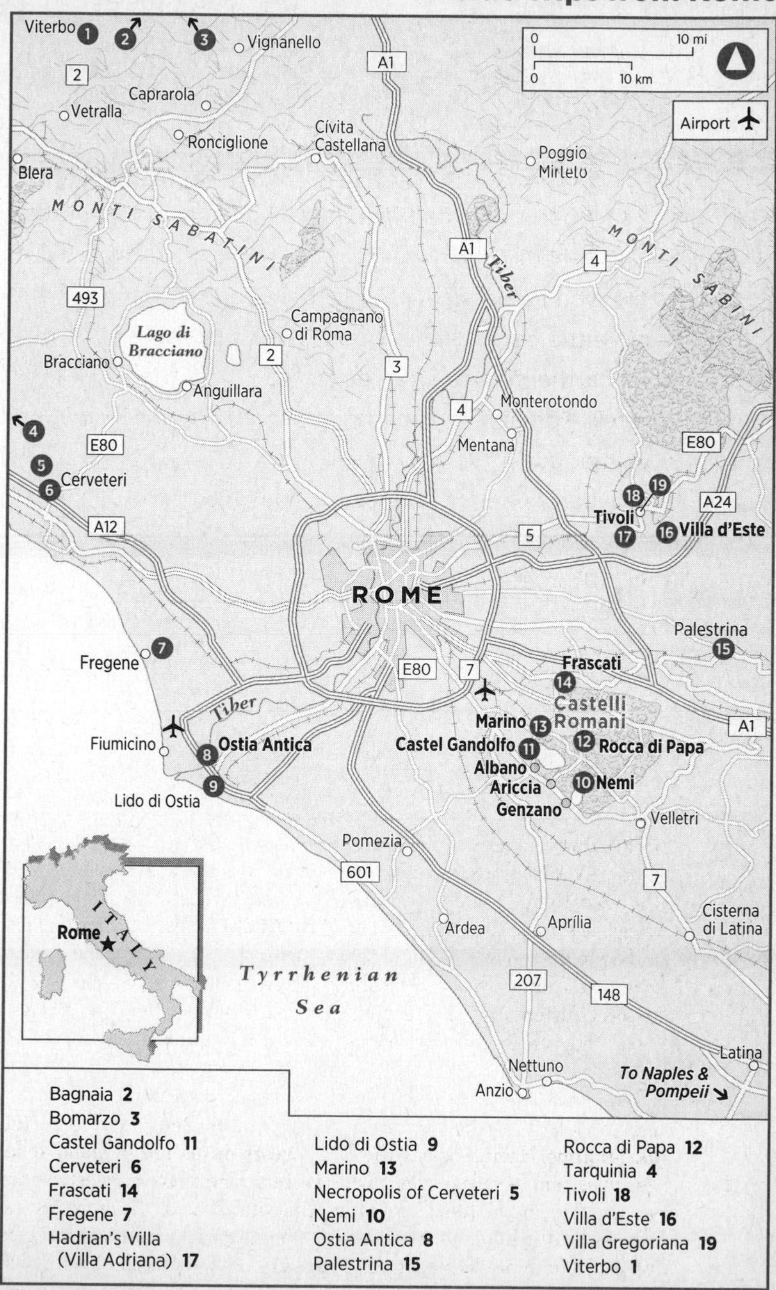

of an architect. His staggering feat of building was more than a villa: It was a self-contained world for a vast royal entourage and the hundreds of servants and guards they required to protect them, feed them, bathe them, and satisfy their libidos.

Hadrian erected theaters, baths, temples, fountains, gardens, and canals bordered with statuary throughout his estate. He filled the palaces and temples with sculpture, some of which now rest in the museums of Rome. In later centuries, barbarians and popes, as well as anyone who needed a slab of marble, carted off much that made the villa so spectacular. But enough of the fragmented ruins remain for us to piece together the story. For a look at what the villa used to be, see the plastic model at the entrance.

One of the two most outstanding and evocative ruins is the **Canopo ★★★**, or Canopus, a re-creation of the town of Canope with its famous Temple of the Serapis. The ruins of a rectangular area, **Piazza d'Oro,** are still surrounded by a double portico. Likewise, the **Sala dei pilastri dorici,** or Doric Pillared Hall, is still a delight. The ruins of the **Baths** remain, revealing rectangular rooms with concave walls. Only the north wall remains of the **Pecile,** or Poikile, which Hadrian discovered in Athens and had reproduced here. The other great ruin, **Teatro Marittimo ★★★**, is a circular maritime theater in ruins with its central building enveloped by a canal spanned by small swing bridges. For a closer look at some of the items excavated, you can visit the museum on the premises and a museum and visitor center near the villa parking area.

Via di Villa Adriana. ✆ **06-39967900.** www.villaadriana.com. Admission 6.50€. Daily 9am-sunset (about 7:30pm in summer, 5:30pm Nov–Mar). Closed Jan 1 and Dec 25. Bus: 4 from Tivoli.

Villa d'Este ★★ Like Hadrian centuries before, Cardinal Ippolito d'Este of Ferrara believed in heaven on earth, and in the mid–16th century he ordered this villa built on a hillside. The dank Renaissance structure is not that noteworthy; the big draw for visitors are the **spectacular gardens** below (designed by Pirro Ligorio).

You descend the cypress-studded slope to the bottom and are rewarded with everything from lilies to gargoyles spouting water, torrential streams, and waterfalls. The loveliest fountain is the **Ovato Fountain (Fontana dell Ovato).** But nearby is the more spectacular achievement: the **Fountain of the Hydraulic Organ (Fontana dell'Organo Idraulico),** dazzling with its water jets in front of a baroque chapel, with four maidens who look tipsy. The moss-covered **Fountain of the Dragons (Fontana dei Draghi),** also by Ligorio, and the so-called **Fountain of Glass (Fontana di Vetro),** by Bernini, are the most intriguing. The best walk is along the promenade, with 100 spraying fountains. The garden provides hours of exploration, but it's a lot of walking, with some steep climbs.

Piazza Trento, Viale delle Centro Fontane. ✆ **0774-312070.** www.villadestetivoli.info. Admission 6.50€. Tues–Sun 8:30am to 1 hr. before sunset. Closed Jan 1, May 1, and Dec 25. Bus: Roma-Tivoli.

Villa Gregoriana ★ The Villa d'Este dazzles with artificial glamour, but the Villa Gregoriana relies more on nature. The gardens were built by Pope Gregory XVI in the 19th century. At one point on the circuitous walk carved along a slope, you can stand and look out onto the most panoramic waterfall (Aniene) at Tivoli. The trek to the bottom on the banks of the Anio is studded with grottoes and balconies that open onto the chasm. The only problem is that if you do make the full descent, you might need a helicopter to pull you up again (the climb back up is fierce). From one of the belvederes, there's a panoramic view of the Temple of Vesta on the hill.

Largo Sant'Angelo. ✆ **0774-311249.** Admission 5€. www.villagregoriana.it. Apr 1–Oct 15 daily 10am–6:30pm; Mar and Oct 16–Nov 30 daily 10am–2:30pm. The bus from Rome stops near the entrance.

Where to Dine

Albergo Ristorante Adriano ITALIAN In a stucco-sided villa a few steps from the ticket office sits an idyllic stop for either before or after your visit to Hadrian's Villa. The cooking is home-style, and the menu includes roast lamb, saltimbocca (veal cooked with ham), grilled tuna with beans, deviled chicken, salads and cheeses, and simple desserts. Two tantalizing specialties include risotto with pumpkin flowers or ravioli filled with ricotta cheese and spinach and served with a fresh tomato and basil sauce. They're especially proud of their homemade pastas.

Via di Villa Adriana 222. ✆ **0774-535028.** www.hoteladriano.it. Reservations recommended. Main courses 10€–30€. AE, DC, MC, V. Mon–Sat 12:30–4pm and 8–10pm; Sun 12:30–2:30pm and 8–10:30pm.

Antica Trattoria del Falcone ROMAN One of the town's better choices lies in the historic core on the main artery leading off Largo Garibaldi. Because of its location, it attracts a lot of visitors, but that doesn't mean that it's a tourist trap. Far from it. The food is regionally inspired by a kitchen that specializes in market-fresh ingredients. Specialties include perfectly grilled fish from the sea as well as saltimbocca. Mixed roast meats, done over the coals, are our favorites. Another dish we like is homemade *crespella,* like a rolled pancake. It's stuffed with ricotta, nuts, and fresh spinach.

Via del Trevio 34. ✆ **0774-312358.** Reservations recommended. Main courses 6€–10€. AE, DC, MC, V. Daily 11:30am–4pm and 6:30–11:30pm.

PALESTRINA

39km (24 miles) east of Rome

Like Tibur, ancient Preneste (as Palestrina was called) was a superb holiday spot. It was a favorite of Horace, Pliny, and even Hadrian, who maintained a villa here.

Getting There

CoTral buses leave every 30 to 45 minutes during the day from Rome; departures are from the Anagnina Metro stop in Rome. It takes about an hour to reach Palestrina and costs about 2.50€.

If you're driving, exit through the Porta Maggiore and travel on Via Prenestina for about 39km (24 miles) or the Autostrada (A1), and get off at Valmontone; the latter route is much quicker.

Exploring the Town

When U.S. airmen bombed part of the town in World War II, they never imagined they'd launch Palestrina as an important tourist attraction. After the debris was cleared, a pagan temple (once one of the greatest in the world) emerged: the **Fortuna Primigenia,** rebuilt in the days of the empire but dating from centuries before. In Palestrina you'll also find a **Duomo** dating from 1100, with a mostly intact bell tower.

Palestrina predates the founding of Rome by several hundred years. It resisted conquest by the early Romans and later took the wrong side in the civil war between Marius and Sulla. When Sulla won, he razed every stone in the city except the Temple of Fortune and then built a military barracks on the site. Later, as a favorite vacation spot for the emperors and their entourages, it sheltered some of the most luxurious villas of the Roman Empire. Its most famous child was Pier Luigi da Palestrina, recognized as the father of polyphonic harmony.

Nazional Archeological Museum of Palestrina ★★ High on a hill overlooking the valley, the Colonna Barberini Palace, the work of both Bernini and Borromini, contains the archaeological museum built on top of the Hellenistic sanctuary of Sanctuary of Fortuna Primigenia.

Worth the trip itself is the **Mosaic of the Nile ★★★**, dating from the 2nd century B.C. The artwork depicts the Nile in flood, and is one of the most significant mosaics in the world. The mosaic also details a shepherd's hunt, mummies, ibises, and Roman warriors. Ancient artifacts such as tombs, statues, and Etruscan are on display.

The Capitoline Triad of Guidonia dates from the end of the 2nd century B.C., consisting of six terraces opening onto panoramic views.

Where to Stay & Dine

Albergo Ristorante Stella (Restaurant Coccia) A contemporary hotel and restaurant, the Stella is in the commercial district of town on a cobblestone square filled with parked cars, trees, and a small fountain. The bedrooms are rather basic but comfortable. The lobby is filled with warm colors and autographed photos of local sports heroes.

The sunny restaurant, open daily for lunch and dinner, serves affordable, zesty Roman cuisine.

Piazza della Liberazione 3, Palestrina, 00036 Roma. ✆ **06-9538172.** Fax 06-9573360. www.hotelstella.it. 28 units. 65€ double; 100€ suite. AE, DC, MC, V. Parking .50€ per hour. **Amenities:** Restaurant; bar. *In room:* A/C, TV, hair dryer.

THE CASTELLI ROMANI ★★

For the Roman emperor and the wealthy cardinal in the heyday of the Renaissance, the **Castelli Romani (Roman Castles)** exerted a powerful lure, and they still do. The Castelli aren't castles, but hill towns—many of them with an ancient history and several producing well-regarded wines.

The ideal way to explore the hill towns is by car. But you can get a limited overview by taking one of the CoTral buses (costing 2€) that leaves every 20 minutes from Rome's Anagnina stop on Metro Line A.

Marino

Marino, the closest to Rome (only 24km/15 miles away), is about 7km (4⅓ miles) off Via Appia Nuova, quite near Ciampino Airport. Much of Marino's original charm has fallen victim to modern builders, but the town is still the place to go each October during the **grape harvest.** Check with the Rome tourist office for the actual dates, which vary from year to year. At that time, the town's fountains are switched from water to wine, and everyone drinks for free.

Rocca di Papa ★

The most attractive of the hill towns lies only some 9.5km (6 miles) from Marino. It's a lovely spot, on the slopes of Monte Cavo facing the Alban lakes. By car, the best route is 217 to the junction with 218, where you make a left turn. Before the intersection, you'll be high on a ridge above Lake Albano, where the views of the lake, the far woods, and the papal palace of Castel Gandolfo on the opposite mountain are superb.

Just before Rocca di Papa is the entrance to the toll road to **Monte Cavo.** A temple of Jove once stood on top of this mountain, and before that, the tribes of the area met with King Tarquin before Rome was a republic. At the top of the mountain is one of the most panoramic views in the hill towns, giving you a wide survey of the Alban Hills and the Castelli Romani. Down below, Rocca di Papa is a tangle of old streets and churches.

Nemi

The Romans flock to **Nemi** (32km/20 miles from Rome) in droves, particularly from April to June, for the succulent **strawberries** grown here, acclaimed by some gourmets as Europe's finest. In May, there's a strawberry festival. To reach Nemi by bus, go to the Anagnini Metro stop in Rome. From here, take the CoTral bus heading for Genzano. At Genzano, change buses, taking the one marked NEMI. Service is about every 30 minutes during the day.

Nemi was also known to the ancients. A temple to the huntress Diana was erected on **Lake Nemi ★**, which was said to be her "looking glass." In A.D. 37, Caligula built luxurious barges to float on the lake. The boats, lavishly fitted with bronze and marble, were sunk during Claudius's reign (he succeeded the insane Caligula) and were entirely forgotten until Mussolini drained the lake in the 1930s. Then the barges were found and set up in a lakeside museum; they remained as a wonder of ancient Rome until the Nazis burned them during their retreat.

At the **Roman Ship Museum (Museo delle Navi) ★**, Via di Diana 13 (✆ **06-39967900**), you can see two scale models of the ships destroyed by the Nazis. The major artifacts on display are mainly copies; the originals now rest in world-class museums. The museum is open daily 9am to 5pm. Admission is 3€. To reach the museum, head from the center of Nemi toward the lake.

The 15th-century **Palazzo Ruspoli,** a private baronial estate, is the focal point of Nemi, but the town itself invites exploration—particularly the alleyways the locals call streets and the houses with balconies jutting out over the slopes.

WHERE TO DINE

Ristorante Il Castagnone ★ ROMAN/SEAFOOD This well-managed dining room in the town's best hotel takes definite pride in its Roman cuisine, emphasizing seafood above meat. Amid neoclassical accessories and marble, you can order delectable veal, chicken, beef, and fish dishes such as fried calamari, spaghetti with shellfish in garlicky tomato-based sauce, and roasted lamb with potatoes and Mediterranean herbs. Other enticing menu items include a salmon and spinach lasagna, risotto with shrimp and zucchini, and egg fettuccine pasta sautéed with porcini mushrooms. As you dine, enjoy a sweeping lake view from the restaurant's windows.

In the Diana Park Hotel, Via Nemorense 56. ✆ **06-9364041.** Reservations recommended. Main courses 12€–23€. AE, DC, MC, V. Tues–Sun noon–3pm and 8–11pm. Closed Nov (dates vary).

En Route to Castel Gandolfo

The road to Gandolfo leads through a few worth-a-visit towns on the way. **Genzano,** on the other side of Lake Nemi, has views of the countryside and a 17th-century palace that belonged to the Sforza-Cesarini.

Ariccia is an ancient town that sent representatives to meet with Tarquin the Proud on top of Monte Cavo 2,500 years ago. After many centuries of changing hands, especially between medieval and Renaissance families, it has taken on a suburban look. The palace in the middle of town is still private and belongs to the Chigi family.

Albano practically adjoins Castel Gandolfo. It has a long history; this is the reputed site of Alba Longa, the so-called mother city of Rome, but it's quite built-up and modern today. Trains going to Albano leave from Stazione Termini in Rome.

Castel Gandolfo ★

The summer residence of the pope, a 17th-century edifice designed by Carlo Maderno, stands practically on the foundations of another equally regal summer residence, the villa of Emperor Domitian. Unfortunately, the palace, the gardens, and the adjoining Villa Barberini can't be visited. You'll have to be content with a visit to **Piazza della Libertà;** its church, Chiesa di San Tomaso di Villanova; and a fountain by Bernini.

If you're here for lunch, as many are, your best bet is **Antico Ristorante Pagnanelli,** Via Gramsci 4 (© **06-9360004;** www.pagnanelli.it), which serves both regional and pan-Italian dishes, with meals starting at 10€ and a high of 18€ for the fresh seafood dishes. The restaurant is open Wednesday through Monday from noon to 3pm and 7pm to midnight.

Frascati ★

About 21km (13 miles) from Rome on Via Tuscolana and some 322m (1,056 ft.) above sea level, Frascati is one of the most beautiful hill towns. It's known for the wine to which it lends its name, as well as for its villas, which were restored after the severe destruction caused by World War II bombers. To get here, take one of the CoTral buses leaving from the Anagina stop of Metro Line A in Rome. From there, take the blue CoTral bus to Frascati. Again, the transportation situation in Italy is constantly in a state of flux, so check your route at the station.

Although Frascati wine is exported and served in many of Rome's restaurants and trattorie, tradition holds that it's best near the vineyards from which it came. Romans drive up on Sunday just to drink it.

Stand in the heart of Frascati, at Piazza Marconi, to see the most important of the estates: **Villa Aldobrandini ★**, Via Massaia. The finishing touches to this 16th-century villa were added by Maderno, who designed the facade of St. Peter's in Rome. You can visit only the gardens, but with its grottoes, yew hedges, statuary, and splashing fountains, it's a nice outing. The gardens are open Monday to Friday 9am to 1pm and 3 to 5pm (to 6pm in summer).

You also might want to visit the bombed-out **Villa Torlonia,** adjacent to Piazza Marconi. Its grounds have been converted into a public park whose chief treasure is the **Theater of the Fountains,** designed by Maderno.

If you have a car, you can continue about 5km (3 miles) past the Villa Aldobrandini to **Tuscolo,** an ancient spot with the ruins of an amphitheater dating from about the 1st century B.C. It offers what may be one of Italy's most panoramic views.

WHERE TO DINE

Cacciani Restaurant ROMAN Cacciani is the top restaurant in Frascati, where the competition has always been tough. It boasts a terrace commanding a view of the valley, and the kitchen is exposed to the public. We recommend the pasta specialties, such as pasta *cacio e pepe* (pasta with cheese and black pepper), or the spaghetti with seafood and lentils. For a main course, the lamb with a sauce of white wine and vinegar is always fine. As is the beefsteak with an artichoke sauce. If you call ahead, the Cacciani family will arrange a visit to several of Frascati's wine-producing villas, along with a memorable meal at the restaurant.

Via Armando Diaz 13. ✆ **06-9420378.** www.cacciani.it. Reservations required. Main courses 15€–17€. AE, DC, MC, V. Tues–Sun 12:30–3pm and 7:30–10:30pm.

OSTIA ★

26km (16 miles) southwest of Rome

Ostia Antica is one of the area's major attractions, particularly interesting if you can't make it to Pompeii. If you want to see both ancient and modern Rome, grab your swimsuit, towel, and sunblock, and take the Metro Line B from Stazione Termini to the Magliana stop. Change here for the Lido train to Ostia Antica, about 26km (16 miles) from Rome. Departures are about every half-hour, and the trip takes only 20 minutes. The Metro lets you off across the highway that connects Rome with the coast. It's just a short walk to the excavations.

Later, board the Metro again to visit the **Lido di Ostia,** the beach. Italy might be a Catholic country, but you won't detect any religious conservatism in the skimpy bikinis on display here. There's a carnival atmosphere, with dance halls, cinemas, and pizzerias. The Lido is set off best at Castelfusano, against a backdrop of pine woods. This stretch of shoreline is referred to as the Roman Riviera.

Ostia Antica's Ruins ★★ Ostia was the port of ancient Rome and a city in its own right. The currents and uneven bottom of the Tiber prevented Mediterranean shipping from going farther upstream, so merchandise was transferred to barges for the remainder of the trip. Ostia's fate was tied closely to that of the empire. At the peak of Rome's power, the city had 100,000 inhabitants—hard to imagine looking at today's ruins. Ostia was important enough to have had a theater, numerous temples and baths, great patrician houses, and a large business complex.

Ostia flourished for about 8 centuries before it began to wither away. By Constantine's time (4th c. A.D.), the worm had turned. The barbarian sieges of Rome in the 5th century spelled the end of Ostia. Gradually, it became little more than a malaria bed, a buried ghost city that faded into history. A papal-sponsored commission launched a series of digs in the 19th century; however, the major work of unearthing was carried out under Mussolini's orders from 1938 to 1942 (the work had to stop because of the war). The city is only partially dug out today, but it's believed that all the chief monuments have been uncovered. Quite a few visible ruins have been unearthed, so this is no dusty field like the Circus Maximus.

These principal monuments are clearly labeled. The most important spot is **Piazzale delle Corporazioni,** an early version of Wall Street. Near the theater, this square contained nearly 75 corporations, the nature of their businesses identified by the patterns of preserved mosaics. Greek dramas were performed at the **ancient theater,** built in the early days of the empire. The classics are still aired here in summer (check with the tourist office for specific listings), but the theater as it looks today is the result of much rebuilding. Every town the size of Ostia had a forum, and during the excavations a number of pillars of the ancient **Ostia Forum** were uncovered. At one end is a

2nd-century B.C. temple honoring a trio of gods: Minerva, Jupiter, and Juno (little more than the basic foundation remains). Also of special interest are the ruins of **Thermopolium,** which was a bar; its name means "sale of hot drinks." The ruins of **Capitolium and Forum** remain; this was once the largest temple in Ostia, dating from the 2nd century A.D. A lot of the original brick remains, including a partial reconstruction of the altar. Of an insula, a block of multiparty apartments, **Casa Diana** remains, with its rooms arranged around an inner courtyard. There are perfect picnic spots beside fallen columns or near old temple walls.

Viale dei Romagnoli 717. ✆ **06-56358099.** Admission 6.50€. Nov–Feb and Apr–Oct Tues–Sun 8:30am–6pm; Mar Tues–Sun 8:30am–5pm. Metro: Ostia Antica Line Roma-Ostia-Lido.

FREGENE ★

39km (24 miles) west of Rome

The fame of this coastal city north of the Tiber dates back to the 1600s, when the land belonged to the Rospigliosi, a powerful Roman family. Pope Clement IX, a member of that wealthy family, planted a forest of pine that extends along the shoreline for 4km (2½ miles) and stands half a mile deep to protect the land from the strong winds of the Mediterranean. Today the wall of pines makes a dramatic backdrop for the golden sands and luxurious villas of the resort. If you'd like to see an Italian beach, head here instead of to the more polluted beaches along Ostia's Lido.

Getting There

You can catch the CoTral bus to Fregene, which leaves from the Cornelia Metro stop in Rome and carries passengers to the center of Fregene. A ticket costs 2.50€, and travel time is 1 hour.

If you're driving, follow SS1 (also known as Via Aurelia) heading west, crossing over the bypass that encircles Rome. After Castello di Guido, 23km (14 miles) west of Central Rome, exit onto the secondary road marked MACCARESE-FREGENE. Then continue southwest for another 16km (10 miles), following the signs to Fregene. There is no tourist information office.

Where to Stay & Dine

La Conchiglia ★ La Conchiglia means "the Shell," and it's an appropriate name for this beachfront hotel and restaurant, with views of the water and the pines. It features a circular lounge with curving wall banquettes facing a cylindrical fireplace. Guest rooms are comfortable and well furnished, ranging from medium to spacious, each with a fine mattress and a bathroom equipped with a shower/tub combination.

It's also possible to stop by just for a good moderately priced meal. Try, for example, spaghetti with lobster and grilled fish, or one of many excellent meat dishes. Meals start at 9€. The restaurant is open daily for lunch and dinner.

Lungomare di Ponente 4, Fregene, 00050 Roma. ✆ **06-6685385.** Fax 06-66563185. www.laconchigliahotelfregene.com. 36 units. 69€–135€ double. Rates include buffet breakfast. AE, DC, MC, V. Free parking. **Amenities:** Restaurant; room service. *In room:* A/C, TV, hair dryer, minibar, Wi-Fi (free).

ETRUSCAN HISTORICAL SIGHTS

Cerveteri (Caere)

48km (28 miles) north of Rome

As you walk through Rome's Etruscan Museum (Villa Giulia), you'll often see CAERE written under a figure vase or sarcophagus. This is a reference to the nearby town known today as Cerveteri, one of Italy's great Etruscan cities, whose origins could date from as far back as the 9th century B.C.

You can reach Cerveteri by bus or car. If you're driving, head out Via Aurelia, northwest of Rome, for 45km (28 miles). By public transport, take Metro Line A in Rome to the Cornelia stop; from the Cornelia stop, you can catch a CoTral bus to Cerveteri; the trip takes about an hour and costs 2.50€. You can visit their website at www.cotralspa.it. Once you're at Cerveteri, it's a 2km (1¼-mile) walk to the necropolis; follow the signs pointing the way.

Of course, the Etruscan town has long since faded, but not the **Necropolis of Cerveteri ★★** (✆ **06-9940001**). The effect is eerie; Cerveteri is often called a "city of the dead." When you go beneath some of the mounds, you'll discover the most striking feature: The tombs are like rooms in Etruscan homes. The main burial ground is the Necropolis of Banditacca. Of the graves thus far uncovered, none is finer than the **Tomba Bella (Tomb of the Reliefs),** the burial ground of the Matuna family. Articles such as utensils and even house pets were painted in stucco relief. Presumably, these paintings were representations of items that the dead family would need in the world beyond. The necropolis is open daily from 8:30am to 1 hour before sunset. Admission is 6€ for adults and 3€ for children 17 and under.

Relics from the necropolis are displayed at the **Museo Nazionale Cerite,** Piazza Santa Maria Maggiore (✆ **06-9941354**). The museum, housed within the ancient walls and crenellations of Ruspoldi Castle, is open Tuesday to Sunday 8:30am to 7:30pm. Free admission.

Tarquinia ★

If you want to see tombs even more striking and more recently excavated than those at Cerveteri, go to Tarquinia, a town with medieval turrets and fortifications atop rocky cliffs overlooking the sea. It would seem unusual for a medieval town to have an Etruscan name, but actually, Tarquinia is the adopted name of the old medieval community of Corneto, in honor of the major Etruscan city that once stood nearby.

The main attraction in the town is the **Tarquinia National Museum ★**, Piazza Cavour (✆ **0776-856036**), devoted to Etruscan exhibits and sarcophagi excavated from the necropolis a few miles away. The museum is housed in the Palazzo Vitelleschi, a Gothic palace from the mid–15th century. Among the exhibits are gold jewelry, black vases with carved and painted bucolic scenes, and sarcophagi decorated with carvings of animals and relief figures of priests and military leaders. But the biggest attraction is in itself worth the ride from Rome: the almost life-size pair of **winged horses ★★** from the pediment of a Tarquinian temple. The finish is worn here and there, and the terra-cotta color shows through, but the relief stands as one of the greatest Etruscan masterpieces ever discovered. The museum is open Tuesday through Sunday from 8:30am to 7:30pm, and admission is 6€ for adults, 3€ for those 18 to 24 years old, and free for those 17 and under. ***Note:*** It is possible to buy a combined ticket for the Tarquinia National Museum and the Etruscan Necropolis. It costs 8€. The museum is closed Christmas, January 1, and May 1.

A fee of 6€ for (adults), 3€ for ages 18 to 25 (free for ages 17 and under) admits you to the **Etruscan Necropolis ★★** (✆ **0766-856308**), covering more than 4km (2½ miles) of rough terrain near where the ancient Etruscan city once stood. Thousands of tombs have been discovered, some of which have yet to be explored to this day. The **paintings** on the walls of the tombs have helped historians reconstruct the life of the Etruscans—a heretofore impossible feat without a written history. The paintings depict feasting couples in vivid colors mixed from iron oxide, lapis lazuli dust, and charcoal. One of the oldest tombs (6th c. B.C.) depicts young men fishing while dolphins play and colorful birds fly high above. Many of the paintings convey an earthy, vigorous sexuality among the wealthy Etruscans. The tombs are generally open Tuesday to Sunday 8:30am to 1 hour before sunset. You can reach the gravesites by taking a bus from the Barriera San Giusto to the Cimitero stop. Or, try the 20-minute walk from the museum. It is closed Christmas, January 1, and May 1.

By car, take Via Aurelia outside Rome and continue on the autostrada toward Civitavecchia. Bypass Civitavecchia and continue another 21km (13 miles) north until you see the exit signs for Tarquinia. As for public transport, a *diretto* (direct) train from Roma Ostiense station takes 50 minutes. Eight buses a day leave from the Via Lepanto stop in Rome for the 2-hour trip to the town of Barriera San Giusto, 2.5km (1½ miles) from Tarquinia. Bus schedules are available at the **tourist office** at Piazza Cavour 23 (✆ **0766-849282**), open Monday to Saturday 8am to 1pm.

VITERBO ★

98km (61 miles) north of Rome

The 2,000 years that have gone into the creation of the city of Viterbo make it one of the most interesting day trips from Rome. Although it traces its history back to the Etruscans, the bulk of its historical architecture dates from the Middle Ages and the Renaissance, when the city was a residence (and hide-out) for the popes. The old section of the city is still surrounded by the thick stone walls that once protected the inhabitants from papal (or antipapal, depending on the situation at the time) attacks.

Essentials

GETTING THERE Take a direct train from Rome (at the Ostiense Station or Roma Trastevere) to Viterbo. The trip takes 1¾ hours, costing 4.50€ one-way.

If you're driving, take Autostrada A1 north to the Orte exit.

VISITOR INFORMATION **Tourist information** is available at Via Ascenzi 4 (✆ **0761-325992**); the office is open Monday to Thursday 9:30am to 1pm and 3 to 6pm, Friday and Saturday 9:30am to 1pm.

Seeing the Sights

The only way to see Viterbo properly is to wander through the narrow cobblestone streets of the medieval town. **Piazza del Plebiscito,** dominated by the 15th-century town hall, impresses visitors with the fine state of preservation of Viterbo's old buildings. The courtyard and fountain in front of the town hall and the 13th-century governor's palace are favorite meeting places for townsfolk and visitors alike.

Just down Via San Lorenzo is **Piazza San Lorenzo ★★**, the site of Viterbo's cathedral, which sits atop a former Etruscan acropolis. The **Duomo,** dating from 1192, is a composite of architectural styles, with pagan foundations, a Renaissance facade, and a Gothic bell tower. Next door is the 13th-century **Palazzo Papale ★★**, which was built as a residence for the pope but also served as a hideout when he was in exile.

The best example of medieval architecture in Viterbo is the **San Pellegrino Quarter ★★**, reached from Piazza San Lorenzo by a short walk past Piazza della Morte. This quarter, inhabited by working-class Viterboans, is a maze of narrow streets, arched walkways, towers, steep stairways, and ornamental fountains.

Worth a special visit is the **Convent of Santa Maria della Verita,** dating from 1100. The church contains 15th-century frescoes by Lorenzo da Viterbo.

Park of the Monsters (Parco dei Mostri) ★ About 13km (8 miles) east of Bagnaia at Bomarzo lies the Park of the Monsters. Prince Vicino Orsini had it built in a deep valley that's overlooked by the Orsini Palace and the houses of the village. Prince Orsini's park, Bosco Sacro (Sacred Wood), is filled with grotesque figures carved from natural rock. Nature and art have created a surrealistic fantasy: the Mouth of Hell (an ogre's face so big that people can walk into its gaping mouth), a crude Hercules slaying an Amazon, nymphs with butterfly wings, a huge tortoise with a statue on its shell, a harpy, a mermaid, snarling dogs, lions, and much, much more.

Villa delle Meraviglie, Bomarzo. ✆ **0761-924029.** www.parcodeimostri.com. Admission 9€. Daily 8am to 1 hr. before sunset. Bus: Take a CoTral bus from Viterbo.

Villa Lante ★★ The English author Sacheverell Sitwell called Villa Lante, located in Bagnaia, a suburb of Viterbo, "the most beautiful garden in Italy." Water from Monte Cimino flows down to the fountains of the villa, running from terrace to terrace until it reaches the central pool of the regal garden, with statues, stone banisters, and shrubbery. The gardens can be visited only on a guided tour. (The gatekeeper at the guardhouse will show you through, usually with a group that has assembled.)

Via Giacopo Barrozzi 71, Bagnaia. ✆ **0761-288008.** www.villalante.it. Admission 2€. Nov–Mar Tues–Sun 8:30am–4:30pm; early Apr and Sept–Oct 9am–5:30pm; mid-Apr to Aug 8:30am–6:30pm. Bus: Take a CoTral bus from Viterbo.

12

FAST FACTS ROME

American Express The Rome offices are at Piazza di Spagna 38 (✆ **06-67641;** Metro: Spagna). The travel service is open Monday to Friday 9am to 5:30pm and Saturday 9am to 12:30pm.

Area Code The area code for Rome is **06.**

ATM Networks & Cashpoints See "Money & Costs," p. 57.

Babysitters Most hotel desks in Rome will help you find a babysitter. Inquire as far in advance as possible. You can request an English-speaking sitter, but you may not always get one. You can also call **American Women's Association** (✆ **06-4825268;** www.awar.org) for a list of reliable babysitters.

Business Hours Most stores open at 10am, closing at 7pm Monday to Saturday. Many still practice the habit of closing for 1 or 2 hours at midday for lunch. Some boutiques and chain stores in the center of Rome are also open on Sunday. In general, banks are open Monday to Friday 8:30am to 1:30pm and 3 to 4pm. Some banks keep afternoon hours from 2:45 to 3:45pm.

Currency Exchange There are exchange offices throughout the city, and they're also at all major rail and air terminals, including Stazione Termini, where the cambio (exchange booth) beside the rail information booth is open daily from 8am to 8pm. At some cambi, you'll have to pay commissions, often 1.5%. Likewise, banks often charge commissions.

Dentists For dental work, go to **American Dental Arts Rome,** Via del Governo Vecchio (✆ **06-6832613;** www.adadentistsrome.com; bus no. 64), which uses all the latest technology, including laser dental techniques. There is also a 24-hour **G. Eastman Dental Hospital** at Viale Regina Elena 287B (✆ **06-844831;** Metro: Policlinico).

Doctors Call the U.S. Embassy at ✆ **06-46741** for a list of doctors who speak English. All big hospitals have a 24-hour first-aid service (go to the emergency room, *Pronto Soccorso*). You'll find English-speaking doctors at the privately run **Salvator Mundi International Hospital,** Viale delle Mura Gianicolensi 67 (✆ **06-588961;** bus no. 115). For medical assistance, the **International Medical Center** is on 24-hour duty at Via Firenze 47 (✆ **06-4882371;** www.imc84.com; Metro: Repubblica). You could also contact the **Rome American Hospital,** Via Emilio Longoni 69 (✆ **06-22551;** www.rah.it; bus no. 508), with English-speaking doctors on duty 24 hours. A more personalized service is provided 24 hours by **MEDI-CALL,** Via Cremera 8 (✆ **06-8840113;** bus no. 86). It can arrange for qualified doctors to make a house call at your hotel or anywhere in Rome. In most cases, the doctor will be a general practitioner who can refer you to a specialist, if needed. Fees begin at around 100€ per visit and can go higher if a specialist or specialized treatments are necessary.

Drinking Laws Wine with meals has been a normal part of family life for hundreds of years in Italy. Children are exposed to wine at an early age, and consumption of alcohol isn't anything out of the ordinary. The legal drinking age is 18.

Driving Rules See "Getting There & Getting Around," p. 49.

Drugstores A reliable pharmacy is **Farmacia Internazionale,** Piazza Barberini 49 (✆ **06-4825456;** Metro: Barberini), open day and night. Most pharmacies are open from 8:30am to 1pm and 4 to 7:30pm. In general, pharmacies follow a rotation system, so several are always open on Sunday.

Electricity It's generally 220 volts, 50 Hz AC, but you might find 125-volt outlets, with different plugs and sockets for each. Pick up a transformer either before leaving home or in any appliance shop in Rome if you plan to use electrical appliances. Check the exact local current at your hotel. You'll also need an adapter plug.

Embassies & Consulates In case of an emergency, embassies have a 24-hour referral service.

The **U.S. Embassy** is in Rome at Via Vittorio Veneto 119A (✆ **06-46741;** fax 06-46742244; www.usembassy.it).

The **Canadian Embassy** in Rome is at Via Salaria, 243 ✆ **06-854441.** The **Canadian Consulate** and passport service is in Rome at Via Zara 30 (✆ **06-854443937;** fax 06-854442905). The **U.K. Embassy** is in Rome at Via XX Settembre 80A (✆ **06-42200001;** fax 06-42202334; www.ukinitaly.fco.gov.uk).

The **Australian Embassy** is in Rome at Via Antonio Bosio 5 (✆ **06-852721;** fax 06-85272300; www.italy.embassy.gov.au).

The **New Zealand Embassy** is in Rome at Via Clitunno 44 (✆ **06-8537501;** fax 06-4402984). The **Irish Embassy** in Rome is at Piazza di Campitelli 3 (✆ **06-6979121;** fax 06-69791231; www.embassyofireland.it).

Emergencies Dial ✆ **113** to call the police; call ✆ **118** for an ambulance; to report a fire, call ✆ **115.**

Holidays Offices and shops in Rome are closed on the following **national holidays:** January 1 (New Year's Day), Easter Monday, April 25 (Liberation Day), May 1 (Labor Day), August 15 (Assumption of the Virgin), November 1 (All Saints' Day), December 8 (Feast of the Immaculate Conception), December 25 (Christmas Day), and December 26 (Santo Stefano). Many offices and businesses also close on June 29, for the feast day of Sts. Peter and Paul, the city's patron saints.

Hospitals See "Doctors," above.

Internet Access Try **Internet Café,** Via dei Marruncini 12 (near Stazione Termini; ✆ **06-4454953**), open Monday to Friday 9:30am to 1am, Saturday 10am to 1am, and Sunday 2pm to midnight.

Language Although Italian, of course, is the official language, English is widely understood in central Rome, especially in the tourist industries such as shops, hotels, restaurants, and nightclubs. To get a leg up, refer to the key phrases and terms in this guide.

Legal Aid The consulate of your country is the place to turn for legal aid, although offices can't interfere in the Italian legal process. They can, however, inform you of your rights and provide a list of attorneys. You'll have to pay for the attorney out of your pocket—there's no free legal assistance. If you're arrested for a drug offense, about all the consulate will do is notify a lawyer about your case and perhaps inform your family.

Lost & Found Be sure to contact your credit card companies the minute you discover your wallet has been lost or stolen, and file a report at the nearest police precinct. Your credit card company or insurer may require a police report number or record of the loss. Most credit card companies have an emergency toll-free number to call if your card is lost or stolen; they may be able to wire you a cash advance immediately or deliver an emergency credit card in a day or two.

If you **lose your card,** call the following *Italian* toll-free numbers: **Visa** (**© 800/819-014;** www.visa.com), **MasterCard** (**© 800/870-866;** www.mastercard.com), or **American Express** (**© 800/872-000,** or collect 336/393-1111, www.americanexpress.com, from anywhere in the world). As a backup, write down the phone numbers that appear on the back of each of your cards (*not* the U.S. toll-free number—you can't dial those from abroad—but rather the number you can call collect from *anywhere;* if one does not appear, call the card company and ask).

Luggage Storage/Lockers These are available at the Stazione Termini. Lockers, which are open daily from 6am to midnight, are on the underground floor of the Termini Wing accessible from the Forum Termini by means of the tapis-roulant, from via Giolitti, or platform 24. The charge is 4€ per piece of luggage per 5-hour period. Luggage storage is also available daily 7am to 11pm in the main arrivals building of the airport, costing 2€ per bag for up to 7 hours of storage, 3.50€ per bag between 7 and 24 hours, and 6€ for oversize luggage per day.

Mail Mail delivery in Italy is notoriously bad. Your family and friends back home might receive your postcards in 1 week, or it might take 2 weeks or more. Postcards, aerogrammes, and letters weighing up to 20 grams sent to the United States and Canada cost .85€; to the United Kingdom and Ireland, .65€; and to Australia and New Zealand, 1€. You can buy stamps at all post offices and at tabacchi, but it's easiest just to buy stamps and mail letters and postcards at your hotel's front desk. You can buy special stamps at the **Vatican City Post Office,** adjacent to the information office in St. Peter's Square; it's open October to June Monday to Friday 8:15am to 6pm, and Saturday 8:15am to 2:15pm; and July to September Monday to Saturday 8:15am to 2:30pm. Letters mailed at Vatican City reach North America far more quickly than mail sent from within Rome for the same cost.

Newspapers & Magazines You can get the *International Herald Tribune, USA Today,* the *New York Times,* and *Time* and *Newsweek* magazines at most newsstands. The expatriate magazine (in English) *Wanted in Rome* comes out monthly and lists current events and shows. If you want to try your hand at reading Italian, the newspaper *La Repubblica* is full of cultural and entertainment listings.

Passports **For Residents of the United States:** Whether you're applying in person or by mail, you can download passport applications from the U.S. Department of State website at **http://travel.state.gov**. To find your regional passport office, either check the U.S. Department of State website or call the **National Passport Information Center** toll-free number (**© 877/487-2778**) for automated information.

For Residents of Canada: Passport applications are available at travel agencies throughout Canada or from the central **Passport Office,** Department of Foreign Affairs and International Trade, Ottawa, QC K1A 0G3 (**© 800/567-6868;** www.ppt.gc.ca).

For Residents of Ireland: You can apply for a 10-year passport at the **Passport Office,** Setanta Centre, Molesworth Street, Dublin 2 (**© 01/671-1633;** www.dfa.ie). In Ireland, infants (up to age 3) are issued with a 3-year passport. Children aged 3-17 are issued with a 5-year passport. Persons aged 18 and over, including those over 65, are issued with a 10-year passport. You can also apply at 1A South Mall, Cork (**© 021/494-4700**) or at most main post offices.

For Residents of Australia: You can pick up an application from your local post office or any branch of Passports Australia, but you must schedule an interview at the passport office to present your application materials. Call the **Australian Passport Information Service** at ✆ **131-232,** or visit the government website at www.passports.gov.au.

For Residents of New Zealand: You can pick up a passport application at any New Zealand Passports Office or download it from their website. Contact the **Passports Office** at ✆ **0800/225-050** in New Zealand, or log on to **www.passports.govt.nz**.

Police Dial ✆ **113.**

Safety Pickpocketing is the most common problem. Men should keep their wallets in their front pocket or inside jacket pocket. Purse snatching is also commonplace, with young men on Vespas who ride past you and grab your purse. To avoid trouble, stay away from the curb, and keep your purse on the wall side of your body and place the strap across your chest. Don't lay anything valuable on tables or chairs, where it can be grabbed up. Children have long been a particular menace, although the problem isn't as severe as in years past. If they completely surround you, you'll often virtually have to fight them off. They might approach you with pieces of cardboard hiding their stealing hands. Just keep repeating a firm *no!*

Smoking On January 10, 2005, a nationwide smoking ban went into effect in bars and restaurants. This law is strongly enforced nationwide.

Taxes As a member of the European Union, Italy imposes a **value-added tax** (called **IVA** in Italy) on most goods and services. The tax that most affects visitors is the one imposed on hotel rates, which ranges from 10% in first- and second-class hotels to 20% in deluxe hotels.

Non-E.U. (European Union) citizens are entitled to a **refund of the IVA** if they spend more than 155€ at any one store, before tax. To claim your refund, request an invoice from the cashier at the store and take it to the Customs office *(dogana)* at the airport to have it stamped before you leave. ***Note:*** If you're going to another E.U. country before flying home, have it stamped at the airport Customs office of the last E.U. country you'll be in (for example, if you're flying home via Britain, have your Italian invoices stamped in London). Once back home, mail the stamped invoice (keep a photocopy for your records) back to the original vendor within 90 days of the purchase. The vendor will, sooner or later, send you a refund of the tax that you paid at the time of your original purchase. Reputable stores view this as a matter of ordinary paperwork and are businesslike about it. Less-honorable stores might lose your dossier. It pays to deal with established vendors on large purchases. You can also request that the refund be credited to the credit card with which you made the purchase; this is usually a faster procedure.

Many shops are now part of the **"Tax Free for Tourists"** network (look for the sticker in the window). Stores participating in this network issue a check along with your invoice at the time of purchase. After you have the invoice stamped at Customs, you can redeem the check for cash directly at the Tax Free booth in the airport (in Rome, it's past Customs) or mail it back in the envelope provided within 60 days.

Time In terms of standard time zones, Italy is 6 hours ahead of Eastern Standard Time in the United States. The E.U. version of daylight saving time runs from the last Sunday in March until the last Sunday in October.

Tipping This custom is practiced with flair in Italy—many people depend on tips for their livelihoods. In **hotels,** the service charge of 15% to 19% is already added to a bill. In addition, it's customary to tip the chambermaid 1€ per day, the doorman (for calling a cab) 1€, and the bellhop or porter 1.50€ to 2.50€ for carrying your bags to your room. A concierge expects about 15% of his or her bill, as well as tips for extra services performed, which could include help with long-distance calls. In expensive hotels, these amounts are often doubled.

In **restaurants and cafes,** 15% is usually added to your bill to cover most charges. If you're not sure whether this has been done, ask, *"È incluso il servizio?"* (ay een-*cloo*-soh eel sair-*vee*-tsoh?). An additional tip isn't expected, but it's nice to leave the equivalent of an extra couple of dollars if you've been pleased with the service. Checkroom attendants expect 1.50€, and washroom attendants should get 1€. Restaurants are required by law to give customers official receipts.

Taxi drivers expect at least 10% of the fare.

Toilets Facilities are found near many of the major sights and often have attendants, as do those at bars, clubs, restaurants, cafes, and hotels, plus the airports and the rail station. (There are public restrooms near the Spanish Steps, or you can stop at the McDonald's there—it's one of the nicest branches of the Golden Arches you'll ever see!) You're expected to leave 1€ for the attendant. It's not a bad idea to carry some tissues in your pocket when you're out and about, either.

Visitor Information On the Web, the Italian National Tourist Board sponsors the sites **www.italiantourism.com** and **www.enit.it**.

For information on the **Vatican,** check out **www.vatican.va**.

In Italy (www.initaly.com) not only contains solid information on Italy and Rome presented in a very personal and friendly way, but it also has one of the best sets of links to other Italy-related sites on the Web.

Another good site, **www.enjoyrome.com**, contains information about walking tours, accommodations, restaurants, side trips from Rome, useful links, and maps. Another helpful site is **www.rome.info.it**.

Information is available at a tourist office at **Leonardo da Vinci International Airport** (✆ **06-06-08, www.rome-airport.info**), open daily 8:15am to 7pm.

More helpful, and stocking maps and brochures, are the offices maintained by the **Comune di Roma** at various sites around the city, with red-and-orange or yellow-and-black signs saying COMUNE DI ROMA—PUNTI DI INFORMAZIONE TURISTICA. The Comune di Roma has a call center for tourist information (✆ **06-36004399**). They're staffed daily from 9am to 6pm, except the one at Termini (daily 8am–9pm). Here are the addresses and phone numbers: in Stazione Termini (no phone); on Piazza Cinque Lune near Piazza Navona (✆ **06-68809240**); at Via Minghetti Marco near the Quirinale (✆ **06-6782988**); on Piazza Sonnino in Trastevere (✆ **06-58333457**); at Via Marsala, outside Termini (✆ **06-4740031**); at Via del Tempio della Pace, near the Colosseum (✆ **06-69924307**), and at Piazza del Campidoglio (✆ **06-6798921**).

Enjoy Rome, Via Marghera 8A, near the train station (✆ **06-4451843;** www.enjoyrome.com), was begun by an English-speaking couple, Fulvia and Pierluigi. They dispense information about almost everything in Rome and are far more pleasant and organized than the Board of Tourism. They'll also help you find a hotel room, with no service charge (in anything from a hostel to a three-star hotel). Enjoy Rome is open year-round Monday to Friday 8:30am to 5pm, Saturday 8:30am to 2pm.

Water Most Italians take mineral water with their meals; however, tap water is safe everywhere, as are public drinking fountains. Unsafe sources will be marked ACQUA NON POTABILE. If tap water comes out cloudy, it's only the calcium or other minerals inherent in a water supply that often comes untreated from fresh springs.

MOLTO ITALIANO

13

BASIC VOCABULARY

English	Italian	Pronunciation
Thank you	Grazie	***graht***-tzee-yey
You're welcome	Prego	***prey***-go
Please	Per favore	**pehr fah-*vohr*-eh**
Yes	Si	**see**
No	No	**noh**
Good morning or good day	Buongiorno	**bwohn-*djor*-noh**
Good evening	Buona sera	***bwohn*-ah *say-rah***
Good night	Buona notte	***bwohn*-ah *noht*-tay**
How are you?	Come sta?	***koh*-may *stah***
Very well	Molto bene	***mohl*-toh *behn*-ney**
Goodbye	Arrivederci	**ahr-ree-vah-*dehr*-chee**
Excuse me (to get attention)	Scusi	***skoo*-zee**
Excuse me (to get past someone)	Permesso	**pehr-*mehs*-soh**
Where is . . . ?	Dovè . . . ?	**doh-*vey***
the station	la stazione	**lah stat-tzee-*oh*-neh**
a hotel	un albergo	**oon ahl-*behr*-goh**
a restaurant	un ristorante	**oon reest-ohr-*ahnt*-eh**
the bathroom	il bagno	**eel *bahn*-nyoh**
To the right	A destra	**ah *dehy*-stra**
To the left	A sinistra	**ah see-*nees*-tra**
Straight ahead	Avanti (or sempre diritto)	**ahv-vahn-tee (*sehm*-pray dee-*reet*-toh)**
How much is it?	Quanto costa?	***kwan*-toh *coh*-sta?**
The check, please	Il conto, per favore	**eel kon-toh pehr *fah-vohr*-eh**
When?	Quando?	***kwan*-doh**
Yesterday	Ieri	***ee-yehr*-ree**
Today	Oggi	***oh*-jee**
Tomorrow	Domani	**doh-*mah*-nee**

English	Italian	Pronunciation
Breakfast	Prima colazione	***pree**-mah coh-laht-tzee-**ohn**-ay*
Lunch	Pranzo	***prahn**-zoh*
Dinner	Cena	***chay**-nah*
What time is it?	Che ore sono?	**kay or-*ay soh*-noh**
Monday	Lunedì	**loo-nay-*dee***
Tuesday	Martedì	**mart-ay-*dee***
Wednesday	Mercoledì	**mehr-cohl-ay-*dee***
Thursday	Giovedì	**joh-vay-*dee***
Friday	Venerdì	**ven-nehr-*dee***
Saturday	Sabato	***sah*-bah-toh**
Sunday	Domenica	**doh-*mehn*-nee-kah**

NUMBERS

English	Italian	Pronunciation
1	uno	**(oo-noh)**
2	due	**(doo-ay)**
3	tre	**(tray)**
4	quattro	**(kwah-troh)**
5	cinque	**(cheen-kway)**
6	sei	**(say)**
7	sette	**(set-tay)**
8	otto	**(oh-toh)**
9	nove	**(noh-vay)**
10	dieci	**(dee-ay-chee)**
11	undici	**(oon-dee-chee)**
20	venti	**(vehn-tee)**
21	ventuno	**(vehn-toon-oh)**
22	venti due	**(vehn-tee doo-ay)**
30	trenta	**(trayn-tah)**
40	quaranta	**(kwah-rahn-tah)**
50	cinquanta	**(cheen-kwan-tah)**
60	sessanta	**(sehs-sahn-tah)**
70	settanta	**(seht-tahn-tah)**
80	ottanta	**(oht-tahn-tah)**
90	novanta	**(noh-vahnt-tah)**
100	cento	**(chen-toh)**
1,000	mille	**(mee-lay)**
5,000	cinque milla	**(cheen-kway mee-lah)**
10,000	dieci milla	**(dee-ay-chee mee-lah)**

ITALIAN MENU TERMS

Abbacchio Roast haunch or shoulder of lamb baked and served in a casserole and sometimes flavored with anchovies.

Agnolotti A crescent-shape pasta shell stuffed with a mix of chopped meat, spices, vegetables, and cheese; when prepared in rectangular versions, the same combination of ingredients is identified as ravioli.

Amaretti Crunchy, sweet almond-flavored macaroons.

Anguilla alla veneziana Eel cooked in a sauce made from tuna and lemon.

Antipasti Succulent tidbits served at the beginning of a meal (before the pasta), whose ingredients might include slices of cured meats, seafood (especially shellfish), and cooked and seasoned vegetables.

Aragosta Lobster.

Arrosto Roasted meat.

Baccalà Dried and salted codfish.

Bagna cauda Hot and well-seasoned sauce, heavily flavored with anchovies, designed for dipping raw vegetables; literally translated as "hot bath."

Bistecca alla fiorentina Florentine-style steaks, coated before grilling with olive oil, pepper, lemon juice, salt, and parsley.

Bocconcini Veal layered with ham and cheese, and then fried.

Bollito misto Assorted boiled meats served on a single platter.

Braciola Pork chop.

Bresaola Air-dried spiced beef.

Bruschetta Toasted bread, heavily slathered with olive oil and garlic and often topped with tomatoes.

Bucatini Coarsely textured hollow spaghetti.

Busecca alla Milanese Tripe (beef stomach) flavored with herbs and vegetables.

Cacciucco ali livornese Seafood stew.

Calzone Pizza dough rolled with the chef's choice of sausage, tomatoes, cheese, and so on and then baked into a kind of savory turnover.

Cannelloni Tubular dough stuffed with meat, cheese, or vegetables and then baked in a creamy white sauce.

Cappellacci alla ferrarese Pasta stuffed with pumpkin.

Cappelletti Small ravioli ("little hats") stuffed with meat or cheese.

Carciofi Artichokes.

Carpaccio Thin slices of raw cured beef, sometimes in a piquant sauce.

Cassatta alla siciliana A richly caloric dessert that combines layers of sponge cake, sweetened ricotta cheese, and candied fruit, bound together with chocolate buttercream icing.

Cervello al burro nero Brains in black-butter sauce.

Cima alla genovese Baked filet of veal rolled into a tube-shape package containing eggs, mushrooms, and sausage.

Coppa Cured morsels of pork filet encased in sausage skins, served in slices.

Costoletta alla Milanese Veal cutlet dredged in bread crumbs, fried, and sometimes flavored with cheese.

Cozze Mussels.

Fagioli White beans.

Fave Fava beans.

Fegato alla veneziana Thinly sliced calves' liver fried with salt, pepper, and onions.

Focaccia Ideally, concocted from potato-based dough left to rise slowly for several hours and then garnished with tomato sauce, garlic, basil, salt, and pepper, and drizzled with olive oil; similar to a deep-dish pizza most popular in the deep South, especially Bari.

Fontina Rich cow's milk cheese.

Frittata Italian omelet.

Fritto misto A deep-fried medley of whatever small fish, shellfish, and squid are available in the marketplace that day.

Fusilli Spiral-shape pasta.

Gelato (produzione propria) Ice cream (homemade).

Gnocchi Dumplings usually made from potatoes *(gnocchi alla patate)* or from semolina *(gnocchi alla romana),* often stuffed with combinations of cheese, spinach, vegetables, or whatever combinations strike the chef's fancy.

Gorgonzola One of the most famous blue-veined cheeses of Europe—strong, creamy, and aromatic.

Granita Flavored ice, usually with lemon or coffee.

Insalata di frutti di mare Seafood salad (usually including shrimp and squid) garnished with pickles, lemon, olives, and spices.

Involtini Thinly sliced beef, veal, or pork rolled, stuffed, and fried.

Minestrone A rich and savory vegetable soup usually sprinkled with grated parmigiano and studded with noodles.

Mortadella Mild pork sausage, fashioned into large cylinders and served sliced; the original lunchmeat bologna (because its most famous center of production is Bologna).

Mozzarella A nonfermented cheese, made from the fresh milk of a buffalo (or, if unavailable, from a cow), boiled, and then kneaded into a rounded ball, served fresh.

Mozzarella con pomodori (also "caprese") Fresh tomatoes with fresh mozzarella, basil, pepper, and olive oil.

Nervetti A northern Italian antipasti made from chewy pieces of calves' feet or shins.

Osso buco Beef or veal knuckle slowly braised until the cartilage is tender and then served with a highly flavored sauce.

Pancetta Herb-flavored pork belly, rolled into a cylinder and sliced—the Italian bacon.

Panettone Sweet yellow bread baked in the form of a brioche.

Panna Heavy cream.

Pansotti Pasta stuffed with greens, herbs, and cheeses, usually served with a walnut sauce.

Pappardelle alle lepre Pasta with rabbit sauce.

Parmigiano Parmesan, a hard and salty yellow cheese usually grated over pastas and soups but also eaten alone; also known as *granna.* The best is *Parmigiano reggiano.*

Peperoni Green, yellow, or red sweet peppers (not to be confused with pepperoni).

Pesci al cartoccio Fish baked in a parchment envelope with onions, parsley, and herbs.

Pesto A flavorful green sauce made from basil leaves, cheese, garlic, marjoram, and (if available) pine nuts.

Piccata al Marsala Thin escalope of veal braised in a pungent sauce flavored with Marsala wine.

Piselli al prosciutto Peas with strips of ham.

Pizza Specific varieties include *capricciosa* (its ingredients can vary widely, depending on the chef's culinary vision and the ingredients at hand), *margherita* (with tomato sauce, cheese, fresh basil, and memories of the first queen of Italy, Marguerite di Savoia, in whose honor it was first made by a Neapolitan chef), *napoletana* (with ham, capers, tomatoes, oregano, cheese, and the distinctive taste of anchovies), *quatro stagione* (translated as "four seasons" because of the array of fresh vegetables in it; it also contains ham and bacon), and *siciliana* (with black olives, capers, and cheese).

Pizzaiola A process in which something (usually a beefsteak) is covered in a tomato-and-oregano sauce.

Polenta Thick porridge or mush made from cornmeal flour.

Polenta de uccelli Assorted small birds roasted on a spit and served with polenta.

Polenta e coniglio Rabbit stew served with polenta.

Polla alla cacciatore Chicken with tomatoes and mushrooms cooked in wine.

Pollo alla diavola Highly spiced grilled chicken.

Ragù Meat sauce.

Ricotta A soft bland cheese made from cow's or sheep's milk.

Risotto Italian rice.

Risotto alla Milanese Rice with saffron and wine.

Salsa verde "Green sauce," made from capers, anchovies, lemon juice and/or vinegar, and parsley.

Saltimbocca Veal scallop layered with prosciutto and sage; its name literally translates as "jump in your mouth," a reference to its tart and savory flavor.

Salvia Sage.

Scaloppina alla Valdostana Escalope of veal stuffed with cheese and ham.

Scaloppine Thin slices of veal coated in flour and sautéed in butter.

Semifreddo A frozen dessert; usually ice cream with sponge cake.

Seppia Cuttlefish (a kind of squid); its black ink is used for flavoring in certain sauces for pasta and also in risotto dishes.

Sogliola Sole.

Spaghetti A long, round, thin pasta, variously served: *alla bolognese* (with ground meat, mushrooms, peppers, and so on), *alla carbonara* (with bacon, black pepper, and eggs), *al pomodoro* (with tomato sauce), *al sugo/ragù* (with meat sauce), and *alle vongole* (with clam sauce).

Spiedini Pieces of meat grilled on a skewer over an open flame.

Strangolaprete Small nuggets of pasta, usually served with sauce; the name is literally translated as "priest-choker."

Stufato Beef braised in white wine with vegetables.

Tagliatelle Flat egg noodles.

Tonno Tuna.

Tortelli Pasta dumplings stuffed with ricotta and greens.

Tortellini Rings of dough stuffed with minced and seasoned meat, and served either in soups or as a full-fledged pasta covered with sauce.

Trenette Thin noodles served with pesto sauce and potatoes.

Trippe alla fiorentina Beef tripe (stomach).

Vermicelli Very thin spaghetti.

Vitello tonnato Cold sliced veal covered with tuna-fish sauce.

Zabaglione/zabaione Egg yolks whipped into the consistency of a custard, flavored with Marsala, and served warm as a dessert.

Zampone Pig's trotter stuffed with spicy seasoned pork, boiled and sliced.

Zuccotto A liqueur-soaked sponge cake, molded into a dome and layered with chocolate, nuts, and whipped cream.

Zuppa inglese Sponge cake soaked in custard.

Index

See also Accommodations and Restaurant indexes, below.

General Index

C

D

N

O

P

R